Gender, Globalization, and Democratization

Gender, Globalization, and Democratization

Edited By
Rita Mae Kelly
Jane H. Bayes
Mary Hawkesworth
and Brigitte Young

ROWMAN & LITTLEFIELD PUBLISHERS, INC.
Lanham • Boulder • New York • Oxford

ROWMAN & LITTLEFIELD PUBLISHERS, INC.

Published in the United States of America
by Rowman & Littlefield Publishers, Inc.
4720 Boston Way, Lanham, Maryland 20706
www.rowmanlittlefield.com

12 Hid's Copse Road
Cumnor Hill, Oxford OX2 9JJ, England

British Library Cataloguing in Publication Information Available

Library of Congress Cataloging-in-Publication Data

Gender, globalization, and gender democratization / edited by Rita Mae Kelly . . . [et al.].
    p. cm.
    Includes bibliographical references and index.
    ISBN 0-7425-0977-X (alk. paper)—ISBN 0-7425-0978-8 (pbk. : alk. paper)
    1. Sex role. 2. Women in development. 3. Women and democracy. 4. International
economic relations—Social aspects. I. Kelly, Rita Mae.

HQ1075 .G427 2001
305.3—dc21
                                                                        00-045720

Printed in the United States of America

∞™ The paper used in this publication meets the minimum requirements of American
National Standard for Information Sciences—Permanence of Paper for Printed Library
Materials, ANSI/NISO Z39.48-1992.

Contents

List of Figures, Maps, and Tables   vii

Acknowledgments   viii

1 Globalization, Democratization, and Gender Regimes   1
Jane H. Bayes, Mary E. Hawkesworth, and Rita Mae Kelly

2 Gender, Globalization, and Democratization: Some Lessons
from Oceania   15
Marian Simms

3 Globalization and Gender: A European Perspective   27
Brigitte Young

4 Gender and Social Implications of Globalization:
An African Perspective   49
Yassine Fall

5 Mexico/U.S. Migration and Gender Relations: The Guanajuatense
Community in Mexico and the United States   75
Laura Gonzalez

6 Globalization and Asian Indian Immigrant Women in the United
States   95
Arpana Sircar and Rita Mae Kelly

7 Income Control and Household Work-Sharing   121
Urvashi Soni-Sinha

8 Japan and the Global Sex Industry 137
Seiko Hanochi

9 Political Spaces, Gender, and NAFTA 149
Jane H. Bayes and Rita Mae Kelly

10 Democratization and Gender Politics in South Korea 171
Bang-Soon L. Yoon

11 Transforming Governance Agendas: Insights from Grassroots
Women's Initiatives in Local Governance in Two Districts of
India
Suranjana Gupta 195

12 Engendering the Japanese "Double Standard" Patriarchal
Democracy: The Case of the "Comfort Women" and Military
Sexual Slavery 205
Kinhide Mushakoji

13 Democratization: Reflections on Gendered Dislocations in the
Public Sphere 223
Mary E. Hawkesworth

References 237

Index 255

List of Contributors 267

Figures, Maps, and Tables

FIGURES

Figure 6.1.   Map of Types of Variables Relevant to Adult
              Political Behavior   96
Figure 11.1   Institutionalization   199

MAPS

Map 5.1.   Guanajuato and Selected Municipalities   76
Map 5.2.   El Bajío means the Lowlands   79
Map 5.3.   Areas and Subareas in El Bajío   80

TABLES

Table 4.1.   Comparative Socioeconomic Indicators   65
Table 4.2.   Estimates of the Rate of Adult Illiteracy by Region   65
Table 6.1.   Demographic Profiles of the Respondents   101
Table 6.2.   Responses to the Index of Sex Role Orientation
              Instrument   104–105
Table 7.1.   Demographic Profile and Socioeconomic
              Background of the Women with Joint Control of
              Income and Joint Sharing of Household Chores   134
Table 10.1.   Women in National Assemblies in South Korea
              (1948–2000)   175

Acknowledgments

This project is the result of a major collaborative effort of the scientific research committee on Gender, Globalization, and Democratization of the International Social Science Council. We wish to acknowledge the ISSC's financial support for all of us to attend the December 1998 meeting in Paris, France, to develop our initial drafts and plans for this book and our other collaborative projects. The work is also the outgrowth of several panel sessions and informal meetings of many members of the Sex Roles Committee of the International Political Science Association in Berlin, Germany in 1994, Seoul, South Korea in 1997, and Quebec City, Canada, in 2000. Follow-up workshops held at the various annual North Texas UN Conferences on Women at the University of Texas at Dallas also moved our work forward. A special thanks is given to all these institutions and many individuals who have encouraged and helped further our studies on these important topics. We appreciate the efforts of the editors at Rowman & Littlefield, especially Cindy Tursman, for overseeing the production of this book. Anyone with an interest in the ISSC research committee on Gender, Globalization, and Democratization should contact Rita Mae Kelly, Professor and Dean, The University of Texas at Dallas, School of Social Sciences, GR3.1, Richardson, TX 75083-0688; email: rmkelly@utdallas.edu.

Globalization, Democratization, and Gender Regimes

Jane H. Bayes, Mary E. Hawkesworth, and Rita Mae Kelly

This book is concerned with three major twentieth-century phenomena—globalization, democratization, and feminization—and their interrelationship and impact on gender regimes in various parts of the world. While many have described both globalization and democratization, few have paid attention to the gendered aspects of these processes. The purpose of this book is to incorporate gender analyses into a critical study of the processes of globalization and democratization.

In the case of globalization, the book focuses on how the economic aspects of twentieth-century globalization—the international movement of capital, goods, and labor—have impacted gender relations or gender regimes, including the movement by women into public arenas, which we term feminization. The nature of gender regimes in a society is critical to the possibility of establishing a full democracy in its richest and most "thick" version, a version that recognizes women as equal citizens of a democratic state. This book argues that a "full democracy" (as opposed to a "limited" or partial democracy) is one that recognizes women as citizens equally with men, one where the institutionalized gender relationships or gender regimes are egalitarian (Mill 1989).

Contrary to prevailing concepts of gender as a role, a norm, or a status category, this book uses Robert Connell's (1987) concept of gender as an active process that creates divisions of labor, power, and emotions between men and women as well as modes of dress, deportment, and identity. Rather than accepting that sex provides a "natural" assignment of roles and responsibilities for men and women, Connell suggests that economic, political, and interpersonal practices create what are taken to be "natural" sex differences. In arguing that gender acts through diverse domains of labor, power, and cathexis, Connell emphasizes that these processes need not reinforce one another. Indeed, tensions among the gender regimes operative in the institutions of family, market, and governance make "lived contradictions" a common experience. A society may include many conflicting gender regimes or it may be more homogeneous.

A major argument of this book is that if established patterns of interaction between men and women in the family, the marketplace, and other nongovernmental institutions in the society deny women physical and economic security, access to education, and access to social and political institutions and offices, then the democratization process, although it may constitutionally claim that men and women are equal, can be no more than a facade, a thin veneer. So long as women are confined to a "separate sphere," confined to reproduction, housework, and child care, so long as women are left uneducated, unable to control their bodies, and unrecognized as citizens on an equal footing with men, democracy, if it exists at all in the form of regular competitive elections, constitutional government, and accountability to the governed, is more a stated goal than a reality. Yet changing gender regimes in a society is no easy task. Economic conditions often establish a division of labor between the sexes, which becomes routinized and institutionalized long after those economic conditions have changed. New economic conditions can create new kinds of division of labor and new gender regimes that can clash with the old forms of gender relationships.

Most of the chapters in the collection explore the complex tensions between the gender regimes that structure work relations and those operative in the family. Several of the chapters examine the complex interplay of gendering processes in politics and sexual practices, while others explore interactions and antagonisms in gender regimes in politics and economics. Collectively, the essays emphasize that gender regimes are in transition under globalization and democratization, but the direction of change is neither unilinear nor inherently progressive. Contradictions in gender regimes in politics, economics, and interpersonal relations create sites of contestation, but the outcome of these diverse and locally specific struggles remains an open question.

While both globalization and democratization have the capacity to alter dramatically gender regimes, the relationship between the two movements is complex. Globalization, both today and in the past, has always had political and economic components that depend heavily on the economy and technology of the period as well as the political ideas and institutions of those who are successful in expanding their operations to other parts of the globe. The idea of conquering foreign lands to generate a political and economic empire is at least as old as Alexander the Great. When Elizabeth I, Queen of England, signed the charter for the British East India Company on New Year's Eve, 1600, she signed a document that was "for the honour of this our realm of England as for the increase of our navigation and advancement of trade of merchandise" (Gardner 1971, 17). England and the other early imperialist nations (Spain, Portugal, the Netherlands) took not only their economic ideas of trade and commerce, but also their languages, political ideas, and political institutions with them as they established settlements and colonies abroad. In their colonial territories, each of these imperialist countries (including France, Belgium, Germany) imposed their political institutions, language, and political ideas as well as their economic means of exploitation. During this period, economics and politics were linked through the rhetoric of nationalism, a rhetoric that these colonies eventually adopted to attain independence.

In contrast, globalization in the late twentieth century links economics and politics primarily through the rhetoric of neoliberalism, which ironically tries to drive a wedge between economics and politics to make each appear independent at a fundamental level. Global corporations with only limited national attachments are the primary engines of production. Yet neoliberalism requires particular functions of government, functions that can be performed by military dictators or juntas, by "thin" democratic states, and even to some extent by socialist and communist regimes. Neoliberalism requires that governments provide for the free movement of capital, the free movement of goods, unrestricted labor markets, responsible banking systems, stable monetary policies, limited fiscal policies, attractive investment opportunities, and political stability. Neoliberalism provides rules for economies, not for societies.

The first argument of this book is that globalization represents a set of economic forces that changes the division of labor between the sexes in many different contexts as well as the nature of the state, creates enormous social disruption and dislocation, and because of all this, can change established gender regimes. The first wave of globalization in the fifteenth century brought Europeans to many parts of the globe intent upon establishing empires, settler colonies, and trading posts. These conquerors and immigrants brought with them their ideas about gender relations as well as their ideas about race and class and imposed them on indigenous populations. Conditions in the new societies or colonies generated further changes (chapter 2). The more recent wave of globalization in the last half of the twentieth century has been fueled by a neoliberal ideology of free trade, free flow of capital, limited governmental regulation, and democratization. Established gender regimes have been altered as the waged labor force has become feminized and women have for the first time in large numbers been drawn out of the household or the family farm into the waged economy (chapter 9 and chapter 6). Gender regimes have changed as foreign investment has disrupted traditional subsistence agricultural communities and encouraged large-scale migration patterns (chapter 5). Foreign lenders, international groups, unions, industrialized governments, and human rights groups demanding human rights for women have been a force for change (chapter 9, chapter 2). States that previously supported a "male bread (or rice) winner" model of gender relations have found themselves compelled to cut social services at the same time that "family wages" are being trimmed to be competitive with the enlarged, feminized, and highly "flexible" global labor force (chapter 3). Multinational global corporations invade on an increasing scale countries in Africa, Latin America, and Asia, making deals with governmental elites to drain valuable natural resources from countries with weak or corrupt governments. In other instances, international organizations promoting the neoliberal capitalist agenda such as the International Monetary Fund and the World Bank demand that export production replace production for domestic consumption in exchange for loans, or the World Trade Organization demands that small, local industries go unprotected in competition with huge global giants. Often these are deals that degrade the environment, upset local economies, disrupt local food supplies, and put women and children into deeper poverty (chapter 4). In some situations, established male-dominant gender regimes are so entrenched they are able to thwart the global trends that would draw women into export production (chapter 7). In other situations, globalization has expanded and internationalized what was formerly a more contained patriarchal gender regime (chapter 8).

Chapters 2–4 provide case studies of specific ways that globalization (either the first wave or the more recent wave) has impacted existing gender regimes. Chapters 5–8 highlight how globalization itself contains contradictions, and the changes it initiates often generate conflicts that can become sites of gender regime contestation. These chapters, and chapter 9 in particular, show how these contradictions offer insights and hope for positive social, economic, and political change for women, how they can create new political spaces for women in both the private and public spheres. The argument in chapters 10–13 is that, in general, the prospects for the establishment of rich and full democracies around the world, democracies where women are recognized as equal citizens with men, still need to be improved markedly.

The impact of globalization on women throughout the world has been as negative and undemocratic as it has been positive and liberating. While some educated women in developed countries have prospered, larger numbers of women in the world have become poorer. The movement of foreign capital into subsistence agricultural communities often induces men to seek waged work elsewhere, leaving their farms to the women and children. The resulting poverty disrupts local social organization, herds people into crowded urban areas and into international migration, and in some parts of the world drives many women and children into slavery, prostitution, and sex trafficking. The same kind of result, as well as a general reduction in the quality of life, occurs for many women in indebted nation-states, in newly democratizing states (as in Eastern Europe), or in those states trying to meet neoliberal deficit standards (as in the European Union countries, Canada, or even the United States). These negative consequences stem from the reduction of housing, food, health, and other social welfare programs or diversion of local resources to export production in order to improve the balance of payments and reduce debt loads. In many Latin American, Eastern European, Asian, and central Asian countries, the mechanisms of old patriarchal gender regimes have reasserted themselves after women mobilized in revolutionary ways to overthrow military dictators (chapter 10) or after unpopular communist regimes fell in 1989. In most northern industrialized countries, women and workers, in general, are losing their battles with the state and the society to retain safety net and social provisions for reproductive work as well as caretaking work, losing the battle to live in a society rather than in an economy.

Faced with the institutionalized sets of gender relationships or gender regimes that perpetuate male dominance in the family, church, temple, mosque, school, university, marketplace, business organizations, military, and in the history and the literary oral traditions of almost all societies in the world, obtaining "full democratization" is a tall order, one that has not yet been attained in any society. Yet the world has definitely become more democratized in the past two hundred years. Political action if undertaken strategically can make a difference. Democratic ideas, once established in at least some institutions of a society, can have a logical progression that presses for greater equality and inclusion for all members of the society. With industrialization beginning in the early nineteenth century—the flourishing of liberal thought, the French Revolution, and the rise of the merchant class—notions of equality, individual rights, and governments authorized by and accountable to "the people" gained legitimacy. In Europe, many monarchies evolved in irregular paths toward constitutional democracies during the nineteenth century. Initially, these constitutional democracies recognized only men as citizens.

Recent feminist scholarship (Kerber 1980; Landes 1988; J. W. Scott 1996; McDonagh 1999) suggests that democratization is not a linear process nor is it the same for men and women. Times of dramatic change are often gendered. As was the case during the Renaissance and the French Revolution (Landes 1988; J. W. Scott 1996), the age of the "rights of man" was an age in which women lost status and power. In the colonial United States, for example, rights of participation were tied to property. When the new states formed constitutions after the Revolutionary War, male gender was added to property as a constitutional requirement for participation. Some propertied women lost their rights of participation. Women who had been politicized and active in the Revolutionary War were privatized by constitutional fiat. The "ideology of Republican Motherhood," which accorded women the narrow political role of bearing children and educating them to be virtuous citizens, was subsequently created to legitimate this restriction of women's political activism (Kerber 1980; McDonagh 1999).

When Elizabeth Cady Stanton called the first Women's Rights Convention together in Seneca Falls, New York, in 1848, women in the United States and Europe were not allowed to own property. With few exceptions, they were unable to attend college, were generally unable to control their reproductive lives, and were unable to vote, to sit on juries, to speak in public, or to serve in elected bodies. Slavery still existed in the United States, and a large percentage of black women in the United States were slaves. Drawing on the ideas and rhetoric of the Declaration of Independence (a document that did not include women), the Seneca Falls Declaration of the Rights of Women declared that all men *and women* were equal and entitled to inalienable rights. As the franchise expanded for men and slaves were freed, women, first in New Zealand and Australia and later in other parts of the world, demanded and received the right to be recognized as voting citizens. The next notable expansion of democratization came after World War II when the United States emerged as the dominant Western economy and the dominant Western power. Japan under the occupation democratized. Germany reestablished its constitutional democracy. India and some African nations broke their colonial yokes to establish fledgling democratic governments. A third wave of democratization came in Southeast Asia and Latin America in the 1980s as popular uprisings toppled military dictatorships and in the 1990s in Eastern Europe and central Asia as communist regimes crumbled. The struggle for democracy for women involves not only the transition of military dictatorships, communist regimes, and traditional monarchies or fiefdoms to political systems that uphold the rule of law, regular competitive elections, and accountable government, but also involves a struggle for the equal recognition of women in and the subsequent democratization of both state institutions, such as legislatures, state bureaucracies, courts, and local governments, and of nonstate institutions, such as the family, the business corporation, religious institutions, and voluntary organizations. Many women participated in the struggles that involved overthrowing dictatorships or welcomed their release from communist regimes only to find themselves marginalized politically and economically in both old and new ways. A partial and thin democratization process may establish ostensibly democratic institutions that operate for men, but tends to exclude women from political participation and the processes of democratic citizenship. A rich and complete democratization process requires significant changes in the traditional relationships between men and women, changes in the socialization of men and women, and changes not only in formal institutions such as parties, legislatures, bureaucracies, and courts, but also changes in the customs and practices of families, religious organizations, businesses, and voluntary associations.

While prospects for democracies that include women equally with men are not good, the situation is not one-dimensional. The contradictions and conflicts created in the sites of gender regime contestation that globalization creates open up political opportunities for gender regime change that can move toward providing the basis for a more full and complete democratization process. For example, women who are drawn into the paid labor force do not all immediately change the gender relationships in their families or in other institutions; however, some gain a certain independence and do become political actors. They change the gender regimes of their families and communities. Migrants moving from societies with patriarchal gender regimes to societies with more egalitarian gender regimes do not all change, nor do they change immediately; but some do and some become politically active.

Globalization and democratization as social movements are peculiarly linked in ways that generate other conundrums and contradictions. The current wave of globalization that promotes and glorifies the rewards of unfettered capitalist markets has its intellectual origins in some of the same seventeenth- and eighteenth-century European thinkers that championed the rewards of democracy, the overthrow of dictatorial tyrannies, and "rule by and for the people." Both valorize the individual either as a free-thinking entrepreneur or consumer or as an independently minded, self-governing citizen (John Locke, Adam Smith, David Hume, Jean Jacques Rousseau). Democratization, even in its thin form that excludes women, depends heavily on the idea of inalienable individual human rights, the concept of a universal juridical male citizen undifferentiated by race, class, ethnicity, or other differentiating characteristics. The logical extension of a rights discourse in a situation of discrimination is to ask (as did Elizabeth Cady Stanton) why should the universal juridical citizen be differentiated by sex or gender? Why should the universal citizen be male only? This question becomes particularly poignant when the forces of globalization are generating conflict in the traditional organization of gender relationships in families and other heavily gendered social institutions.

Certainly in the last half of the twentieth century the global human rights movement has been extremely important in legitimating the global demand for women's political citizenship. The human rights agenda supports an undifferentiated juridical citizenship for all human beings regardless of sex or gender. A major symbolic and conceptual breakthrough on this issue occurred at the United Nations Human Rights Congress held in Vienna in 1994, when the delegates agreed that women's rights are human rights. At the same time that the global economic expansion in the 1990s has enabled global corporations to challenge the sovereignty of nation-states, erode the accountability of ostensibly democratic governments, propagate and support neoliberal ideas that fuel debt crises, deregulation, privatization, and structural adjustment policies, the same neoliberal forces and governments have also advocated and supported ideas of individual human rights and even the idea that women's rights are human rights.

The relationship between globalization and democratization and the political citizenship of women has been quite different outside Europe and the United States. Liberal ideas do not dominate most cultures as they do in the United States (chapter 12). In these situations, international public opinion and the influence of Western liberal ideas become factors that can generate contestation. The recent institution of quota systems in a large number of European, Latin American, and Asian countries is an example of trying to enforce gender regime change from the top down. Since many countries have entrenched patriarchal gender regimes that prevent women from running for office or standing for party seats, quotas have been adopted as a solution to help break this impasse (chapter 11). Whether this practice improves the political potency of women is a topic of considerable debate. Another site of contestation is in the international organization of nongovernmental organizations to oppose some of the dictates of global financial and trade organizations. The existence of the fax machine, Internet, and e-mail as well as global news broadcasts such as CNN make it possible to organize environmental, labor, women's groups, and human rights advocates to engage in global political activities such as the Seattle protest in November 1999 against the World Trade Organization.

Both globalization and democratization (including a human rights agenda) are processes supported by the U.S. government since 1945 in the form of tax breaks for direct foreign investment by U.S. multinational firms, foreign aid, military assistance, direct contracts for democratizing countries, structural adjustment policies that link aid to the development of competing party systems, and the establishment of thinly democratic legislatures and court systems. Yet globalization and democratization processes are often quite separate. The U.S. government and other developed "democracies" have also been eager to give aid to dictators who support global capitalism. When these industrial economies do encourage democratization, their insistence on democratic procedures rarely goes beyond the imposition of a thin democratic facade that rarely includes an insistence on the equal participation of women. This is due in part to the fact that even the advanced "democratic" capitalist countries pushing this agenda are incompletely democratized themselves. Here, too, women struggle to compete on an equal footing with men.

In the most recent globalization movement of the last half of the twentieth century, the life prospects and opportunities for political participation have improved for some women, but for many others, globalization has meant social and economic dislocation, the separation of families due to migration, interruption of food supplies, environmental degradation, increased poverty, and a decline in the public welfare role of the state. Social disruption is particularly intense in certain sites such as global cities where immigrants from many different cultures congregate and different social classes live next to one another, in areas where capitalist agriculture has displaced traditional farming, in areas where women are for the first time drawn into the waged labor force, in situations where rights-based legal systems clash with legal systems unsupported by an individual rights discourse, and in situations where international human rights, labor, environmental, and women's groups can advertise the injustices generated by globalization. All of these sites of contestation are arenas for political action, places where the gender order is permeable (in Connell's terms), places where change from patriarchal gender regimes may be changed to more egalitarian ones. Quota systems, international organizing efforts in sites of gender regime contestation, and human rights work are all strategies that deserve support and continued effort. However, as both Mushakoji (chapter 12) and Hawkesworth (chapter 13) note, major conceptual changes are also necessary in both "old" and "new" "democracies" if democratization is ever to be full and complete.

GLOBALIZATION AND GENDER REGIME CHANGE

Chapters 2–8 identify some of the characteristics of globalization from different regional perspectives and also identify and discuss the impact of globalization on established gender relations in various societies. Marian Simms of Australia (chapter 2) argues that the globalization of the last half of the twentieth century is nothing new, but rather is a continuation of a previous wave of globalization that created settler societies and colonies bent on exploiting the raw materials of any new lands they could conquer, invade, and control. She traces the consequences of this interaction in Oceania as it impacted political institutions and suggests that Oceania's response to globalization, its decentralization and reliance on federalism, and its linkages with the international community have much to teach the rest of the world in dealing with the most recent wave of globalization. She notes that in settler societies, immigrants brought with them the "male breadwinner" gender regime, wherein the male is expected to earn a "family wage" and the female is to occupy a separate unwaged wife and family sphere. However, she notes that the economic conditions in settler societies, especially Australia, New Zealand, Canada, and the United States, encouraged the development of a "partnership" gender regime where men and women were related to each other in a more equitable partnership in making a living.

Brigitte Young (chapter 3) from Germany presents a European perspective on globalization. Her particular concern is the change that recent globalization forces have imposed on European states, states that prided themselves on having highly developed "societies" with well-established social safety nets, health care systems, and provisions for reproduction and child care as well as well-developed "economies." Young notes that globalization has changed the focus of the state from the overall welfare of its citizens and directed it instead toward competing in the global economy, often at the expense of its citizenry, especially its women and children. Young draws upon the theoretical insights of the French Regulation School, which stipulates capitalist modes of production as a series, but not necessarily a linear projection, of different historic regimes of accumulation and modes of regulation. Young links recent periods of capitalist accumulation with gender regimes. In particular, she examines the complex connection between the transformation from the Fordist regime of accumulation and the construction of new gender regimes.

In chapter 4 Yassine Fall from Senegal examines gender and globalization from an African perspective. As in Oceania and Central and Latin America, globalization has a long history in Africa. African economies have been integrated into global networks for hundreds of years as sources of raw materials and labor. African labor was first internationalized through the slave trade and later through the development of colonies founded to serve the needs of colonial powers. In the 1960s and 1970s many newly independent African states borrowed international funds at high interest rates in attempts to modernize their economies. The resulting accumulation of debt has resulted in the stabilization and structural adjustment policies prescribed by the International Monetary Fund and the World Bank. These policies that stress production for export draw both men and women out of agrarian subsistence economies into an urban context, into a variety of informal economy activities, and into the migrant worker labor force. The international private sector has been empowered by these processes, while African women have been particularly hard hit by policies that reduce the domestic food supply and reduce government spending on services and infrastructure in favor of earning foreign exchange to repay accumulating national debts. The impact of globalization forces in recent years has been to continue the exploitation of African raw resources for the benefit of global corporations and industrialized countries. African rulers and governments often become complicitous partners in these activities. While a few token women may sit on boards and committees, decisions affecting the lives of women and families in Africa continue to be made by foreign private interests and African male elites. Three case studies illustrate these points: debt management and the highly indebted poor countries (HIPC) debt relief initiative, the Chad oil pipeline being built by a consortium of outside interests, and the Lomé Agreement allowing European trawlers to decimate the local fish supply by fishing in West African waters.

In chapter 5 Laura Gonzalez focuses on the impact of globalization on the gender regimes of particular areas of Guanajuato, Mexico. Large-scale capital intensive agriculture has moved into the fertile area of Guanajuato in the past thirty years. In addition, *maquiladora* factories have also been established in the region. Using extensive interviewing techniques, Gonzalez found that gender regimes changed in the agricultural areas depending on the quality of the land and the availability of irrigation. Large-scale capitalist agriculture financed by foreign direct investment occupied land next to the river that could be irrigated. While many had to leave this land and join the migrant labor force moving to the city or north, the large-scale agricultural operations continued to hire a number of year-round agricultural workers and pay them well enough to support a nonwaged wife and children. In this area, the tortilla or breadwinner model prevails. In nearby areas that depend partly on irrigation and partly on rainfall, farms are smaller and worked by families who do more sharing of the labor. Often men leave to go north (to the United States) to earn money to supplement the meager farm produce. This leaves wives in charge of the household and the farm for long periods of time. In the most desolate and rocky land dependent only on rainfall, men often go north and never return, although some do send money home. These are the poorest areas. With no men around for years at a time, and then only for short visits, the women in these areas become totally self-sufficient as single heads of household. They live very hard lives, but they perform all the duties in the community, including political duties. Gonzalez also traces immigrants to the United States and reports on the interaction of Mexican gender regimes as they interact with those found in the United States.

Like Gonzalez, in chapter 6 Arpana Sircar and Rita Mae Kelly report on another female immigrant population in the United States and the gender regime conflicts they have experienced in moving from India to the United States as well-educated professional workers. These Indian women from traditional patriarchal gender regimes were divided in their reactions to the social and economic changes they experienced. Some lived dual lives, being independent and equal at work while assuming an inferior role to their husbands at home. Most considered themselves as being more progressive and Americanized than their Indian counterparts who remained in India, but less independent than U.S.-born professional women.

In chapter 7, Urvashi Soni-Sinha reviews the literature on the feminization of waged labor in export industries before reporting on her study of a handmade gold jewelry production sector in the Noida export processing zone near Delhi. Governments usually establish export zones as a means of reducing taxes to encourage production for export. Usually women are recruited to work in these zones as docile and cheap workers. Unlike other export industries, Soni-Sinha finds that women are often *excluded* from work in this industry. Instead the industry often prefers to rely on child labor and trainees to maintain its "flexibility." Here established traditional gender regimes operate to prevent women from this kind of employment and instead use precapitalist kinship systems to recruit young male workers, often children, to learn the trade. The work is hard, the hours long, and a system of subcontracting makes security nonexistent.

In chapter 8, Seiko Hanochi highlights how sexual trafficking of women has persisted through centuries of diverse forms of internationalization and globalization. She notes that the unwanted commodification of women's and children's bodies is comparable in many ways to the military enslavement of women for sex purposes that was done in the past.

PROSPECTS FOR DEMOCRATIZATION AND GENDER REGIME CHANGE: CAN POLITICAL ACTION HELP?

Chapters 9–13 identify and evaluate the prospects for gender regime change and increased democratization that will benefit women using a variety of case studies from around the world. In chapter 9 Jane H. Bayes and Rita Mae Kelly identify three ways that gender regimes can change in sites of contestation generated by globalization and provide specific examples drawn from the experience. The first way is when outside forces threaten the family's and women's ability to perform their family and reproductive responsibilities as defined by current gender norms and culture. This is illustrated by conditions in central Mexico where subsistence agriculture is being replaced by large-scale capitalist enterprises. A second way is when women enter the waged labor force and experience a different gender regime or through their work obtain resources that allow them to challenge the traditional gender regime of their upbringing. The employment of Mexican women in the *maquiladora* industry illustrates what can happen to gender regimes under these circumstances. A third way that gender regime change can occur is when the international norms of human rights are applied as a standard to evaluate extant gender relations, practices, and legal codes. Such change can happen when the laws governing the gender codes in one nation clash with those in another nation. Pregnancy testing and sexual harassment are examples of this on the U.S.-Mexican border.

Do these changes necessarily mean that political spaces will open for women in the political arena as democratization occurs? The answer to this question is mixed at best. The analysis of the role of women in the democratization of South Korea by Bang-Soon L. Yoon (chapter 10) indicates that patriarchal ideological and structural counterforces often block the gains women have made in the labor force and at the household level when it comes to democratization of the political system.

Over the past decade, women have been actively involved in the initial and most dangerous stages of democratization within nation-states, organizing against oppressive regimes, mobilizing as citizens to demand the transformation of the political system, and standing publicly against authoritarian rule. Women's presence in the democratization process, however, has often been quickly supplanted by women's marked absence from public life and from political roles in the phase of "democratic consolidation." As political parties, interest groups, civil society, and capitalist markets are reconstructed in emerging democracies, women have been markedly underrepresented in campaigns, elections, and in elective offices.

A major mechanism to include women in democratization, even if national gender orders are hostile to women being equal political participants, is the establishment of quotas. Suranjana Gupta (chapter 11) describes India's efforts to implement the 73rd Amendment to the Indian Constitution, which mandated in 1993 that 30 percent of all local elected offices must go to women. This forced entrance of women into political spaces creates many challenges. Contexts and processes for women to participate effectively must be designed and built. Participation involves capacity building. Gupta finds that women's groups, especially credit unions organized by women, are important ways to build this capacity. These groups provide support for women both formally and informally that is vital to implementing the government's mandate that 30 percent of India's local government consist of women. Gupta's study, in addition to providing insights into how quotas both help and hinder efforts to include women systematically in democratization, reinforces the point made earlier that the international women's movement, women activists within nation-states, and the universalization of international human rights and notions of citizenship for all are very critical to the inclusion of women into democratization.

Kinhide Mushakoji, in chapter 12, uses these latter two examples to show how the inclusion of women in democratization and the prevention of them from becoming victims of globalization requires a reconceptualization of some existing basic concepts and terms. In spite of its presumed democratic constitution and competitive elections, the imposition of a human rights discourse with its *gesellschaft* assumptions upon the *gemeinschaft*, traditional Japanese society has been incomplete, which helps to explain why the current constitutional democracy continues to be unable to take responsibility for the military sexual slavery imposed during wartime. As Mushakoji notes the traditional assumptions and traditional gender regimes tend to be invisible, but they need to be addressed if democratization is to include women in Japan.

In chapter 13, Mary E. Hawkesworth asks why democratization has produced gendered redistributions of resources and responsibilities that make women worse off. She explores the processes by which political space has been constituted and is being reconstituted as male space and to identify mechanisms that might produce a more gender-inclusive and gender-balanced polity. Despite two hundred years of feminist political mobilization, women hold less than 12 percent of the formal political offices in nations across the globe. In more than one hundred countries, women hold no elected offices in their national assemblies. Hawkesworth concludes that one source of the problem lies in the fact that many of the processes traditionally associated with democratization are gendered. Democracy as a mode of governance is most widely understood as a Euro-American model of male-dominant democratic elitism. The "democratic" concepts and institutions (both political and economic) that are exported to other countries carry with them this bias. Modernization theory, for example, assumes that women once drawn into the paid labor force will become independent individuals, free of the patriarchal ideology that has justified their exclusion from economic and political activity in the past. The need to address gender relations in the private sphere and gender biases in democratic ideologies is not recognized. Western democratic ideas would predict that the institutionalization of civil society or the revival of political parties in former authoritarian regimes would be progressive accomplishments for women. In practice, this has not been the case. Instead, public space in these Western institutions has consistently been reclaimed as male space. Hawkesworth suggests that the globalization of ideas from the international women's movement, such as those concerning implementing gender quotas, gender impact analyses, and elements of the International Human Rights Movement, such as the Convention to Eliminate Discrimination Against Women, can make a positive contribution to this situation. Her central point, however, is that women need to become aware of the fact that democratization as it is currently understood institutionalizes practices that can be and often are hostile to women. These practices reaffirm male-biased gender regimes both within the household and within the public, political sphere. They preclude women's mobility and regulate women's access to political decision-making. Contesting the reconstitution of political space as male space can illuminate the gulf between democratization and democracy in ways that may help women in "mature" liberal democracies learn from the experience of women in democratizing nations.

CONCLUSION

This book includes and focuses on gender in its analysis of both globalization and democratization. Women constitute over 50 percent of the world's population. They are heavily involved in production, reproduction, commerce, culture, education, trade, and social organization, yet most mainstream accounts of both globalization and democratization omit or ignore women, their activities, and their contributions. The field of economics is notorious for its exclusion of reproduction, caring, and nurturing as vital social and economic activities requiring resources and labor. The concepts of the discipline are often male biased. For example, the very definition of work has been confined to the waged economy thereby excluding from consideration all the unwaged work that women do to keep an economy running. The important role of the informal economy is often ignored. Women's vital contributions as educators and perpetuators of cultural, social, and economic practices have only recently been recognized by Western developmental economists. This book seeks to show how concepts can reinforce or challenge gendered relationships and demonstrates that sites of contestation include conceptual understandings. This book shows how vital women are to both globalization and democratization processes and challenges those discourses and practices that would keep women invisible.

This book also contributes to the capacity building of women by identifying and evaluating strategic sites for gender regime change and by studying the successes and failures of mobilizing efforts in these areas. Globalization creates certain kinds of gender regime disruption in different global and domestic arenas. Disruption increases the probability that gender regime change can occur. This volume illustrates the complexity of understanding globalization and democratization from a gendered perspective and should be a valuable tool for scholars, activists, and policymakers.

This book is intended to be an interdisciplinary scholarly contribution. It should be of interest to those concerned with globalization, democratization, and gender in the fields of economics, sociology, anthropology, political science, and development studies. It should be appropriate for use in both upper-level undergraduate and graduate courses.

2

Gender, Globalization, and Democratization: Some Lessons from Oceania

Marian Simms

From the perspective of Oceania, globalization is not new but is a process that began almost two hundred years ago. Historically speaking, the European powers were beneficiaries of the early global colonization processes and consequently, except for a few Marxists and others concerned about imperialism, analysts did not generally define these processes or outcomes as problematic. Other types of societies, in other parts of the world, did not tend to be beneficiaries. Although, ultimately some of the "new societies" (e.g., Australia, Canada, and the United States), which had been formed on the basis of European expansion and were acutely aware of international processes especially those of trade and migration, did become independent and did benefit.

The Oceania region includes a range of different types of societies that share long histories of the internationalization of capitalism. Geographers define Oceania as the lands between the continents of Asia and the Americas and south to Australia and New Zealand (see Australian Geographic Society 1988: 2142). Sometimes it refers to the islands of the South Pacific, namely, Polynesia, Melanesia, and Micronesia. As far back as the eighteenth century European organizations, such as the Catholic Church, used the term to refer to Australia, New Zealand, the Pacific Islands, and the Philippines. Currently, Oceania most often refers to civil society rather than to the state. For example, the Roman Catholic Church has an Oceania synod and the International Soccer Federation has an Oceania subgroup. This chapter will use the broader definition, namely, the countries between the continents of Asia and the Americas.

Most of the discussion below will draw upon the history of the "new settler societies" of Australia and New Zealand and use examples from former colonies such as the Philippines, Papua and New Guinea, and the Pacific Island countries.

NEW SETTLER SOCIETIES

In addition to Australia and New Zealand, South Africa, Argentina, Chile, and Uruguay are normally included to make up the full listing of the "new settler societies" (Denoon 1983). Other lists also include Canada and the United States (Hartz 1964). The former listing includes countries heavily dependent on export earnings from raw materials, which distinguishes them from the other so-called advanced industrial societies, including the United States and Canada. These "new societies" are also termed settler states, as they were formed on the basis of settling permanent populations, rather than as simply establishing military or trading outposts, as was the case with the Philippines, for example.

Under English common law the contrast has also been drawn between "settled" and "conquered" states. Settler Societies are those where the migrating population from Europe encountered no established population. Colloquially, this could be termed vacant possession—the legal term was *Terra Nullius*. The latter were places that had established populations that needed to be subdued or "conquered" before European settlement could take hold. The early adoption of the legal doctrine of *Terra Nullius* by the colonial Australian court system in the first half of the nineteenth century effectively denied any prior rights of the apparently nomadic indigenous Aboriginal people. This gave the European settlers more or less free rein over the land. In contrast, the indigenous Maori population of New Zealand gave clear evidence of agricultural settlements and waged war on the European intruders. The resultant Treaty of Waitangi signed in 1840 gave recognition to the prior rights of the Maoris and ensured the legal and constitutional basis for the maintenance of their independent culture (Mulgan 1989).

In both Australia and New Zealand predominantly Anglo-Celtic populations had established societies, which by the end of the nineteenth century were widely seen as fragments of the United Kingdom, without its tops (the aristocracy) and tails (the urban poor) (Reeves 1902). As was the case with the United States and Canada, streams of European travelers (most notably the novelist Anthony Trollope and the political commentator Lord Bryce) passed through Australia and New Zealand during the nineteenth century and penned reasonably favorable accounts of their societies and political progress.

International migration was critical to the formation of Australia and New Zealand (Castles 1998). The sheer scale of the global movement of people in the second half of the nineteenth century was greater than at any previous time in recorded Western history. The next great wave occurred after the dislocation caused by World War II. Both "waves" were possible, inter alia, due to the modernization of transportation and information flows caused by technological change.

International trade allowed both economies to prosper and act as magnets for further immigration, again predominantly from the United Kingdom. Economists (Slaughter and Swagel 1997) have demonstrated that international trade movements peaked in the early twentieth century, subsequently bottomed out due to the two world wars and the Great Depression, and then rose again in the 1970s and 1990s. During the key international decade, the 1890s, other parts of the Oceania region were not booming. For example, Papua was an Australian colony until the 1970s and New Guinea was a German colony until the 1890s.

DEMOCRATIZATION IN THE NEW SOCIETIES

Australia and New Zealand were not simply "fragments" of the Old World but from the second half of the 1850s moved firmly toward the orderly transition to independence from the United Kingdom and then toward democracy. In fact, democratization was a product of globalization. These societies were able to achieve a measure of democracy because they were without the established political and economic elites of the Old World. Hartz's (1964: 8) very influential fragment theory posits that "Australian radicalism . . . remains morally fixed at the point of its origin," namely, the radicalism of Richard Cobbett. Particular social groups were bearers of radical democratic values. English and Irish radicals, including the Tolpuddle Martyrs and Chartists, were transported as convicts to Australia in the mid-nineteenth century (Hughes 1988).

Manhood suffrage (1856), the invention of the secret ballot (1856), the establishment of effective labor parties (1890s), and then female suffrage (1894) had all been concluded by the beginning of the twentieth century in Australia and New Zealand (Reeves 1902). Other colonies were slower on both scores. In 1902, the year after federation and the establishment of the Australian nation, most Australian women over twenty-one were allowed to vote in the federal (national) elections. Aboriginal "natives" were specifically excluded, unless they had through a quirk of fate already gained the right at a state level.

The Australian political compact specifically excluded "colored" people and the indigenous Aborigines in a variety of ways. "Colored" men were specifically excluded from being granted "miners' rights," without which they could not legally seek gold or any other mineral or ore. In the Australian colonies "miners' rights" were one important basis on which voting rights were gained, and they marked the beginning of inroads into property qualifications. (Technically speaking they were also property rights of a kind, but clearly not of the typical kind.) In fact, the right to maintain discrimination against "coloreds" by the government was extensively discussed and formally agreed to by the Australian founding fathers during the official federal convention debates of the late 1890s.The colonies had treated their Aboriginal minorities in, at best, a paternalistic way. The colonies, therefore, fought strongly to keep legislative control over those populations for themselves. They had no wish to cede their powers to the newly formed federal government at the turn of the century. Aborigines were subsequently denied political rights until well into the twentieth century and only gained the federal franchise in 1962.

In New Zealand, the indigenous Maori people fared better. They had the basis of formal recognition through a treaty. This subsequently led to the achievement of separate Maori constituencies in the New Zealand legislature. More generally, according to Lyall Allan (1990: 372), the New Zealand practice of political separatism can be termed the "Maori option," which many saw as "peculiar," "not particularly progressive," or even as "offensive to democratic theory." The Maori political culture did not easily fit in with the dominant Anglo tradition of majoritarianism. However, the New Zealand option must be viewed as better political practice than the Australian one. Moreover, by the late 1990s, the Maori option has garnered considerable support (see for example the discussion in the New South Wales Issues Paper: *Aboriginal Representation in Parliament* 1998).

Clearly it was a white man's political paradise. White men's political rights had been advanced in nineteenth-century colonial Australia. These rights were advanced after federation (1901) through the key institutions of the parliament, the bureaucracy, and the political parties. These institutions remained heavily dominated by white males until the 1970s. The democratization anomaly of Australia and New Zealand was that white men held the keys to power, and they governed on *behalf* of indigenous and white women.

GLOBALIZATION AND GENDER RELATIONS

A long if scattered literature discusses the specific impact of colonization upon gender relations. In addition, a stream of scholarship within feminist political economy has charted the impact of industrial capital upon marriage and the family (Hamilton 1978). Feminist political economists argue that with the advent of industrial capitalism, all members of the family were drawn into the paid workforce, causing the home gradually to shift from a place of production to a place of consumption. Before industrialization, the household functioned to produce clothing, household items, and food. The same strictures did not identically apply to those women whose husbands and fathers owned the factories or were self-employed in business or the professions, such as farmers. In these households women and children were not forced into paid employment. In fact, the middle-class wife became the "Angel in the House" with largely decorative and social roles. The literature on the origins of the suffrage movement in nineteenth-century Europe pays tribute to the activities of precisely such women.

Contemporary commentators (such as de Tocqueville 1988) saw that the absence of hereditary classes among men extended to the relations between men and women. Marriage was no longer concerned chiefly with inheritance of land (especially under a system of primogeniture) but with other social goals. He was referring to the nature of the house on the prairie (de Tocqueville 1988: 733). His main argument was that in democratic societies, as compared with aristocratic ones, men and women might unite on the basis of feeling rather than property. Consequently, he maintained, that in the United States marriages tended to resemble partnerships whereas in more traditional Europe they were more hierarchical.

Historian Patricia Grimshaw (1972, 1983) has explored the character of the prevailing models of marriage in nineteenth-century United States, New Zealand, Australia, and the Pacific. She found the partnership model to prevail among the European settlers. The domestic partnership model was then used as a rationale for public activism by a variety of women leaders. The question was posed as follows: If women have their own sphere within marriage shouldn't that sphere and they also be recognized with political status? Also, the issue of excessive drinking was a reminder that men not only could not be trusted to look after the interests of women and children in the political realm but also that their political interests frequently oppose those of women.

Double standards for men and women regarding sexual behavior also increased political tension. Grimshaw and May (1994) charted some of these other gender sources of conflict in their study of the destructive effect of the European settlers upon Aboriginal marriages and family life. Sexuality was one source of the friction between white and indigenous women in settler societies. In the outback, white men spoke of "black velvet" and respectable white women looked the other way. This issue is still mostly discussed through fiction rather than in official white political circles and history books.

In settling frontiers, white women's work was invaluable and is recorded in poetry and song as well as in more formal historical accounts. A tendency, however, emerged for the partnership model to incorporate separate spheres. Consequently in the rural/farming sectors, women's work was identifiably different from that of males. In the towns, when opportunities arose for paid work, women tended to work in different industries, such as clothing and textiles, than men. Women struggled for equality in the newly established labor movement that was focused on the "family wage" (1907), which would give men an advantage in the workplace. Hence, women gained higher living standards as wives at the expense of financial independence and labor market equality. In Australia and New Zealand the good economic conditions delivered by world trade conditions were translated, via national institutional decisions, into good household incomes. In other words, financial incentives existed for marriage until the second wave of globalization and the shift in the 1970s toward wage justice at the individual level and the end of the "family wage" model.

The major social issue uniting white women in the early twentieth century in most settler societies, including that of the United States, was their opposition to excessive male drinking. Grimshaw (1972) has explained this on economic grounds as well as for partnership reasons; namely, that wives had implied rights conveyed through the marriage relation. By drinking, men were depriving their wives of their rights to shared income. The most prevalent form of female activism in the nineteenth-century colonies was around the temperance issue. The

Woman's Christian Temperance Movement was the most significant force lobbying for votes for women at this period (Grimshaw 1972).

The first wave of the Australian and New Zealand women's movements tended to be divided between those who accepted women's separate (but equal) role and those who struggled against the notion of equality. Both sections of the movement projected different models of the "political" than did the male political institutions (Sawer and Simms 1984). The separate but equal faction tried to bring "private" issues, such as maternal and child welfare, into public consideration. Voluntary organizations, such as the Country Women's Association, set up their own welfare infrastructure. Those who accepted subordination and difference pursued politics into the economic realm and lobbied in the workplace and in the labor movement. Both wings actively lobbied local (in New Zealand) and state (in Australia) governments. In other words, divided government was not necessarily negative for women's interests. White men had carved up the spoils of national power, but this left unguarded many local political spaces, especially for white women.

THE FEDERAL EXPERIMENT

The Oceania case also shows clearly that the nation-state has neither been a pervasive nor necessarily a defender of the weak. To suggest that the nation-state was a bulwark against capitalist exploitation and protector of women until its position was challenged by the current wave of globalization is not supported by Australian history (nor by U.S. history). To suggest that the breakup of strong nations necessarily leads to anarchy and decay is also incorrect (Giddens 1998). The experience in the "new world settler societies," to the contrary, reveals that federalism enabled greater democratization, greater balance of forces within the nation-state, and more political spaces for women to operate.

Bhiku Parekh (1998, 274) has persuasively argued that the idea of the nation-state is by no means self-evident or inevitable. Yet many accounts of globalization (Young, chapter 3 below) indicate that the nation-state is in decline, and that this is necessarily problematic. Other accounts, such as that of Anthony Giddens (1998), also note that the nation-state has limited power to deal effectively with the power of capital without borders. This assumes that the state has historically favored the rights of consumers over capital. At the very least, this assertion would require demonstration. The state, in newly industrializing countries, such as the Philippines, has consciously fostered the interests of local and international business at the expense of consumers. A brief history of the Australian federal compact in the Oceania region shows that the nation-state is relatively new and has not been as pervasive as suggested in some of the globalization literature. From the Oceania perspective forms of governance other than the nation-state may instead provide exemplars for dealing with the power of global capital.

According to international relations scholars, the Westphalian model provides the basis for the "sovereign territory ideal" of the modern nation-state. The so-called Philadelphian system is different and less well described by international relations scholars. Under this model, sovereignty is shared between two or three different levels of government within the same territory. The latter system is better known outside international relations as federalism. Also well known is the fact that federalism was chosen by many "New Societies." In the United States the idea of federalism supported the eighteenth-century ideal of limited government. In the nineteenth century, federalism was chosen by Canada and then by Australia. In both cases, the justifications were practical rather than philosophical.

Colonial politician and political scientist Reeves (1902: chap. 4) has listed the practical reasons for federation, including fear of external attack and desire to remove boundaries to intercolonial trade. He has also noted that federalism has a conservative aspect, as reflected in his comment that it would provide a "steadying influence" (p. 150) against the excesses of the newly formed labor parties. Incidentally, labor parties were scarcely represented among the founding fathers of either the United States or Australia who were mostly men of property (Denoon 1983: chap. 1). While the central government conducted foreign relations, the state governments dealt with the bulk of government/business relations, including international mining and manufacturing firms (Bell and Head 1993). The central government coordinated labor relations involving centralized wage fixing rather than collective bargaining. In contrast, in the United States, business has dealt with all levels of government. New Zealand followed Britain in opting for a unitary system, but even under that model, local governments have played important roles in business relations.

FEMINIST POLITICAL STRATEGIES

Women, both European and indigenous, were largely left out of the process of establishing political compacts in both Australia and New Zealand, as well as in the United States and Canada. However, the original social roles of European women were highly significant. For example, in the subduing of traditional societies in the region, their work as missionaries and "civilizers" was crucial (Grimshaw 1983; Grimshaw and May 1994).

White Australian and New Zealand women were politically active long before they gained the right to vote. Yet they tended not to lobby with or on behalf of indigenous women as their equals. White women's activism was predicated on raising indigenous women to white standards, in line with white women's roles as civilizers.

The "first wave" of feminism was nothing if not international (Banks 1981). The Australian and New Zealand contingents were among the strongest adherents to internationalism, in spite of the vast distances involved in attending meetings in

Britain and Europe (Anderson 1920). Australian and New Zealand women lobbied for women's suffrage in Britain long after it had been achieved "down under."

Vigorous debate exists as to the impact of women's suffrage and feminist lobbying upon public policies. Critics (such as Bryce 1921, 3:339) maintained, with specific reference to New Zealand in the early years, that women made "no practical difference . . . apart from . . . drink questions." Defenders, such as Anderson (1920: 280), measured the feminist impact by "laws relating to the drink traffic, in those relating to women and children, and in the altered status of women."

The women's movement in both Australia and New Zealand was most active at the local levels of government (Sawer and Simms 1984, chap. 2). In Australia, with its federal system, this also meant state government. The women's movement tended to be most focused on health, welfare, and service delivery matters, which, in most political systems, are dealt with at local/regional/state levels. The focus on the national government came only in the 1970s. Even then women focused attention on the lower rungs of the state. In Australia, the first legislative packages on equal opportunity and antidiscrimination questions were first introduced at the state level.

The nation-state did not become a major focus of attention of Australian women until the 1970s when the second wave of globalization became a vital force impacting gender relations around the world. The court's interpretation of the "foreign affairs" power of the constitution meant that the central government could make policy on areas over which it did not have strict authority if the area was subject to international treaty. International policy was seen as an important leverage to force domestic governments to toe the line. Recognizing this power, Australian and Filipina women have been among the most active in international women's groups, particularly those associated with the United Nations (Simms 1989). Although local and state governments have been a major focal point for women in Australia during the second wave as well as the first wave of globalization, the nation-state has not been irrelevant for women's groups. In fact, if central governments control much of the national budget, then nation-states are crucial, even if regional governments deliver services.

Catherine Mackinnon's (1983) point that feminists have neglected to theorize the state is not only still more or less true, but was also acknowledged to be true for Australia and New Zealand (Franzway 1989). Ironically, the Australian feminist practice since the 1970s of establishing a presence of feminist activists (femocrats) in the state bureaucracy has been accompanied by a lack of sustained analysis of the process. The extensive Australian literature has tended to examine the role of particular individuals and described particular policy initiatives, such as gender analyses of national budgets.

Many writers (Franzway 1989; Simms 1981, 1993) have noted the ambivalence of the Australian women's movement toward the state. The current debate over globalization and democratization draws attention to the strong history of localism and voluntarism in the women's movements of the New World. In contrast to Europe, where the women's movement during the first wave of globalization was facilitated by the existence of the servant class, in Australia, the United States, and other settler societies, it was assisted by the "family wage," which gave upper-middle-class women free time to be politically active. Class ideology and structure, as well as globalization, impact not only gender relations but also the types of political space and processes that have been available for women.

As the second wave of globalization since World War II has pulled more women into the labor force and raised new questions about equality in the workplace, feminist strategies for dealing with gender relations have also changed in settler societies. For example, by the 1970s sufficient numbers of women had become part of the Australian state government that they became independently powerful. Australian femocrats (women activists who were in high positions in the civil service) were strongest in the 1970s when they were able to secure funding for initiatives started in civil society by women's groups (Franzway 1989). These groups provided women's services such as domestic violence refuges, health centers, and rape crisis programs. They also improved women's career prospects in public bureaucracies through equal employment opportunity (EEO) programs (Sawer 1990). At this time in Australia and New Zealand, the women's movement saw workforce participation (often compelled by the globalization and free trade forces) as the key to women's freedom. Australian and New Zealand women have had among the highest workforce participation rate in the world.

By the mid-1980s the neoliberal programs of the second wave of globalization adopted by the state and federal governments began to restrict femocrats' efforts. Clare Burton, one of the leading femocrats in the EEO field, complained in 1998 that an emphasis on individualism and diversity had eclipsed EEO programs. Federal government employment programs began to read like a cross between a neoliberal document and a postmodern treatise.

Yet, at the same time as official state feminism was declining in the wake of neoliberalism, the same neoliberalism was delivering jobs for some women. The service sector, always an important source of female employment, has burgeoned under globalization (Kirkby 1992). Manufacturing, a male employment area, has shrunk, as has rural employment. Recent newspaper reports *(Sydney Morning Herald* Jan. 5, 1999) explain that retrenched women workers in "white collar" areas are finding new jobs more quickly than men due to women's greater networking skills. Hence, the impact of the second wave of globalization on women's status and on gender relations has numerous positive as well as negative elements.

INDIGENOUS CHALLENGES TO EUROPEAN GOVERNANCE

In indigenous communities women have been and remain key community leaders. The indigenous populations both of Australia and New Zealand have fostered alternative models of government (Jennett 1990; Mulgan 1989). Mulgan (1989) has noted the inconsistencies between the majoritarianism of the British parliamentary tradition and the indigenous Maori political traditions. A similar point could be made about Australian Aborigines, although an Australian equivalent to Mulgan's New Zealand book-length study does not exist. Fletcher (1994) has described several case studies of Aboriginal communities adapting Western institutions to suit them. This basically means taking white-established, hierarchical, bureaucratic institutions and making them more community-focused. In the Australian case, necessity rather than choice (Commonwealth of Australia 1997: 560) forced indigenous populations to be innovative in their tactics and strategies, often because these groups have not been included in the mainstream institutions, such as parliaments and political parties. One of Fletcher's (1994) cases involved a traditional community that achieved a degree of self-government through becoming a local government authority (see also Jennett 1990).

Australian Aborigines have been less successful in their search for formal parliamentary representation than their New Zealand counterparts, who early on achieved a level of guaranteed minimum representation. Maoris have also been active in the mainstream political parties. Their current economic status is considerably higher than that of the Australian Aboriginal or the North American Indian populations. Most recently, two of the six Australian states have seriously examined the New Zealand option of guaranteed separate representation. Partly on account of being relatively unsuccessful using formal means of electoral representation, Aborigines have utilized other avenues. For example, they have lobbied international agencies, especially the United Nations, to embarrass the domestic government (Jennett 1990). Aboriginal activists have marshaled arguments from international human rights law to lobby for legal changes and reparations for past injustices.

Simultaneously, Aboriginal women and men have been using the British common law tradition. In 1992, the Australian High Court reversed the original doctrine of *Terra Nullius*. The High Court recognized native title as a form of land tenure and noted the following: "Aborigines were dispossessed of their land parcel by parcel, to make way for expanding colonial settlement. Their dispossession underwrote the development of the nation" (quoted in Commonwealth of Australia 1994: iv).

CONCLUSION

These cases show that the nation-state has, at times, acted cruelly toward its inhabitants. They also show that globalization played out differently in the early years of Oceania than it did in Europe. They also suggest that the existence of indigenous peoples, the more egalitarian marital relations in the "settler states," and the adoption of the Philadelphian (federal) rather than the Westphalian form of the nation-state has created a very different playground for current globalization processes, particularly as they affect women and gender relations in general. Nonetheless, in Australia as well as in Europe, the United States and Canada, and other advanced industrial countries, a generally common gender regime tended to prevail. This regime divided men and women into the public and private spheres, identified men as the bread (rice) winner, and emphasized a separate but equal notion of complementarity between the sexes as the foundation for political citizenship. This gender regime solidified during the Fordist period of capitalist accumulation, as noted by Young in the following chapter, but is now, in Oceania as well as elsewhere, being challenged by the new characteristics of the late twentieth-century globalization.

3

Globalization and Gender: A European Perspective

Brigitte Young

GLOBALIZATION

As we enter the twenty-first century, globalization is best understood as an open and contradictory process that entails restructuring the nation-state–bounded economic system and the Keynesian institutional regulatory structures that came to dominate the post–World War II era. More specifically, European nation-states are facing a process of denationalization of the political and economic spaces that symbolized the preceding period of capitalism, generally referred to as the Fordist regime of accumulation (Aglietta 1979; Jessop 1988). In contrast to the belief that the global restructuring process is nothing new (as highlighted by Marian Simms in the previous chapter), I suggest that the current phase of the world economy is characterized by significant discontinuities with the preceding periods (Sassen 1996).

After 1945, Fordism came to mean the highly successful synchronization between mass production and mass consumption. The novelty of the post–World War II Fordist regime was based on the way liberal democratic societies were able to assert themselves against the destructive forces of the market. At the center of the unique historic Fordist compromise was the synchronization of real (male) wages with productivity growth, and the national anticyclical monetary and fiscal policies that led to one of the longest growth periods in history. The Keynesian welfare state was key in stabilizing consumer demand and expanding social rights to average citizens who, for the first time, were given access to mass consumer goods. Since 1973, the "virtuous circle" between mass production and mass consumption has come under increasing stress. The neoliberal answer to the crisis has been the deregulation and flexibilization of the nationally bounded economic and social system. Whereas the Fordist model assumed relatively full employment in the formal economy, the neoliberal post-Fordist model sees labor as a more flexible commodity employed both in the formal and the informal economy (flexibilization).

Accordingly, globalization cannot be reduced to a quantitative comparison of international trade and financial statistics as many critics of globalization assert. Hirst and Thompson (1996) cite export quotas and data for direct investment between 1870 and 1973 to show that the process of globalization is nothing new. These scholars maintain that the present global trade and investment data do not significantly differ from those of the imperialist period. But globalization is not about quantitative indicators. In contrast to globalization, internationalization prior to World War I was based on an exchange between nation-states. It starts with the nation-state as the central actor in this exchange (Strange 1996). The major difference between internationalization and globalization is that in the late twentieth century national economic and political actors were exposed to the logic and conditions of global competition. The nation-state continues to be important, but is forced to adjust to the economic logic of the global economy. The state logic no longer is that of Keynesian demand management. Hirsch (1995) refers to the new state as a "competition state." The state acts primarily as a geo-economic actor, and its traditional role as geopolitical actor becomes secondary (Altvater and Mahnkopf 1996).

For the first time in history, the global economy has the capacity "to work as a unit in real time on a planetary scale" (Castells 1996, 92). Whereas the space-time relations in modernity were shaped by the separation between time and space—it was the invention of the mechanical clock that first made possible a precise classification in space and time zones—globalization meant an expansion of such processes. In other words, a network architecture was emerging as a form of connection between different social contexts and regions across the entire global surface (Giddens 1995). The many "times" across different continents shrink to one world time. This process of creating "a timeless time," despite events that happen at different times, has produced an artificial "world rhythm," making it difficult to discern between the "real" and the "virtual." In this "hyperreality," citizens of the first world live in the "time." These inhabitants, linked via telecommunications and computer technology, experience the globe as a village. Their spatial environment is increasingly minimally restricted. Inhabitants of the developing world experience the space-time dimension in reverse to the people of the first world. They live in a "space which is heavy, indestructible, untouchable, . . . [tied down by time,] and . . . beyond the control of its inhabitants" (Bauman 1996, 661).

In this "hyperreality" in which the spatial and temporal distances between local and global events are "stretched," a complex relation develops between "local involvement" (a situation of simultaneous presence) and the "interaction across distances" (connections between presence and absence) (Giddens 1995, 85). With globalization, an intensification of global social relations spanning local and distant social events starts to take effect. One gets the impression that with economic globalization all other social relations also become globalized, even those aspects that cannot be subsumed under capitalist forms of utilization (Altvater and

Mahnkopf 1996, 13). As a result, globalization always also encounters barriers. Not everything that comes in contact with globalization can be subsumed to the logic of capitalism. Globalization is thus not only a process of expansion and breakthroughs of political, economic, social, and ecological barriers. It always also involves the development of counter-tendencies, those that set barriers to globalization.

This chapter is guided by the central question of how an increasingly border-less global market and the territorially bounded concept of democracy can be re-constituted so that they can include women, and how gender regimes and orders are reconfigured in the new "network societies." The theoretical insights of the French Regulation School provide the basis for explaining the complex connection between the transformation of the Fordist regime of accumulation and the re-configuration of new post-Fordist gender regimes and order. To explore this ar-gument I focus first on the decline of industrial capitalism and the present rise of "informational capitalism" with its new network structures (Castells 1996). I pro-ceed with an analysis of why and how globalization has undermined the Fordist gender regimes and discuss the emerging new "flexible" gender orders. Finally, I explore the significance of these changes for feminist state theory and practice.

"INFORMATIONAL CAPITALISM" AND THE DEVELOPMENT OF NETWORK STRUCTURES

The globalization literature defines the new mode of production emerging in the late twentieth century as a transformation from industrial production to a service economy. The existing data provide some evidence for this assumption. Not only has the share of the service sector in the United States risen to 70 percent as part of the gross domestic product, in other industrial countries as well the share of the service sector has increased while the share of industrial production has declined (Thurow 1997). From this, a linear sequence of historic regimes of accumulation is extrapolated: agrarian capitalism until the nineteenth century, followed by in-dustrial capitalism, and now the rise of the tertiary economy. These different ac-cumulation regimes vary fundamentally in how profits are extracted. In agrarian capitalism, profits were appropriated through the extensive use of land and labor power in the production process. Industrialism relied on the intensification of technology and labor power, made possible by the fossil fuel revolution. Not only was it feasible to abstract high energy efficiency with low amounts of energy input, the profits from this production process were used to advance social, po-litical, cultural, and economic living standards of the population (Altvater and Mahnkopf 1996). Energy efficiency is no longer the basis for profit accumulation in the emerging informational capitalism. At the center of the present value gen-eration is the quantitative and qualitative intensification of electronic information and communication processes (Castells 1996).[1]

The source of productivity lies, as Castells points out, in the technology of knowledge generation, information processing, and symbol communication. "What is specific to the informational mode of development is the action of knowledge upon knowledge itself as the main source of productivity. . . . [Information processing is focused on a "virtuous circle" of] interaction between the knowledge sources of technology and the application of technology to improve knowledge generation and information processing" (1996, 17). While industrial capitalism pursues the goal of maximizing output, informational capitalism is oriented toward technological development: the accumulation of knowledge toward higher levels of complexity in information processing. This information production does not take place in an abstract space. It is embedded in material production processes. As a result, neither industrial nor agrarian production loses its economic importance in the global economy despite the continuing decline in overall numbers. On the contrary, as a result of the new information technology, for example in genetic engineering, new horizons appear for the agricultural and the medical and pharmaceutical sectors, which were inaccessible until now. The tapping, manipulation, and decodification of human, animal, and plant life and the future reprogramming of genetic codes of living material open new doors, however critically this is viewed from an ethical standpoint. We are not even able to fathom the effects on human beings and nature at the moment (Haraway 1996; Wichterich 1998). To quote Castells once again, "what characterizes the current technological revolution is not the centrality of knowledge and information, but the application of such knowledge and information to knowledge generation and information processing and communication devices, in a cumulative feedback loop between innovation and the uses of innovation" (1996, 32). The present interpretations of the sequential development from agrarian to industrial, and now to a service economy, represent a simplification of the very complex interconnection of different production developments.

The change in the technology paradigm has also led to fundamental transformations in the types of economic organizations and control mechanisms. The new types of organizational structures are based on a combination of features inherent in the market and the state. On the market side, the characteristic plurality of autonomous actors is combined with the typical capacity of the state to coordinate strategies for the purpose of achieving specific goals (Messner 1997, 57). Castells defines the emerging plurality of the interorganizational weblike connections as a network society. Networks are the new instruments for a global economy based on innovation, globalization, and decentralized concentration, "for work, workers, and firms based on flexibility, and adaptability; for a culture of endless deconstruction and reconstruction; for a polity geared towards the instant processing of new values and public moods; and for a social organization aiming at the supersession of space and the annihilation of time" (1996, 471). The new economy no longer relies on the vertical organizations of the multinational era, described by Alfred Chandler (1977) as the prototype of efficiency during the

Fordist era, but is organized around global enterprise networks of capital, management, and information, whose access to technological innovation is the driving force for competition. The new logic of this network society not only pervades the economy, it substantially alters the entire social structure and dramatically reorganizes existing power relations. According to Castells, "switches" connecting the networks are the new instruments of power. Financial flows that take control of media empires influence political processes and furnish the interoperating codes and switches that shape social processes and the social structure. This type of capitalism differs from the previous industrialization first in that it is global and second, in that it is structured largely around a network of financial flows located in a few strategic "global cities" (Sassen 1996). Profits are mainly accumulated in the sphere of circulation and no longer in production. Whatever is extracted as profit "is reverted to the meta-network of financial flows, where all capital is equalized in the commodified democracy of profit-making" (Castells 1996, 472).

The transformation from vertical structures of industrial organization to the new interconnected global networks has fundamentally changed the gender-specific Fordist division of labor between the highly paid male industrial workers and the female part-time earners. I will now examine how and why this has occurred and explore the reconfiguration of gender regimes in the context of the emerging global "flexible regime of accumulation" (Harvey 1989). In the new decentralized "flexible accumulation" processes the organization of work is based on the spatial dispersal of informal subcontracting and outsourcing activities to a wide net of contractors, subcontractors, and sub-subcontractors. The preferred workers in the "global factories" specializing in cheap electronic, textile, clothing, and shoe products are young, uneducated, poor rural women who are strangers to labor organization. Women no longer earn money only as an additional source of income to the male breadwinner. They increasingly subsidize the seasonal work of their husbands through their permanent integration in the labor force, or their wage labor functions as the sole income to feed the family (Ward and Pyle 1995).

Associated with this spatial dispersion of economic activities, we witness a new division of labor between an international, hypermobile, professional class of "information carriers"—mostly white and male—and the low-skilled, place-bound workers of all colors. In her studies on "global cities," Saskia Sassen (1996) criticizes the mainstream accounts on globalization for operating like a "narrative of eviction." These narratives concentrate on the global culture, the hypermobility of capital, and the power of transnationals. By neglecting the material production sites for running the advanced information and global communications technologies, we miss the place-bound capital that is at least still partly embedded in national territories. Focusing on the *practices* that provide the infrastructure for the production and reproduction of global capital, we recover a multiplicity of work cultures ranging from immigrant to female cultures where the work of globalization gets done. These include secretaries, pizza delivery persons, cleaning crews, truck drivers, industrial service workers, maids, and a host of other low-skilled, blue-collar workers that have become "invisible" in this narrative of hypermobile capital. The invisibility of the material work culture has produced a change in the valuation of labor inputs. Increasingly, many of the unskilled jobs are regarded as irrelevant and no longer needed in the global economy. Sassen warns that the corporate culture, with its emphasis on specialized information services, is overvalued while other kinds of work cultures are devalued. In simple terms, it is the work of women and immigrants that has become devalorized. Thus we need to proceed from the bottom up in studying how the global economy works. "Power is not a silence at the bottom; its absence is present and has consequences" (Sassen 1996, 21). If we include the precarious activities of women and immigrants as part of the capital-bound globalization process, then women and the ethnic economy are important components of the global information economy.

The informal sector of the global economy employs many more women than the formal sector.[2] The major "carriers" of the informal economy are the subcontractors that produce for the transnational corporations. Particularly in the free export zones, found anywhere from Central America to parts of Africa and East Asia, a new type of "global factory" has emerged. On the border between the United States and Mexico these global factories work on a contract basis for American transnational corporations, such as J. C. Penney, Sears & Roebuck, Wal-Mart, and Montgomery Ward. The "*maquila* businesses" profit from the high unemployment rates in these regions, and from the desperate need of women and men to earn a living.[3] These export zones benefit from the extraterritorial status they enjoy. Import and export activities are handled in these zones and are cut off from the national territory; companies in the zones do not provide living space for their workforce; buildings and factories are exempt from taxes; the enterprises do not pay local, land, corporate, or income taxes; imports and exports are exempt from tariffs; the host countries provide infrastructure, build streets and harbors, and offer telephone, water, and energy services at low prices (Lemoine 1998). The new cheap-wage "*el dorado*" countries in Asia at the turn of the twenty-first century are Vietnam, Cambodia, Laos, and China. These countries are replacing the former cheap-labor countries of South Korea, Taiwan, and Hong Kong in the 1970s, followed in the 1980s by the Philippines, Thailand, and Indonesia (Wichterich 1998).

Transnational production is increasingly associated with local informal activities that range from sweatshops and home-based work to street alleys and backyard conditions. Increasingly, the rural countryside is opened up for even cheaper sources of labor. Transnational corporations take advantage of the still-existing household economies by paying below the subsistence minimum. As a result, the subsistence work of the women in the household economy relieves the companies from paying even the minimum wage. The search for ever-cheaper production sites means that the firms are constantly on the move either to locate their businesses to cheaper areas, taking advantage of further outsourcing into back alleys and sweatshops, or rationalize the production process and thus get rid of most of the labor force (Ward and Pyle 1995).

In contrast to the Fordist production techniques, the new flexible accumulation can be housed in small and mobile "global assembly lines." The new precarious, unregulated, and very exploitative activities of the informal economy have also appeared in Western industrial countries. In Eastern Europe and in the periphery of Europe, the interaction among globalization, informalization, and transnationalization has promoted the flexibilization of the workforce and strengthened the gender-specific division of cheap labor (Wichterich 1998; Mahnkopf 1997). Transnational labor-intensive corporations are found from Greece, Spain, and Ireland to the United States. Many of the European textile and clothing industries, the Italian producer Benetton for example, are marketing enterprises that coordinate globally their cheap-labor subcontracting firms dispersed among networks of worldwide sweatshops (Harvey 1989). In the United States, labor-intensive transnational corporations are found in the same industries (for example, electronics and the clothing industries) as in cheap-wage countries of the developing world. In contrast to the widely held belief that the low-skilled and work-intensive industries have migrated to Third World countries, the United States shows exactly the reverse. The clothing and textile industries are not shrinking sectors. The number of workers in the clothing industry alone is greater than the combined workforce in the auto, steel, and electronic industries (Fernández-Kelly 1989).

Despite important differences there are commonalities between the Eastern European transitional societies, parts of the Third World, and the industrial countries: everywhere we find "cheap-wage zones" (Mahnkopf 1997). These enclaves of the informal economy have become a permanent feature of the formal economy. The informalization of the economy is thus no longer a marginal or transitional phenomenon. It is an immanent part of economic globalization. In the Northern Hemisphere, increasingly we see conditions of the "South," and in the South centers emerge that have much in common with the "North" (Die Gruppe von Lissabon 1997). New hierarchies of class, gender, and race emerge in this system of flexible accumulation. In the textile industry in Miami, for example, the producers are mostly Jewish men, the subcontractors are overwhelmingly Cuban men, and Cuban women fill the sweatshops (Fernández-Kelly and Garcia 1992). Globalization and the spatial dispersion of economic activities have thus created new gender hierarchies, which are intensified through class, ethnic, and national membership. Males overwhelmingly control the unregulated area of subcontracting while women (particularly immigrants) are found in the sweatshops of the "global factories" (Fernández-Kelly and Sassen 1995).

GENDER REGIMES: FROM FORDISM TO GLOBALIZATION

Methodologically, the argument presented here rests on the assumption that the transformation of specific historic regimes of accumulation go hand in hand with the reconfiguration of gender regimes and gender orders. With the concept of *gender*, the social construction of masculinities and femininities is emphasized rather than the biological definition of the sexes. Linda Gordon (1993) defines gender as a series of meaning systems that are socially constructed as sexual differences within the context of systemic male domination. Gender thus refers to societal networks of hierarchically regulated social relations, which are ordered along a socially dividing line that places women on one side and men on the other (Kreisky and Sauer 1995). The concept of *gender regime* is used here to refer to institutionalized practices and forms of gendered systems of domination that are constituted as social ordering principles in all societies. Social norms, rules, regulations, and principles are not gender-neutral entities, but are inscribed with specific norms for the roles men and women are designed to play in the polity. The networks of overlapping social and cultural mores then become embedded in the institutional structures of the polity. These institutionalized gender practices are far from being static entities, but are continually reproduced through the organization or structure of practice that persists in its effects on subsequent practices. Institutionalization means, as Connell points out, creating conditions that make cyclical practice probable (1987, 141). Finally, *gender orders* are the aggregate of these gender regimes at the level of macropolitics. The interaction between state powers that bear on gender relations, cultural definitions of gender, and the historical possibilities in gender relations makes up these orders. They are stabilized through the various micro- and mesopractices that ensure the reproduction of these macropolitical orders. Stabilized means that gender regimes and orders become sufficiently institutionalized as a result of specific historic regimes of capital accumulation. At the same time, the ongoing gender practices stand in "reflexive relations" (Giddens 1984) to the existing power structure of the sexes. Women and men continuously renegotiate the meaning of gender identity, struggling over the formation and dissolution of accepted categories and the reconfiguration of institutional relations (Connell 1987, 139). Gender regimes represent a symbolic gender order that is at the same time an arena of power in which the boundaries are part of a struggle between the sexes to define their contours. Given the dynamic process of gender regimes and orders, there is not only one historical "masculinity" or an unchanging ahistorical "femininity." Masculinities and femininities abound in their plurality in terms of both their spatial and temporal contexts. Gender regimes and orders are utilized in this study as heuristic devices to delineate and analyze the development and subsequent reconfiguration of these categories within specific historical contexts.

These conceptual tools provide the foundation for explaining the complex connection between the transformation of the Fordist regime of accumulation and the reconstruction of the new gender regimes and orders. In this context, I draw upon the theoretical insights of the French Regulation School, which stipulates capitalist modes of production as a series—but not necessarily a linear projection— of different historic regimes of accumulation and modes of regulation. The central question of this chapter is how is the transition of the Fordist regime of accumulation to a flexible global regime of accumulation related to the reconfiguration of new gender regimes?

Gender Regimes During the Fordist Period

The Fordist phase of capitalism (1950–1973) has already entered the history books as "the golden age of capitalism." The particular compromise between capital and labor was surely "the golden age" if one was a white male industrial worker living in a Western capitalist country. A look backward through the prism of gender analysis tells a different story of the gender regimes and orders that accompanied the golden age. Beginning at the turn of the century, Fordist industrialization replaced the extensive mode of production associated with agrarian capitalism and transformed the existing gender regimes based on the unity of the private and the public production spheres. In contrast to the agrarian period, the Fordist production model elevated the white male to the center of industrial capitalism. Males entered this new production paradigm both as managers in the newly emerging vertical organizations of the multinational firms (Chandler 1977) and as factory workers herded together in the places of mass production. The workplace and "his" family wage were tailored to the needs and interests of the male worker and "his" dependent family. The conditions for this Fordist "breadwinner model" were negotiated in the hierarchical, exclusionary, male-biased bastions of labor unions and employers' associations. These collective bargaining institutions possessed a monopoly in the formulation and implementation of wage-bargaining decision-making (Schmitter 1974). The corporatist organizations were deeply male-biased in their organizational, membership, decision-making, and leadership structures. Women were rarely found in leadership positions; they were absent from employers' associations; corporatist negotiations among labor, state bureaucracies and ministries, employers' associations; and from economic "think tanks." Decisions affecting the entire economy and not just workers and employers were made in these para-statal organizations,[4] bureaucratic administrations, and economic interest groups. The male industrial worker was at the center of this production model. In this gender-specific arrangement capital and labor were quite united. While they stood on opposite sides on class interests, capital and labor shared a common interest in reproducing the existing hierarchical Fordist gender order.

Yet the Fordist accumulation regime was not completely exclusive of women, but included them in a specifically dependent role. Inclusion was achieved through the status of the husband and in women's assigned social role as "career housewives." Women were not completely absent from the labor market. Integrating women into the labor force was certainly functional for increasing consumer demand. As pointed out earlier, the key to the Fordist production paradigm lies in the rising access of average citizens to mass consumption. One way to integrate women was via the expansion of the Keynesian welfare state. Women were hired for the care of the elderly and children, as nurses, teachers, and to provide other services for dependents. At the same time, women were hired for low-skill jobs in the social service hierarchy as social workers. Women were thus tied to the welfare state through a three-tier chain: as social workers, clients, and consumers of public services. In virtually all Western industrial countries, public services expanded in the Fordist period, and this proved beneficial for women. Yet this statement has to be qualified. The newly created social service jobs were in no way comparable to the well-paid industrial jobs of the male workers. The labor market remained highly segregated, replicating the sexual division of labor between production and reproduction. Elisabeth Hagen and Jane Jenson are right in pointing out that "the stereotypes, based on the deeply rooted assumptions about proper gender roles and gender relations, shaped labor markets no less in 'progressive' and egalitarian countries like Sweden than elsewhere" (1988, 9). This is not surprising given that the Fordist production model produced a gender order that, despite some differences, shared the overall characteristics of the "breadwinner model." Feminists have shown that European countries can be categorized as strong, weak, or medium breadwinner models (Ostner 1995). Despite these differentiations, none of the Western industrial capitalist countries have developed a gender order that is outside the breadwinner system. Aside from the job opportunities in care-giving and social services, women also found new opportunities at the lower end of the production line. Gaining entrance onto the factory floors had to do with the fundamental economic restructuring that started in the 1970s. With the process of economic rationalization, male jobs were increasingly sacrificed at the expense of cheaper and less-skilled labor. Highly paid industrial workers became redundant and women were hired for the low-skill assembly line jobs instead. That they succeeded in entering the factories did not mean that the few remaining well-paid industrial jobs were open to them.[5] The labor market remained sharply segregated, and the jobs available to women were at the lower end of the occupational hierarchy and were generally the undesirable positions. As in the public sector, the private sector seemed to replicate the sexual division of labor. The gender order reflected the social norms of a gender-specific separation between the public and the private. In this process, the nonmonetized housework of women became largely devalued; women, despite their integration in the labor market, were subordinated to the male breadwinner, and their activities were regarded as a secondary earning source to be spent only for consumption purposes (Hagen and Jenson 1988; Kurz-Scherf 1996).

The gender orders of the Fordist period can be summarized as consisting of three central elements:

1. The role of women, despite their integration into the labor markets, was tied to the reproductive and private spheres.
2. The role of women identified with the private arena corresponded with the male's role as the "breadwinner."
3. A gender-specific separation between the private and the public characterized the Fordist period.

In the geometry between class and gender, men were subordinated directly to the market. Women, on the other hand, were subordinated directly to men and only indirectly to market forces.

The present restructuring of the global economy and the increasing internationalization of capitalism has, as I will show in the next section, undermined the existing Fordist regime of accumulation and modes of regulation. The link between mass consumption and mass production has collapsed, and we seem to face a new uncertain economic regime without an institutional structure to control the unfettered forces of the market. This fundamental restructuring toward a system of "maximal markets" and "minimal states" has also weakened the male breadwinner model and the entire gender order that has been associated with the Fordist period. That global restructuring is occurring on a gendered terrain is largely forgotten in the mainstream accounts (Bakker 1994), a point to which I will return in the subsequent section.

THE NEW GENDER ORDERS

Can we identify a new configuration of gender order(s) that is emerging in response to these dramatic changes in both the production paradigm and the social structure? I start with the assumption that the three central aspects of the Fordist gender order are being fundamentally transformed. To recall, the three elements of this order are: (1) the male breadwinner model; (2) women associated with reproduction and the private sphere; and (3) the gender-specific separation between the private and the public arenas. The reconfiguration, which can only be inferred at this point and not tested as a hypothesis, seems to take place on many different levels. First, the Fordist model of the male breadwinner is a phenomenon of the past. Second, the stark gender-specific separation between the public and the private and the associated assignment to the reproductive and productive economies no longer reflect the reality of the situation. Third, while equality has increased among men and women of the middle class, we witness an increasing rise of inequality and differentiation among women depending on their racial, class, and national belonging (Friese 1995). Finally, a new gender-specific social division is emerging between those (mostly male, but including some females) who frequent the hypermobile "money society" and those (mostly female and unskilled, including males) who remain bound to the national "work territory." These changes do not imply only negative consequences for women. They also have the potential of weakening and dissolving local, patriarchal cultures and systems of male domination.

The Disappearance of the Fordist Family Breadwinner Model

Globalization has eroded the material conditions for the male breadwinner and his dependent wife and family. The increasing rise of double wage-earners since the 1970s is a byproduct of this development. Double wage-earner families can be divided into two groups. On the one side are the relatively well-off professionals who are part of the formal economy. A much larger group can be found in the medium and lower levels of the economy who rely on the additional wages of women to maintain or improve their living standards. There is also the group of single parents (mostly female), whose numbers have increased dramatically. In the United States, 67 percent of single mothers and 53 percent of mothers with children under three years old worked for wages in 1998. Of the double wage-earner families, 53 percent had children (Fernández-Kelly and Sassen 1995; Ward and Pyle 1995). The increasing "feminization of the labor process" has undermined the family wage system. Most wages in the informal economy are no longer adequate to support a family or provide economic security.

The increasing integration of women in the labor market has promoted new definitions of gender roles and has led to changes in the social value structure. The Fordist norm of women dependent on the male breadwinner is being replaced by the increasing individualization of women. Women from Mexico, living in the United States, express this value change as follows. Previously when a woman worked outside the household, everybody knew that she only did this to help the man; it was his duty to support his family. Now it is women's duty. Women are expected to work outside the household whether they want to or not (Fernández-Kelly and Sassen 1995, 112, 113), though it must be acknowledged that most women now do prefer working outside the home.

The Reconfiguration of the Public/Private and Production/Reproduction

The informalization of the labor market has greatly undermined the separation between the productive and reproductive economies. This separation was once the hallmark of the Fordist gender order. Increasingly the processes of production and reproduction (also of social reproduction) are played out in a wide spectrum ranging from the informal, formal, and household economies.[6] The conceptual separation between the private and the public does not take into account that the daily work of many women is done in a "triple shift" (Hossfeld 1990) among formal, informal, and family or subsistence activities.[7] Whether this work is done by women in the Caribbean, in Asia, or in Silicon Valley, its common feature is that women's work is a combination of activities in formal transnational production, informal sectors, and the subsistence economy. The borders of this "triple shift" are quite fluid for women, but relatively rigid for men. In order to secure their survival, women often spend up to sixteen hours in this "triple shift." In contrast, males are rarely found in the household economy and work either as subcontractors in the informal economy or in the formal economy (Ward and Pyle 1995).

In the 1970s, feminists pointed out that the gendered opposition between markets on the one hand, and family on the other, expresses an ambiguity that is full of contradictions. Regina Becker-Schmidt has argued "that what we generally understand as public (i.e., the social market economy) has as a capitalist economy many private property characteristics, and vice versa, the most private institution (i.e., the family) carries out public functions in education, reproduction of the labor force, care for the elderly among many other public activities" (Becker-Schmidt 1993, 44).

The feminist expansion of the concept of "work" to include the nonmonetized sector of the reproductive sphere remains, however, tied to the conventional idea of two complementary spheres. To the degree that the male breadwinner role is pushed more and more into the background, women are forced to earn their livings in a combination of the private and the public spheres. Increasingly large numbers work on-call in paid tele- and home-based activities in their homes (private sphere), are found in sweatshops (neither private nor public), or with their babies on their backs in the "global factories" (mixture of production and reproduction). Among other things, this means that the concept of a regular, statistically defined worktime utilized in the formal economy is no longer adequate to define the new forms of the "feminization of work." Joan Smith and Immanuel Wallerstein pleaded in the 1970s for a reconceptualization of "work" in the spheres of family, production, and the public. Instead of using the concept of "family" and separating monetary production from nonmonetized reproduction, they use the concept of the "household." Households are groups of family members, unrelated members sharing the living quarters, and neighborhoods that share resources. In this concept, no difference is drawn between the monetized and nonmonetized economies, and among family members, friends, and neighbors. The notion of "income" is expanded to include such barter services as subsistence production and is extended to neighborhood services and help (Smith and Wallerstein 1992, 6–9).

These new forms of "work" are also redefining existing gender identities. While the woman was identified with the family and subordinated to the male in the Fordist period, she is "reduced" to an individual in the global economy. The informal economy is only interested in "her" labor power. Reconciling the need to have a job and raise children at the same time is no longer an issue. From an economic standpoint, reproductive activities are made "invisible." Any demands for child care or other social services are silenced. Whether a sick child or an elderly parent hinders a woman worker from appearing at the doors of the free export zone is her "private" concern. Her place is taken by somebody else (Lemoine 1998). Women have finally reached the long-awaited abstract equality with men! Not in terms of wages, but in terms of an abstract notion of individualism that is free at last from child care. Despite its private seclusion, the reproductive work during the Fordist period was at least socially recognized. Now with the flexibilization of the labor market, child rearing has, once again, become an economic and social externality, and the dialectical relations between market and nonmarket activities has disappeared from the neoliberal discourse of the global economy (Elson 1994; Mann 1994).

The Increasing Inequality Among Women

The rising integration of women into the labor force has also meant a greater disparity among women of different classes, races, and national belonging. Although the new members of the new "club society" are mostly the "new boys," as Wendy Larner (1996) calls the new global players of the neoliberal New Zealand model, professional white middle-class women in the knowledge and information industries are no longer a rarity. Linda McDowell (1997) has shown in her study of the male financial stronghold of London that a slight crack did open for a new class of female professionals. As a result of the expanding international service economy, young, well-educated females succeeded in entering the middle and upper echelons of the finance and business world in the "global cities," although with the caveat, as Sassen has pointed out, "that notwithstanding the growing number of top level women professionals in global economic activities and in international relations, both these worlds can be specified as male-gendered insofar as each in its distinct way has the cultural properties and power dynamics that we have historically associated with men of power, or least some power" (1996: 10).

Labor market segmentation into a high-paid "post-Fordist informational economy" and the expanding informal sector of the "laboring poor" has increased the disparity among women. Low-skill service jobs are not just an important part of the infrastructure of the formal economy. They also allow socially privileged women in Europe, North America, and in other regions access to a professional career. As long as women, independent of their social class, remain responsible for reproductive work, the conditions upon which women enter "male" structures are gender-specific. Socially privileged females have the advantage of falling back upon mostly cheap, often illegal immigrants, to perform household tasks and child rearing. Without adequate public child care services, and without the fall-back position on women from developing and transitional countries, women would not be able to climb the professional ranks that demand great personal mobility and flexibility. Whether these activities are performed by mostly overqualified Polish women in Germany, or African American and Latin American immigrant women in the United States, they lead to a new international division of labor at the household level. On the one side is the "mistress" and on the other stands the "maid," separated by different racial, ethnic, and national backgrounds. A professional woman's career of the European or American middle or upper class is thus possible only in the narrow confines of ethnicity, class, and gender (Friese 1995; Mahnkopf 1997).

Gender-Specific Social Divisions

Globalization has led to a social division between those who remain tied to a territorially bounded "work society" and the "money society" that no longer is constrained by national boundaries. This opposition between the global money society and a national "work society" resulted from the "disembedding" of the monetary sphere from the productive economy (Altvater and Mahnkopf 1996). Huge profits are now made in the sphere of financial circulation and not in material production. As a result, finance capital has become dominant in the global economy.

The separation between finance capital and place-bound capital also explains the present crisis of the welfare state. Despite a "borderless" global economy, the majority of women and men continue to depend on the solidarity and the "community of fate" of national societies. It was after all the nation-state that extended political rights to the working class and integrated them as citizens. The territory of the nation-state thus became the "political and social home" of the working class. Within the boundaries of the national territory, the Keynesian full-employment guarantees provided the economic stability criteria for the Fordist model. The nation-state was also the vehicle for creating a national identity. I have already alluded that these political rights, as Carole Pateman (1988) pointed out, went hand in hand with a specific modern form of patriarchal welfare state.

Members of the money society, mostly white, upper-class, and male, do not depend on the solidarity of the national territory. They are members of a global "club society," in which the code of money is the medium for global identification. Voting for many of these individuals in national elections is no longer an expression of national identity. Electoral politics is at best a vehicle to stop tax increases or programs for social distribution. Financial elites are still pro forma citizens of their respective states, but they do not depend on national solidarity and the "community of fate." They invest in the stock market now to provide for retirement later. For these members, the provisions of the Keynesian social state have outlived their usefulness. Their needs are fully met and bought on the free market. Formal rights of citizenship have thereby not changed. But the conditions for citizenship rights have been undermined by the "borderless" global economy. The basis of the "work society" has been the

Keynesian social compromise between those that have and those that are less well-off. Under the conditions of global competition and the push for the lowest "single price," the logic of the global economy is on a collision course with the logic of the Fordist social compromise.

In their triple dependence on the welfare state (as social workers, clients, and consumers), women are particularly hard hit by the social welfare crisis. As a result of the reduction of public services, they are "punished" in various ways. First, reducing social services means that these services once again become part of the nonmonetized private sphere. Cutting costs for the care of the elderly, in the health sector, and for education places care burdens again on the shoulders of women. Second, the present privatization of these social services destroys the very conditions that have made the integration of women in the labor market possible. Particularly for women in the lower-skilled professions, publicly provided child care services often make the difference between seeking employment or staying home. Finally, social service jobs generated by the Keynesian welfare state disappear with the dismantling of public services (Jenson, Hagen, and Reddy 1988).

Globalization has thus fundamentally challenged the very notion of what is public and what is private. In the process, it has worsened gender-specific social division. The neoliberal "reprivatization discourse" (Fraser 1989) seeks to repatriate the economic and social to the former domestic enclave. Reprivatization of the domestic, as Janine Brodie argues, has elevated and revitalized the hetero-patriarchal family (Brodie 1994: 57). It rests on the dubious assumptions that the family is responsible for social reproduction, and that a family still consists of the male "breadwinner" and his dependents. Aside from the conservative and ideological premise of these assumptions, they neglect to take into account the changing reality of the family. The Fordist gender order no longer exists. Today's reality is that women—even if they wanted to—no longer have the "luxury" to remain as caretakers in the home. In ever-greater numbers, women have joined the labor market, while labor market participation rates for males have stabilized or even declined. How the reproductive issues will be resolved in this "borderless" global economy is the million-dollar question.

Finding a gender-conscious resolution of the tasks connected with human reproduction is made all the more difficult by the changes in the social structure and the reorganization of existing power relations. As pointed out earlier, the state no longer is guided by a Keynesian logic, but is driven by the logic of competition. These changes have also produced fundamental reorganization within the state apparatus itself. Departments associated with the Keynesian welfare states, such as labor and social and human services, have all been devalorized at the expense of the valorization of economic and financial departments. The reorganization has not weakened, hollowed out, or marginalized the authority of the state, as is suggested by a majority of the globalization literature. True, the singular focus on the decline of public services may support such a view. However, this one-sided focus on the welfare state has failed to take into account new power centers that have arisen in the state and are closely tied to the global financial and economic interests.

This reorganization within the state has produced tremendous battles between those who celebrate the unfettered workings of the global markets and those who are disillusioned by the destructive effects of the unregulated free market. Both sides invoke language that is a stark reminder of the ideological struggle of the Cold War. Not only is the battle fought over the superiority of respective economic models, the arguments are also very much about the moral superiority of "free trade faith" versus "regulated free trade faith." Whereas the former camp sees the liberal market economy as "the Highest Stage of Mankind" (Martin 1997), the latter invokes the Keynesian state as "the Highest Stage of the State" (Jessop 1994). Absent from any of these studies is any awareness of the differential impact globalization has had on men and women.

A FEMINIST AGENDA

Feminist scholars are now confronted with new challenges. The question is no longer whether the nation-state is in its very structure male biased, or whether state structures and offices can be used to promote women's rights and interests. Feminists are now challenged to make visible the new centers of structural and strategic disparities in the network societies. Paradoxically, just as German feminists no longer reject the state outright as an apparatus of male control and domination[8] and even rally around the "patriarchal welfare state," the state is no longer the site of sovereignty and the exclusive subject of domestic and international politics (Sassen 1996; Strange 1996). The increasing acceptance of the state as a vehicle for feminist activities in the 1980s and the shrinking capacity of the state to control domestic economic activities are both closely tied to Thatcher's and Reagan's neoliberal revolution of the late 1970s and early 1980s. The "neoliberal utopia," as Bourdieu (1998) calls the transformation toward a pure market-oriented economy, with its disregard for the values of collective solidarity and national belonging, has raised[9]—if not the level of general politicization of the feminist movement—the insecurity of feminists of all ranks. The neoliberal "backlash" (Faludi 1991) against the still mostly marginal and often symbolic achievements in political and economic equity between the sexes in Western capitalist countries has signaled a more concentrated feminist interest in the properties of the nation-state being reconfigured in light of global economic restructuring.

International feminist discourse on the state can be divided into two major theoretical strands: the widely cited Anglo-American and Scandinavian "state feminism"[10] on the one hand, and the dominant discourse in the German-speaking countries on the structural characteristics of "male-bonding" in the state, on the other (Kreisky and Sauer 1997; Kulawik and Sauer 1996; Kerchner and Wilde 1996). The concept of state feminism refers to the role of state structures and offices in promoting women's status and rights. Adherents of this school start with the assumption that state structures can be used to promote the interests of women (Stetson and Mazur 1995; Eisenstein 1990). In contrast to these liberal notions of feminism, the goal of German research is to deconstruct the "maleness" of the state and through feminist intervention engender the very structure of the state. Skepticism toward the state and the almost complete rejection of participation in political institutions is a particular feature of the German "autonomous feminist movement." Due to the authoritarian and undemocratic legacy of the German state, the feminist movement perceived these institutions as unchangeable. Only a politics outside of these political state institutions promised to reflect the interests of women. With the increasing institutionalization of the Green Party in the 1980s, the autonomous feminist movement redirected its strategy and became more open to established political forces (B. Young 1999; Lang 1997; Kulawik 1991–92). Despite the differences in discourses, practices, and strategies of "state feminism" and the German analysis of the state institutional structure, both frameworks remain wedded to the classical concepts of the nation-state and the welfare state (B. Young 1997; Demirovic and Pühl 1997).

The continuing focus on nation-states can be explained in part by the increasing attack on public services and the rising degree of privatization since the 1980s that hit women in particular as clients, state workers, and beneficiaries of the Keynesian social state. While the authority of the state has declined within its territorial borders, the nation-state is still the institutional encasement of the national territory providing average citizens with political influence and an avenue to exercise their democratic rights. As a result, the nation-state is still the only place and space in which the irreconcilable principles of the market and democracy can come together and citizens can achieve and share a common identity of a "national community of fate" (Held 1991). These national communities of fate are the result of long and brutal struggles between the bourgeoisie and the monarchy first, and subsequently between capital and labor. The social democratic compromise between capital and labor did alleviate the worst economic inequalities, and the inequalities of the market were further minimized by the introduction of political equality among (male) citizens (*citoyens*), and by providing some minimal aspects of social equity (Altvater 1997). That this political and social equality was deeply biased against women has received much attention from feminist scholars (Pateman 1988; Nelson 1990; Gordon 1990; Fraser 1990). Feminists have tried to deconstruct the "two-channel welfare state" and have challenged social theory and practice to reexamine the welfare state in a more gender-conscious light (Nelson 1990). That feminists continue to focus on the nation-state as an important transformative agent for achieving a gender-neutral "national community of fate" is thus quite understandable. Yet the question arises whether economic globalization and the resulting denationalization of politics has not made the focus on the nation-state an anachronism. Today feminists of all persuasions are being called upon to come to grips with the new realities of the spatial dispersal of global economic activities and the decline of the sovereignty and exclusivity of the nation-state.

Global actors sharing the power with the state include transnational corporations; financial markets; insurance, information, and rating agencies; international institutions such as the World Trade Organization (WTO), the World Bank, the International Monetary Fund (IMF), and the Organization for Economic Cooperation and Development (OECD); transnational trading and economic blocks such as MERCOSOR, ASEAN, NAFTA, and the European Union (EU); nongovernmental organizations (NGOs) as, for example, Amnesty International, the Olympic Sports Organization, and the Catholic Church; and transnational associations and networks, including the Mafia and international speculators (Strange 1996).

The expanding interconnections between state and nonstate organizations, and among domestic, international, transnational, and supranational activities, can no longer be analyzed with the theoretical and methodological instruments available from such disciplines as political science, sociology, or economics. The network society with its reorganization of social structure and power relations has fundamentally contributed to what Sassen (1996) calls the emergence of a "new geography of power." That economic activities have become global and the institutional encasement of the nation-state reconfigured means that feminist research has to focus on the new gender-specific institutional materiality of these networks. How these networks reconfigure gender orders and power relations in the network society is both a theoretical and political challenge feminists face.

At the same time, globalization should not be looked upon only as a negative phenomenon for gender relations. The informalization and flexibilization of the labor market have opened up new opportunities for women. In the export-oriented "global factories," it is women who are the preferred workers. That the cost has been high is also no secret. On average, the "feminization of labor markets" has expanded flexible labor market structures, replacing the life-long, secure Fordist (male) employment patterns. Despite the low wages and the exploitative conditions that are part of the free export zones, studies also show that, in contrast to national firms, the transnational corporations provide higher wages and better working conditions (Lemoine 1998; Ward and Pyle 1995).[11] Furthermore, the integration of women into the labor force has also helped lessen dependence on husbands and families. Finally, women are by far not the passive victims in these "global factories," as the globalization literature seems to suggest. Newer studies show that women increasingly join labor unions in South Korea, the Philippines, and South Africa and actively fight against the practices of wage dumping, deskilling, and other tactics of transnational corporations (Ward and Pyle 1995). The picture of the passive working woman is thus not only an ideological caricature, it also shows the contradictory process of globalization. Women are the preferred workers in the "global factories" because they are presumed to be passive and difficult to organize in labor unions. But the very experience with such exploitative working conditions also politicizes women to struggle against such conditions. That most labor struggle successes are only of short-term duration, addressing mostly local situations, and therefore have no long-term effect on transnational corporate behavior is also no secret (Ward and Pyle 1995).

The integration of women into the global market has another unintended side effect. It can also weaken local patriarchal structures. Once again this process is contradictory. Through integration in the global economy, women can resist male domination to some extent. They also lose in this process the protection that this local patriarchal culture offers. This loss of local protection can be redressed through international conventions on human rights, such as the Fourth World Conference on Women in Beijing in 1995 and the official Platform for Action and the Beijing Declaration. As a result of these international conferences, we are witnessing the ascendancy of new human rights regimes. Through these new legal mechanisms women can gain more representation in international law in matters involving human rights and refugees. While rooted in the legal codes of nation-states, international human rights can challenge the exclusive authority of the state over its citizens. Since all residents, whether citizens or not, have the right to claim human rights, "human rights begin to impinge on the principle of nation-based citizenship and the boundaries of the nation" (Sassen 1996: 33). This strengthens individual actors and nongovernmental organizations to challenge the state as the sole subject of international law. These new legal regimes also have implications for the concept of citizenship. Women, either as individuals or as a collective, can be recognized as subjects within international law. Human rights organizations and feminists have demanded for some time to redefine the anarchic conception of international relations and develop international mechanisms to intervene domestically if human rights are endangered. With the slogan, "Women's Rights Are Human Rights," women have created in Beijing a basis from which to make claims for their protection overriding decisions made by their own states. Skeptics may reply that this slogan is little more than a "tiger without teeth." But one should remember the Helsinki Declaration of 1975 and the adoption of Charter 77. It was this rather benign document that proved the basis for the Eastern European opposition to launch their "velvet revolution."

Globalization cannot be viewed only as a nightmarish scenario. It is neither theoretically helpful nor does it promote political action for women to turn into frightened rabbits when confronting the "snake" of globalization. Undeniably, economic globalization has constrained the political scope of nation-states and narrowed the capacity of citizens to claim gender-neutral social rights from the state. However, one also has to recall that the reconfiguration of the Fordist gender order also offers an opportunity for women to develop new concepts and strategies to achieve equality on a global scale.

NOTES

1. Castells introduces the concept of "informational capitalism" to differentiate this type from "industrial capitalism."

2. The informal sector consists of a vast array of work ranging from legal to illegal activities, including "home-based" work; work in the free export zones; sweatshop activities; street vendors; maids; illegal farm labor; prostitution; and many other such activities that are precarious and unregulated (Mahnkopf 1997; Ward and Pyle 1995).

3. Women provide the majority of the labor in these "*maquila* businesses": 58 percent in Mexico (1995); 60 to 62 percent in Costa Rica; 70 to 75 percent in Honduras; 78 percent in Guatemala (1993); and 60 percent in the Dominican Republic (1992) (Lemoine 1998).

4. Para-statal refers to a level of organizational structure to be found between the state and society. These organizations, if not created by the state, are recognized by the state as sole representatives of societal interests. This para-statal level of organization is often associated with corporatist bargaining among the state, labor unions, and employers' associations. In Germany, these institutions can also be found in many other areas such as the health system and other social systems.

5. Women workers had staffed factories since the beginning of industrialization. They also occupied the factories during World War II as the men were shipped to the front. With the beginning of Fordism and the emphasis on the male breadwinner model, women were increasingly excluded from the center of industrial work and only integrated selectively or temporarily.

6. These labor market conditions are still overwhelmingly restricted to the new industrial countries and the transitional societies. However, this form, as the American example increasingly shows, has also expanded rapidly in Western industrial countries.

7. Formal work is defined as regulated and socially insured; informal work is flexible and unprotected; and family and subsistence work is neither regulated nor paid.

8. Rejection of the state as a repressive force is not shared by all European feminist theorists. In contrast to the German antistate tradition, Scandinavian and other European feminists were from the start more state-oriented and chose "the march through the institutions" (state feminism) as the strategy to change the social and political role of women (Stetson and Mazur 1995).

9. Baroness Thatcher declared that, for her, societies no longer exist; only individuals.

10. Hester Eisenstein speaks of "femocrats" in state bureaucracies and institutions, who try from within to attain political change for the equality of the sexes.

11. For example, the minimum wage in the Honduran *maquila* is on average 40 lempiras per day versus 30 lempiras in national industries (Lemoine 1998).

4

Gender and Social Implications of Globalization: An African Perspective

Yassine Fall

GLOBALIZATION: AN OLD PARADIGM

Globalization is not a new phenomenon. Classical pharaonic Egypt, Rome, Greece, Persia, the British Empire, the Chinese dynasties of the Ming period, the Arab territories of the classical jihad periods represent early signs of globalization understood as the primitive stages of military and economic imperialism.

From the Industrial Revolution initiated by Europe and more particularly by England prior to World War II, globalization moved to a higher stage characterized by an unprecedented development of markets, primary resources, and technology under the wings of capitalism. From the end of World War II to the 1970s, globalization was mainly sustained through mass markets and mammoth production levels, an unprecedented level of capital flow, and a fast-growing maturation of transnational political, economic, financial, and military powers.

The 1970s and 1980s displayed an entirely different map of globalization: the capitalist system was in crisis and that led to global threats (east/west and north/south tensions aggravated by military buildup and the widening economic and technological gap between industrialized and underdeveloped countries). During this period, crises erupted on all fronts (financial instability with excess of money supply; ecology disasters; global environmental threats; social upheavals; neglected pandemics such as HIV/AIDS in Africa, malaria in Asia) and plunged the Third World countries into a state of poverty and human despair perhaps unequaled in the past two centuries.

The past two decades have witnessed the collapse of the Berlin Wall and the subsequent rise of the United States as the only twenty-first-century superpower. In a complex web of mechanisms, processes (such as the speedy unification of markets and capital), and technological advances, accelerated by the marriage among computers, communications satellites, and submarine and fiber optic cables, globalization has reached its highest stage.

From a twentieth-century point of view, globalization is a combination of several phenomena occurring simultaneously. It refers to trade as well as financial capital, global mobility, fluidity, speed of growth, circulation, and outreach capabilities. Globalization also implies the weakening of national policies as well as the increasing role played by technological innovations and value-added information. Globalization refers as well to knowledge generation, processing, storage, and accumulation, and above all, to a central drive for the conquest of markets and the commercialization of a greater variety of products and services. Globalization has reversed the meaning and centrality of power. The volume of financial growth has become more important than that of productive output. This reality has led to various positions according to the source of the analysis, and some view this as dangerous for economic and social development, which could lead to anarchic financial behavior, deflationist tendencies, and recession. Other sources describe this financial dominance as healthy and necessary to prepare for the ultimate success of capitalism.

Globalization has moved in a drastic fashion the seat of power from traditional politicians and power brokers to gigantic financial conglomerates controlling all government branches and supranational bodies, such as the World Trade Organization (WTO), that can determine to a large extent the fate and destiny of humankind.

Women are marginalized in this global picture. They are still fighting to have their fair share of resources, services, and opportunities in the workplace, which is overwhelmingly dominated by male if not chauvinistic (and perhaps sectarian) powers. The shift in power allows transnational corporations to set up mechanisms and strategies, enabling them to manipulate political leadership and protect themselves from the control of already weakened states (Amin 1996; Gaye and Dansokho 1997).

From an African perspective, the latest tides of globalization represent a new manifestation of the same exploitative institutional mechanisms and relationships begun in the fifteenth century when Africa was introduced into the world market as a net provider of slave labor and cheap raw materials. With the end of slave trade, European powers established a colonial trading system with Africa that continued to use gunboat diplomacy to extract raw materials and exploit cheap African labor for agricultural and mineral production. Globalization in the twenty-first century is Africa's principal contradiction. International agreements, such as the Lomé Convention, and the most powerful international institutions (the World Trade Organization [WTO], the International Monetary Fund [IMF], and the World Bank) use neoliberal ideology to justify the establishment of trade and financial conditions, thus giving the cutting edge to global corporations in areas such as mining, agricultural, and oceanic and extra-atmospheric resources.

Africa's disastrous situation may be largely explained by this fundamental imbalance between dominant categories of power and the periphery of global capitalism. The internal contradictions (artificial ethnicization of conflicts, corruption, weak governance systems, inadequate public services, and so forth) described at length by superficial analysts are the tip of the iceberg. The root causes for poor governance must be found elsewhere and particularly in the structure and function of international and regional relations.

GLOBALIZATION AND ITS PREEXISTING INSTITUTIONAL MECHANISMS

The Atlantic Slave Trade

Africa's encounter with the Western world intensified with the European invasion of America as labor became the focal commodity in international trade. The Atlantic slave trade, which started in the fifteenth century and developed until the nineteenth century, tied Africa as a net provider of slave labor and cheap raw materials. Ten to sixteen million Africans were exported as commodities in the Americas between 1451 and 1870. The population of slaves was estimated to be 60 percent male and 40 percent female (Zeleza 1993). Zeleza rightly suggests that most Western scholars tend to minimize the impact of the Atlantic slave trade on Africa's present social situation and industrial retardation. Western development specialists often shy away from discussing this human rights violation and crime against humanity. They have managed to reverse responsibilities by transferring to Africans the guilty feeling of discussing slavery and presenting it as a global economic problem. These Western experts are projecting corruption that has infiltrated all strata of the African states and leaders as the only factor responsible for the level of poverty and despair the continent is experiencing. The real issue is to know how forty years of state mismanagement and corruption can erase and annihilate the impact of four hundred years of slavery (Zeleza 1993). How can we forget this costly and tragic experience when analyzing Africa's integration into global trade?

The Colonial Trade Economy

The colonial exploitation system was set up through militarism and trade. A closer examination of the trading system shows its asymmetric aspect at the expense of African products and in favor of European manufactured products. Colonial trade companies had the same peculiarities and trade patterns. Whether they were British headquartered in Manchester or Liverpool, French based in Bordeaux or Marseille, or German based in Bremen or Hamburg, they were all buying cheap and very poor quality goods in Europe that were conveyed to be sold in the colonies at extremely high prices. At the same time, colonial powers were using forced labor to minimize the cost of agricultural and mineral products as well as to build the railroads and ports necessary to support trading companies' activities (Suret-Canale 1964). Every infrastructure put in place during the colonial period was meant to facilitate European capital accumulation through trade. As a matter of fact, infrastructures clustered around "useful" coastal agricultural and mining areas with a particular emphasis on telecommunication infrastructures were used as a backbone for trading, administrative, and military endeavors (Sy 1996).

AFRICA IN THE GLOBAL ARENA

Prior to the fourth wave of globalization in the 1970s, Africa had been integrated in the international division of labor and pillaging of resources. It was already at the bottom of the global economy. Extroverted economic policies developed mechanisms that created and maintained a situation of extreme poverty both in economic terms and with regard to access to health, education, and general welfare.

Most African countries are not semi-industrialized, intermediary, or emerging economies. Agriculture is the primary sector. It is in this sector where most Africans work. Of the world's thirty-six poorest countries, two dozen are in sub-Saharan Africa. They belong to the highly indebted poor countries (HIPC) group. Statistics show that the gap is widening at an amazing pace between the HIPC group and the richer countries. In 1960, the gap between 20 percent of the world's richest people and 20 percent of the world's poorest people was 30 to 1. In 1990, the gap grew to 60 to 1. In 1960, 20 percent of the world's poorest populations held 2.3 percent of world income and 20 percent of the world's richest individuals held 70 percent of world income. In 1990, each group respectively had 1.4 percent and 85 percent of the world's income (UNDP 1997b, 1998).

Global trade mostly bypasses the highly indebted poor countries. At the end of the twentieth century, 10 percent of the world's poorest populations engaged in 0.3 percent of global trade (two times lower than ten years ago). The conditions of trade have also been worsening. The market price of raw materials has decreased by 45 percent during that decade. The same downward spiral crippled foreign direct investment. In 1995, the forty-seven countries of sub-Saharan Africa attracted only 3 percent of the flow of direct foreign investment into the developing world. In contrast, Latin America and the Caribbean received 20 percent and East Asia and the Pacific received as much as 59 percent (*The Economist* 1996).

In 1998 sub-Saharan Africa was ranked as having the lowest human development index (HDI). This score is even lower when computed on the basis of gender-desegregated statistics. Among the forty-five least-developed countries in the world, thirty-five are from sub-Saharan Africa. In addition, sub-Saharan Africa's adult literacy rate is 47.9 percent for women and 66.2 for men, compared to 61.7 and 78.8 respectively in other developing countries. Forty-eight percent of people in sub-Saharan Africa do not have access to clean water or health services compared to 29 percent and 20 percent of the people in other developing countries. In at least half the African countries, one woman dies every three minutes from childbearing-related reasons (UNDP 1998).

Life expectancy represents a significant measure of human underdevelopment. In 1997, almost 20 percent of the people in developing countries were expected to die before the age of 40 compared to 5 percent for industrialized countries and 33 percent for sub-Saharan Africa. During the same year, maternal mortality was estimated at 971 per 100,000 live births compared to 471 for the developing world (UNDP 1997b). The AIDS virus has aggravated Africa's already chaotic social situation. It was estimated in 1995 that one adult among ten in the Ivory Coast, 4.1 percent of Nigeria's population, and 32 percent of pregnant women in Harare were HIV-positive. This explains the increased death rate in particular for women and children. In 1998, infant mortality increased by 150 percent in Zimbabwe and 100 percent in Kenya. It is expected that Africa's life expectancy will fall much faster and drastically due to the fact that forty million people will be infected with AIDS worldwide by the year 2000, two-thirds of them being in sub-Saharan Africa. Without AIDS, life expectancy at birth in 2010 would be estimated at 61 years in both Burkina Faso and Botswana. With AIDS, and if the present trends remain unchanged, life expectancy at birth in Burkina Faso and Botswana for the same year is estimated to be respectively less than 35 and 33 years (UNDP 1997b). These figures are increasingly getting worse for women and children (populations at risk) trapped in the battlefields of ethnic and military confrontations.

Sub-Saharan Africa has one of the highest illiteracy rates in the world. Its rate of school enrollment is not keeping pace with its population growth rate. The region's illiteracy rate was twice the world's average rate in 1990. It doubled the world's average rate in the year 2000. The gap between women's illiteracy level and that of men is above 20 percent. According to a UNESCO study on the state of education in Africa, one of the characteristics of the African school system is the consistent decrease in its enrollment rate. This decrease is observed at two levels. The growth rate of the overall student population enrolled in schools has fallen since 1960. Also the farther up the school ladder, from elementary school to the higher education levels, the fewer the number of students. The education system in Africa has made some progress during the post-independence period in particular between 1975 and 1980. Since then the population of enrolled students has been declining despite the demographic boom experienced in the continent (UNESCO 1995).

Finally the foreign debt of African nations is staggering, equal to the gross domestic product (GDP) of Africa for a year. Interest payments owed by governments often amount to 20 percent or more of all government spending, or as much as 6 percent of GDP. If a country is unsuccessful in meeting its payments in a given year, the debt load becomes even larger the following year. An analysis of factors contributing to the debt cycle in sub-Saharan Africa may be summarized in the following sequence.

- The rise in international oil prices during the early 1970s pushed upward the prices of certain commodities like agricultural products, which sub-Saharan

Africa was exporting. As a result of this substantial increase in its export earnings, sub-Saharan Africa gained a satisfactory level of credit worthiness in the eyes of the international financial institutions.

• However, this increase in oil prices placed sub-Saharan Africa's extroverted post-colonial economy in need of increased financial borrowing to purchase fuel-derived commodities.

• This period of sub-Saharan Africa's credit worthiness and critical need for financial assets coincides with the European and American banks' desperate need to find market outlets for their excessive Eurodollars in order to avoid a financial crisis.

• Very attractive credit conditions were offered to developing countries, including African countries.

The increasingly mounting debt burden of sub-Saharan Africa may best be explained by the fact that countries were encouraged to borrow very large amounts of money with no conditionality and no monitoring of the destination of the funds disbursed. Sub-Saharan African governments showed very irresponsible spending behavior with no priority given to the development needs of the moment. Expensive, environmentally detrimental, and ill-conceived projects were financed with no economic or social benefits for local people (Fall 1996).

In the 1980s, when industrialized countries' financial situation stabilized, they tightened lending conditions through interest rates three times higher than previously. Moreover, they decreased the prices paid for commodity exports from sub-Saharan African while increasing the prices of their exported manufactured products to sub-Saharan Africa. African countries were hit hard by the deterioration of terms of trade particularly because the agreements they signed under the Lomé Convention encouraged them to continue producing the same raw material to satisfy the needs of their former colonies instead of diversifying their economy through industrialization.

The 1980s ignited a severe multifaceted crisis throughout the Third World. The African, Caribbean, and Pacific countries lost U.S.$147 billion between 1980 and 1987 as a result of the fluctuation of the world market value of their raw materials (Adams and Soloman 1991). The new unfavorable terms of trade required that the countries increased their external borrowing in order to sustain their levels of expenditures. But borrowing was now under new terms: skyrocketing interest rates, much higher debt servicing, and tighter conditionality to implement harsh economic adjustment policies under the control of the Bretton Woods institutions.

Sub-Saharan Africa's total debt kept growing at an amazingly fast pace. From U.S.$6 billion in 1970 it climbed to U.S.$134 billion in 1988 and by 1992 reached a level of two and a half times its 1980 level. In 1985 the region's debt was equivalent to 2.7 of its exports earnings. By the end of 1988, it reached 3.5 of its exports earnings (World Bank 1989). From an annual average of 27 percent of the region's exports earnings in 1985, the debt service continuously climbed to reach 47 percent of exports revenues in 1988. The number of countries who serviced their debt on a regular basis between 1980 and 1988 did not reach thirteen. Most countries rescheduled their debt or accumulated more arrears of payment. Twenty-five sub-Saharan African countries rescheduled their debt 105 times between 1980 and 1988 (World Bank 1989).

GLOBALIZATION AS AN INSTITUTION

A typical modern neoliberal recipe for addressing Africa's socioeconomic problems involves:

- A budgetary policy aimed at mobilizing domestic resources and increasing public savings through: (1) reducing budget deficits and raising public revenues; (2) reducing consumer surplus by increasing sales and excise taxes; (3) privatizing and curtailing subsidies to public and semiprivate enterprises; (4) freezing wages and hiring employees in the public sector, decreasing public salaries through dismissals with or without compensation and encouraging early retirement, or ceasing to hire university graduates; (5) mobilizing public savings by channeling grassroots initiatives and community-based projects toward government savings frameworks.
- Monetary policy acting on the money supply through the control of interest rates and reduction of national demand. Monetary policy reforms are usually aimed at strengthening existing formal and informal financial systems to mobilize household savings, reorienting credit policies inclusive of risk and costs factors associated with loan allocations, and adjusting interest and exchange rates to so-called market equilibrium "rules." The international financial institutions (IFIs) advocate the introduction of differential and higher bank margins for customers borrowing small amounts of money and offering little guarantees in comparison to a creditworthy customer borrowing a large amount of money.
- A structural policy reform emphasizing the creation of enabling conditions to attract producers in the private sector. According to this policy an investment of at least 25 percent of GDP needs to be generated and channeled to improve physical infrastructures in sectors reflecting private (foreign) businesses' priorities. This reform supports the opening of the economy and the creation of a supportive and enabling environment for foreign direct investment in order to increase the production capacities of the countries.
- An exchange rate policy that is supposed to boost the export-oriented production. This policy also suggests a more "efficient" use of imports (favoring increased capital goods imports) in view of satisfying foreign investors' infrastructure needs.

- A foreign debt policy whose main objective is to align national economies with foreign capital financing (Fall 1996).

Various international agreements (Lomé I, II, III, and IV) and global watchdog institutions (e.g., WTO, IMF, and the World Bank) in close cooperation with transnational corporations are positioned to encourage and enforce these neoliberal policies.

THE LOMÉ CONVENTION

During the post-independence period, trade continued to play a central role in reinforcing Africa's peripheral position in the international division of labor. Crafted after independence in 1958 to define new trade and cooperative relations between Europe and its former colonies the Yaoundé Convention followed in 1975 by the Lomé Convention signed by the European Economic Community and forty-six African, Caribbean, and Pacific countries sought "to promote the economic and social development of these countries and territories" by eliminating duties on certain African products and stabilizing with guaranteed returns the export earnings from specified African products. This practice has continued the unfair practice of giving European states and companies easy access to African raw materials at low costs. Under this agreement, only African products that were not in competition with European products were allowed to enter Europe free of tax. Meat or manufactured African products such as roasted coffee, fruit juices, and margarine were not allowed into European markets. They were highly taxed to prevent them from being in competition with European products.

Every time a tax-free African commodity started being competitive to the point of threatening a European product, the country in question would retaliate by diminishing its imports of that product and increasing its subsidies for the competing European products. These strategies supported the creation of semimonopolies for European commodities, both at home and in Africa. These steps worked against Africa's industrialization efforts and attempts to diversify its economic activities. Such actions were taken for two reasons. Through this mechanism African companies would not need a considerable quantity and variety of raw materials; therefore, demand for inputs would be controlled and prices would not be competitive. Further, slow industrialization for Africa meant less competition and more markets for European products at home and abroad.

The competition of European products versus African products is not only in the area of manufactured products but also includes agricultural crops. African onions, potatoes, tomatoes, and other vegetables are not exported to Europe and are thrown away in large quantities because Europe's subsidized crops invade local African markets. Unsubsidized farmers who go into debt to buy agricultural inputs cannot sell their products at competitive prices. Such a situation creates instability in farm production and food insecurity for a country's population. The impact on women farmers are multifold. Women's noncash crops are sidelined, as their crops are not included on the lists of products selected for importation into European markets. The competition brought forth by manufactured products has a negative impact on the production of cereals such as millet, the Sahelian main staple food. European wheat flour replaces millet for bread production in spite of the poor nutritional value of bread made from imported wheat. This represents a threat to local food security, women's and children's nutritional health, and crops mostly grown, transformed, and sold by women, who are ultimately excluded from cash crop farming.

The drop in international prices of African agricultural products and raw materials was the result of several factors including global competition, market diversity, and the movement of European industries into new sectors. Further deterioration of the terms of trade and devaluation of African raw materials has jeopardized the continent's capacity to pay its debt or provide adequate social services to its constituencies. Because European priorities have shifted from the African markets it controlled for centuries to the newly built European Union market and other emerging economies in different parts of the world, Europe can afford at this stage in international relations to snub its "traditional" African allies and ask them to "diversify" their products (Dembele 1999).

Another devastating impact of the Lomé Convention is the outcome of the European Union (EU) agreement on fisheries. This agreement allows huge boats to deplete the oceanic resources of the African coastal countries, completely disrupting the marine biodiversity. Various species of fish have been totally endangered by the size, speed, and fishing techniques of the EU boats, in countries where fish is the only nutritional source of protein for the people and in particular children. Recent fishing agreements have threatened the livelihoods of many people in the industry, especially women. Women in fisheries have multiple economic roles in selling, processing, and trade activities. The agreement to export fish and sell it to export processing industries reduces its supply. This affects the price of the fish and consequently decreases the incomes of people involved in fisheries.

CORPORATE POWER, FINANCIAL, AND TRADE INSTITUTIONS

Bretton Woods and WTO

The Bretton Woods institutions, initially created to regulate and build the capitalist world after World War II, have become the major force regulating the developing world. They represent today the institutional brokers of the corporate and financial system. Their power is more ideological and political than monetary. They give their green light to private investors and private banks interested in private investment, and they sound the alarm to warn Organization for Economic

Cooperation and Development (OECD) countries and corporations of possible risks, thereby discouraging private investment. Despite all its rhetoric and gesticulations, the IMF controls less than 1.8 percent of world imports. In contrast, the IMF's political power is so strong that it has been seeking to play a role in dispute settlements within the WTO. This move generated resistance among developing countries who perceived it as an attempt on the part of the Bretton Woods institutions to extend their control over and influence on WTO.

Neoliberal ideology is the philosophical base of globalization. The Bretton Woods institutions promote export-driven economic models as *the* best alternative for developing countries, a policy that contributes to and accelerates the uneven distribution of resources. In the case of Africa where most countries are HIPC, this model ensures that government revenues generated from exports are used to pay the external debt. Exports also contribute to the country's balance of payments, a key indicator of the country's increasing integration into the global economy. Debt management policies are indeed tools for controlling African governments and telling them what to do. Little evidence exists to support the view that revenues generated from growth trickle down to reduce poverty, yet the Bretton Woods institutions use this argument relentlessly to maintain and expand their hegemony over countries to make them abide by their neoliberal rules. The totalitarian position of the Bretton Woods institutions has been widely condemned by developing countries that accuse the IMF and World Bank of antidemocratic practices, as the cost of stabilization and liberalization is increasingly borne by women and the poor.

In order to reinforce the existence of formal transactions rules at the global level, the World Trade Organization was created in January 1995 as an international body dealing with trade regulations among nations. Agreements under WTO are the legal ground rules for international commerce and trade policy. Negotiated and signed by governments, these agreements include contracts binding nations to keep their trade policies within agreed limits.

The establishment of the WTO symbolizes the ultimate phase of the Uruguay Round, which was the last round of negotiations under the General Agreement of Tariffs and Trade (GATT). WTO represents a major step in the trade liberalization agenda. The GATT was amended and incorporated within the WTO. There are some differences between GATT and WTO. GATT was small, provisional, and not legally recognized as an international organization. GATT only dealt with trade in goods. Under WTO agreements, multilateral also referred to activities on a global or near-global level. It contradicts actions taken regionally or by other smaller groups of countries. WTO rules have the supremacy over national or regional regulations. However, WTO rules were supposed to be "transparent" and "predictable."

Another WTO major feature is dispute settlement that is supposed to take place within a "neutral" forum where conflicting interests based upon a legal foundation are debated and resolved under "true" principles of governance. (OECD website, http://www.oecd.org)

The establishment of WTO and the implementation of its regulations were found insufficient by free market ideologists. In addition to trade liberalization, investment and other critical sectors of the economy had to be deregulated in order to allow globalization to reach its ultimate goal. In the Americas, where free market supporters were most powerful, the North American Free Trade Agreement (NAFTA) was created to ease the flow of investment and trading among Canada, Mexico, and the United States.

The Multilateral Agreement on Investment

International financial corporations and governments from the OECD held various consultations during which they examined the rationale and conditions allowing the creation of a multilateral body similar to NAFTA. Under NAFTA's formal investment rules, corporations have the right to directly sue governments and consequently request monetary compensations for both actual or presumably future damages as well as reparations for tarnished images (*Ethyl Corporation vs. Government of Canada*).

OECD is an international body comprised of the world's wealthiest and most powerful nations, including Austria, Australia, Belgium, Canada, Czech Republic, Denmark, Finland, France, Germany, Greece, Hungary, Iceland, Ireland, Italy, Japan, South Korea, Luxembourg, Mexico, New Zealand, the Netherlands, Norway, Poland, Portugal, Russia, Spain, Sweden, Switzerland, Turkey, the United Kingdom, and the United States. The following justifications for its existence were as follows:

- The existence of more than 1,800 bilateral trade and investment agreements often created confusion and conflicting framework mechanisms.
- The need to build investor confidence, provide a better legal protection to multinational corporations, cancel out discriminatory regulations on foreign investors, place domestic private sector and investors on a same-level playing field with international corporations.
- The need to provide investors with a more secure environment and reduce costly government regulations in order to stimulate higher investment levels and promote economic growth and jobs.

In 1995, OECD countries negotiated the establishment of the Multilateral Agreement on Investment (MAI) as an international economic agreement aimed at easing the movement of capital—both monetary and production facilities—across international borders. This international agreement would therefore limit the power of governments to restrict and regulate foreign investment. It would apply the extreme deregulatory agenda of the WTO to any other vital economic and financial sector not already covered by its rules. This would mean redefining the terms and conditions for organizing investment for services and manufacturing, monetary flow and exchanges, ownership of land and natural resources, broadcasting and entertainment, and so forth. Unlike the GATT, the MAI treaty does not have a general exception to its rules for national laws protecting public morals, human health or life, animals' health or life and the conservation of exhaustible natural resources. The MAI gives the choice on these protections to foreign companies and investors (OECD website, http://www.oecd.org).

The specific objectives of the MAI were to:

- Open all economic sectors, including real estate, broadcasting, and natural resources to foreign ownership;
- Disregard any particular advantage given to local, domestic firms or vulnerable groups;
- Restrict the ability of federal, state, and local legislators to regulate business in favor of public interest;
- Allow investors to directly sue governments for compensation if they believe that a national, state, or local law violates the MAI or poses a barrier to investment flow;
- Set up international dispute resolution panels through which lawsuits would go and whose decisions would be binding to all nations and interests involved;
- Allow OECD countries to be eligible to file a list of specific laws or general categories of laws that the treaty will not apply to in their country;
- Prevent developing nations excluded from OECD negotiations from having the right to file exemptions to the MAI for their protection or benefit. They are only expected to sign in and submit to MAI rules.
- Prevent, through a standstill clause, the introduction of any new laws violating or limiting the influence of the MAI, as the MAI is a Binding Treaty (*MAI and Human Rights* 1998).

The secrecy under which the MAI legislation was crafted had prevented governments from developing countries and most branches of government from OECD nations to be aware of its existence. This wall of silence and secrecy was first broken in 1997 when a group of nongovernmental organizations (NGOs) got a copy of the document and confronted the U.S. authorities that were denying the existence of such a text. In France authorities like the chairman of the Foreign Affairs Committee in the National Assembly who was highly involved in the MAI negotiations continuously rejected the fact that he knew something about the agreement and those supposed to negotiate it, until he was publicly proven wrong. While establishing the MAI, the United States designed an investment and trade treaty that would link it with Africa under new deregulated terms.

The Africa Growth and Opportunity Act (AGOA)

On March 11, 1998, the U.S. House of Representatives passed a bill, the African Growth and Opportunity Act, that was supposed to be introduced later to the Senate for debate and consideration. The argument behind this bill was that in order to sustain economic growth, sub-Saharan Africa had to implement sound and sustained free market policies. The specific features of the bill are:

- more benefits in favor of large foreign and multinational investors;
- endorsement of privatization at the utmost level and under any circumstances;
- absolute right given to foreign interests to establish themselves in any African country without fulfilling any conditionality;
- obligation by African governments to treat foreign investors the same way as domestic investors;
- obligation of African nations to cut corporate taxes as a condition for receiving U.S. aid and trade benefits.

Despite the fact that governments, transnational corporations, and international finance institutions support these policies, agreements, and instruments (WTO, MAI, AGOA, and so forth) and lobby for their maintenance or implementation, a growing and powerful movement has emerged from academic circles and citizens from around the globe to call for more transparency and accountable governance to protect people and the environment against the growing power of corporations (Lal 1998; Letter of Transafrica President, Randal Robinson; *Ethyl Corporation vs. Government of Canada*; Warning 1999; Sen 1999). Their argument is that growth and liberalization do not guarantee improved living standards. Liberalization and competition give companies the freedom to use any means to minimize costs and maximize profits. Weak companies will be closed down and the rest will be drawn into fierce competition. Large companies from developed countries will take over. Labor market deregulation will annihilate workers' protection and minimum ceilings for wages. Small nations unable to catch up with the new rules of the global economy will be further isolated. Globalization will increase the living standards of the upper social classes in industrialized countries and selected elites in developing countries, leaving the large majority of populations in the poor agricultural countries of Africa in an increasingly desperate situation. As an illustration, gains from trade that are supposed to increase global income by an estimated amount of U.S.$212 to $512 billion between 1995 to 2001 will benefit a few countries and corporations and make many countries and communities more miserable. Comparatively, gains from trade will also create losses amounting to U.S.$600 million a year for the least-developing countries and U.S.$1.2 billion a year for sub-Saharan Africa (UNDP 1997b).

The political and economic legitimacy of all these institutions have been in question in different circles all over the world including in the United States. They, however, remain powerful and confirm the supremacy of the economic over the political as advocated by neoliberal economists. A comparison of the WTO, the MAI, and the AGOA shows a striking similarity on the rationale and provisions behind these formal trade rules and enforcement institutions. The common features shared by all three institutions are as follows:

- They violate in different degrees, principles of good governance by excluding African and developing countries. All these instruments were crafted without the participation of African and developing countries in general. In the case of the MAI, proceedings were conducted in secrecy. For both the MAI and the WTO the records are not publicly accessible.
- They represent a serious threat to African local or domestic firms, in particular women's opportunity for building enterprises from their active work in the informal economy. Opening the economic sphere to foreign ownership reverses the particular advantage given to women's enterprises. It also restricts the ability of state and local legislators to regulate business in the public interest.
- They threaten community investment in economically deprived areas and put at risk positive discrimination programs aimed at closing economic gender gaps. Any foreign company or investor could challenge poverty, economic empowerment, or small-business assistance programs.
- They establish an uneven playing field that provides corporations a new way to impose their laws through market and unregulated price mechanisms. Powerful countries, mainly the OECD members, will be able to negotiate with foreign investors and corporations while developing nations, in particular the weakest of African countries, will not have the same leveraging opportunity while negotiating with multinational corporations.
- They all promote and reward neoliberal economic policies without consideration for the political and social consequences these instruments bring to African people, especially women and children.

THREE CASE STUDIES:
DEBT MANAGEMENT AND THE HIPC INITIATIVE,
THE CHAD OIL PROJECT, AND PRIVATIZATION IN SENEGAL

Three case studies illustrate why neoliberal economic policies and institutions are questioned in Africa and around the world. The HIPC debt relief initiative is a structural adjustment program that calls on poor countries to face three to six years (or even longer) of structural adjustment including liberalization of finance, labor, goods, and services as well as privatization of public enterprises and reduction of public spending. The Chad oil project raises the question of whether investing large amounts of money to generate growth through transnational corporations is the best way to reduce poverty and promote sustainable engendered development. It also questions whether the use of financial resources especially reserved for development and poverty programs to implement an oil pipeline in Chad promotes or undermines the economic rights and well-being of the poor, in particular, poor women. Senegal's privatization experience raises the question of who privatization benefits and for what purpose. Each of these cases is described in more detail below.

The Highly Indebted Poor Countries (HIPC) Debt Relief Initiative

After many calls for action to address the debt problem of countries with the largest portion of their population under abject poverty, and after the multiple rescheduling exercises performed under the prescriptions of the Paris or Naples Club, the World Bank and the IMF proposed to the world a new debt relief program. This initiative was proposed to poor countries' governments with very heavy conditional ties. They negotiated and accepted it without any consultation with their constituencies or involvement of any independent technical advisory group. Adopted in September 1996, the HIPC initiative was presented as a multilateral debt relief framework with a new mechanism of burden sharing among creditors. Sub-Saharan Africa has the largest number of countries involved in the HIPC process. The HIPC countries include: Angola, Benin, Bolivia, Burkina Faso, Burundi, Cameroon, Central African Republic, Chad, Congo, Côte d'Ivoire, Equatorial Guinea, Ethiopia, Ghana, Guinea, Guinea Bissau, Guyana, Honduras, Kenya, Lao People's Democratic Republic, Liberia, Madagascar, Mali, Mauritania, Mozambique, Myanmar, Nicaragua, Niger, Nigeria, Rwanda, Sao Tome and Principe, Senegal, and Sierra Leone.

The HIPC initiative is guided by the following principles:

- Each country is taken on a case-by-case basis.
- Each HIPC will have to undergo a three-year performance screening while implementing the IMF Enhanced Structural Adjustment Facility Program (ESAF). The ESAF lending funds were set up in 1987 and became operational in 1988. These funds are to benefit only countries eligible for the World Bank International Development Association (IDA) loans. A country can borrow from ESAF provided it undertakes structural adjustment and stabilization programs with rigorous performance criteria and follows a strict monitoring mechanism. The monitoring tools are the World Bank Country Assistance Strategy (CAS) and the IMF Policy Framework Paper (PFP). Both documents are signed by governments after being drafted in the countries under the guidance and tight technical supervision of officials from these two institutions. ESAF's aim is to create enabling conditions for growth, to minimize trade restrictions, and to create smooth relations between member countries and their creditors. While implementing ESAF, member countries' PFPs are evaluated and reviewed annually, which often lead to adding new economic requirements such as restoring a viable balance of payment, implementing stronger measures to promote economic growth, and maintaining an acceptable inflation rate, increasing efficiency and competitiveness.

- Each country has to show to the World Bank and the IMF a good track record of performance. The country will have to negotiate with the Paris Club in order to benefit from additional funding with rescheduling programs on the basis of the Naples terms. Bilateral and multilateral creditors will also be asked to support the country with an important amount of funding.
- The three-year period that represents the first phase of the HIPC will be concluded with a debt sustainability analysis (DSA) undertaken during the last year of ESAF. This first phase will be terminated with a *decision point*.
- The World Bank and the IMF, on the basis of the country's performance in meeting the objectives defined in the PFP, determine if there is a satisfactory track record. The performance criteria are rank-ordered as follows: (1) macroeconomic performance measured by the usual economic indicators; (2) implementation of structural reforms (i.e., liberalization reforms of financial and labor sectors; reforming goods and services markets; privatization programs); (3) social reforms aimed at "alleviating" (not eradicating) poverty.
- The DSA will determine the country's eligibility for debt relief. Debt sustainability refers to the level of indebtedness under which a debtor country is able to pay its present and future debt service obligations. Further, a country reaches a sustainable debt situation when it is able to keep an acceptable level of economic growth, does not accumulate loans, or does not need to request debt relief or debt rescheduling. In addition to the economic criteria described above, some social factors, not systematically specified, are supposed to be taken into consideration in the debt sustainability analysis.
- If the DSA shows that the country is unable to sustain its debt, the World Bank and IMF subscribe a new performance program for three additional years. The Paris Club is called again to support the country's good intention for showing good track records in applying economic reforms. The Paris Club offers more rescheduling and financial flows. The country also receives assistance from bilateral and commercial sources. A second DSA is then undertaken at the completion point of the second round of the three-year period of economic reforms. If the country is found still unsustainable for debt payment, bilateral and commercial creditors will provide financial assistance. Multilateral organizations will also intervene to support the country. All the institutions providing support will finally share the costs of assisting the country to reach a sustainable debt level.

Under the poor economic and financial conditions reflected in table 4.1, the HIPC countries are expected to implement the ESAF framework. These HIPC countries have very poor public revenues with a very limited tax and economic base. Their capacity to fund their social programs is almost nil because of their commitments to service their debt. For example, Mozambique spent only U.S.$1.5 per person on health in 1994 while disbursing U.S.$4 per person in 1980 already in debt payment (WILPF 1994). The prospects for education are also bleak.

Table 4.1 Comparative Socioeconomic Indicators*

Regions	Real GDP per capita (PPP$)[a]	Life Exp. at Birth	Adult Literacy	Gross Enrollment Ratio[b]	HDI Value
WORLD	5,428	63.0	76.3	60	0.746
DCs	15,136	74.3	98.3	82	0.909
LDCs	2,696	61.5	68.3	55	0.563
SSA	1,288	50.9	55.0	42	0.379
Dif.[c]	1,408	10.6	13.8	13	0.184

*All figures are for the year 1993.
[a]Value in Current Dollars measured at purchasing power parity.
[b]Combined first, second, and third gross enrollment ratios.
[c]Difference between Less Developed Countries (LDCs) and Sub-Saharan Africa (SSA) figures.
Source: Dembele, 1996.

Africa is the only region in the world not increasing its per capita expenditure on education: U.S.$26 in 1985, $28 in 1990 and 1992 as opposed to $27 in 1985, $39 in 1990, and $49 in 1992 in developing countries as a block. In 1990, illiteracy rates for women were higher than 60 percent in many African countries, which has adversely affected the ability of women to empower themselves as meaningful change agents and decision-makers (UNESCO 1995). Women's participation in higher education is also low; in 1991 there were only 27 percent of women in sub-Saharan Africa's global student population as opposed to 33 percent in East Asia and 36 percent in South Asia. The same year, there were 5,000 students per 100,000 people in North America, 2,500 students per 100,000 in most developing countries, and only 100 students per 100,000 people in sub-Saharan Africa (UNESCO 1995). A further look at adult illiteracy by region is shown in table 4.2.

Table 4.2 Estimates of the Rate of Adult Illiteracy by Region

Regions	1990 Men (%)	1990 Women (%)	2000 Men (%)	2000 Women (%)
Arab States	35.7	62.0	27.1	49.4
East Asia/Oceania	11.8	28.1	7.7	16.4
Latin America/Caribbean	13.6	16.6	10.3	12.7
OECD/Europe	2.6	3.9	1.0	2.0
South Asia	40.9	67.8	33.8	58.8
Sub-Saharan Africa	40.5	64.4	29.8	50.4
World	17.8	32.7	14.7	25.8

Source: Dembele, 1996.

The microeconomic implications of the new macropolicies spearheaded under the HIPC initiative will thus worsen Africa's situation given the state of persistent and rising poverty with a growing number of people living below the poverty line. The six years of ESAF implementation will represent a very highly paid social cost borne mostly by women and the poor. Budgetary levies will deepen the gaps in the distribution of wealth, aggravate gender and social disparities, and frustrate large sectors of poor populations from accessing meaningful social services.

The time frame given to countries to perform and apply reforms through DSA and presenting acceptable track records to international lending institutions is questionable. A country that is extremely poor and highly indebted would have enormous difficulties undergoing six years of ESAF and in the end reach a satisfactory level of DSA. When the track record for consistent payment is being monitored, large amounts of financial resources are taken from millions of women dying during childbirth or from children, in particular girls, who are denied their basic rights to education. Even in countries that are being presented as having high growth rates, poverty among women is increasing (UNDP 1995). The debt service payment represents a drain on poor government resources while women are in dire need for social services. It is a financial hemorrhage that is literally killing millions of African people while condemning to death certain millions of malnourished babies whose brain cells are progressively destroyed because of a lack of adequate food and vitamins and as a direct result of morally unsustainable budgetary, fiscal, and social reforms.

This judgment may sound biased to some readers but the bottom line is that Africa is weakened by policies imposed upon its people against their will and above all contrary to Africa's long-term strategic and security interests. Africa's internal contradictions and ultimately its political and economic responsibility are not ignored in this tragic situation. On the contrary, under the conditional ties described above, one can clearly see the linkage between internal and external factors. External factors in this particular instance have overpowered and determined the fate of internal factors, although the latter are engineered in great part by local dynamics and subsequent class and gender contradictions and struggles. Since the 1960s, very few African political leaders had the opportunity or willingness to explore alternative development pathways. Those who tried mostly failed under adverse conditions aggravated by former colonial powers (i.e., Julius Nyerere of Tanzania, Kwame Nkrumah of Ghana, Modibo Keita in Mali), while all the other tyrants were tolerated if not encouraged or empowered by financial lending institutions and Western powers under the pretext that democracy in its tropical version was unable to grasp the principles of fairness, good governance, and the rule of law. As evidenced by the recent tide of democratization that neutralized many African dictatorships, these ideological clichés are superficial.

The Chad Oil Project

The Chad oil project is a World Bank multibillion-dollar financial initiative. It consists of oil exploitation by a consortium formed by Exxon, Shell, and ELF (ELF stands for Enterprise de recherches et d'activités Pétrolières, or more commonly ELF-ERAP. Over time it became known as ELF, one of its gasoline brand names). The project will undertake the construction of three oil fields in the Doba basin of southern Chad and the building of a 6,000-mile-long pipeline that is planned to go from Chad and pass through Cameroon to reach the Atlantic Ocean. Additional plans include the construction of a pump and storage station in Chad and a storage and off-loading station to be built in Cameroon. This project was initially funded with U.S.$120 million from the World Bank IDA and U.S.$250 million from the International Finance Corporation (IFC). Above all, the World Bank involvement represents a political warranty for the consortium. By being associated with the World Bank, the oil consortium will be protected against any kind of political or financial risk that may be encountered in these countries. Contributions from the IFC, the World Bank wing that finances the private sectors, represent an encouraging invitation to other big investors to participate in the venture. The IDA funding was later withdrawn after international pressures from groups in Africa and the United States, in particular due to the campaign organized by the Association of African Women for Research and Development (AA-WORD).

Chad is one of the poorest countries in the world with one of the lowest Human Development Index (HDI) ratings. It ranks 164 of 175 countries covered by the survey. Chad's HDI has even declined from 0.296 in 1992 to 0.288 in 1994 (UNDP 1995, 1997b). Chad is among ten countries having the lowest Gender-related Development Index (GDI) and Gender Empowerment Index (GEM). The GDI assesses the level of human development inequality between women and men, while the GEM shows the level to which women have been empowered. Given the very high degree of extreme poverty and gender inequality in Chad, the choice made by the World Bank to support transnational corporations for an oil pipeline raises fundamental questions regarding its commitment to gender equality.

This project is described as having detrimental environmental and social consequences for the population. Forests will be destroyed, the water will be polluted, and the agro-ecological equilibrium will be disrupted. As an environmental defense fund officer, Korina Horta wrote, "the region has the potential to develop another Ogoniland scenario" (*Africa Agenda*, no. 11, June 1997, p. 30). Many people will be displaced and have their land taken away from them. Given the large gap in gender disparities, women will be last to be served in case any reallocation of land to resettlers ever takes place. What would women and the poor gain from a pipeline after being expelled from their communities, losing their forests and the land they use for cultivation, seeing their biodiversity severely damaged and their drinking water, a most valuable resource for women farmers, polluted? Because many women are food providers, the differential gender impact this project will have on food security has not yet been fully assessed or understood. Gender implications are an overriding concern here because women are not only poorer than men, but they experience poverty in a more dramatic way given biases against them (in training, ownership of assets, employment, and participation).

The World Bank and the Chad government have shrouded this project in secrecy and share very little documentation with the public. No one is allowed to come close to the oil exploitation site. The political climate is getting worse and this project is planting the seeds of future conflicts in the region at a time when many agencies and development actors are discussing peace-building and warning against the economic, physical, and emotional distress women suffer under conflict situations.

The people are being denied their economic and social rights as well as their rights to information. By excluding the people from the conception of this project, the World Bank encourages corruption and undermines democratic processes and good governance practices. This is in direct opposition to the World Bank's call for participation, ownership, and national consultation. The World Bank has taken no serious effort to take into account the demands of human rights groups, women's groups, and the overall nongovernmental community in Chad.

Even if the Chad and Cameroon governments get a percentage of the benefits generated by the oil companies, this extra revenue will be used to pay for a larger amount of the countries' debt service and to purchase arms. On the one hand, expenditures for the provision of social services to respond to women's needs are a small percentage of government expenditures, and the amount of money that would be allocated to that sector would be marginal. On the other hand, the debt service payment, the buying of arms, and the transfer of profits from the oil consortium to Western banks will represent an important shift of financial resources to northern countries at the expense of women's rights to economic livelihoods.

Privatization in Senegal in Response to Globalization

The case of privatization in Senegal demonstrates how policy levies introduced through adjustment programs have created enforcement mechanisms that accelerate the country's integration into an increasingly globalized world economy. Senegal played an important geopolitical and economic role in Africa during the trans-Saharan trade and the Atlantic slave trade periods. It continued to represent a strategic point of convergence during the colonial period, with the hosting of the French colonial capital for West Africa and the African representation of major French trading companies from Bordeaux and Marseille. Several studies have described the nature and impact of French colonialism (Suret-Canale 1964).

Informal trade rules in Senegal are an inheritance from both the traditional exchange system and the colonial trading system. Since independence, Senegal has attempted to develop formal rules to create an environment enabling trade to flourish. Adjustment policies implemented in the early 1980s emphasized a structural policy reform that would set in motion structural programs leading to an enabling environment for foreign private corporations. The Bretton Woods institutions asked the government to channel at least 25 percent of its GDP toward the improvement of physical infrastructure in sectors that would reflect investors' priorities. The reform also supported the revision of labor regulations, the lowering of producers' taxes, and the opening of the economy to foreign investment in order to increase the country's production capacities.

Privatization is one of the major policy instruments Senegal has used in the structural adjustment era. It was initiated in 1989 out of the urgent need to balance the budget by eliminating government expenditures on public enterprises and increasing government revenues with the sale of major public enterprises to private firms. Ten years after privatization, the Senegalese people and development specialists joined other Africans who wondered about the efficiency of such privatizations. They saw this exercise as a mere transfer from state monopoly to the monopoly of foreign private corporations, a process that encourages corrupt government officials to receive bribes. Further, corporations proposing to purchase would-be-privatized enterprises would negotiate the best conditions for themselves, knowing that the government was pressed by the Bretton Woods institutions to respect promises to privatize. Their own respective governments backed these corporations during negotiations. It must be stressed that these governments maintained dominating power relations with African countries. One strategy used by European companies is to time negotiation sessions during an official visit of their minister of cooperation to make sure they get the market. Such strategies worked in almost all cases, particularly where old colonial ties exist.

European companies, mainly French and North American companies, have taken over the public enterprise sector in Senegal. In the case of the telephone company SONATEL, the Senegalese telephone service provider was sold to France Telecom. The government has permitted the buyer to hold a seven-year monopoly on telecommunication services. The French RATP transport authority, buyer of Senegalese public transportation company SOTRAC, and the French company SDE, which bought the Senegalese water company SONES, have negotiated very favorable conditions in their own terms with the authorities. The same scenario prevailed when Hydraulique Quebec, a Canadian company that purchased SENELEC, the national energy provider. The sale of SENELEC took the Senegalese people by surprise and caused total shock because this public enterprise was doing well in terms of profit generation and management. The sale of SENELEC put the country in a state of political crisis with a major confrontation between the government and the workers because the government had promised the workers and the management that the company would not be privatized if the management and financial situation were satisfactory. The Minister of Energy publicly recognized that the government promised not to privatize but was obliged to honor its obligations with the international financial institutions. Union leaders were jailed and consumers suffered unprecedented levels of electricity disturbances and shortages.

Privatization policies have not delivered the expected results. Prices of water, electricity, telephone, and transport have gone up while services delivery is as distorted as before. In the case of water supply, several families in the urban areas have gone back to the old way of getting water from public fountains. This means increased working hours and heavier workloads for women who have to carry water buckets several times for domestic usage. As a result of privatization in water delivery service, public fountains made available by the government to the very poor in urban areas are no longer free. Having to buy water at the public fountain creates a new income deficit, aggravating women's poor living standard and obliging them to carry heavy buckets of water considerable distances after having bought it at highly prohibitive prices. It is hoped that future evaluation of privatization policies will factor in their impact on women's income, reproductive health, and their ability to find free time for other monetary activities, as women's domestic work, however harsh, is mostly not counted or valued.

Privatization policies have also undermined people's opportunities for increasing their livelihoods or building a local private enterprise. Workers are unhappy because jobs and social security are shuttered while expatriates with huge salaries are being hired. Women are being hired as temporary workers on daily-paid jobs with no access to minimum wage security. Privatization has placed at risk local private enterprises as well as women's opportunities for emerging as an economic force in the informal sector. Women's access to local as well as international markets is made difficult because of their inability and uneasiness to compete with foreign companies. In the local market, women are pushed away by competition from foreign corporations. The heavy social cost of these reforms has not provided a more secure economic environment in the country, and the expected "trickle down" results in terms of stimulating greater levels of investment, advancing economic growth, and increasing jobs has not occurred.

CONCLUSION: REGIONAL INTEGRATION AND GENDER EQUALITY, A MUST

Overall, the institutions and processes of globalization in Africa are aggravating Africa's marginal position in the international division of labor. Neoliberal policies favoring growth of global market economy over the well-being and even survival of Africa's people are part of the problem. The actions of the IFIs and a countless number of global corporation executives pursue growth-oriented development strategies at the expense of engendered human development strategies pursuing the objectives of self-reliance and self-sustainability. The support given to the Exxon/Shell/ELF's oil consortium is a clear illustration of this. The rationale is that resources generated from growth will trickle down to alleviate poverty. But the World Bank has recognized on many occasions that even in those sub-Saharan African countries showcased as having a satisfactory growth rate, poverty has increased during the past decade.

Structural adjustment policies are meant to sustain and reinforce conditions that will invite foreign investors to exploit either the labor or natural resources of a country to produce foreign currency for balance of payments purposes and to repay national debt. They encourage the use of a country's resources for export development rather than for domestic development (again to produce foreign currency to repay debt). They encourage the privatization of services, which reduces the autonomy of local governments and often generates massive unemployment. They encourage cuts in health, education, and social welfare budgets for the purpose of reducing deficits, leaving people, especially women and children who are already impoverished and disadvantaged, in desperate and life-threatening situations.

Supporters of structural adjustment programs argue that trade liberalization will bring growth and in the long run spread the advantages that would benefit everyone and eliminate poverty. But how much more plundering and depravation can Africa undergo? Is there enough time left before tackling Africa's social illnesses?

Very fundamental questions must be raised here. Is the state responsible for allocating resources and determining which and whose wishes will be satisfied? Will African societies be better off if the mobilization and allocation of resources are left to foreign private firms primarily motivated by wealth accumulation or to international financial and trade institutions or to bilateral development agencies? What is the potential of political intervention in promoting or impeding social welfare or striking a balance between public outcomes and foreign private interests? Should French and Canadian companies be running the water and telephone companies of Senegal when the national private sector could be empowered to do so? Can African countries compete against European and American corporations and pharmaceutical companies who have the knowledge and power to patent seeds or medical products and prevent others from using them for developmental objectives? Who should make choices about which economic sectors should receive investment or what constitutes a "good track record" in meeting structural adjustment requirements? Should people, including women, have a voice in these decisions, or will the decisions continue to be made by international bankers and global corporation executives controlling international capital?

Many more questions emerge regarding debt management. How relevant are the criteria used to define debt sustainability? How are countries differentiated in specific situations? In what ways and at what level are factors such as gender and overall human development considered when assessing debt sustainability? How can a country be very poor, very indebted, and undergo six years of enhanced structural adjustment facility before being eligible for debt relief? To what extent have the research results that positively correlate ESAF policy instruments with mechanisms that aggravate the poverty of women been taken into consideration (Fall 1996)? Why should only the World Bank and IMF decide on which indicators to use? Why is the IMF asking industrialized countries to continue to commit their resources to HIPC without any substantial evidence that the initiative, which causes such pain and suffering, is effective in resolving the debt problem?

The debt problem is a problem of economic justice, not simply a technical macroeconomic issue, because expenditures on debt service endanger women's right to human development. Much more money is used to service the debt than to support social spending at a time when the continent is faced with outstanding problems of poverty, illiteracy, and disease.

African women need to get clear answers to these questions. They must be actively involved in the assessment of the HIPC process. The initiative involves a range of economic reforms and raises very critical gender and social policy issues. Sustainable human development should be the ultimate aim of development and an inalienable right of both women and men. The World Bank–IMF criteria must consider the state of human development in the classification of criteria.

Africa must tackle globalization with a strategy oriented toward economic integration and cooperation because globalization will prove that national development is an impossible task within the framework of the unequal international division of labor and the place assigned to Africa in that context. With the limited market outlets, the lack of communication and transport infrastructures, the low level of income, and the states' weak institutional capacity, few African countries will be able to develop a sound economic policy on their own.

Africa must integrate its production structures and create economies of scale within regional markets and harmonize investment, fiscal, customs, and trade policies. A common policy framework toward the WTO regulations will give countries greater bargaining power in negotiating the time frame necessary for decreasing custom tariffs.

Regional cooperation can be built through the following principles:

- Creation of a free trade area involving the removal of trade and nontrade barriers;
- Establishment of a custom union under which trade restrictions are eliminated and a common external tariff is applied by all signatory countries;
- Creation of an economic union guarantee to member states that have harmonized monetary, fiscal, structural, and social policy frameworks;
- Creation of a supranational body.

Other actions may be taken such as:

- Better coordination and integration of subregional market entities;
- Inclusion of social and gender indicators in trade policy reviews carried out to assess every country's effort and progress;

- Widening of the consultation process on the social clause in all sectors of civil society;
- Reinforcing, democratizing, and genderizing labor standards and their implementation processes;
- Pressuring the WTO to accept the social clause with binding effect;
- Strengthening women workers' organizations.

In addition, the following conceptual issues should be critically examined in order to strengthen further the link between macro-, meso-, and micropolicies in development programs:

- The conventional wisdom that economic policies and, more particularly, trade policies, are gender neutral should be reassessed and challenged based on factual evidence showing quite the contrary;
- African women researchers and activists should join hands and undertake a systematic statistical data compilation and analysis of national accounts bringing in the informal sector activity and women's contributions to gross national product. Such statistical exercises are a prerequisite for adequately designing economic policies based on a clear representation of traditionally marginalized economic actors and a good and fair understanding of women, the poor, and gender interhousehold differences in production, consumption, decision-making, and access and control over resources;
- Economic models that will be able to deal effectively with gender inequality and poverty eradication need to be designed. Globalization as the highest stage of imperialism cannot target gender equality, especially in the African context, as an objective because it is solely concerned with competition and profit maximization;
- Women NGOs should cooperate with other UN agencies such as the United Nations Development Program to call on the expertise of women economists to develop gender indicators of economic performances or economic failures; and
- Mechanisms enabling women and community-based organizations to participate more meaningfully in national and international macroeconomic policy choices must be set up. Such mechanisms should include information exchange mechanisms that would enable women to develop strong policy advocacy skills.

The large majority of African women have very low incomes and face difficult humanitarian problems. Transfers from public spending programs are critical to their survival, even though it may not solve all their problems. African economies' dependency on the Bretton Woods institutions is chronic. The essence of adjustment conditionality denies women the right to participate in economic policy formulation and to identify the economic models that suit the conditions

under which they live. An assessment of the role and work of international financial and trade institutions has proven that these institutions of twentieth-century
globalization are not concerned with people-responsive governance and the promotion of women's right to development. We should not be apologetic for exposing them and their policies as major contributors to the demise of African
women's well-being.

Sustainable development will not be promoted if countries do not develop policy priorities that privilege human capacity building, food security, and a strong
environmental culture that positions forestation programs and the fight against
drought before the short-term objectives of stabilization and liberalization.
Women must exercise their right to play a central role in evaluating the costs and
benefits of policy choices in all national economic sectors, and governments, corporations, and globalization institutions must recognize that neither governments
nor societies nor economies will be sustainable without the full participation of
Africa's women.

Regional integration is a pressing priority that Africa and the world must pursue to help Africa improve its economies and position in the global economy.
Only through regional integration can Africa begin to obtain some bargaining
power to address its debt, infrastructure, and human capacity-building problems
and its need to improve its relative position in the global economy. Women and
women's NGOs are important links in the democratization, cooperation, and participation processes that will be necessary to fulfill the strategic need for an in-
ward integration of Africa's economies, markets, infrastructures, societies, and
institutions of higher learning.

5

Mexico/U.S. Migration and Gender Relations: The Guanajuatense Community in Mexico and the United States

Laura Gonzalez

Globalization is not only about the movement of capital and production across national borders. It also includes labor. Labor migration from Mexico to the United States is a good example of labor transcending political boundaries. The economic development of the southwestern United States was made possible in part because of Mexican laborers who helped build the railroads, mines, and ranches in the latter part of the nineteenth century. Since then, Mexican laborers have migrated in large numbers to all parts of the United States, forming heavy concentrations in Texas and other states in the Southwest.

This chapter presents the different gender regimes found in rural Guanajuato, gender regimes that correlate with the type of agriculture being practiced and accompanying migration of labor to the United States. (See map 5.1 for the location of Guanajuato in Mexico.) Gender regimes found among migrant and immigrant Guanajuatense populations will also be covered. The information in this chapter is based on twenty years of fieldwork both in Guanajuato and in the United States, particularly Texas, California, and Pennsylvania.[1] The examination of labor migration from Guanajuato to the United States provides an opportunity to see how globalization in the form of imported mechanized agricultural methods and in the form of demand for labor in the North has affected traditional gender relations both in Mexico and the United States.

GUANAJUATO, MEXICO

In rural Mexico, women's participation in market and subsistence activities is directly affected by changes in the productive structure initiated by national agrarian policies and development programs. This became particularly evident after the agrarian reform efforts of the 1930s. In that decade, the Mexican state created the *ejido*[2] and the Indian community as the basic units of social property

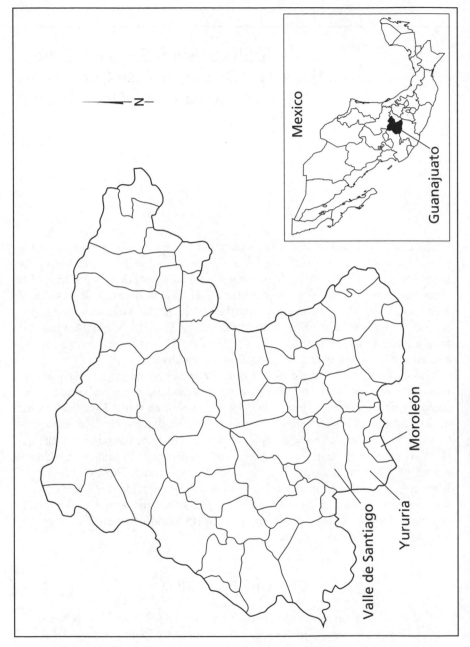

Map 5.1 Guanajuato and Selected Municipalities

and agricultural production, as social and cultural entities, or gender regimes in which men and women, children, youth, and the elderly occupy defined places or positions and perform specific roles. In most of the households of these rural communities, women played the fundamental roles of maintaining family and community cohesion, transmitting cultural norms and social mores (Arizpe and Botay 1987). They engage in cooking, cleaning, taking care of the children and the elderly, activities that can be viewed only as reproductive. However, peasant women were also agricultural producers. The social structure appeared to be patriarchal in nature but the gendered division of labor was subject to the equilibrium inherent in the peasant economy (Arizpe and Botay 1987). Rather than a male-centered farming system, Mexican and Latin American peasant farming in general was best characterized as a family system (Deere and León 1987). A farming system constitutes an integrated set of activities that involves more than just crop production and participation in fieldwork. Animal husbandry, agricultural processing, product transformation and transportation, natural resource management, marketing, and decision-making are also important aspects of the whole system. Women's participation in the production process is significantly higher when all these activities are taken into account.

Over the past fifty years, the impact of the Green Revolution[3] and other local restructuring phenomena—imposed by the Mexican state, the world market economy, and the globalization processes—have transformed the internal social organization of peasant households, *ejidos*, and Indian communities. The local responses to these macropolitical and economic processes have centered on labor migration, which differs from one region to another according to the type of environment, agricultural system practiced, type of state intervention, and pattern of migration. As shown in other works (Gonzalez 1992; 1996a), a major peasant response to the Green Revolution in the state of Guanajuato, Mexico, has been the permanent and temporary displacement of labor from agricultural work that results in international migration.

This pattern of international migration may be described as analogous to a flowering plant rooted in Guanajuato with its stems and flowers stretching into all corners of the United States. Like seedlings in a nursery, migrants are born and nurtured in Guanajuato. They then move north forming small and large enclaves in all the states of the United States. International migration should not be seen as only a unilinear process but rather as permanent and a cyclical movement of people. Under this portrayal Guanajuato is the flowerpot where Guanajuatenses are "inexpensively" reproduced and later transplanted into other states and countries ensuring an abundant source of young, healthy, hard-working, and docile workers.

THE MAJOR REGIONS OF GUANAJUATO

The state of Guanajuato is considered the heartland of Mexico, the cradle of the Independence Movement from Spain in 1810. Since the 1920s, it has been the seat of independent political movements and an entrepreneurial elite that opposes the central government and ruling party, the Partido Revolucionario Institucional (PRI), based in Mexico City. In 2000, it was a former governor of Guanajuato Vicente Fox, who defeated the PRI, which had dominated Mexico for seventy-one years. Guanajuato is unique ecologically, socially, and politically. Its uniqueness can be divided in three main regions: the *Bajío* region, the industrial corridor, and the arid North (see map 5.2). Each of these regions has its own climate, soil, terrain, infrastructure, and economic possibility that requires a specific division of labor and generates its own kind of gender regime.

The *Bajío*

The southern part of the state, the lowlands crossed by the Lerma River known as the *Bajío*, is made up of prime lands (see map 5.3). Irrigation is possible thanks to the Lerma River, its affluence, and thousands of wells drilled during the past thirty years. Generally, the *Bajío* lands produce two crops per season in a year: sorghum and maize during the summer, wheat and barley during the winter. Agricultural production in this area, traditionally considered the breadbasket of Mexico, is highly capitalized and mechanized. It is the region where the Green Revolution was first implemented and, as a result, today its farming is modern.[4]

More recently, the *Bajío* lands have been producing fruits and vegetables. Agribusiness is growing strawberries, broccoli, tiny carrots and zucchini, squashes, tomatoes, chiles, peppers, onions, and garlic for national and international markets, using very labor-intensive agricultural systems. Coexisting with one of the most modernized agricultural systems in the world, *huamiles*, or traditional agricultural systems where subsistence farming takes place, are also found. As shown in other works (Gonzalez 1992; Valencia 1981) *huamiles* use no capital and are very labor intensive; produce multiple diverse crops; and occupy steep and stony terrains where *huamileros* (*huamil* producers) grow corn, beans, squash, fruits, herbs, roots, and edible weeds.

In the *Bajío* region, the international migration flow started with the Revolution of 1910 and continued with the *Cristero* movement, the *Bracero* program, and the modernization of agriculture. Migrants, mostly men who work in agriculture, have moved to the north of Mexico and to the southwestern United States. These men are from 15 to 40 years old and have little formal education. They are hard-working people who are used to long hours of work in harsh conditions including hot dusty weather, rain, and mud.

Industrial Corridor

Stretching from the southeast to the northwest and connecting medium-sized cities such as Querétaro, Celaya, Salamanca, Irapuato, León, and San Francisco del Rincón is an industrial corridor along a major highway in which more than

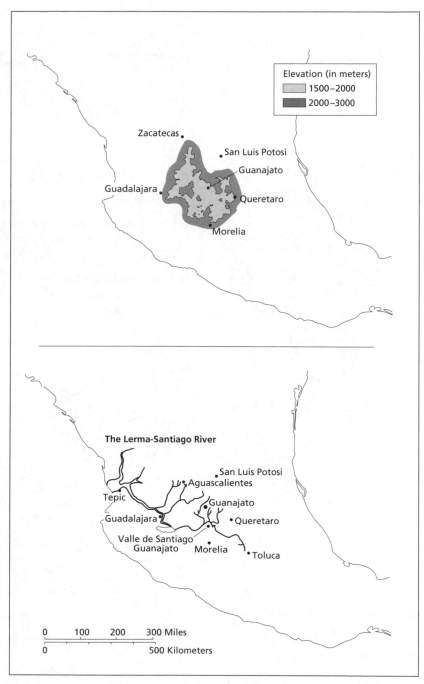

Map 5.2 *El Bajío* **Means the Lowlands**

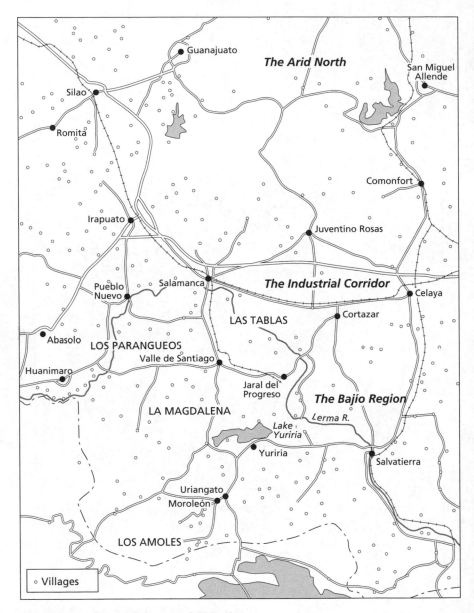

Map 5.3   Areas and Subareas of *El Bajío*

two thousand industries are located. These urban centers and cities are home to 60 percent of the total population of the state. Transnational and national companies are located in and around cities, and make use of the best access to roads, airports, trains, the most fertile lands, easily accessible water, electrical lines, and better medical and legal services, schools, shopping malls, and entertainment.

These urban centers are also exporting labor to the United States. All the forty-six municipalities of the state of Guanajuato are exporting laborers for different reasons. As pointed out earlier, the *Bajío* region is sending people north because modernization of agriculture means displacement of labor, and the industrial corridor cities are doing the same for other reasons. One explanation is that wages are low in the area. Another reason is that new industries do not hire local laborers but employ their own specialized workers brought from Mexican industrial cities such as Monterrey, Puebla, Toluca, and Mexico City, or directly from the United States. More explanations are that better-educated people born and/or raised in the cities of this industrial corridor in Guanajuato are finding better opportunities in the United States, better schools for their children, less crime, less corruption, and more economic opportunities than in their homeland.

Young men and women with more years of formal education work in the industrial corridor. For example, General Motors, Green Giant, and Del Monte require workers to have a high school diploma and basic knowledge of the English language. Japanese firms are opening technical schools and universities to supply their own demand for professionals. In the industrial corridor, both men and women work in packing sheds and the oil refinery, and do loading and unloading of goods, repairing machinery, and preparing food. Some work as bricklayers, mechanics, drivers, and maintenance workers. Others work as waiters or bartenders in restaurants and bars, or as male and female prostitutes and drug dealers for the increasingly affluent society growing in these small and medium-sized cities.

Arid North

The northern portion of the state of Guanajuato is part of a cultural area outside of Mesoamerica known as arid America. The *Chichimecas*, a generic term that includes tribal people who speak Otomí, Pame, Jonás, Capuz, Samue, Guaman, and Guachichil, have inhabited this territory since pre-Hispanic times. The environment of this northern tier of the state consists of poor soils, drought, and low population densities. Agriculture in this region is risky, even with access to irrigation. The local people describe conditions as "one good year in five." Cattle-raising, scattered populations, and Indian communities characterize this part of the state of Guanajuato and its neighboring states of Querétaro, Zacatecas, and San Luis Potosí.

The people from the arid North region were the first to migrate north, mainly to Texas and the U.S. Southwest to work in agriculture, to develop the railroad systems and the mining centers, and later as contract workers under the *Bracero* program. As a consequence, today more Ocampenses and San Felipenses live in the Dallas–Forth Worth area in northern Texas than in the entire municipalities of Ocampo and San Felipe in northeastern Guanajuato. Cemetery evidence in Texas indicates that these men and women from northeastern Guanajuato were in Texas by 1907, but our hypothesis now is that Guanajuatenses arrived before the railroads, during the late 1870s.

Today, the inhabitants of the arid North are mostly children, some women, and the elderly, living in scattered communities. Some raise cattle (cows, horses, and goats). When irrigation is possible, some families grow small plots of maize for subsistence and commercial crops such as hot peppers and sorghum. Inhabitants of small cities, like San Miguel de Allende, have developed tourist attractions or, like Dolores Hidalgo, work the clay to make and sell ceramics.

The rural area of Guanajuato (the hundreds of communities with less than 2,500 inhabitants) still has a characteristic *norteño* flavor: empty houses during ten or eleven months per year; and during the winter months, the money flows abundantly, especially dollars, which benefit small businesses and the whole regional economy. With each passing year, there are more *casas de cambio,* literally "exchange houses," where dollars are exchanged for pesos and vice versa; there are more vehicles with Texas, Illinois, California, Georgia, Florida, North Carolina, Colorado, and Oregon license plates; houses with two floors, garages, and satellite antennas; children playing Nintendo and wearing T-shirts with American logos, sneakers, tattoos, baseball caps, and all those clothes with the gang colors of Los Angeles, Chicago, Houston, or Miami. In the summertime, rural communities look empty, but during the winter months everything is happiness, and is noisy, and money flows abundantly because the *norteño*, the people who stay in the United States for most of the year, come back to their houses and communities to celebrate the local fiestas with their families, neighbors, and friends.

THE *BAJÍO* REGION:
AGRICULTURE, MIGRATION, AND GENDER REGIMES

Because Guanajuato has a variety of localized agricultural systems as well as an urbanized industrial region, a comparison of economic structures, migration patterns, and gender regimes among regions is possible. Four different agricultural systems and international migration patterns exist in the *Bajío* region, and each area exhibits a distinctive pattern of gender relations. The regions are similar in a small-scale way to the major regions of Guanajuato, although all four of these subareas are located in the *Bajío* region. (1) *Las Tablas* represents a large-scale, irrigated, capital intensive, mechanized kind of agricultural region, similar to most of the *Bajío* region. (2) *Los Parangueos* is a combination of smaller irrigated lands combined with rain-fed lands under subsistence production. (3) *La Magdalena* is marginal subsistence farming on hilly, rocky land. Because of the terrain, neither machinery nor animals are used in production. (4) *Los Amoles* is a group of small communities practicing similar subsistence agricultural systems found in both *La Magdalena* and in *Los Parangueos*. The difference here is that *Los Amoles* is close enough to *maquiladores* in the region to make waged employment and piecework possible. Each of these regions exhibits characteristics similar to one of the three major regions of Guanajuato, the *Bajío* region, the industrial corridor, or the arid North. Each also exhibits different patterns of gender relations peculiar to its economic and migratory circumstances.

Las Tablas is located within the oldest irrigated subarea of the municipality of Valle de Santiago, dating from the seventeenth century, when the engineers from the Augustine order of Yuriria diverted the flow of the Lerma River and created the Laguna de (Lake of) Yuriria. The area consists of privately owned (lots of 10, 50, or 100 hectares) and *ejido* lands (plots of 4, 6, and 8 hectares) with permanent access to irrigation producing at least two crops per year (sorghum or corn during the summer and wheat or barley during winter). Agriculture is highly mechanized, capital intensive, and performed by men. All the roads in this zone are in use year round. The local population travel daily in the pickup trucks, cars, buses, and bicycles that frequently pass by the communities.

Men are always present in *Las Tablas*, especially during harvest, planting, and weeding periods. When not working in the fields, men go to the city to buy food, to secure or repay loans, to buy seeds and machinery, to get their machinery repaired, to drink alcohol at the *cantinas*, to hang around with friends in the main plaza, and to see what is going on in politics and the markets for their products. Women stay at home except for Sundays, when they go to church, to the market, to see the doctor, and to visit family and friends. During the week, women cook for the whole family and send the children to school. If the family owns cattle, they milk cows and prepare cheese, which they store, give away, or sell to friends, family, and neighbors. Women and girls clean the house, do the laundry, cook and serve meals, and preserve food. Women have no authority in terms of spending money, except for the small amounts of cash they receive from selling their chickens, turkeys, eggs, or handicrafts (embroidered napkins, pillowcases, tablecloths, linens for wrapping tortillas, and bread baskets). The money obtained through these economic activities is spent on Sundays at the pueblo for toys, medicine, or candy for the children. Men "accompany" their wives, mothers, and daughters and pay in the stores for the sugar, soap, meat, and basics (toilet paper, soap, matches, fruit, vegetables, oil, salt, bread, sugar, and light bulbs) the family buys every week.

More cash circulates in this subarea than in any other of the three subareas. They buy and sell animals and pay for bus tickets. The population of this area is close to the city and has access to the money obtained through the selling of their agricultural goods at least twice a year. When growing vegetables, owners and farm workers get cash money more frequently. Young and old men drink beer, tequila, and brandy, and gamble (cards, cock fights) and do not help women with household chores. They "help" women by bringing the food from the pueblo, by carrying heavy things like gas cans, large sacks of beans, and boxes or furniture, by cleaning the pig sties, taking care of cows, horses and donkeys, and by repairing electrical appliances, walls, roofs, and wash tubs and sinks. The consumption of alcohol as well as violence against women, against children, and among young males are greater in this subarea than in the other subareas, perhaps because there are more men and cash is more readily available.

Los Parangueos is a mixture of rain-fed and irrigated agricultural systems. The area has different types of land (pasture, rain-fed and irrigated, private property, *ejido*, and communal lands). One of the largest haciendas[5] in Mexico existed in this area. *Los Parangueos* is a little more isolated than *Las Tablas*, with less movement of vehicles and people as well as less use of cash for transactions. Men and women go to the local stores to buy food and other basic necessities, and the clerks keep a list of the things bought, as the local people say: "*compran todo fiado* [bought on faith]," on credit. Later, with the money obtained during the harvest, men and women pay their debts. Men go north, to the United States, once or twice a year, usually after planting or harvesting. They send back money every two or three weeks, and decide how to spend both the money obtained by the selling of the commercial crop (sorghum), or by selling their labor in the United States.

Housewives help to harvest the corn, the beans, and the chick peas. When men are in town and cultivating the land, women cook and take or send the lunch to the field. Women take care of the household chores, doing the laundry, processing and preserving food, and taking care of the children, the sick, and the elderly. Traditionally, when men leave to go north to work, wives stay at home with their in-laws, or with their own parents, and take care of their children, and/or raise some small animals such as pigs, poultry, and bees.

The typical family in *Los Parangueos* is a trigenerational group comprised of grandparents, children, and grandchildren. Old men and children take care of one or two cows, the donkeys used to transport the harvest, and a few goats. Livestock serve as a form of liquid capital, or *imprevistos,* to pay for medicine for an illness or any other emergency. However, since 1986, more women are joining their husbands and fathers and traveling to the United States to work. Some elementary schools are seeing reduced numbers of children because whole families are leaving for the United States. At the same time, junior high and high schools, locally known as *telesecundarias* and *preparatorias*, are opening in the area and are attended mostly by girls. More girls than boys comprise the secondary education population because all the young men are traveling north, following the example of their grandparents, parents, uncles, brothers, and cousins. Women are consequently becoming more highly educated than men.

La Magdalena is one of the most traditional communities found in the *Bajío* region with hilly, steep, and stony lands, and small and isolated sets of houses around the Laguna de Yuriria. In *La Magdalena*, small landholdings occupy the larger part of the territory. The holdings are very reduced in size, most of them smaller than 1 hectare, rarely exceeding 4 hectares, and most of them are located on steep hills and mountains. All the agricultural production is for subsistence and depends on rain. The smallness of the plots is the result of land inheritance and high population density. The *ejidal* territory is 80 to 85 percent hilly. Another characteristic of *La Magdalena* is the lack of modern agriculture. However, these steep and stony lands have been opened to cultivation and are adequately exploited through the agricultural system known locally as *huamiles*.

Huamiles are small areas of half or a quarter hectare, or less, with uneven and stone-covered surfaces. The areas have to be worked with family labor, using the hoe and the machete, because neither machinery nor animals can work the land. In these small gardens, the *huamilera* or *huamilero* (respectively female or male cultivator) and their family produce corn, beans, squash, and pumpkins for subsistence. The *huamiles* are fenced with *cacti, pitahayos, garambullos*, or some other fruit-bearing trees, and medicinal weeds, all of which are consumed by the family. The state has no programs for this traditional type of production and, as a result, does not have a say in the production. Consequently, these peasants are more independent than those of *Las Tablas* or *Los Parangueos*.

In the *huamiles*, men, women, children, and the elderly spend many hours per day, many days per year on the land. They cultivate the land, they clean it, make piles and fence it with stones, and spend time collecting medicinal and edible weeds and fruits. They eat there, they take naps, they feed their goats, and they even make love in the fields. Their relationship with the land is total. Early on, children learn about nature and how to protect it.

In the flat lands of the *Bajío* where commercial monocrops are cultivated, the relationship to the land is different. For example, women and the elderly do not go into the fields. Even men and male children do not touch the ground because they are using tractors, or because the land is contaminated with pesticides, fungicides, and fertilizers. Modern agriculture has divorced these people from their land. In contrast, traditional agriculture roots the people to their land because they learn to respect and protect the environment. In the *huamiles* nobody uses chemicals.

The terrain of *La Magdalena* does not permit the commercial cultivation prevalent in the rest of the region. The low agricultural productivity of the area compels a large part of the population to migrate to other regions in search of waged work. This practice has created a particular economic organization in which local families organize their resources in connection with the temporary or permanent labor migration of men (mainly to the United States) and with the agricultural production of the women, elders, and children, who stay and work the *huamiles*. In *La Magdalena*, the linkage of the families with the capitalist sector is through the sale of male labor, whose reproduction is supported by the subsistence agricultural production carried out by the women (Margolis 1982).

Because men leave to work in different parts of the United States, they are not present during most of the year, and for many years of their life cycles. They leave women completely in charge of the land, in charge of the family, the cattle, the children, and the elderly. Women in this situation have much more opportunity to become empowered and politically active. Some women from communities like *La Magdalena* have become local authorities such as *delegadas*, or *presidentas del comisariado ejidal*, board secretaries during elections, presidents and secretaries of school boards, and they are making decisions in terms of spending money at home and for public works. While the women have more autonomy and independence in *La Magdalena*, life for these women is difficult. They live in areas that barely support subsistence agriculture and, singlehandedly, manage to do both the productive and reproductive work of raising families and surviving. Because the men are absent either permanently or for long periods of time, the women are overworked, sometimes to the point of exhaustion. *Huamileras* are tough women with rough hands, strong muscles, and dry skin. Life expectancy is shorter than in other areas, and many women in their late thirties and forties appear to be in their sixties and seventies. Increasingly, women from *La Magdalena* and from many other similar rural communities are migrating and immigrating to the United States. Once they join their husbands, their gender roles revert to a more traditional pattern. They come to Texas, California, Illinois, and Georgia to help their husbands and children, keeping house, cleaning and cooking for them, and helping to raise their grandchildren, while they work as babysitters, housekeepers, or as caregivers for the ill and the elderly.

Los Amoles is a set of communities located southwest of the textile cities of Moroleon and Uriangato, on the northwestern slope of the highest mountain of the area called *Los Amoles*. La Ordeña, Las Peñas, Pamaseo, and Caricheo are some of the communities in this subarea. This rural area is characterized by small valleys and hilly terrains covered with stones, where peasants grow mostly maize and beans for subsistence and very small amounts are sold in local markets. Wild cacti of more than twenty varieties and a great range of weeds, harvested for medicinal uses by local folk, make up the natural flora. The annual rainfall is around 700 millimeters, making agriculture possible, though risky without irrigation. During the rainy season, from June to September, surface water is limited to small streams that eventually evaporate. Underground water sources are scarce and too costly to locate, tap, and pump. Although local land is more suitable for pastoral activities, such as cattle-raising, subsistence agriculture is the dominant activity. Until the 1940s, the two *haciendas* in the region mainly raised cattle for the market and allowed their workers to grow crops for their home consumption (Pimentel Rodríguez 1995). Today, some families continue with this tradition. They raise a few head of cattle, mainly cows that provide milk for home consumption and that they occasionally sell to kin, friends, or neighbors with small children.

The producers are *pequeño propietarios* (small landowners) and *ejidatarios* (title-holders or renters of *ejido* plots) with small parcels, reduced in size (2, 4, and 6 hectares) from larger landholdings over time as a result of land inheritance practices. The number of *ejidatarios* and small landowners is difficult to determine. An approximation is not possible because some *ejidatarios* own private property, and others migrate to the United States and rent their *ejido* parcel or set up a sharecropping arrangement with kin or close friends. Most of the parcels are smaller than 1 hectare and rarely exceed 4 hectares. Maize, squash, garbanzo beans, and peppers are grown on these parcels. Surrounding grazing land is used for raising cattle and small livestock, such as goats and sheep.

Women, elders, and children carry out various economic activities in the region, and the men migrate to the United States and return home according to the agricultural cycle. When the migrants have papers, that is, green cards or citizenship, they make the trip back home to plant seed, harvest the crops, and visit their families. When the migrants have no documents, they stop coming back to their homes for four, five, or eight years, because they cannot afford to be caught and deported and/or to pay again the U.S.$800 to $1,200 fee the coyote (a smuggler of human-beings across the U.S.-Mexico border) charges to cross illegally.

Besides being responsible for domestic work, such as cooking meals, caring for children, and cleaning the home, women in *Los Amoles* help to seed and harvest the fields, take care of domestic animals, and engage in other economic activities that allow them to earn money. Washing clothes, cooking meals, and performing other service work for local families are a few examples. The preparation of foods, such as *chicharrones* (pork rinds), *carnitas* (barbecued pork), and cheese that are sold locally, is another. Young women, with the help of family members, assemble clothes in their homes for clothing *maquiladoras* (assembly plants) in nearby Moroleón and Uriangato. Some of them commute daily to work in these shops, sewing sweaters, blouses, shirts, dresses, and pants; ironing, embroidering, knitting, crocheting, putting in zippers, and sewing on buttons. Work in the garment industry generates income for the coffers of many families, but according to many parents of these young women, the social cost is too high. Rural young women are victims of the older males, patrons, and managers who overexploit these girls when they do not sexually harass them, rape them, and abandon them after they get pregnant.

The small factories, shops, or *talleres* that use piece workers produce sweaters, blankets, and pants during the winter months and dresses, sheets, underwear, suits, wedding dresses, first Holy Communion dresses, baptism dresses, and *quinceañera* (fifteenth birthday, "coming out") dresses during the rest of the year. All the days of the week, except Tuesdays, hundreds of shops both permanent and temporary open from 9:00 A.M. to 7:00 P.M. to sell "*al mayoreo y al menudeo*" (wholesale or by the piece) to the thousands of clients who come from all the states of Mexico, as well as California, Texas, Arizona, Colorado, and Pennsylvania. Mexicans from the entire country go there to buy or sell clothes. The Moroleón and Uriangato garment industry provides and does *maquila* work for the best clothing stores in Mexico City, such as Palacio de Hierro, Liverpool, Coqueta, and Calvin Klein, and even for very wealthy individuals.

The textile industry offers hundreds of temporary jobs for young females, single and married. Many housewives do piecework in their homes four or five hours a day to make 30 or 50 pesos (U.S.$3 or $5) per week. The highest salary for a well-trained seamstress, paid by work done and not by time, is 450 pesos per week (U.S.$45). The large majority of rural women who daily commute to work in these shops make 200 pesos (U.S.$20) per week. Older women cannot work because their eyes become too tired. Some owners of *maquiladores* confide that seamstresses last only a few years, from eight to twelve years, when they are healthy and energetic.

Both the men and the women who go to the United States and return to Guanajuato bring back ideas from the North with them, yet the local culture remains strong. Men who do laundry, wash dishes, and cook in the United States "forget" or stop doing these chores when they return to visit or to live in Mexico. Although not yet a pattern, increasingly more and more independent single women, returning Mexican women from the United States, Protestant converts, and educated women are becoming empowered in Mexico and are transforming their communities. Some become schoolteachers, nurses, and state administrators, but many more become entrepreneurs, successful businesswomen who create their own offices and later become political leaders at the local, regional, and international levels.

LOCAL MEXICAN ECONOMIC SYSTEMS, MIGRATION, AND GENDER REGIMES

The above review of four subareas in Guanajuato suggests a link between the nature of the local economy, the pattern of migration in the area, and the resultant gender relations. In *Las Tablas,* the agricultural economy is modernized, capital intensive, and relatively prosperous. While many men have been displaced and have migrated north, enough jobs remain to support a significant male population year round. In these regions characteristic of much of *Bajío*, a gendered division of labor exists whereby men do the work outside the home and men control most decision-making both inside and outside the home.

In areas like *Los Parangueos*, with some irrigated farming and some rain-fed, subsistence farming, both men and women share in many of the agricultural tasks when the men are home. Most men leave for the North, send money back home every two weeks, and come back twice a year to harvest and plant. Traditional gender relations prevail, given that men maintain control over decisions involving farming and the spending of money. Women are expected to perform cooking, cleaning, and caring functions as well as help with the agricultural work. Because the men are absent much of the time, the gendered division of labor is less clear-cut than in *Las Tablas*. In *Los Parangueos*, women and men are more likely to share chores and duties; however, men traditionally remain in control. The culture of migrating north for young men, combined with the Mexican government's building of many more schools, is persuading more girls than boys to continue their schooling.

La Magdalena has such poor agricultural possibilities that almost all the men migrate out in search of employment, either permanently or for long periods of time. Women have traditionally remained in the area to perform all productive and reproductive activities as single mothers. Women in *La Magdalena* have become empowered by the absence of men. They control the land, the local businesses, and even the local political systems. The cost of empowerment for these women, however, is overwork, exhaustion, and early aging.

Los Amoles, with its proximity to the *maquila* garment industry, illustrates the impact of a waged (minimally waged) economy on the gender relations in a subsistence family farming system, similar to that of *Los Parangueos*. While this empowers some women because they are able to earn a wage and have some money to spend of their own, many young girls and women work for their families, not for themselves. Their wages add to the family income but do not empower them. Many young girls and women are sexually harassed on the job, raped, seduced, and in other ways sexually exploited. Those who avoid these dangers must still cope with eyestrain and other unhealthy working conditions while earning very low wages.

GUANAJUATENSES IN THE UNITED STATES

People originally from Guanajuato live in all of the United States with particular concentrations in Texas (800,000), California (700,000), Illinois (300,000), Salt Lake City (80,000), Southern Chester, Pennsylvania (12,000), and Lexington, Ontario, Canada (1,000).

Guanajuatenses in California work primarily in agriculture, mainly in the San Joaquin valley, and the central coastal valleys but also in cities, such as Los Angeles, mainly in the service sector as gardeners, as day workers in restaurants and hotels, as janitors cleaning offices, and as mechanics and drivers. In the construction industry, they work as bricklayers, plumbers, carpenters, and electricians. They also work as housekeepers, live-in all-purpose workers, babysitters, and caretakers of the elderly and ill people in the home care industry. Many Guanajuatense women live in the homes of very wealthy people taking care of the elderly, the sick, and children.

In Texas, Guanajuatense males work mainly in the building industry as bricklayers and carpenters, but also as gardeners on golf courses or cleaning offices and streets. Women work in homes performing different types of housekeeping, taking care of children, the elderly, and the sick. They also work as janitors cleaning offices, shopping malls, universities, schools, airports, banks, and health clubs.

In Pennsylvania, Guanajuatense men work in the mushroom industry harvesting and packing mushrooms, as well as taking care of gardens. Some work in factories, dry cleaners, and restaurants. Almost all Guanajuatense migrants in Pennsylvania are male. However, more and more women are arriving to join their husbands and fathers and start working in packing sheds, factories, restaurants, dry cleaners, and local stores.

The Guanajuatenses in Chicago are the elite of this population because they have more years of formal education. Most of the Guanajuatenses who live in Chicago have finished high school, earn an average of U.S.$36,000 per year, and most of them are bilingual and bicultural. Also, in political terms, the Guanajuatenses who settled in different parts of Illinois and Michigan seem to be very active and well organized.

GENDER REGIMES IN THE UNITED STATES

The largest and oldest Guanajuatense enclave is in the Dallas–Fort Worth area, where early members arrived at the turn of the century, if not before. Overall, about 85 to 90 percent of all Guanajuatense migrants are male and, as a result, gender relations in the United States are skewed. However, the number of women is growing, a growth made possible by the legalization programs of the Immigration Reform and Control Act of 1986.[6] In Texas, thousands of women from Guanajuato come from a range of socioeconomic backgrounds, from rural and urban areas, some uneducated and some with more formal education, some bilingual and some monolingual. They are entrepreneurs, students, housekeepers, single heads of households, typical housewives, and single mothers. Those women who are not educated, not bilingual, undocumented, and/or recent arrivals are likely to continue under the control of their husbands, fathers, brothers, and sons or daughters who become bilingual. Their employment options are limited to household work, cleaning, caretaking, and perhaps illegal sweatshop or piecework labor. In general, they maintain traditional gender roles. Many are subject to abuse and exploitation both by male employers and by men in their own families who mistreat them physically, verbally, psychologically, or who constantly threaten to call *la migra* (the Immigration and Naturalization Service) if they do not obey or please. Many of these women see upward mobility as something they desire for their children, if not for themselves, in the United States.

If documented, skilled, and able to earn a living wage in the United States, Mexican women are able to assert some independence in household and community affairs. In the United States, these women are exposed through the media and by example to a range of role models for women. Some Guanajuatense women from rural areas become entrepreneurs, taking advantage of opportunities in the United States. They create their own businesses and often create jobs for other family members and employees. Many of these women have been instrumental in establishing Casas Guanajuato in twenty-nine locations in the United States. These are local nonprofit organizations that help migrants deal with their problems. Some women are the presidents or founders of these Casas Guanajuato. These organizations are linked together in networks that maintain contact with the government of the State of Guanajuato.

As mentioned above, men too are influenced by their work circumstances—by U.S. customs and by the absence of women during their sojourns north. Certainly many of these men who live alone or with a group of men in the United States must do their own laundry, cooking, and cleaning. One of the main differences of Guanajuatense gender regimes in Mexico and the United States is that Mexican men in a nuclear family in the United States are more likely to help with or take care of housework, especially if the wife works outside of the household. However, when the same man goes back to Mexico to visit, he stops helping with housework.

CONCLUSION

A careful examination of the gender relationships or gender regimes in four different types of agricultural areas in Guanajuato, Mexico, suggests a close interrelationship among agricultural systems, immigration patterns, and predominant gender regimes. Areas suitable for capital-intensive agriculture primarily employ men who tend to stay in the area all year. The men who are displaced by this less labor-intensive way of farming migrate north. With a critical mass of men present, the division of labor and gender relations remain traditional. Men control decision-making both outside and inside the home. In areas with subsistence farming, women are still governed by the traditional division of labor, but much less rigidly. Women continue to do all housework, food preparation, and domestic chores. They also help with agricultural production work. Usually, they do not control decisions concerning household spending or the agricultural operation but may share in this decision-making. In subsistence farming areas where men are absent, women assume economic and political responsibility. They perform all the roles. They also make all the household spending decisions, farming decisions, and local public spending decisions. Some hold political office. Wage work in the *maquiladoras* provides jobs for women in a traditional agricultural setting. For some women in a traditionally male-controlled household, the extra cash can supply a bit of independence and autonomy for the wage-earning women. However, the pay is too meager to make much of a difference for most. For many women, the workplace is but an extension of male family control and domination and not a source of empowerment.

The gradual appearance of more education for women and girls, more single independent women, more female Protestant converts, and more Mexican women returning from the North are small signs of empowerment for a few women. The possibility for democratization in areas that are not based on subsistence agriculture, however, appears to be reduced by capital-intensive agricultural systems that employ only men. In these situations, new forms of patriarchal, authoritarian, and patron-client relations appear. In very poor subsistence farming areas where all men leave, democratization is highly advanced as women perform all household, economic, and civic functions. For those women who receive money from the North to supplement the family income, the situation is much better than for those women who do not.

Once in the United States, Guanajuatense men and women are exposed to and participate in other economic systems and other kinds of gender regimes different from those of rural Mexico. Their response depends largely on their education, their ability to speak English, and their marketable skills. Women who migrate from Guanajuato are of all classes, with different educational backgrounds. Those with more resources in United States are often able to provide leadership for others. The formation of the twenty-nine Casas Guanajuato throughout the United States creates new spaces and new opportunities for political education and political participation for Guanajuatense men and women. Many of them are becoming well established in the the United States and are able to organize politically and to work collectively.

Globalization processes that allow people to move from one region to another are generating a political infrastructure that links Guanajuatense enclaves in the United States with each other and also to their home communities in the State of Guanajuato. The two million Guanajuatenses involved in the process of international migration, including the migrants and their U.S.-born children, are permanently or temporarily living in another state or country, but they are maintaining important economic and increasingly political relations with their families and communities both in the United States and in Guanajuato. The remittances of these migrants to Guanajuato are the most important source of revenue to a state with no oil to export and a tourist sector that has not been developed to its full potential. Recognizing this fact, the government of Guanajuato, since 1997, has sought to nurture and foster the migrant networks of Guanajuato. It has sponsored a newspaper, *Boletin Pa'l Norte*, by funding research on Guanajuato migrants, and establishing an office (headed by a woman) in Dallas, Texas, to concentrate and coordinate political and economic efforts in order to advance the well-being of compatriots in the United States. This "new political system" has a very different gender regime from those of traditional Mexican politics where women, especially rural women, are normally excluded. The Casas Guanajuato not only include women but are sometimes organized and led by women. This, along with increased levels of education for girls and women and the subsequent ability of more Guanajuatense women to break out of sex-segregated, low-wage, service jobs in the United States economy and in the Mexican economy, is the key to increased democratization for Guanajuatense women.

NOTES

1. The research started in Valle de Santiago, Guanajuato, in 1976, when a group of professors and students installed the long-term project Agricultura y Sociedad en el Bajío, funded by an interinstitutional agreement among Universidad Iberoamericana, Universidad Autonoma Metropolitana, Iztapalapa, and el Centro de Investigaciones Superiores en Antropologia Social (CIS-INAH), today's Centro de Investigaciones y Estudios Superiores en Antropologia Social (CIESAS) (Gonzalez 1992). The research continued in California, Pennsylvania, Guanajuato, and Texas, using the same methodologies and theoretical framework, thanks to the research projects funded by the University of California, Santa Barbara; Indiana University of Pennsylvania; the U.S. Census Bureau in Washington, D.C.; Universidad de Guanajuato, Mexico; and the University of Texas in Dallas (see Garcia 1992, 1995; Palerm 1993, 1998, 1999; Garcia and Gonzalez 1995, 1999a, 1999b, 1999c; Gonzalez 1996a, 1996b, 1999; Gonzalez and Hernandez 1998).

2. *Ejido* is an agricultural community and a unit of production established after the Mexican Revolution. Peasant men who qualify and vow to comply with the requirements of the Agrarian Law of 1917 are granted usufruct rights to the land (4 to 6 hectares per person in the *Bajío* region). It cannot be sold, rented, mortgaged, traded, or abandoned. If it is, the *ejidatario* loses all rights to the land. For a comprehensive discussion of the *ejido* in Guanajuato see Gonzalez 1996a, chapter 2.

3. The Green Revolution is a development program designed to increase crop production by implementing new farming technology. This new technology includes improved and hybrid cereal seeds, large landholdings, and modern farming implements, such as machinery, fertilizers, insecticides, fungicides, and herbicides, and an inexpensive, temporary, and abundant labor force (Gonzalez 1992, 1996a, chapter 3; Griffin 1972; 1974; Hewitt de Alcantara 1976; Gonzalez 1992).

4. The Green Revolution was the result of a Mexican agricultural program from the 1940s through the 1960s. It originated in a joint U.S.-Mexico technical program designed to raise agricultural production. In 1943, with support from both governments, a group of scientists, sponsored by the Rockefeller Foundation, began to work closely with Mexico's Office of Special Studies in the Ministry of Agriculture. The binational venture reached its peak in the mid-1950s, when the Office of Special Studies employed eighteen U.S. scientists and over one hundred specialists, at a cost of U.S.$1.6 million annually (Hewitt de Alcantara 1976). The objectives of the U.S.-Mexico team were to increase crop yields by developing new hybrid seeds, improve soil by using fertilizers, and control pests and plant diseases. The United States provided technical assistance and Mexico backed the project with capital and the development of rural infrastructure. Overall, the Green Revolution accomplished its goals. In four years, from 1947 to 1950, agricultural production increased by 9.4 percent annually, an unprecedented rate. Overall, agriculture grew at a rate of 6.3 percent per year from 1940 to 1960, an increase comparable to the highest rates in the world. However, this success was achieved at high environmental and social cost. The irrigation projects and other innovations developed by the Green Revolution benefited only landowners with large landholdings and capital. The large majority of the *Bajío* peasants did not have the needed resources, such as water and capital, to participate fully and profit from the change. The Green Revolution was well organized and orchestrated by the state. State industries opened shops locally and produced sorghum hybrid seeds and Mexican

fertilizers to be used in the production of major Green Revolution crops such as sorghum and wheat, the major export crops. In addition, banks sanctioned by the government offered credit, machinery, and technical personnel, such as agronomists, topographers, and agricultural extensionists, to farmers who would grow these crops. Green Revolution hybrid crops, such as wheat and sorghum, replaced subsistence crops, such as maize and beans, and displaced hundreds of thousands of peasants, who had no work during ten months per year. The Green Revolution meant displacement of labor and degradation of the environment (see Gonzalez 1992, 1996a, 1996b).

5. The *hacienda* was the dominant unit of production up to about World War II, based on private property and wage labor. The size of the landholdings varied from 100 to 20,000 hectares. The best lands, usually under irrigation, were cultivated with wheat; lands without irrigation were used to grow maize and other subsistence goods; and the second- and third-class lands were dedicated to cattle-raising. A small number of permanent workers and their families lived on the estate; and temporary workers were contracted from neighboring Indian communities during peak production periods. Some *haciendas*, such as *Los Parangueos*, included peasant communities within their territories who worked for a salary in the commercial agriculture and cattle-raising areas of the *hacienda*, or became sharecroppers in times of bad markets.

6. The Immigration Reform and Control Act of 1986, known by its acronym IRCA, was designed to halt illegal migration and immigration into the United States. It was to accomplish this ambitious task through employer sanctions that would make it illegal for employers to hire illegal workers. Employers, if caught, would be fined and in some cases imprisoned. Additionally, IRCA would legalize workers and their families already residing and working in the United States. The legalization programs—the Special Agricultural Workers (SAW) Program and the General Amnesty Program—would allow those granted amnesty to sponsor the immigration of their spouses, children, and other close kin.

6

Globalization and Asian Indian Immigrant Women in the United States

Arpana Sircar and Rita Mae Kelly

Understanding the sociopolitical behavior and workforce participation of women as well as men depends on many classes of variables, all of which contribute to a life cycle of socialization. Globalization with the migration that it promotes disrupts traditional socialization and presents counterforces that can, and typically do, open doors for new types of behavior. In this chapter, using data on upper-middle-class Asian Indian working women, we examine some of the central ways that globalization changes women's expectations, abilities, and capacities.[1]

As a broad model for presenting our data we use the categories of variables presented in figure 6.1 (see Kelly and Boutilier 1978). The box I variables in figure 6.1 concern our sociopolitical and cultural heritage and the interrelationship this heritage has with the box II variables, which deal with socialization. Typically the box V variables have the most important impact on our political and public participation behaviors. Globalization produces a major intervention in the socialization processes in that the typical linear patterns of a society for socializing girls and women get interrupted in the family, community, church, school, and among one's peers. The obligations and responsibilities available as an adult for participation in the workforce and establishing one's socioeconomic self also change, creating new options and new choices. The transformation of women from private persons to public, political ones is often more difficult than it is for men because historically women have been given the task of maintaining and passing on their ethnic and national sociopolitical and cultural heritage. Hence, even when opportunities unfold for them to become political actors, they often do not. Cross-pressures from their ethnic and national sociopolitical and cultural heritage can block the exercise of the new options globalization creates in their adult lives in a new culture. This study of Asian Indian immigrants enables us to explore how these classes of variables are interacting among one group of well-educated working immigrant women in the United States to both promote greater empowerment and to impede the exercise of such empowerment.

Figure 6.1 Map of Types of Variables Relevant to Adult Political Behavior*

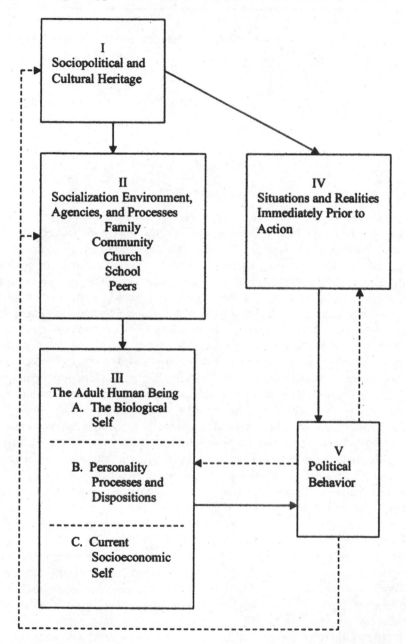

Adapted from M. Brewster Smith, "A Map for the Analysis of Personality and Politics,"
Journal of Social Issues *24 (July 1968): 17.*

Because one of the unique aspects of migration in this globalization era is bringing well-educated, new ethnic and racial groups, especially Asians, to more advanced countries such as the United States, we will first discuss how the current wave of globalization has changed Asian Indian migration patterns to the United States in general. Then, focusing on twenty professional Asian Indian women, we examine how this interruption of their lives has impacted their empowerment within and beyond the household.

ASIAN INDIAN MIGRATION PATTERNS TO THE UNITED STATES

Migrants from the Indian subcontinent have been coming to America since the early decades of the nineteenth century (Dasgupta 1986). The century from 1830 to 1930 is now considered by historians to be a period of heightened international migration of large worker populations from less economically developed countries to the more developed richer nations, causing severe social and political dislocation in both the sending and receiving countries (Jensen 1988). The first Indians to arrive on America's shores in significant numbers (only a few thousand of the millions in the diaspora) were primarily male farmers from northern India (mostly Sikhs from the Punjab) who came between 1907 (after the 1882 Chinese Exclusion Act and the 1907 Gentlemen's Agreement with Japan restricted the supply of cheap Asian labor to work in California's thriving, large-scale agribusiness) and 1917, until the "Barred Zone" Immigration Act stopped almost all Asian immigration to the United States except for Filipinos who had the peculiar status of "U.S. nationals" (Leonard 1992:18–19). These Indians settled on the west coast of the United States, intermarried with Mexicans, and created a distinct hybrid bi-ethnic community popularly known as Mexican Hindus, although there were Muslim Indians in the group. Some members of this group elect to include themselves in today's official census category of "Asian Indians." Asian Indians were not identified in U.S. Census data prior to 1980. They were included in the category labeled "Other Races." Their small numbers, determined by the national origin quota law that allowed severely restricted entries each year, may have inspired this policy.

Records of the U.S. Immigration and Naturalization Service show a total of 40,796 Asian Indians coming to America between 1820 and 1970; 31,214 came between 1961 and 1970 (U.S. Bureau of the Census 1970: 61–64). A quantum jump in the numbers occurred following the liberalization of immigration laws under the Johnson administration and the Immigration Act of 1965. According to immigration data, 176,800 Asian Indian immigrants came to the United States between 1971–80; 261,900 came during 1981–90; and 191,548 came between 1991–95. The total for the ethnic population listed in the 1990 U.S. Census was 815,000. It was the fourth-largest Asian ethnic group in the United States after the Chinese, Filipinos, and the Japanese (U.S. Bureau of the Census 1997). At its current growth rate, the present size of this ethnic population is possibly close to one million. This ethnic community fluctuates in size as temporary residents such as students, management trainees, and visiting academics and technology specialists arrive in and leave the United States.

The Immigration Act of 1965 built in a preference system for immigrants from Eastern Hemisphere countries. Visa applicants with professional educational and occupational skills were given higher preference, thus encouraging the entry of these professionals. Consequently, Asian Indians can be characterized as an affluent group in the U.S. today. In 1994, according to the U.S. Congressional Caucus on India and Indian-Americans, their median household annual income was U.S.$59,777, the highest of all Asian ethnic groups. The average per capita income in the group was 25 percent higher than the national average and second highest (behind the Japanese) among all U.S. ethnic groups. This relative affluence is explained by the high human capital of the majority of these immigrants. In 1994, 87.5 percent of Asian Indians had completed high school, with 62 percent having some college education, and more than 58 percent having bachelor or post-baccalaureate degrees—the highest percentage among all Asian American ethnic groups. In 1990, 170,844 of 391,949 Asian Indians in the workforce (aged 16 and over) were employed in "managerial and professional specialty occupations," over 30 percent of them in "professional specialty occupations," compared with 13 percent of all U.S. workers. Twenty percent of foreign-born Asian Indian professionals are physicians; 26 percent are engineers; and 12 percent are faculty members at U.S. colleges and universities, according to the Washington D.C.–based Center for Immigration Studies (Mogelonsky 1995: 33–37).

This so-called new immigration from the Indian subcontinent reflects a much larger trend of global migration in the wake of the restructuring of the global capitalist economy and a changing world order. In this order, Asian immigration is not only a product of the restructuring, but also a contributing factor. The Asia-Pacific region that includes the countries termed "mini-dragons," namely, Taiwan, South Korea, Hong Kong, and Singapore, and other developing countries such as Thailand, India, Indonesia, Malaysia, and the Philippines, is experiencing a large-scale growth with capital and labor flowing in both directions. U.S. immigration policy had hitherto been severely restrictive toward Asians. The 1965 shift in the policy was indicative of rapidly expanding U.S. economic and political interests in the region. It is in this larger context that the nature of the Asian Indian immigration to the United States must be understood (Ong, Bonacich, and Cheng 1994).

While the shift toward higher-educated professional immigrants is a product of U.S. immigration laws that give preference to highly trained people, it cannot alone explain the numbers. In order to move up the stratified global econopolitical ladder, India and other developing Asian countries have been encouraging higher education, particularly in science and technology. Since the 1950s, India has pursued an aggressive educational development program by expanding its educational facilities. As a result of this expansion, coupled with the fact that the Indian labor market did not have the capacity to absorb them, a highly skilled group of professionals trained both in India and in the United States were ready to peddle their skills to suitable overseas bidders. By 1967, there were 100,000 unemployed and 300,000 underemployed university graduates in India. One out of every ten university graduates went abroad, including 11 percent of scientists, 10 percent of doctors, and 23 percent of engineers (Domrese 1970: 221–236). The most popular destination was the United Kingdom until it tightened its immigration policies in 1962. After 1965, the United States, along with Canada and Australia, became the biggest draw for Asian Indians (Domrese 1970: 218–219). This continuing flexible pool of transmigrants contributes to the "internationalization of the professional-managerial class" (Cheng and Evans 1991). In the service-oriented U.S. economy, some of these technology specialists are hired through direct recruitment to fill critical shortages in health, engineering, and scientific fields that are the results of the country's cutbacks on social spending, including spending for education, as well as its relentless pursuit of technological innovation and consumerism.

The Asian Indian U.S. community is primarily urban with 91 percent of its members living in urban areas. Most of its members are foreign-born (over 75 percent in 1990). The median age for the group in 1990 was 29.4, 30.1 for males, 28.6 for females (U.S. Bureau of the Census 1990: 13). The community as a whole can be considered traditional since an overwhelming majority of the families are male-headed nuclear families (Dasgupta 1986: 297). Only 4.5 percent of Asian Indian households have no husband present, and another 1.3 percent have an unmarried couple. The 1990 U.S. Census located 285,000 (35 percent) of Asian Indians living in the busy urban areas of the Northeast, 146,000 (17.9 percent) in the Midwest, 196,000 (24.0 percent) in the South, and 189,000 (23.1 percent) in the West. Texas is now one of five states with the highest concentration of Asian Indians, 55,795 in 1990, up 138 percent from 23,395 in 1980. In 1994 alone, Texas admitted 2,254 immigrants from India (U.S. Bureau of the Census 1997). This study took place in the Dallas–Fort Worth metroplex, which had an Asian Indian population of over 17,831 in 1994. The demographic characteristics of the local population resemble those of the larger ethnic community, except for the fact that fewer of the earlier Asian Indian immigrants settled here.

This study focuses primarily on working Asian Indian immigrant women. The gendered perspective in research on immigrants is particularly warranted because the experiences of immigrant men and women generally differ significantly in all groups. Current research on migration shows that the push and pull factors for immigrant men and women are not necessarily the same (Friedman-Kasaba 1996). Coming in associational migration (wives accompanying their husbands) as dependents of the "real immigrants," immigrant women are legal and actual dependents of their husbands. Often, the women are forced to leave their original homes by circumstances beyond their control, be they political, social, or economic (Buijs 1993). The women are unable to participate fully in the host society due to limited educational and employment opportunities, as well as a lack of adequate knowledge of the official language. Although the educational and occupational qualifications of the subjects of this research are, on average, quite high, associational migration remains the principal pattern of female Asian Indian migration to the United States. Furthermore, migrating women face the potential of finding themselves leading a paradoxical existence. On the one hand, there is the promise of the fulfillment of "old world" dreams in a new land or, at least, a degree of emancipation from restrictive old customs and relatively greater self-determination. On the other hand, migration can intensify existing subordination due to a greater dependency on men in the unfamiliar/hostile and stressful/insecure environment in the host country. Migration can also introduce new forms of subordination, namely, racism-ethnicism and nativism, into their lives, which U.S. immigrant women at the turn of the century experienced (Friedman-Kasaba 1996).

The expectation of finding conflict and resultant adjustments being negotiated by immigrant Asian Indian women also stems from the anticipation of changed circumstances in the lives of many of these women who became wage-earners only after coming to the United States. According to the 1990 U.S. Census, there were 362,764 women in the Asian Indian community, of whom 268,649 (74 percent) were foreign-born. Of the 391,949 Asian Indians (aged 16 and over) in the labor force at the time, 180,048 or 46 percent were women. With the total number of women, aged 16 and over, in the ethnic community being 260,532 in 1990, the labor force participation rate for this sex group stood at 69 percent. Of these employed women 168,911 or 94 percent were foreign-born. Of all Asian Indian women in the labor force 49,322 or 27 percent were employed in "managerial and professional specialty occupations." Of these, 46,649 or nearly 27 percent were foreign-born (U.S. Bureau of the Census 1990: 119).

SCOPE OF THIS RESEARCH

This study focuses primarily on the traditional hierarchical gender system in both the U.S. and Indian societies. The study acknowledges the facts that: (1) important changes have taken place globally in the degree and type of gender hierarchy; and that (2) gender is largely a personal experience determined by the intersection of biography (lifetime socialization), history, and social structure. A triangulated research method was employed to collect data, involving: (1) a paper-pencil questionnaire; (2) taped face-to-face interviews and telephone follow-ups; and (3) field notes on physical cues provided by the subjects. Twenty Asian Indian women were recruited from the Dallas–Fort Worth area using the snowball method. The selection criteria called for each subject to be a married Hindu and a working, immigrant woman with a college-level education. First, the subjects were asked to fill out a paper-pencil questionnaire to provide demographic information and sex role orientation data. Further attitudinal and behavioral information was gathered in in-depth, semistructured, face-to-face interviews and follow-up telephone interviews. While the interviews were taped for subsequent transcription, additional information was recorded from observable physical and environmental cues from the subjects and the settings in which they were interviewed. Data collected in the questionnaire were analyzed using descriptive statistics, while data from the interviews were analyzed using the tools of the "grounded theory" approach.

As table 6.1 shows, the earliest of these twenty respondents to arrive on America's shores came in 1967, followed by four (20 percent of the sample) who came in the 1970s, eleven (over 50 percent) who came in the 1980s, and four (20 percent) who came in the 1990s, the most recent one arriving in the summer of 1997. Most of the cases were examples of associational immigration, that is, they were dependent wives of immigrant males. Five (25 percent) single women came alone, four as

Table 6.1   Demographic Profiles of the Respondents

ID/Age	Marital Status	Caste	Education	Occupation	Working Since	US Arrival
A/40	Married	Kshatriya	B.A.	Clerical worker	1976**	1982
B/42	Married	Vaishya	B.A.	Administrative asst.	1978	1982
C/49	Married	Brahmin	M.S.S.W.	Psychotherapist	1978	1967
D/46	Married	Kshatriya	Ph.D.	Software consultant	1980	1978
E/34	Married	Brahmin	Ph.D.	University professor	1985**	1988
F/35	Married*	Brahmin	Ph.D.	Research scientist	1986	1980
G/40	Married	Kshatriya	M.A.	Schoolteacher	1992**	1985
H/31	Married	Brahmin	M.S.	Electrical engineer	1988	1989
I/38	Married	Brahmin	M.A.	Salesclerk	1983	1991
J/51	Married	Brahmin	M.A.	Accountant	1984	1971
K/35	Married	Kshatriya	B.A.	Accountant	1993**	1986
L/24	Married*	Kshatriya	M.S.	Software engineer	1997	1995
M/55	Married	Brahmin	B.A.	Clerical worker	1958	1986
N/46	Married	Kshatriya	M.S.	Clinical analyst	1976**	1974
O/35	Married	Kshatriya	Ph.D.	Research scientist	1990	1985
P/43	Married	Brahmin	M.Sc.	Medical technician	1992	1988
Q/34	Married*	Brahmin	Ph.D.	College professor	1992	1983
R/63	Widow*	Shudra	Ph.D.	Administrator	1958	1978
S/27	Married	Brahmin	M.S.	Software engineer	1993	1992
T/51	Divorced*	Vaishya	M.B.B.S.	Physician	1972	1997

*Indicates cases of divorce, remarriage, widowhood, hypergamy (marrying up)/hypogamy (marrying down).
**Indicates intermittent work pattern.

graduate students, which is a sure sign of independence and ambition. Except for the newly arrived woman, the rest found their mates here, which is yet another sign of self-determination. Sixteen subjects (80 percent) had U.S. contacts such as relatives or friends, a fact that has historically spawned ethnic conservatism in the United States. Three women (15 percent) stated that their stay in the United States was to be temporary, one woman (5 percent) was unsure at the time of the interview; the rest (80 percent) said they were here permanently. Based on this information, the "sojourner" element that motivates immigrants to stay loyal to their ethnic cultures does not appear to be a big issue for this group. At the same time, almost all of the respondents stated that they participated only in ethnocultural organizations, yet another immigrant phenomenon that contributes toward the ghettoization of immigrants. Some reasons for immigration offered by the respondents were: marriage for fifteen women (75 percent); higher education not only for the five single immigrant women, but also for five others (50 percent) who came with their spouses, which shows long-term personal educational and occupational goals of some of the respondents; and a better life for most. A majority of the respondents were in middle adulthood, only two (10 percent) were in their twenties, and the oldest was in her sixties. Most (90 percent) were married. There was one divorcée and one widow in the sample. Most of the women lived in nuclear families. Two had an additional relative living with them. The number of children ranged from one to three. Six women (30 percent) had children under the age of six; eight (40 percent) had older children including teenagers; and four (20 percent) had adult children. Three women had no children. Five (25 percent) of the women married outside their castes on their own volition, which is a mark of nontraditionality and independence. Among the five were the two divorcées in the sample, another uncommon phenomenon in the Asian Indian subculture. Most of the women (85 percent) came from the higher two castes, which could be a contributing factor to their high educational qualifications, given India's long history of unequal socioeconomic opportunities for members of the various castes and other social categories. Relevant to this issue is the fact that two of the professional women, the physician and the zoologist turned social worker, came from the lower two castes.

As a group, the respondents had significantly high human capital at their disposal. Their educational backgrounds ranged from two B.A. degrees (10 percent) to six Ph.D.s (30 percent) with several professional degrees in between (Certified Public Accountant, M.D., M.S. in Social Work, M.S. in Engineering, and M.S. in Public Health). Occupationally, the group was composed of three clerical workers, one schoolteacher, one retail salesperson, one psychotherapist, three software consultants, one electrical engineer, two professors, two accountants, two clinical analysts (one chemist, one microbiologist), two research scientists (one molecular scientist, and a physician). The human capital of most of the respondents was remarkably higher than those of their parents. Except for three engineers, a geophysicist, and a lawyer, the fathers of the subjects were/are nonprofessionals, one with only an elementary-grade-level education. Most mothers were full-time homemakers. Only three, including a lawyer, were wage-earners. The contrast in the educational and occupational backgrounds of the mothers and daughters reflect trends of significant socioeconomic changes in postindependence India, as discussed by researchers (Ong, Bonacich, and Cheng 1994). Eight of the subjects (40 percent) were in the labor force while in India. The remaining twelve (60 percent) became wage-earners after coming to the United States. Four of the women (20 percent) came independently to the United States as graduate students and joined the workforce upon graduation. The women's share of their annual family earnings ranged between 10 percent and 100 percent. The professionals in the group contributed between 25 percent and 100 percent of their annual family incomes that ranged from U.S.$60,699 to over $100,000.

SEX-ROLE ORIENTATIONS: EMPOWERMENT WITHIN THE HOME

An instrument titled the Index of Sex Role Orientation (for the specific items see table 6.2), containing closed-ended questions with fixed scaled responses, and hitherto referred to as the ISRO, was used in this research to collect information about the gender attitudes of the subjects. The ISRO measures gender-traditional/gender-nontraditional attitudes, not behaviors. Ten (1, 2, 3, 5, 7, 9, 11, 12, 16, and 17) of the seventeen questions have gender-traditional content, while seven have gender-nontraditional content. In this section, the respondents' sex-role orientation will be determined using the frequency distribution patterns of their responses to five clusters of questions having five distinct conceptual themes. The five themes are: affirmation of gender-typed separate spheres of activity; affirmation of the motherhood mandate and domesticity for women; conflict between family and career in a working woman's life; gender equality in the workplace; and working women negotiating family, career, and independence. Frequency distributions of responses are shown in table 6.2.

In their responses to the ISRO survey most of the twenty Indian women revealed a dramatic break with the traditional sex-role ideology that held being a wife, mother, and submissive homemaker as the most important thing in a woman's life. The attitudinal survey supports the view that these Indian women immigrants had gained power and parity within their own households as the result of being pulled into the labor force. Nonetheless, the follow-up interviews and data on actual behavior indicated that the reach of the traditional gender ideology was still impressive.

Economic power is acknowledged by sociologists to be a determinant of one's status in the family as well as in the larger society. The differences in the economic resources that husbands and wives control result in a normative spousal power hierarchy. As this resource equation changes due to the wife's workforce participation in advanced market economies, so should the spousal power hierarchy (Sanday 1981). Others (Yans-McLaughlin 1974; Blumberg 1984; Bloom

Table 6.2 Responses to the Index of Sex Role Orientation Instrument (N = 20)

Statement	Strongly Agree	Agree	Neutral	Disagree	Strongly Disagree
Cluster 1. Gender-typed Separate Spheres of Activity					
1. Women should take care of running their homes and leave running the country to men.	5%	0%	5%	40%	50%
7. Except in special cases, the wife should do the cooking and house cleaning, and the husband should provide the family with money.	0%	0%	5%	30%	65%
16. I could not respect a man if he decided to stay at home and take care of his children while his wife worked.	15%	0%	25%	45%	15%
17. A woman should realize that just as she is not suited for heavy physical work, there are also other jobs that she is not suited for, because of her mental and emotional nature.	5%	40%	5%	40%	20%
Cluster 2. Affirmation of Motherhood and Domesticity for Women					
5. A girl proves she is a woman by having a baby.	10%	0%	15%	15%	60%
9. Women are much happier if they stay at home and take care of their children.	0%	0%	20%	35%	45%
11. Women should be concerned with their duties of child rearing and house tending rather than with their careers.	5%	5%	0%	50%	40%
12. Although women hold many important jobs, their proper place is in the home.	5%	5%	0%	30%	55%
Cluster 3. Family versus Career					
2. Most women who want a career should not have children.	0%	5%	5%	55%	35%
3. A preschool child is likely to suffer if his mother works.	20%	25%	15%	40%	0%
Cluster 4. Gender Equality in the Workplace					
8. A woman should have exactly the same job opportunities as a man.	75%	15%	10%	0%	0%
15. Men and women should be paid the same money if they do the same work.	80%	20%	0%	0%	0%

Table 6.2 Responses to the Index of Sex Role Orientation Instrument (N = 20) (Continued)

Statement	Strongly Agree	Agree	Neutral	Disagree	Strongly Disagree
Cluster 5 Working Women Negotiating Career, Family, and Independence					
4. Having a job means having a life of your own.	15%	45%	20%	10%	10%
6. A woman should not let bearing and rearing children stand in the way of a career if she wants it.	20%	45%	0%	25%	10%
10. A working mother can establish just as warm and secure a relationship with her children as a mother who doesn't work.	65%	30%	0%	5%	0%
13. A wife who has no children should not ask for alimony when getting divorced.	10%	10%	15%	45%	20%
14. I approve of a woman providing the financial support for the family while the husband does the household chores.	15%	35%	30%	20%	0%

Source: The original ISRO instrument was developed by Dreyer, Woods, and James, 1981: 176–177 and used by Arpana Sircar (2000) to collect the data for this study.

1985), however, argue that wage-earning by women does not result in a status increase because men still control decision-making power in the family and the society. Yans-McLaughlin (1974) points out that a false consciousness on the part of the women helps sustain the spousal hierarchy. To some extent this argument is supported by data generated in this study.

The first cluster consists of four ISRO questions (1, 7, 16, and 17) that assert the principle of gender-typed separate spheres of activities. As table 6.2 shows, respondents as a group disapproved of the principle of separate spheres of activity for the two sexes. They clearly rejected the premises of questions 1 and 7 that "Women should take care of running the homes and leave running the country to men" and that "Except in special cases, the wife should do the cooking and house cleaning, and the husband should provide the family with money." The pattern, however, changes somewhat with the other two ISRO questions (16 and 17). Although the majority of the respondents disagreed with the statement "I could not respect a man if he decided to stay home and take care of his children while his wife worked," more ambivalence exists regarding whether "A woman should realize that just as she is not suited for heavy physical work, there are also other jobs that she is not suited for, because of her mental and emotional nature." Follow-up telephone interviews explained the position of those in the middle and those who are in agreement. Women who had neutral responses did not like the idea of strict spousal role reversal but said they can accept it as an internal arrangement of a family, not to be judged by outsiders.

Those who disapproved of the concept of a househusband thought that clear demarcation between the public and the domestic was impractical. If the man chose to stay at home, leaving the difficult task of breadwinning totally to his wife, it reflected negatively on him. A significant number of respondents believed in essential biological differences between the sexes that justify gender-typing of "some tasks," but not all. On the whole, responses to questions in cluster 1 suggest that the respondents did not like many of the traditional restrictions placed on women, but at the same time, they could not or would not wipe out all sex-role distinctions. They all maintained, however, that difference did not mean hierarchy.

There are four questions in cluster 2 (5, 9, 11, and 12) that affirmed motherhood and domesticity. By an overwhelming majority, the respondents rejected these two mandates. Upon being probed, even those who strongly disagreed that to be a woman one must be a mother and a housewife, they acknowledged that there were plenty of women who were happy to be homemakers and mothers, just as there were many who were not. Their reactions are focused more on the moral aspect of the mandates than on the behavioral ones. Their status as working women might have biased these women's responses. Either they believe what they said and that was why they were active in both domains, successfully as most of them claimed during face-to-face interviews, or they were taking logical stances since doing otherwise would discredit their own choices. When asked how Asian Indian working women were handling the demands of their domestic and work lives, all felt that the process was stressful but rewarding and Asian Indian women were doing a creditable job, some better than others, of course. They stressed compromise and organization as keys to success. The majority of the respondents could not imagine being full-time homemakers.

The two ISRO questions that formed cluster 3 posited that children of working women suffer. The responses that these questions generated showed curious attitudes. The proposition in the first of the two questions, that career women should not have children, was summarily dismissed. The vote was overwhelmingly (18–1) against, with one respondent abstaining. However, the group was split almost evenly, with three in the middle, about the assumption that preschool-age children of working mothers suffer. Telephone interviews revealed the sentiments behind the responses. These women believed that a working woman could balance family and career in general, but they also agreed that very young children generally suffer if the mother is not around. The consensus was that the mother is still the best caregiver for her children because of both biology and social conditioning (none of these women knew the term "socialization" until their interviews). When asked then why working women should have children, the respondents explained that compromises had to be made by way of either spouse having flexible schedules, members of the extended family taking care of the child, reliable hired help, or some combination thereof. The mother giving up her career for the welfare of the child was viewed as an option only when no satisfactory child care was available.

The fourth cluster of questions consisted of two ISRO questions with a theme of gender equality in the workplace. Question 8, mandating the same job opportunities for the two sexes, generated widespread agreement. Two who were neutral, accountant J and charity administrator R, stated in follow-up questioning that they did not think all jobs should be offered to both sexes because there are differences in suitability. Responses to the question stressing equal pay for equal work were unequivocally affirmative, varying only in intensity.

The fifth cluster of ISRO questions had an empowering theme that upheld a working woman's ability and right to negotiate the balance between family and career according to her own needs. This cluster stressed independence and self-reliance in a woman even to the extent of a complete spousal role reversal. Responses to the first three questions show a majority of the women favoring gender-nontraditional positions. Especially noteworthy are the numbers yielded by question 10, which argues that working mothers can have secure and warm relationships with their children just like stay-home mothers. There was only one instance of disagreement. Charity administrator R, who had a terminally ill son, responded that women with very young children should either not work or work part time so that they can devote more time and energy to their children.

Many of these same women also agreed with a question in an earlier thematic cluster that states that very young children of working women suffer because the mother is not around to care for them. The apparently inconsistent reactions generated by the two questions stem from the age factor of the children. In question 3, preschool children's well-being is the issue, while question 10 does not mention any specific age group. The respondents treated the latter question in a more academic manner and voiced their resounding approval. The very next question, number 13, which encourages women to be self-reliant, drew very different reactions from the women. The majority of them disagreed, which indicates that these women want a childless divorcée to demand alimony. Follow-up phone interviews clarified the responses further. Those opposed feel that if the woman is not skilled enough to support herself, as many traditional women were not at the time of divorce, alimony should be paid until she had an adequate income of her own. The respondents also feel that the wife should have a share of the family assets that she helped build.

SEX-ROLE ORIENTATION OF THE SUBJECTS

Although almost all of these twenty women have a relatively feminist egalitarian stance on most of these items, they nonetheless stopped short of demanding full equality. Even women who had voiced strong support for formal spousal status parity felt that the husband ought to occupy the "head of the household" status even if his wife was the main breadwinner in the family. They said it provided clarity of roles and not a hierarchy. Some of them said that husbands were better decision-makers because they were more analytical and had more knowledge and experience of the "real world," especially money matters. They believed wives were too emotional and indecisive. This sentiment is a clear reflection of the essentialist belief that differences exist in the natural abilities of the two sexes. When these same women were asked about their behaviors in the workplace, they pointed out that they were decisive and unemotional at work because this was an occupational imperative. The situation changes at home as cultural tradition takes over. A majority of the subjects admitted that they liked their husbands' leadership and support and thought most Asian Indian immigrant women felt the same way. They did not see it as dependency. Only a small minority of professional women acknowledged feeling guilty about their psychological dependence on their husbands and were critical of the inconsistency it created in their lives.

This affirmation of innate gender differences and spousal hierarchy by the subjects along with the acknowledgment of their psychological dependency on their husbands debunks the long-held view that as immigrant women pass through "the golden door" their acquiescence to the demands of patriarchy disappears. If anything, these attitudes of the respondents lend credibility to a contrary position offered by Sanday (1981), who argues that male dominance increases under the insecurities of migration and the resultant cultural disruption.

BEHAVIORAL DUALITY

Findings of this study strongly support the conclusions of existing research (Siddiqi and Reeves 1986; Dasgupta 1989) about the dualistic attitudes and behavior of Asian Indians. Siddiqi and Reeves (1986) interpret this inconsistency as an example of what Berger, Berger, and Kellner (1973) call "creative schizophrenia," which suggests a pluralization/fragmentation of life worlds in modern societies. Dasgupta (1989) views it to be a product of the educational system in India, which blends categorical and instrumental values. Products of that system thus cherish the Hindu principles of holism, hierarchy, and continuity in their social and familial lives while pursuing the secular Western goals of individual achievement and success in education and occupation. The subjects of this study were as dualistic in their behaviors as in their attitudes. The majority of them stated that they and other Asian Indian working women whom they knew were gender-nontraditional in their public (work) roles, doing whatever they needed to do to be effective workers. Nontraditionality varied according to the respondents' ages (younger members as a group claimed to be more nontraditional, and most of them are in cross-sex professional occupations) and educational-occupational backgrounds (professional women as a group were more nontraditional). Respondent S, a young software engineer with a major airline company, made the following comment: "'Nontraditional' is a relative term in this situation. We are more traditional than White women, but less traditional than traditional Asian Indian women in the U.S., who are less traditional than traditional women in India." Several of the respondents, professional and semiprofessional, acknowledged being less assertive than their white counterparts. Contrary to what existing research (Faver 1984) posits, the number of children or their ages were not significant factors in the sex-role orientation of the respondents. Four of the women each had two grown children and showed considerable traditionality. Others who were gender-nontraditional on most issues had children ranging in age from less than a year to twelve years, and in number from one to three.

CORRELATES OF GENDER ORIENTATION

Factors often associated with gender orientation for immigrants are the extent of acculturation to the new society, age and education, participation in the social and cultural organizations of the new society, participation in the labor force, and racism and sexism in the United States.

Acculturation

The older view of immigrant adaptation, characterized as the human capital approach, measures acculturation, education, and occupational training of individuals.

Acculturation judged by physical characteristics such as clothing and hairstyle is not a good indicator of sex-role orientation of the subjects of this study. For example, two of the more visibly acculturated women, clerical worker A and charity administrator R, were very gender-traditional on several individual issues. Software consultant D and clinical analyst N, who were not outwardly too "Americanized" (an Asian Indian term for acculturation), were gender-nontraditional on many issues. The pattern persisted even when two other indicators of acculturation, command of English and length of stay, were taken into consideration. Respondents A, R, and D spoke the language fluently. In contrast, N possessed a working command of the language, even after being in the country for twenty-four years. A was schooled in a prestigious English missionary school in India and had been in the United States since 1982. Psychotherapist C, who took gender-traditional stands on quite a few issues, spent part of her early life in England where she attended school. Also, of all the respondents, she had been in the United States the longest (since 1967). D and R both came to the United States in 1978, but showed different levels of acculturation. Most of the women who had come more recently showed stronger gender-nontraditional orientations on most issues, and yet displayed varying degrees of acculturation. Ralston's (1996) study of the lived experiences of South Asian women in Atlantic Canada found a similar ambiguity in the role of acculturation, particularly length of stay, in its subjects' adaptation.

Participation in mainstream American sociocultural and political organizations was also used as an indicator of acculturation. Only one respondent, clinical analyst N, acknowledged being a member of a political (Democratic) party. The rest of the women participated only in ethnocultural organizations, which were considered a hallmark of ethnic solidarity and fulfilled a need for a separate ethnic identity. The remaining indicator of acculturation—citizenship—was not a significant factor since only three of the respondents had U.S. citizenship. Interestingly, although scholars of modern/postmodern global migration (Pozzetta 1992; Ong, Bonacich, and Cheng 1994) believe America to be a lengthy but temporary stop in a multistep journey in the lucrative multinational labor market, all but three respondents of this study stated that they planned to stay in the United States permanently. The sojourner motive, which inspires cultural loyalty, can be ruled out as a significant influencer of cultural continuity among the subjects. However, the yearning for an eventual return to their homeland and the resultant ethnic loyalty, termed the "myth of return" by Anwar (1979), may not be. The group's reaction to the status of their citizenship, which ranged from embarrassment ("We never got around to doing it!") to pragmatism ("Why give it up if you don't really need to?") and acute ethnic pride ("Give up Indian citizenship? No way!"), can be viewed as an indicator of the myth. Also, as Steinberg (1981) contends, the instant middle-class status acquired by "middlemen minorities" (Bonacich 1973) like the Asian Indians in the United States, who have high human capital and an achievement orientation, may reduce the need for cultural adaptation among the respondents, unlike among immigrants with class disadvantages.

Age and Education: The Generation Factor

One of the most interesting findings of this study was the effect of age on the subjects' sex-role orientations. There are distinct differences in the stances of the two age cohorts on many of the gender issues. The older group (aged 38–63) was more traditional than the younger group (24–35). Age was expected to be a significant variable, but not such a strong one. The literature suggests that age-correlated adult development has several dimensions: age cohort (group of people born at the same time), generation (people subjected to common historical events), and life cycle/life course (stages of life). According to Bernard, "One's world is different according to when one is born, when one grows up, when one marries, bears children, loses a husband, or becomes widowed. . . . Each age cohort may be thought of as representing a past 'culture' level or . . . 'world' obtained during its early years of socialization" (cited in Faver 1984: 3). Her conclusion holds particularly true of the women in this study.

Much of the inconsistency in the respondents' stances on individual issues can be understood using the concept of age-correlated development. For example R, the oldest member of the group, who is one of the two most gender-traditional subjects, grew up in pre-independence India when the country was engulfed in an intense freedom movement. Women ventured into the public arena mostly as secondary freedom fighters, except for a handful of upper-class women leaders. The gender referents in society, especially the rural society of farmers in which R grew up, were still very traditional. The older age cohort can be called India's "transitional generation," much like the "baby boomers" in the United States (Dinnerstein 1992). Most of these women grew up in post–World War II, post-independence (1947) India. The country was busy implementing an economic expansion and industrialization-modernization plan that opened up educational and occupational options for its people, including women. At the same time, the emphasis on marriage and motherhood continued. It was a scenario similar to that existing in postwar America, especially during the two decades immediately following the war. The academic training provided by their families to women in cross-gender technological fields was a reflection of the changing times in which men and women both had to participate in nation-building. In other cases, however, education was insurance bought for attracting better marriage prospects, as some of the respondents themselves acknowledged. Writing at the time, Ross notes, "although girls are attending schools and colleges in ever increasing numbers and more young women are taking outside jobs, it is still not a generally accepted idea that middle and upper class women should have careers. The central goal of a girl's life is marriage rather than career" (1960: 61). Nearly two decades later, another researcher of the South Asian sociocultural scene, Smock (1977) concluded that most South Asian women chose studies that would enable them to be highly cultivated wives who could enhance their husbands' social statuses.

The ambiguities were felt intensely by the subjects of the study within their own families. Their full-time homemaker mothers were unhappy with their circumscribed traditional roles, and yet were unable or unwilling to do anything about their situations, particularly because there was little encouragement to pursue careers. The conflict witnessed early left indelible marks on the daughters, many of whom became determined not to follow in their mothers' footsteps, especially since they knew they had greater options. For these women, the generation factor, which refers to people in an age group subjected to common historical events, was India's independence from two hundred years of British rule. Rather than World War II this event was the main catalyst for the new sociopolitical order in India. The decades immediately following India's independence ushered in a period of nation-building during which indigenous cultural traditions were emphasized. Being "Westernized" or "Anglicized" was taboo during this period; it was seen as a direct threat to Indian morality and national identity. The ideology that influenced contemporary Indians had the millennia-old wife and mother roles for women at its center. That was the mainstay of traditional Indian culture, and changes meant jeopardizing the essence of the culture. Being in the labor force was not the norm among women of the middle-middle and upper-middle classes who were embodiments of that essence. Most of the subjects of this study came from these social classes. Only four of the older subjects were in the labor force in India, while the rest became wage-earners only after coming to the United States, although all but two had career goals while growing up.

Women's educational training in math and science was also not the norm in India until the decade of the 1970s was well under way (Liddle and Joshi 1986; Ramu 1989). This fact surfaced in the demographic data furnished by the subjects. A majority of the older subjects had studied traditionally feminine academic disciplines. Fewer than half trained in nontraditional math and science fields. In contrast, all of the younger women were employed in professional fields, seven with gender-nontraditional science-math or technological education.

The generation factor for the younger age cohort was a combination of (1) a significantly more egalitarian educational structure in India during the 1980s and early 1990s, when they were college students; (2) a more open and gender-nontraditional labor market that increasingly incorporated women professionals; and (3) a sociocultural environment receptive of American cultural exports sweeping much of the world in this period. Only one of the eight women in this group was in a gender-traditional educational field (liberal arts) in India. Interestingly, even she had become a professional in her adopted land, like the seven other members of her cohort. Immigration and marriage to a male of the same age cohort with more current perspectives acted as the catalyst of change in her case. Whether in India or in the United States, not having a career would have been the exception for the younger women, not the norm. Education for these women was a logical step toward career paths. Also noteworthy is the higher aggregate level of educational and occupational qualifications of the parents of these younger subjects who themselves grew up in post-independence India.

Waged Labor

The majority of the subjects agreed that waged labor certainly enhanced a woman's status and power in the family, in addition to heightening her sense of self-worth and confidence, as the literature suggests (Kelly 1991). Not everyone thought that having a well-paying or professional job had an additional impact on the spousal power relationship. The personalities of the spouses played a role as well. A few of the women mentioned successful physician friends who were submissive to their own domineering husbands. Some of the professional women said that having a well-paying, cross-sex job mattered because money aside, people including their husbands recognized their abilities. Interestingly, the professional women admitted that ultimate household authority remained very much in the hands of the husband. More of the nonprofessional women with lower personal incomes stated that there was status equality in their families. Almost all the women, including the professionals, acknowledged normative spousal hierarchy in Asian Indian households and asserted that decision-making in their families was shared, with one spouse sometimes getting the upper hand depending on who had the needed expertise in the issue under consideration. The majority of the respondents were convinced that the status of head of household was rightfully a man's because of the natural abilities he possessed. Some felt it added clarity to the family structure. Income had nothing to do with it. Others did not want the status for themselves because they knew their husbands would resent the shift in power. Ideological, coercive, and voluntaristic bases of spousal hierarchy, which are macro- and micromechanisms of gender (Chafetz 1990; Nielsen 1990), were apparently active in the lives of these respondents, in spite of their independent incomes.

Racism-Sexism in U.S. Society

Impediments faced by Asian Indians have been significantly fewer compared to those faced by ethnic immigrants who came earlier, but they still face racism and nativism (Mazumdar 1989; Sethi 1998). Why then do these Asian Indian women feel they face far less prejudice than do African American and Mexican women? A simple explanation could lie in the high human capital of these women, which translates into high-income occupations and a fairly high purchasing power that leads to homes in upscale neighborhoods and late-model imported cars—two outward signs of prosperity that most Americans recognize. Roediger (1994), however, says that in U.S. history, victims of prejudice and repression redirect their biases in a pecking order, as the Irish and Italians have done against blacks and other newer nonwhite ethnic groups. It is a powerful way of transforming their own identities as "outsiders" to "insiders" or "Americans." This false consciousness is created by the white/black racial dichotomy in U.S. society. Historically Eurocentric, anthropologically Caucasian Asian Indians find it hard to identify with people of color. The bias that the respondents uniformly acknowledged facing to some extent was sexism, which is still pervasive in mainstream U.S. culture. Nonetheless, because the sexism in the United States regarding women working is less than in India, immigration did act as a catalyst for change for a majority of the Asian Indian women in one particular sense: it inspired and guided their evolution from playing traditional feminine sex roles of wives and mothers to combining these with careers. The subjects of this study came to a U.S. society that was and still is somewhat paradoxical in its adherence to many traditional gender norms and patterns but is generally accepting of women in work roles. After an initial period of adjustment, Asian Indian women have been in waged labor in numbers comparable to the rate for U.S. women's workforce participation (47.4 percent) (U.S. Bureau of the Census 1995). Several of the subjects candidly admitted that had they stayed in India, they might not have had ongoing careers like they do now. Paid work in the old country might have been an on-again off-again proposition for them personally because of the primacy of family life and the lingering structural and familial constraints for married women in that society. The "golden door" (of immigration) did work for these women insofar as it enabled them to become wage-earners.

The admission that without immigration they probably would not have pursued careers reinforces Chodorow's (1978) theory of daughters being influenced by their mother's role choices and the critical importance of one's cultural heritage and of the socialization environment, agencies, and processes both as a child and as an adult. Most of these women had full-time homemaker mothers. Only three had mothers in the workforce. In view of the social-psychological benefits available to working women with meaningful jobs (Lindsey 1994; Kelly and Stambaugh 1997), immigration and the less gender-traditional U.S. sociocultural environment have certainly been empowering forces in the lives of these women, as traditional theories of migration suggest (Friedman-Kasaba 1996; Groneman 1978; Pleck 1983). The ability to earn money in a burgeoning capitalistic economy is a powerful resource for household bargaining and for self-empowerment.

Regarding political awareness, the subjects of this study demonstrated the heavy hand of their sociopolitical and cultural heritage about the role of the sexes in public leadership positions. Political awareness of women's issues was far from mature among these Asian Indian immigrant women. Participation in any kind of political activism was practically nonexistent. Any change linked to political behavior will take time and probably require serious and extensive consciousness-raising by Asian Indian women activists.

This lack of interest in politics is an extension of the lack of interest in community leadership and not just a matter of role overload that most respondents used as an explanation. For these Asian Indian immigrant women, the separation of the two spheres of activity—public and private—is unacceptable because it mandates that women should not be in the workforce and men should not do housework and child care. However, they considered the public sphere activities of politics and community leadership to be distinctly masculine vocations requiring masculine traits. These women prefer domestic territoriality for themselves. As respondent K commented, "these immigrant women are happy to trade selfhood for a good life." A simpler explanation for this phenomenon could be the sociological theory of ethnomethodology, which suggests that members of a community interact using certain "background rules" known to all members (Garfinkel 1967).

Among a number of traditional gender attitudes expressed by the women was a very negative view of feminism and feminists, which was shared by most respondents. Dasgupta's study (1986) found the same widespread skepticism about Western feminism. The persistence of antifeminist attitudes may well stem from the widely held belief among Indians that Western womanhood is different from Indian womanhood and not a model of emulation (see below). All but two voiced an intense dislike for feminists and their political agenda. Feminists were viewed as bra-burners. At the same time, they were well aware of the tenets of feminism. The two women who stood apart had firsthand knowledge of feminist activism, either through direct participation or through a friend. Yet, although they did not empathize with feminist activism, there was a growing activism among them against domestic violence. The community runs battered women's shelters in the major metropolitan areas of the United States, which are staffed primarily by women.

An interesting finding of this study is that Asian Indian immigrant women in the United States are using contemporary women in India as their reference group, rather than mainstream U.S. women. In this respect, they resemble Chinese immigrant women in the United States earlier in the century who looked to women in revolutionary China for role models (Yung 1986). Emulating American women does not appear to be on the minds of these Asian Indian women, perhaps because acceptance into the mainstream is unlikely and also because cultural pluralism validates separate ethnic identities. A further motivation for this may be found in the dichotomous concept of "Indian womanhood" and "Western womanhood" that surfaced in the literature and proved to be very much a part of the subjects' psyches (Chatterjee 1989; Chakrabarty 1992). Like contemporary women in India, these immigrant women want behavioral freedom and freedom of personal life choices within the existing social organization.

SEX-ROLE REORIENTATION

To understand the reconstitution of these women's lives, it is necessary to view them as engaged historical agents within hierarchically organized households, communities, and broader global cultural and econopolitical structures. The on-going daily performance of sex roles in these immigrant families is more traditional than not. A noticeable area of change is that the husbands are helping with the household chores more. Role overload for women still persists in these families, however, as does spousal hierarchy, although blind deference to husbands appears to be a thing of the past.

As might be expected, the stories of the twenty individuals in this study are nuanced in terms of empowerment and personal autonomy. Even with significant commonality in educational-occupational and social class backgrounds, the subjects within age cohorts and subgroups gave individualized responses to work and family issues. This underscores the variability in how individuals negotiate structural and cultural boundaries of masculinity and femininity on the basis of personal circumstances, temperaments, interests, and talents. To use Dinnerstein's (1992) taxonomy of women's role overload, there are, among these Asian Indian women, the "accommodators" like A, E, G, P, and Q, who give in to tradition and do most of the housework; the "negotiators" like B, C, D, F, and N, who are able to get some help from their spouses; and "equalizers" like I, K, M, O, and S, who have established a more balanced sharing of household responsibilities. These behaviors seem to affect the women's work lives, judging by their accounts of how supportive their husbands are of their careers, extra help they have, and special circumstances such as a late start of a career, taking time off from career, faltering professional careers, and failed marriages resulting from pursuit of careers. Most of the women were fortunate enough to have realized their career goals, while some claimed to have fallen short because of the demands of family life.

Behavioral Duality

With the exception of two, all the subjects in the study claimed to behave non-traditionally at work and traditionally at home and in the ethnic community out of necessity as well as choice. While this duality may appear to be confounding, Berger et al.'s (1973) theory of "creative schizophrenia" argues that people in increasingly complex modern societies fragment their personalities to survive in multiple life worlds in which they have to operate. Particularly noteworthy is the fact that while a few older professional women with long-term careers, as well as most of the younger professional women, expressed dissatisfaction with this behavioral duality, most older women felt quite comfortable saying it came naturally and was very effective. One woman, N, commented, "It's like taking off your overcoat when you come home from work during the cold weather." Those who disliked the practice thought it is tantamount to having multiple persona and is stressful and hypocritical. Electrical engineer H reflected, "It feels like you leave an important part of yourself outside as you enter the house." It appears that the professional women in nontraditional fields have been equals with men throughout their educations and beyond in their careers, so they find it particularly difficult to adopt a deferential role with their husbands. In contrast, women who find the duality natural are those who started their careers late in life or are low-level workers accustomed to being deferential.

The significant findings of the study reflect important trends and transitions taking place in most societies. Work outside the home is becoming the norm for women as it has been for men for centuries. More importantly, it is becoming the norm for mothers as it has been in the United States for some time. National surveys indicate that women view work as central to their lives. They would choose employment even if they could do without the earned income. "This shows a generational transition toward expression of women's achievement orientation through career activity" (Faver 1984: 138). All of this points toward a trend of permanent or lifetime labor force commitment and attachment for women—similar to that of men (Kamerman and Kahn 1981). The majority of the Asian Indian women in this study expressed a similar attachment to their careers, although the two age cohorts demonstrated distinct attitudinal and behavioral patterns related to career commitment. Members of the younger cohort, most of whom are professional women educated and employed in gender-nontraditional fields, were generally more loyal to their careers than some of the women in the older age cohort who placed family ahead of career.

Occupational attachment is not confined to professionals only though. A, an intermittent clerical worker in the older age cohort, trying to finish her U.S. undergraduate degree in art history and eventually work in the field, felt this was her chance to do something other than the mundane roles she played: "I want to do something for myself. I want to accomplish something more. All this other stuff—I do it for others. I know I am being egoistic, but I want to contribute something. I think I can." In Hong Kong, where her husband was a visiting professor, she was frustrated because her degree plans had to be postponed.

> I feel like the itsy bitsy spider climbing up the spout. It seems like there is always some family priority that pushes me down. But that is all right. I am not giving up. The process is as important to me as the end. I will much rather keep on trying than give up altogether. Besides, maybe my daughters will learn from my struggle!

GLOBALIZATION, IMMIGRATION, AND EMPOWERMENT

"For women, global migration and becoming a person are two sides of the same coin" (Friedman-Kasaba 1996: 192). Immigration has been empowering for the participants in that it has enabled them to realize their lifelong goal of being in the labor force. This was acknowledged by all the subjects, even the professionals in technological fields. Of course, the class privileges of these women have also been factors. Their husbands' financial resources made it possible for the women to advance their educational and occupational qualifications, which translated into better jobs and occupational status. For the four single younger women who migrated on their own, migration was an opportunity for a free-choice marriage; for the rest who accompanied their husbands, escaping the gender restrictions on women in India was an attraction. Living in nuclear families without the in-laws also allowed more behavioral freedom for these couples. Furthermore, despite their claim that they did not emulate the gender models in mainstream U.S. society, the changing cultural milieu could only facilitate innovative alternative models when adopted by the participants of this study. All of these emancipating and empowering experiences of the subjects lend credibility to the push-pull/modernization theory of immigrant adaptation (Friedman-Kasaba 1996).

The most significant sign of change and empowerment of the subjects is the conviction that housewifery and motherhood are not the ultimate tests of womanhood. The women seem to have developed a sense of selfhood that includes labor force participation as its key component, as existing theories of women's workforce participation posit (Faver 1984). Autonomy for women is often connected to education and professional advancement. The Asian Indian women in the study lend credibility to this. When asked why work is so important to her, clerical worker A said: "I can assert myself. It makes me feel good about myself. I do what I want to and not just what I have to." "Becoming a person" thus means becoming a wage-earner. It boosts self-esteem, pride, and sense of accomplishment, all of which are reflected in respondent A's remarks. For software consultant D, work tied into self-identity on a different level: "My work makes me grow intellectually. It keeps me in touch with state of the art technology, although I use it and do not invent or develop it which I would rather do. It gives my whole life a new meaning. It is very rewarding."

This quest for personal growth is yet another syndrome prevalent among immigrant women. The sense of selfhood or personhood is a subjective side of self-determination. It develops as the immigrant woman imagines, identifies, and defines herself as an entity apart from identities by which others define her. This growing sense of selfhood is more remarkable with regard to this study's older age cohort representing India's "transitional generation," most of whose members followed the traditional path of marriage and motherhood at first and took on work roles much later. The following is an apt description of these women: "They are not passive. None of the women . . . was content to stay home and do nothing. They pursued either education or a career and, by doing so, broke out of the ghetto of passive domesticity for women" (Kramer and Masur 1976: xv). The attitudinal and behavioral adjustments these women have made in their lives are of huge proportions when taken in context. Becoming waged workers has given them a confidence and self-definition that they may not have anticipated while growing up in India. This newly acquired self-definition is slowly tipping the balance of the old spousal power hierarchy toward a more even keel.

The selfhood and empowerment of these immigrant women are not tied to just waged work; they are multifaceted. One dimension of this is connected to their sense of ethnic identity that they try to retain by conforming to their cultural traditions, including gender traditions, at home and in the ethnic community. Co-ethnic conformity and association reported by these educated women is thus not blind loyalty, but a conscious choice. Theorists (Geertz 1973; Triandis 1989) identify this trend as a hallmark of Asian cultures that stresses the collective self over the individual self and that has a strong in-group out-group distinction determining social behavior. It can also be explained by the motive of transmigration (Friedman-Kasaba 1996).

Modern migrant workers are transmigrants attracted from impoverished peripheries of the global political economy to the core countries like the United States (Pozzetta 1992; Ralston 1996; and Friedman-Kasaba 1996). They often make several stops along their routes of migration and develop a transnational identity that encompasses both their sending and receiving societies and their peoples. Some of the respondents in this study seem to fit this model. Administrative assistant B spent some years in England where her family relocated before she joined her husband in the United States; psychotherapist C attended school in England while her father was working there. Software consultant D has one sister in England and one in South America whom she visits regularly. Soon after her interview, clerical worker A accompanied her husband to Hong Kong for a two-year stay and is working there as an elementary schoolteacher. A few others mentioned trading visits with uncles, aunts, and cousins living in different parts of the world, in addition to regular visits back to India. A few even mentioned plans for eventually returning to India. Transnational or multicultural, the ethnic identity Asian Indians in the United States have developed is a hybrid identity. S, the airline software engineer, pointed out that the standards of traditionality among U.S. Asian Indians are not the same as those in India. They are much more lax here and have a distinct local flavor. This aspect of the women's lives, combined with their stated lack of interest in assimilation, lends support to the world systems theory of immigrant adaptation and transmigration (Friedman-Kasaba 1996).

CONCLUSION

Looking back at figure 6.1 we can see that globalization and socioeconomic development and participation along with increased ideological support for both citizenship and independence for women within India as well as the United States have empowered these Asian Indian working immigrant women to have more control over their life space. They are now on the threshold of becoming political beings. One has joined the Democratic Party, others have become involved in establishing and maintaining domestic violence shelters. But something else still has to happen for politics to become politically salient enough for most of these women to counter the cultural heritage of essentialism that grants men a privileged position in political spaces. This wave of globalization clearly has moved these Asian Indian women more toward being public, political actors, but not sufficiently yet so that they are willing to counter this basic gender and spousal norm. We might need to wait for the next generation of Asian Indians to support the proposition that women as a group have the same capacities as men as a group to be legitimate heads of households and political leaders. As Gupta discusses in more detail in chapter 11 in this book, active political mobilization by the government itself through the establishment of quotas by constitutional law might be the most effective way of immediately disrupting the powerful cultural heritage that socializes both men and women to discourage capitalizing on the political spaces globalization is opening for many women.

NOTE

1. More details of the data used in this chapter can be found in Arpana Sircar, *Work Roles, Gender Roles, and Asian Indian Immigrant Women in the United States*. Lewiston, N.Y.: Edwin Mellon Press. Copyright 2000 by Arpana Sircar.

7

Income Control and Household Work-Sharing

Urvashi Soni-Sinha

The Noida Export Processing Zone (NEPZ) is one of the seven export processing zones in India. NEPZ was set up in 1985 in the Ghaziabad district of the northern state of Uttar Pradesh and is about twenty-four kilometers from Delhi. Gems and jewelry are the primary exports from this zone, constituting 33 percent of its aggregate exports. This chapter is based on the case study of sixteen married women workers in the machine-made jewelry production sector in the zone. The study seeks to explore the implication of women's waged work on the gender relations in the family. Elson (1995: 1) defines gender relations as "the gender dimension of the social relations structuring the lives of individual men and women, such as the gender division of labor and gender division of access to, and control over resources." The gender relations approach helps to contextualize the differences among women and the ways in which they experience gender. This chapter will focus on the changes in the "gender regime" in the institution of the family brought about by the participation of women in waged work. Agarwal (1994: 51) describes gender relations as relations of power between women and men and the ascribing to them of different abilities, attitudes, desires, personality traits, and behavioral patterns. According to Connell (1987: 120), "The state of play in gender relations in a given institution is its 'gender regime'". The main focus of this chapter is to examine the income control and domestic work-sharing experiences of women, engaged in wage work in machine-made jewelry production in NEPZ.

HOUSEHOLDS AS SITES OF "COOPERATIVE CONFLICTS"

Neoclassical economics treats the household as a unified whole. Sen (1983) has labeled the different approaches to the household as a unit of analysis in neoclassical economics as the glued-together family, the despotic family, and the super-trader family. The first approach to the household assumes that there are no variations in the interests of the household members. The second approach does allow for variations within the household but assumes that a despotic head of the family makes decisions for them. In both these approaches the welfare of the household is represented by the joint utility function. Becker (1981) puts forth the super-trader model, which treats the household as a market. Such a model treats the distribution of resources and allocation of work as resulting from individual choices, freely exercised. Household unity is the outcome of these individual decisions. This model does not take account of differences in power among different family members and the manner in which it could affect the outcome.

Sen (1990) provides a useful insight into the working of the households by treating it as a site of "cooperative conflicts," where the members of the household cooperate to increase the total availabilities but there is conflict in dividing the availabilities among the members. A useful conceptual tool to understand the nature of cooperative conflicts is the bargaining model of Nash (1950, 1953) and to start to see household divisions as "bargaining problems." In this model the "bargaining powers" of the respective parties depend on the breakdown position in case of bargaining failure. The solution also depends on "perceived interest" and "perceived contribution" of the persons in the group, which as indicated by Sen are neglected in the "bargaining problems" formulations of household economics.

Sen (1990: 148) indicates that women's earnings from outside not only contribute to the overall affluence of the family but also influence the relative share by affecting the "breakdown positions" of women and also the perception of women's "contributions" and "claims." However, the empirical evidence on the implication of women's waged work on their empowerment and increased claim over resources is not uniformly positive. Class and economic status of the husband emerge as important in influencing the implication of women's waged work on her empowerment. It is to some of this empirical evidence that we now turn.

FAMILY PERCEPTION, CLASS, AND WOMEN'S CONTROL OF WAGES

Studies on the familial consequences of women's waged work have indicated that the perception of women and the family concerning women's income has important implications for the power dynamics in the household (Hood 1983; Pyke 1994). Studies have shown class as an important variable in determining the perception of husbands toward their wives' income, which influences the control of income of women and their power within the families. Safilios-Rothschild (1990), in her study of Greece, Honduras, and Kenya, notes that the ability of wives to translate income into family decision-making power depends on the class position and economic security of the husband. In general the poorer the husband, the more likely he is to feel threatened by his wife's income and attempt to control it. On the other hand, husbands with a stable and sufficient economic base allow their wives greater autonomy and control over income. Pyke (1994) studies marital power among white women in America in the context of gendered meanings couples give to potential resources. Her study shows that men who are less successful in their occupation are likely to view their wives' market work as a threat and not as a "gift." Wives in these situations respond by not resisting the dominance of men. Kabiria's (1995) study of women garment workers in Bangladesh shows that whereas urban working-class women handed over their wages to the male head of the family, the lower middle-class women kept their wages with permission. According to Kabiria, neither of these patterns question the existing patriarchal relations in the family.

Working-class men associated women's wage work with their own economic impotence; seizing control of women's income was a gesture that affirmed their economic headship. In contrast, lower-middle-class men affirmed their economic authority by allowing women to control their wages (Kabiria 1995: 306). Thus all the above studies indicate a positive relationship between class and women's control over their wage income. In other words, women coming from higher socio-economic backgrounds had better control over their income. However, much of the evidence from India (Devi 1987; Sharma 1986, 1990; Standing 1985) indicates little relationship between control of income of women and their entry into the paid labor force. According to Sharma (1986: 99–100), of the women who were employed all but a few kept and disposed of their own wages, but this in itself cannot be taken to mean that they necessarily had greater decision-making power than those who did not earn wages. Often a wife who had a job would be given no allowance by her husband but would be expected to meet all regular household expenses out of her wages, giving her little effective choice as to how to spend it. Thus, there is a need to distinguish between budgeting and control of income. While control over income indicates who makes the policy decisions as to how intrahousehold resources are to be allocated, budgeting entails the implementation of the decision. However, it is also important to note that in working-class and low-income households, there might be little relevance of the distinction between budgeting and control, for there would be in many cases little income left after meeting the bare necessities. None of the studies in India have compared the implication of class and social status on the women's control of income. The studies indicate little reversal of power or change in the domestic responsibility of women. It is to the evidence on negotiation of domestic chores and changes in the responsibilities of the spouses with the entry of women into wage work that we now turn.

WOMEN'S WAGED WORK AND THE SHARING OF DOMESTIC CHORES

"New home economics" developed by the Chicago School of Economics (Becker 1981) uses the theory of comparative advantage to justify the sexual division of

labor and almost exclusive responsibility of women to carry the burden of the reproductive economy. Becker argues that women have a comparative advantage
over men in childbearing and childrearing, which justifies their specialization in
household labor given constant or increasing returns to scale in production with
specific human capital. Becker's argument of comparative advantage as given
seems to rest on biological determinism. He fails to distinguish between biological reproduction and social reproduction and the role of norms, institutions, and
customs in shaping the latter.

Sen, in putting forth the theory of "cooperative conflicts" of the household,
sees the entry of women into waged work resulting in their increased "bargaining
power." The central question of interest is whether empirically the participation
of women in waged work results in their increased bargaining over household
work and in their partners' sharing of household chores.

Hartmann (1994: 184), in her analysis of empirical studies relating to housework, notes that women who do wage work find that their husbands spend very
little additional time on housework on average than the husband whose wife is
not a wage worker. She also notes that women are primarily responsible for child
care, and that the burden of increased workload with increases in the family size
largely falls on women. Hartmann (1994: 184) notes few differences in the "patriarchal benefits" in housework across class, race, or ethnicity. On the basis of
her review of the empirical evidence, she concludes that the increase in women's
wage work alone will not bring about any sharing of housework with men, and
that a continuous struggle will be necessary.

Most studies in India suggest little positive effect of women's waged work on
the sharing of household chores by husbands. Sharma (1986: 144), in her study
of women in Shimla, notes that "women's employment does not lead to any substantial redistribution of domestic work between the sexes, although it may lead
to redistribution of tasks among the available women." Liddle and Joshi (1986:
149) in their study of professional women in India note that "in the joint family,
the women who have solved the problem of domestic work are those who have
achieved a more democratic relationship in the female hierarchy and negotiated
work-sharing arrangements." They further note (p. 150) that women in the nuclear families solve this problem by using their class privilege to buy the domestic labor of lower-class women and men. Ramu (1989), in his time budget study
of Bangalore, also notes that husbands in dual- and single-earner families spend
little time on domestic chores, and that for working women this meant shifting
some household chores to other women—either kin or domestic servants. Thus,
in none of the cases does entry of women in paid work result in any significant
sharing of household work by the spouse.

The existing literature on the implication of women's paid work on household
work-sharing by spouses almost uniformly indicates little increase in husbands'
contribution to household work or child care. Whereas studies of the First World
show little difference in the household workload of women across different

classes, in the case of India there is an indication of a decline in the workload of professional women due to use of paid domestic help.

STUDY METHODS

This chapter is part of a larger study of the gems and jewelry sector in NEPZ in India, conducted in 1996–97. As a part of the study I interviewed owners/managers and male and female workers in the gems and jewelry sector. Twelve women were interviewed in the factory, of which six interviews were followed up at the residence. Four interviews were held only at home. The initial interviews for the twelve workers were carried out in the factory premises and each lasted for over an hour. Follow-up visits to the homes of six workers were made where many questions were asked in depth in a less structured manner. Contacts were established with four more workers at the residence. The interviews were conducted in Hindi and were tape recorded and later translated and transcribed. For maintaining anonymity the names of the companies and of the respondents has been changed in the text.

THE EVIDENCE

I focus here on the experiences of sixteen married women working in the machine-made jewelry sector in terms of their control of income, decision-making, and sharing of household chores. The ages of these women varied between twenty and thirty. Seven of them did not have any children. Of the nine others, seven had at least one child under the age of five.

There are wide variations in the education levels of the women workers, varying from two years in elementary school to high school graduation. Three women had primary level educations, seven had been to school between eight and ten years, four between eleven and thirteen, and two were high school graduates. The wide variations in the education levels of the workers occurred due to wide differences in the education levels of women workers in Dimple Jewelers, many of whom had primary level educations, and BharatRatna Jewelers, where most women workers were educated up to year twelve or above. The median education is year ten (or eleven years in school). Of the sixteen married women workers, fourteen were migrants from different states—Bihar, West Bengal, Madhya Pradesh, and Tamil Nadu. Some migrated from other districts of Uttar Pradesh. A majority of the migrant women came from villages, where they lived in extended households and the family-owned small plots of agricultural land. Of the sixteen women, ten lived in nuclear families and one in an extended family. Of the other five, four had at least one person from the in-law's family living with them and one had her sister living with her. Even in the case of nuclear families, many women depended on their mother for child care and many expressed obligations toward the in-laws. There are variations in the cultural traditions of different states in India from which the women in my sample have migrated. However, a discussion of this is outside the scope of this chapter.

Of the sixteen married women respondents, twelve were working in the wax department. Of the four other women, three were in quality control and one in metal allocation. Eight women in the sample earned wages above the stipulated minimum of Rs15,002 (at the time of the survey 43 Rs equaled U.S.$1) per month for a skilled worker in NEPZ. Eight others were getting wages less than the stipulated minimum for a skilled worker.

The literature (Kabiria 1995; Pyke 1994; Safilios-Rothschild 1990) indicates a positive relationship between husbands' occupational success, class, and economic stability to women's control over their income. Any empirical study on class and socioeconomic status presents many problems of measurement and definition. According to Rosemary Crompton (1993: 10) "the use of the single word 'class,' [*sic*] therefore may describe legal or traditional rankings, social prestige or material inequalities, as well as revolutionary or conservative social forces." Due to problems in measurement of the husband's class position, I concentrate on the husband's income as a denominator of economic stability of the husband. I present my findings according to the patterns of work-sharing and income control discerned in the study and analyze the variability of the husband's economic position and stability across the group. The categories that emerge are:

• men control income with no sharing of household chores,
• men control income but share in household chores,
• women control income but husbands do not share in household chores,
• joint control of income with sharing of household chores.

These categories broadly represent a continuum of dependence and autonomy for women. There are no cases of women controlling income and household work-sharing or of joint control of income and no sharing of household chores by the husband. Since the issues around control and budgeting of income are complex and vary with income level of the household, I have not differentiated between control and budgeting of income in my initial categorization.

Men Control Income and Do Not Share in Household Chores

The experiences of three women fall into this category. Again there are wide differences in the socioeconomic backgrounds of these women.

Meena is a twenty-one-year-old Bengali woman who migrated from the Howrah district of West Bengal to Delhi after her marriage. She has been married for eight months. She had been working in a garment export factory for three years prior to her marriage. She is educated up to year ten. She joined Pratap Diamond Jewelers two months after migration and drew a salary of Rs1,100 per month for three months, after which she was terminated. She has lately gotten a job in an electronic company in the zone. Her husband, Ajit, works as a polisher in Ajay Diamond Jewelers and draws a salary of Rs1,900 per month. He is a high school graduate. I had held an interview with Meena's husband at the company, and it was through him that I got to interview Meena.

The case of Meena is typically that of a male-dominated family. Many times Ajit intervened in the course of the interview and answered on behalf of Meena. When I asked Meena about her work perception, she said that she worked because she got bored in the house. "What will I do sitting idle at home?" Thus she undervalued her household work and her financial contribution. Meena told me that she handed all her income over to her husband. At that point Ajit intervened and said, "I do not touch her income. I put her salary in her account and save it for our child." Clearly here, Ajit has the real control over income, though the account is in Meena's name. In this case we find that by this gesture Ajit tried to assert his image of a breadwinner. On the one hand, he did not allow his wife to control her income, and on the other hand, he did not use it on household expenditures. His domineering role became obvious many times during the course of the conversation with Meena. At one point he said, "I will let her work for two to two and a half years, after which we will have our child and she will leave work."

In the case of Meena it is difficult to say whether she did try to "bargain" with her husband and failed or did not start to "bargain" at all, given her husband's domineering nature. Conducting the interview in the presence of her husband made it difficult to discern the issue in depth. However, downplaying her productive and reproductive role, Meena did not seem to negotiate either for household work-sharing by her husband or for control over income.

Alka is a twenty-six-year-old woman. She has been married for five years and had migrated four years prior from a small town in Uttar Pradesh to join her husband. She lived in an extended family there. Now her mother-in-law lives with her. She has no children. She has had eleven years of schooling. She has worked in the wax department of Ajay Diamond Jewelers for a year and a half. She had worked in the jewelry line for two years prior to this. She earns a salary of Rs1,900 per month. Her husband was a junior manager in a jewelry company earlier where he earned Rs15,000 per month. He is a high school graduate. Now he has a joint business with his brother and has started manufacturing artificial jewelry with him. The average profit is Rs20,000 per month.

Alka said that she handed over her income to her husband and then he allocated some money for household budgeting to her. As to the perception of work she said, "I do not work for financial reason but because I get bored sitting idle in the house. I have no child. At least when I go out I meet a few people." In the case of Alka, engagement in the "public" world was like a compensation for being childless. Alka's income is a very small proportion of the household income. However, despite this her husband did not allow her control over her income.

This case again contradicts the expected increase in autonomy of the wife with better financial security of the spouse. As to decision-making, she said that her husband, she herself, and her mother-in-law together made most of the decisions. Her husband did not share in any household chores. Again Alka's perception that she was working because she was idle led to a poor "bargain" for her, based on the underestimation of both her paid and unpaid work.

Savita is a twenty-six-year-old woman. She has had her education up to year eleven. She has been married for seven years and had migrated from a village in Madhya Pradesh. She lived in the village in an extended family. She has three children, six years, three years, and seven months old. She has been working in Pratap Diamond Jewelers for six years. She is a wax department supervisor and earns a salary of Rs2,800 per month. Her husband is finishing high school and he works in Madhya Pradesh. He previously worked in Maharishi Ayurved in NEPZ. He now commutes on the weekends. He earns a salary of Rs3,500 per month.

When asked about her perception of work, Savita said that she is working for financial reasons and that she felt too tired. She would give up her job when her husband gets a permanent one. Her husband had never shared in any household chores and she felt that he was very demanding. Her mother-in-law looked after her children in her absence and shared in some household chores. She gave her husband all her salary and kept only Rs100 for expenditures on the children or some small requirements. However, she said that her husband had no personal expenditures and that he deposited part of her salary in the bank in her name as they were saving for a house. She had little say in decision-making and her husband made almost all the decisions.

The analysis of these three cases shows that a wide diversity in the husband's economic position and the proportionate contribution of women to the family income could still result in similar experiences in terms of control of income and domestic work-sharing by the husband. Meena and Alka undervalue their roles in the productive and reproductive sphere, whereas Savita is clear in her perception of her financial contribution. For Meena paid work was a temporary phase until she had children, whereas for Alka it was compensation for being childless. Savita thought of leaving paid work because she felt overburdened. In the above cases none of the women seem to engage overtly in bargaining with their husbands over income control or household work-sharing. Only Savita clearly recognized her own contribution and sought more work-sharing by her husband and greater control over her income. But in this case, bargaining is avoided as she foresees little better outcome, except confrontation.

Men Control Income and Share in Household Chores

There are three women whose experiences fall in this category, Purnima, Lakshmi, and Swarna. Purnima is a twenty-six-year-old woman who had married at the age of thirteen. She had studied up to year two in a small village in Bihar. She stayed with her in-laws in the village for two years and then migrated to Delhi to join her husband. Her husband is a security guard and earns Rs1,300 per month. She has three children, ten, six, and four years old. Purnima has been working in Dimple Jewelers for the past three and a half years. She does not have any previous experience of waged work. Purnima's perception of her waged work reveals the many conflicts in the minds of some women about waged work.

> When I saw other people work, I also thought of working. I have three children and it was difficult to manage on my husband's salary. When there is difficulty one has to like the work. Otherwise who will like to work? What can I do, I am under a compulsion to work. If I do not work my children will not be able to study. How can they?

Purnima was not satisfied with her job because of its temporary nature, low salary, and unavailability of *crèche* (day care). She thought she would prefer not to continue with the job if her husband could get a salary of Rs5,000 per month. Regarding control and budgeting of income, she handed over her salary to her husband and asked him for money for her requirements. When I asked her about decision-making in the house, she said that she would let her husband make all the decisions, so that she does not have to bear the responsibility of any wrong decision. However, on probing further she did reveal that she participated in almost all the decisions in the house, and also that she decided to work in the company on her own, though her husband did not wish her to do so. Purnima did not want to project the image of an individual with an independent will, and by adopting the strategy of conforming to the patriarchal ideology overtly, she was able to assert herself indirectly. Similarly with regard to household work, though initially she did not elaborate on the extent of work her husband did, she said "he gets water from a nearby tap—what else will a man do?" Later she did say that since she is also working, her husband should and did actually share in the household tasks with her. Her husband took care of the children in her absence as he had night duty. Though she did mention that her say in the house had increased after she started to work, she did not emphatically link the two and said that it could be because as a family they were better off now.

Lakshmi is a twenty-four-year-old woman. She migrated from Tamilnadu to Delhi after her marriage, two and a half years earlier. She graduated with a degree in botany and has been working in the metal distribution department of Bharat-Ratna Jewelers for the past two years. She had no experience of working before. She draws a salary of Rs4,000 per month. Her husband is a computer programmer and is also earning Rs4,000 per month. She has an eight-month-old child whom she has left with her mother in Madras. She and her husband decided to do that because their son would not have been looked after well in the *crèche* and because he would not then experience the cultural aspect of southern India.

On asking Lakshmi about how she perceived her waged work she said that she is working for the future of her family, to be able to get a good education for her son. She said that initially she had no plans to take up paid work, but her husband wanted to pursue his higher education and had asked for her support. She began to work to finance her husband who was studying for his M.B.A. She said she would give up the job when her husband is able to earn Rs8,000 or more per month. She said that she felt overburdened and that she would have liked to be with her child and see him growing.

Regarding other decisions in the house she said that they made most of the decisions together. She thought that her husband was like her friend and did not suppress her. In terms of control of income she said, "traditionally or otherwise, we are told that my husband and me are the same. So there is no point in keeping any money separately. If I want any money I can take it from him. He will not refuse." With regard to sharing household chores her husband helped her with cutting vegetables and with cleaning the house. He washed his own clothes and they did household shopping together.

Swarna is a twenty-two-year-old woman who has worked in the quality control department of Victor Jewelers for the past six years. She is educated up to year ten. Her father also works in the same unit as a polisher. Swarna draws a salary of Rs2,100. Her husband works in a leather showroom. Swarna was the only woman respondent who did not know her husband's salary. When asked about control over her income she said, "Why will I keep it with myself? I give it to my husband. If he gives some to me I keep some." However, in terms of household chores, her expectation was not traditional: "Yes, my husband has to share in household chores as I am also in service. He does all the work. I have taught him all the household chores, which he did not know before. He would do ironing and shopping and would cut vegetables." Nonetheless, she said that her husband made most of the decisions.

When one looks at the motivation of the women one finds that whereas both Purnima and Lakshmi say that they work for their family and not for themselves, Purnima does not completely merge her interest with her family. She took up waged work despite her husband's objection, whereas Lakshmi started working because of her husband's wish. Swarna has been working since before her marriage and thinks she will continue to work in the future.

The case of Purnima shows the manner in which "gender contestations" can work in a subtle manner. Though Purnima did not confront her husband overtly, she did get to have her say in many matters and also was able to negotiate with him to do household work and take care of their children. Her handing over her wages to her husband was not because her husband wanted to control her income, but more because she did not want to confront his "breadwinner" role and preferred to negotiate around it. In the cases of Lakshmi and Swarna, their handing over their wages to their spouses is the influence of tradition, and there is little contestation around it.

The cases show little relationship between the husbands' financial security and women's control over their wages as indicated in the literature (Pyke 1994; Safilios-Rothschild 1990). In the case of Purnima, her husband, who is relatively poor, does not overtly take control of her income, but it is Purnima who strategically hands it over. In the cases of Lakshmi and Swarna, their decision to hand over their income to their husbands is the influence of tradition. The above cases show that despite a vast diversity in the socioeconomic backgrounds, experiences of control of income and household work-sharing can be very similar.

Women Control Income but Husbands Do Not Share in Household Chores

The experiences of two women, Preeti and Amita, fall into this category. Preeti is a thirty-year-old woman. She migrated from a village in Bihar five years ago. She has been married for seventeen years and has two children, fourteen and twelve years old. She has six years of education. She has been working in Dimple Jewelers for three years in the quality control department. She had earlier worked in a tire manufacturing company for one year. She earns a salary of Rs1,450 per month. Her husband is a manual worker and draws a salary of Rs1,000 per month. When asked about her waged work she said:

> Initially when we came to Delhi from our village we were in great difficulty. My husband was also sitting idle. It was so difficult to manage with two children. We were staying in my brother-in-law's place in Suraj Kund and he used to buy us the ration. My husband used to think that he would take up only a good job. I used to ask him to start working; when one has no choice, one should take what is available. But he would not listen. So one day I told him in anger that you sit, I will take up a job and run the house. Then I started looking for a job. I was new to the place and it took me sometime to find out about the jobs.

This highlights the independence of Preeti, who now earns more than her husband. However, in the course of the conversation she said that had her husband been more responsible and earning more, she would not have taken up wage work and would have looked after her children. She also felt that her salary was very low and she was dissatisfied with her job.

Preeti said that she controlled and budgeted the joint income, but that she had little money left for any personal expenditure. Thus, when I asked Preeti whether she kept something for her personal expenditure she said, "No, nothing. If I have to run the house, I have to think about the essential expenditures in the house first. Only if something remains, can I think about my requirements." Regarding decision-making she said, "I have always taken all the decisions. My husband just wants food and drink after his duty. I have to think about everything." Regarding household work, her husband did not share in any household chores. According to Preeti, "What will he do? I have to even look after his personal needs like getting his bath water ready." Her daughter helped with some household chores.

The case of Preeti is one of the few where she is earning more than her husband. Though we see that Preeti controls and budgets all the income as well as makes all the decisions in the house, she attributes this to the irresponsible nature of her husband and not to her wage work.

The second case where the woman controls her income but there is no sharing of household chores is that of Amita. Amita is a thirty-year-old woman. She has eight years of education. She has been married for thirteen years and has three children, twelve, ten, and seven years old. Her husband is a retired army soldier who works as a security guard. Amita migrated from Garhwal three years earlier. She did farming in Garhwal. She has been working in Dimple Jewelers for two years. Prior to that she worked in a toy company. She gets a salary of Rs1,325 per month. Her husband earns a salary of Rs2,000 per month.

Regarding control of income, Amita kept her income to herself, but since she budgeted the funds she had little left for personal expenditures. Her husband contributed only Rs1,000 per month to the domestic budget and kept the remaining Rs1,000 for his personal expenditures. Unlike some other women, Amita was very critical of her husband's noncontribution to household chores and his keeping 50 percent of his income for himself. She said, "He gets Rs2,000 in hand after a provident fund deduction. He has his personal expenses like smoking, typical of an ex-serviceman. He is not very responsible. He hands me only Rs1,000." She did not keep any money for herself, but she saved some money to get household durables, such as a cooking gas stove and a television. She had also built a house in her natal village and earned a rent of Rs200 per month from the same.

In terms of decision-making she said, "I take all the decisions. I pay the fees and run the house. My husband is just like that. No one listens to him. I have always been responsible for taking all the decisions." When asked about her perception of her waged work she said that she had decided to work on her own but she did tell her husband about it. She added, "I feel that my position and the position of my children have improved since I have started working." She liked to work and said that she would continue to work. Regarding household work, she said that she had to do all the work and neither her husband nor her children shared in any of the household chores. Thus, according to Amita, "He does not do anything. Absolutely nothing."

The experiences of Preeti and Amita resemble each other in many ways. Both Preeti and Amita do not particularly like to be responsible for all decision-making and budgeting of income. While both Preeti and Amita have control over their incomes, they have little left for personal expenditures. Whereas for Preeti taking up waged work is a means of reconciling to her situation, Amita liked the challenge. Gender relations here question the traditional gender regime of a patriarchal family, with women's substantial contributions to the family income and control over their income. However, it does not change their domestic responsibilities and results in a double burden of work for the women in these cases.

Neither Preeti nor Amita engage in any overt bargaining with their husbands to control their income; nor were their actions based on a "perception of interest."

Rather, it was more in the nature of taking on the responsibility of managing the joint income in the interest of the family. In the case of Preeti, while her husband handed his whole salary over to her, Amita's husband gave her only part of his salary. However, these women's waged work does not lead to any reduction in their domestic responsibility. This was not because they did not "bargain" for it, but rather because they thought it useless to "bargain" for household work-sharing with an "irresponsible" person. An important point to note in the context of both Preeti and Amita is that though both were critical of their husbands and were not happy in the marriage, neither of them thought of leaving their marriages nor did they look upon paid work as a fallback should a divorce occur.

Joint Control of Income and Sharing of Household Chores

The experiences of eight women fall in this category. It is not possible to go into the case studies of all the women for lack of space. However, I will go into the important aspects of the case studies to highlight the dynamics of the agency of the women and the manner in which they arrive at joint control of family income and the sharing of household chores. Differences exist in the extent of control of income and in the sharing of household chores.

Table 7.1 shows the demographic profile and economic position of the eight women workers whose experiences broadly fall in this category. The workers have been arranged in ascending order of their husbands' income. The salaries of the husbands vary diversely, from Rs1,100 to Rs8,000 per month. There are wide variations in the education levels of the women, from as low as year six up to graduation and of family income from Rs2,000 to Rs13,500 per month. The percentage of contribution of women to the family income varies from 25.1 to 51.85 percent.

In terms of perception of work, three of the eight women—Alka, Sulekha, and Roopa—said that their husbands were not particularly happy that they were doing waged work. Alka and Sulekha said that their spouses objected to their starting to work. While Alka started to work without telling her husband, Sulekha started working after much negotiation with her husband. Roopa had been working prior to her marriage and said that her husband was not particularly keen on her continuing to work. Both Sulekha and Roopa also said that though they did not live in extended families, they did feel the pressure from their in-laws to give up work. Sunyana, Sushila, and Mrinalini did not face any objection from their husbands regarding their work. Thus diversity exists in the perceptions of the spouses about their wives working for wages. However, contrary to Pyke's (1994) finding that women's control of income was greater if the husband considered her wage work as a "gift," in these cases the differences in the initial perception of the husband does not affect the control of income of the women. Sulekha said she managed the expenditures but her husband gave her Rs2,000, after keeping Rs500 for his personal expenditures. She said that there were little savings. The women perceived

Table 7.1 Demographic Profile and Socioeconomic Background of the Women with Joint Control of Income and Joint Sharing of Household Chores

Worker's Name	Age	Education (Years)	No. & Age of Children (Years)	State	Years of Migration	Nature of Work Done in the Co.	Work Experience in the Co. (Years)	Salary (Rs per Month)	Husband's Salary (Rs per Month)	Family Income (Rs per Month)	Women's Salary as a % of Family Income
Sunyana	20	10	None	West Bengal	1	Wax stone Setting	1	1,100	1,100	2,200	50.0
Alka	27	6	3 (5,8,10)	Uttar Pradesh	6	Wax	2	1,350	2,000	3,350	40.0
Jyoti	20	9	1 (1)	West Bengal	3	Wax	2 & 6 mos.	1,350	2,000	3,350	30.2
Sushila	24	12	1 (2)	West Bengal	8	Quality control	9 mos.	1,600	2,500	4,100	39.0
Sulekha	20	8	None	Madhya Pradesh	1	Wax	9 mos.	1,342	3,000	5,342	25.1
Roopa	23	10	None	Uttar Pradesh	NA	Wax dept. supervisor	2 & 6 mos.	3,200	3,500	7,700	41.5
Mrinalini	26	12	None	Nepal	NA	Wax dept. Supervisor	3	7,000	6,500	13,500	51.8
Meeta	25	BA	1 (2)	Uttar Pradesh	5	Wax setting supervisor	5	3,500	8,000	11,500	30.4

Source: The table has been constructed from the data collected during fieldwork in India between May 1996–Jan. 1997.

that their work was related to their income, the level of their husbands' income, and the number and ages of their children. Thus, Sulekha and Jyoti, who had children under five years old, thought they would not have worked if their husbands' income were better. This was particularly so because they found their wages to be very low. However, Meeta was satisfied with her job and her salary and liked to work, despite her husband's relatively better salary and a two-year-old child.

Control over income also varied by case. For Sunyana joint expenditures meant little freedom for personal expenditures and little margin of savings because of the low family income. For Alka, Jyoti, and Roopa joint control meant some freedom for personal expenditures. However, their spouse controlled major expenditures as well as savings. For Meeta and Mrinalini joint control of income meant joint budgeting of expenditures and a joint savings account. In the case of Meeta her husband operated the account. Mrinalini is the only woman who admitted to me that she supported her natal family financially. She said that her mother was a widow and that she regularly sent Rs1,000 per month to her. One could link her empowerment to her large contribution to the family income. However, there is no straightforward link between the percentage share of a woman's contribution and the extent of control of income and empowerment in all the cases.

Regarding household work-sharing, most of the women said that their husbands did share in the household chores like cutting vegetables, washing dishes and clothes, and shopping but that the prime responsibility was theirs. As to the perception of the benefits from wage work Sulekha, Jyoti, and Sushila thought that their position in the house had not changed much since they started working and that they always had a say in the house. However, Alka, Mrinalini, and Meeta considered their wage work as important in empowering them. For Alka it meant greater flexibility in spending on herself. Meeta and Mrinalini had been working before marriage and thought it to be important not just for financial gain, but also for self-actualization.

The above case studies show that women with differing levels of economic standing from their husbands broadly have some similarity in their control over their income and in the household work-sharing. However, there are individual differences in the way women perceive their wage work, and the manner in which their control over their income is achieved.

CONCLUSION

Through the analysis of these sixteen case studies of married women working in NEPZ, I show that wage employment of women often opens up new dimensions for change in the traditional gender regime in the family. Although many women do not perceive their interest as separate from that of the family and do not report contestations or overt confrontation with their husbands, they are able to negotiate and strike a better "bargain" implicitly. Ten of the sixteen women have part or full control over the income; and the spouses of eleven share in the household chores. The study shows variations in the extent of control over income but does not support the hypothesis of increased control of income simply with improvement in socioeconomic background. The study also contradicts the previous evidence in the literature of little sharing of household work by men on entry of women into waged work.

This study shows that the breakdown of the traditional gender regime of a male breadwinner and the entry of women into waged work can open new spaces of empowerment for women. The changes in the gender relations get reflected in better control of women over resources and some sharing of household chores by the spouse.

8

Japan and the Global Sex Industry

Seiko Hanochi

Every society includes a sector that is suppressed from its collective conscious-ness and corresponds to the darker side of its double standards. This is particu-larly true of sexuality in the patriarchal "social order." The suppressed area func-tions as a "safety valve," curbing forces detrimental to the patriarchal order and helping to preserve the societal structures of production and reproduction. This function is fulfilled by means of exploitation, by sacrificing the freedom, basic rights, and security of those who work in brothels or similar institutions that are tolerated by the patriarchal state in the name of maintaining "law and order." Prostitution is based on various patriarchal systems of ethics that are adjusted to the gender culture dominant at the time in question. Although the patriarchal structures of feudal societies are generally considered to be the most inequitable, it is in capitalist societies that prostitution is most exploitative. This is particularly true of societies such as Japan, in which precapitalist, community-oriented con-cepts of gender relations combine with the objectified, capitalist economic de-velopment to produce socioeconomic conditions that favor the commodification of the female body in a master-and-servant relationship. This relationship is then exploited by traffickers, owners, and male clients. The patriarchal capitalist soci-ety establishes rules under which this sector is tolerated, and the trafficking of women and exploitation of prostitution are institutionalized. While these rules impose certain restrictions on the sector, they also serve to further its acceptance.

THE HISTORICAL BACKGROUND

In the premodern Japan of the Edo period, the hierarchical order was based on the patriarchal domination of the *samurai* class, and the prostitution sector emerged as a "free space" for men from different social backgrounds. As this domain was excluded from the hierarchical order, men of differing social status were able to interact "freely," a phenomenon that contributed to the development of a bourgeois culture in Japan. This "free space" was, however, based on the sexual exploitation of the women who prostituted themselves in the public houses, many of whom had been trafficked from the poor rural periphery of feudal Japan. The emergence of this *kuruwa* sector of the patriarchal Edo society was supported by the existence of a large bachelor population, consisting mainly of *samurai* separated from their families on the one hand, and the development of an early capitalist economy during the *sakoko*, or "closed-door policy" of national seclusion on the other (Nishiyama 1979).

Modern Japan developed a new domestic order that corresponded to the requirements of a modernizing capitalist state with an expansionist orientation. The Japan of the Meiji period consisted of a patriarchal state, which was equated with the Japanese people, at the head of which was an emperor who functioned as a *pater familias* for the "familial-capitalist" system and was a unifying figure for this despotic model of development.

The prostitution sector served to guarantee the reproduction of this modern patriarchal order by dissociating the sexual satisfaction of the male members of the familial-capitalist society from its productive and reproductive activities, thus ensuring that men and women in the formal sector could devote themselves entirely to these two activities. This distorted specialization of prostitution led to the segregative nature of the prostitution sector (based on a complex system of class, ethnic, and gender discrimination) typical of modern Japanese society. New institutions were developed to meet the specific needs of each of the different stages in Japan's modernization process. The *kuruwa* tradition, which was based on the trafficking of young women from the poor peripheral areas of Japan, was expanded to include the international trafficking of Japanese women to the more affluent regions of Asia. Many young girls from Nagasaki and other poor areas of Japan were sold to brothels in the Southeast Asian colonies of the Western powers (e.g., Malaysia and Indonesia). These women were known as *kara-yuki-san*—girls bound for *kara*—and while *kara* literally means China, it was later also used to refer to other parts of Asia.

The modernization of Japan can be broken down into three phases: domestic democratization and external expansion (1870s–1920s), military expansionism in which the development of democracy was suppressed (1930s–1945), and democratization and economic growth (1945–1970s). Each of these phases had a particular effect on the sex industry, and the same is true of the current phase of globalization (since the 1980s) (Fujime 1998).

When Japan evolved from a peripheral state in East Asia to a regional hegemony, taking control of the neighboring countries by invasion, colonization, and occupation, the situation was changed by means of brutal military force. A unique form of military sexual slavery emerged in the occupied territories, and enforced prostitution, the victims of which were euphemistically labeled "comfort women," occurred throughout the military expansionist era.

After its defeat in 1945, Japan once more began to advance from the periphery to the core of the world system. This trend was reflected in the structures of the sex industry in the region. The military regime of sexual slavery was replaced by a commercial system characterized by the sex tourism of Japanese males and by *japa-yuki-san*—girls bound for Japan. This marked a reversal in the direction of trafficking since the days of the *kara-yuki-san*. Now that Japan was at the center of the world system, women from the poorer Southeast Asian countries were sent to the more prosperous Japan.

Before reaching this stage in the 1980s Japan had witnessed an earlier phase of democracy in the 1920s. With the ratification of a convention for the suppression of prostitution in 1921, radical changes in the prostitution sector had been envisaged. However, the military elite, which constituted the core of the emerging fascist movement, soon put an end to this democratic period.

Since the Meiji Restoration, and especially since World War I, political life in Japan had been characterized by fierce competition between two opposing camps: the modernizers who wished to see Japan industrialized, modernized, and integrated into the international community on the one hand, and the traditionalists who wanted to resist modernization, and to maintain the feudal, patriarchal values and institutions that they regarded as the roots of Japanese power on the other. The system of state-regulated brothels also became a point of contention between the modernizers, who aimed to abolish the system, and the conservative political forces who wanted to preserve it.

These two opposing coalitions reflected the polarization of the modernizing Japanese society. The traditional elite of local and national patriarchal communities resisted the challenge issued by the Western-trained liberal intellectuals and liberal feminists, many of whom were strong supporters of the antiprostitution campaign organized by the Christian Women's Union for Public Morality. At the same time, the impoverishment of the nonindustrialized regions provided ideal conditions for traffickers to find women to sell to brothels in the industrial centers of Japan. The counterattack of the brothel owners and traffickers received widespread support from the traditional forces, all the way up to the Ministry of the Interior. A traditionalist, patriarchal alliance of local elites, including nationalist and right-wing politicians, was formed to oppose the coalition of liberal forces and those politicians who advocated the abolition of the public brothel system out of concern for Japan's international image. This right-wing alliance laid the foundation for a system of military sexual slavery in which women from the occupied countries were forced into prostitution.

THE "COMFORT WOMEN"

The case of the so-called "comfort women" (Tomioka and Yoshioka 1995) is a brutal example of institutionalized sexual slavery that reveals the true nature of the patriarchal Japanese state at the time of World War II. The various discriminatory structures of the state were combined in this institution. To an even greater extent than the state-regulated brothel system typical of peacetime, it served the sexual interests of the male military aggressors by violating the human rights of the women, by sacrificing their dignity, their mental and physical well-being, to sexual exploitation.

The aggressive character of the "comfort stations" is characterized by two parallel aspects. First, it was the state of Japan that enslaved the victims who, as citizens of the colonized and occupied states (Korea, Taiwan, China, the Philippines, and Indonesia), were both powerless and helpless. This is a striking example of a powerful state threatening the human dignity and security of the citizens of weaker states and occupied nations. Thus, the power relationships between the states were at the root of this institution. Second, the "comfort stations" were a military variant of the state-run brothel system that is an integral part of the Japanese patriarchal society. They were based on gender-specific exploitation, on the commodification of the female body, which has a long tradition in Japanese culture. The patriarchal values in the center of the system led to suppression and exploitation on its periphery.

This dual aspect of the case of the "comfort women" became a matter of public interest in the 1990s as a result of the debate triggered by the Asian Women's Fund. The Japanese government rejected legal responsibility for the enslavement of the "comfort women," thus ruling out any compensation for the victims, and set up the fund in order to appease its critics. The United Nations Special Rapporteur on violence against women, Radhika Coomaraswamy, made it clear that while the fund could be recognized as an expression of the Japanese people's moral concern for the fate of the "comfort women," it could not obviate the need to make reparations; this was the legal responsibility of Japan as a state.

The dual responsibility of the people/nation on the one hand and the state on the other is a difficult concept for the Japanese. In Japan, it is customary for the state to be seen as equivalent to the nation, with the exception of the emperor who is neither one of the people nor a member of the nation. Refusing to accept the legal responsibility of the state is thus an important mechanism by which the emperor can be protected and the Japanese people called to account in his place. This obscures the issue of the Japanese patriarchal system in which a "familial" state was established, with the people cast as the obedient children of the patriarch and the Imperial Army declaring itself to be one with the supreme commander who embodied the state. The patriarchal Japanese state was now to fulfill its obligations, however, and compensate the victims of enforced sexual labor.

In addition to accepting legal responsibility, Japan would also have to alter its approach to prostitution in order to overcome the patriarchal structures that allowed military sexual slavery to occur. The current discussion about the fate of the "comfort women" shows that this goal is still far from being achieved. The end of the war in the Pacific did not mark the end of military sexual slavery. At the same time, however, a new phase began, characterized by the expansion of commercial sexual slavery.

THE EMERGENCE OF THE MODERN SEX INDUSTRY AFTER 1945

The Japanese defeat on August 15, 1945, marked the end of the state-run military sexual slavery of the "comfort women." On the same day, the Tokyo police organized a meeting of representatives of the Tokyo brothel owners in order to discuss the provision of "comfort facilities" for the occupying forces. Such "comfort facilities" were set up in Omori, Mukojima, Yoshiwara, and Siiuzaki with funds provided by the Kangyo Ginko Bank. An association founded especially for this purpose coordinated them. So although state-run military sexual slavery was ended, a commercial military sex industry under the administration of the Japanese police immediately took its place. This was the first example of a commercial sex industry organized around an American base for the benefit of its male personnel. With the Korean War and the setting up of military bases in East and Southeast Asia, the network of the military sex industry soon spread throughout Korea, the Philippines, and other countries. Thailand, in particular, became an important center during the Vietnam War. This network of military sex institutions provided the ideal basis for the development of a global trafficking network run by transnational brokers, expatriate Chinese, Japanese, and other local operators. Thus, the globalization of the sex trade was accelerated and intensified by the military sex industry, which was soon opened to nonmilitary clients.

In 1956, after a "process of democratization" initiated under American occupation, Japan became a member of the United Nations and ratified the 1949 Convention Against Trafficking and the Exploitation of Prostitution of Others. This meant that the gradual process of abolishing the state-run brothel system that had been rudely interrupted by World War II was now to be resumed. Like the 1921 convention, the decision to ratify the 1949 convention was motivated by the need to demonstrate to the international community that Japan was a civilized nation. Japan was thus forced to deal not only with issues of national security, but also those of personal security.

In the same year, Japan passed a new law to implement the convention. To some extent, this was the result of decades of campaigning for the abolition of prostitution. However, closer inspection of the law shows that it was but a hollow victory, as one of the main demands of the abolitionists—the punishment of male clients—was ignored. Only those who employed sex laborers, or enforced, facilitated, or exploited the prostitution of others could be punished. The formal change in the law had no effect on the double standards or the structure of the prostitution sector in the modernized patriarchy. True enough, the traditional brothel owners lost their privileges; however, they were replaced by modern exploiters of prostitution such as the "Turkish bath" owners. The actual practices of prostitution and trafficking were merely adapted to the growing Japanese economy and its central position in the region, without any improvement in the fate of the women working as prostitutes.

The Prostitution Prevention Law was riddled with loopholes and permitted the development of a whole variety of forms of prostitution and trafficking. The closed baths, which became known as "soaplands" rather than "Turkish baths" after a complaint from the Turkish government, were centers for prostitution. The rapid growth of the Japanese economy was thus accompanied by a flourishing sex industry. One unexpected change brought about by the new law was the modernization and internationalization of the sex trade. Before the law was enacted, the Japanese brothel system had a particular culture that did not permit non-Japanese women to become prostitutes, as they were viewed as being unable to behave according to the traditional rules of the brothels.

Another important change brought about by the internationalization of Japanese trafficking in women was sex tourism. This began in 1965 when Japan entered into a bilateral treaty with the Republic of Korea. Tourism had been under strict control in Japan due to the shortage of foreign currency, but it was deregulated in 1964 in view of the Olympic games to be held in Tokyo. When Korea was reopened to Japanese tourists by treaty, a new form of sexual exploitation known as *Kinseng* tourism (named after the famous Korean women entertainers) opened the Korean sex industry to Japanese clients. This exploitation of Korean women by Japanese sex tourists met with strong opposition from the Korean women's movement. Japanese feminists began to cooperate with their Korean counterparts, and in the 1970s conducted an intense discussion of the issue of Japanese sex tourism. One of the results of this collaboration was that the fate of the "comfort women" was brought to the attention of the world public. It was a different matter on the government level, however. As part of the economic cooperation stipulated in the bilateral treaty, the Japanese government began financing measures to support the Korean tourism industry. One such project was the development of the "night life" on Cheju Island, the primary targets of which were (male) Japanese tourists.

Sex tourism was one of the ways in which Japanese businessmen could establish a sense of community with their male customers and among one other. After Korea, other Southeast Asian countries such as the Philippines, Thailand, and Indonesia became destinations for sex tourism. The organization of this transnational sexual exploitation led to the forging of links between the sex industries of East and Southeast Asia. The Japanese sex tourists profited from the fact that while the dollar lost its power after the American defeat in Vietnam, the yen continued to grow in strength until the latter half of the 1970s.

THE GLOBALIZATION OF THE SEX INDUSTRY IN JAPAN

The globalization of the sex industry was accelerated by the strong yen of the 1980s. This was the time of the first *japa-yuki-san*, or women bound for Japan. Instead of Japanese women being sent to the European colonies of Southeast

Asia, as was the case in the 1920s and 1930s, women from the Southeast Asian countries were now trafficked to Japan. These trafficking routes mirror the economic and political relationships between Japan and the countries of Southeast Asia. After a military period during which the powerful Japanese state forced East and Southeast Asian women into military sexual slavery, the victims of commercial trafficking began to be sold to Japan.

The trafficking of women to Japan began in 1979 and continued to increase until 1993, when the speculative bubble burst and the entire Japanese economy—including the sex industry—went into decline. The expanding sex industry forged links between Japan, a "recipient" country, and the developing Southeast Asian "supplier" countries, and an independent sex market emerged. This market was based on the characteristic combination of free competition and chumminess (cf. Yamawaki 1996). The development of the trafficking network echoed the economic growth in the region. Korea, Taiwan, and Thailand—originally "supplier" countries providing women for the Japanese market—now became destinations for women trafficked from less-developed countries. The development of the Korean economy, for example, first resulted in sex tourism to East Asia and China, and later in the trafficking of women from these regions to Korea. In Thailand, economic prosperity led to the development of trafficking networks with the poorer neighboring countries—Burma, Vietnam, Laos, Cambodia, and China. Taiwan soon also joined the ranks of the new destination countries. These recipient countries retained an important function as trade centers for the trafficking of women to other countries.

In the 1980s, as the recession spread to Mexico and other Latin American states, these countries also began to supply women for the Japanese market. Women from Mexico, Colombia, and Argentina were trafficked to Japan via various connections including the Medellin drug cartel. Further expansion occurred after the end of the Cold War, when Eastern European and Russian women began to arrive in Japan. The globalization of trafficking in women thus reflects the structures of global interdependence, trafficking to Japan representing only a fragment of the global trafficking in women.

SEXUAL EXPLOITATION IN EUROPE AND JAPAN

The globalization of the capitalist economies led to the emergence of a new form of sexual slavery. The female body became a marketable commodity within the globalized economy. Some governments have legalized prostitution, causing even more difficulties for the victims of trafficking. In countries such as Switzerland and Germany where prostitution is legal, foreign women are often unable to work legally as prostitutes, as they do not have the necessary residence or work permits. They are thus forced into sham marriages or into complete dependency on the traffickers/owners. While such situations exist throughout the world, they are particularly frequent in Europe, where prostitutes are often regarded as free workers. This supposed "freedom" is of little use to the victims of trafficking, however, who are further enslaved by debts and their "illegal" status.

In Europe, both feminists and the sex industry support the legalization of prostitution. For feminists, legalization is a means to secure the rights of the sex workers; for the sex industry it is a way to guarantee future growth. The globalization of the free market would appear to make it possible for the right of self-determination to be exercised, but only a very few well-situated women are able to exercise their rights in the sector of prostitution. Some Asian women now consent to being sold into prostitution, as they are otherwise unable to find work. Such women prefer to come to European countries where prostitution is legalized. Instead of having the same opportunities as the local women, however, they find themselves at the very bottom of the occupational ladder. Among the sex workers, too, there is a hierarchy of discrimination based on the women's country of origin.

In Asia, the situation is different but not better. The idea of legalizing prostitution and recognizing the rights of the sex workers has been imported from Europe to Japan and is starting to become a topic of feminist debate. Japanese feminists have frequently tried to emulate their European sisters, and the discussion of women's rights and human rights has always been regarded as an integral part of Japan's modernization. However, Japanese feminists also have fundamental problems with the legalization of prostitution, as this would mean accepting that the female body is a commodity, a position that is not only at odds with public morals, but which threatens the human dignity of the women in question.

THE FATE OF THE WOMEN TRAFFICKED TO JAPAN

The women trafficked to Japan face various problems depending on their country of origin and the conditions of the sex industry in the particular area. Both state and society contribute to the vulnerable position of these women. From the societal point of view, trafficked women are at the very bottom of the hierarchy of sex workers in the Japanese sex industry. The highest-ranking sex workers—with respect to both societal recognition and earnings—are Japanese schoolgirls and students, often with excellent educational qualifications, who only occasionally work as prostitutes via "telephone clubs." Next come the hostesses who work in luxury bars and cabarets, most of whom are also Japanese natives. The lowest rank is held by the "illegal" women who have been sent to Japan to work in second-rate bars, "soaplands," or clandestine, illegal brothels. Although most of these women come from Asia, the number of women from Latin America and Eastern Europe is on the increase.

The majority of foreign women trafficked to Japan still come from the Philippines and Thailand. Some of the Filipinas entered Japan with legitimate entertainer's visas and were able to stay legally. However, most of these women came to Japan as tourists and were compelled to work illegally in the establishments of the sex industry without any form of protection and with none of the employee benefits guaranteed to legal workers. These women are not only overworked, they prostitute themselves under the constant threat that they will be denounced and deported. They are often confronted with "debts" for their travel costs and living expenses and are forced into prostitution in order to repay these debts.

The number of Filipinas working in the Japanese sex industry rose steadily until the middle of the 1980s. The Filipinas speak English and have a meeting point where they can exchange information and seek support, namely the Catholic Church. Since the traffickers and brothel owners prefer to keep their victims in as vulnerable a position as possible, Filipinas have become less attractive and Thai women more attractive. Since the latter half of the 1980s, the number of women trafficked from Thailand has risen dramatically. Unlike the Filipinas, these women do not speak English and have no ready meeting points.

Trafficking scenarios vary from country to country. In the case of Thai women, each stage involves a different agent. First, brokers contact the women in their apartments and persuade them to work in Japan. Recruitment in the neighboring countries of Burma, Vietnam, Cambodia, and China also follows this pattern. Difficulties often occur here because many women have neither a birth certificate nor proof of nationality. If the Japanese authorities later establish that their papers are false, the women become stateless. After this first stage of recruitment, other traders "export" the women to Japan. In Thailand, the women are sold to Japanese traders for 1.5–2 million yen, often with the consent of the local dignitaries and the woman's relatives. After being sold to agents of the *yakuza* (the Japanese mafia) and having their papers confiscated, they are auctioned for 3–4 million yen. There were in 1995–96 an estimated one hundred Japanese traders, backed up by extensive *yakuza* networks. The victims of trafficking are forced to work to pay off their "debts" for a period of many years before they are permitted to keep any of the money they earn. This "released-slave" system is typical of the global development of the sex trade in Japan (cf. HELP 1996; Supapung 1996).

CONCLUSION

Prostitution is not a women's institution (by women and for women). It is an institution run by men and maintained by intimidation, cultural practices, and violence. Its primary purpose is to exploit girls and women for the pleasure and profit of men. Its character depends heavily on economic and political conditions as it tends to exploit arenas of poverty and powerlessness to benefit the wealthy and powerful. In times of isolation, prostitution in Japan was an integral part of the social hierarchy. In feudal Japan, the victims were primarily poor young Japanese girls from rural areas. In times of international commerce, both Japanese and non-Japanese prostitutes become international commodities to be bought and sold as sex slaves. When Japan was a marginalized state, Japanese women were trafficked to other Asian countries. Now that Japan is a regional and global economic leader, prostitutes from other countries are imported to Japan to augment the local supply. In times of war, non-Japanese prostitutes and sex slaves were instruments of the Japanese war machinery used to service Japanese military men in foreign countries. As those in destitution and poverty shift economic and political conditions, so too does the international trafficking in women, a situation that reflects the shifting international division of labor between the powerful core and the marginalized poor of the global capitalist economy.

9

Political Spaces, Gender, and NAFTA

Jane H. Bayes and Rita Mae Kelly

Globalization, with its disruption of economic, political, and other social structures and patterns, creates the potential for opening political spaces for women. Political spaces are arenas for political thought and action. Historically, women have been excluded from the public, political sphere and from most political spaces. Being viewed as different, "The Other," as beings who resided almost fully in the reproductive and nurturing realm of life, women have not been recognized as citizens, or certainly not as citizens equal to men with equal rights, duties, and responsibilities. The purpose of this chapter is to begin the development of a conceptual framework that will facilitate further analyses of the political spaces opening for women in this period of globalization of both economies and notions of human rights. To accomplish this purpose we first draw on the earlier discussions of globalization that constitute the background and create the potential for social change in and among women at this point in history. Second, we highlight Connell's (1987) notion of gender regimes to identify some of the institutions where gender regimes are embedded and where change can occur. We also review arguments concerning how individual women can move from being powerless and politically inactive to becoming politically aware and/or politically active. Third, we draw on Sassen's (1996) notion of strategic sites of globalization to identify two geographical areas—Chiapas, Mexico, and the U.S.-Mexico border—to assess how particular circumstances arising as a result of, or as a concomitant of the North American Free Trade Agreement (NAFTA), can change gender regimes in particular institutions and raise political consciousness among Mexican women to impel them to act politically to change gender relations in these situations. The methodology involves identifying and examining specific instances of gender regime change or gender regime contestation to identify and assess the forces and circumstances that make such a change or contestation possible.

147

GLOBALIZATION AND WOMEN

Globalization of security, trade, production, financial markets, and the knowledge function has set in motion the restructuring of the labor force, welfare regimes, development strategies, the sovereignty of nation-states, citizenship rights, democracy, markets, and gender relations. The shift of power to other nonstate authorities raises new questions about the nature of sovereignty, the dispersion of power, and political control. It also raises questions about how gender relations are being impacted, and how women, in all their diversity, are interacting with and being influenced by the new global economy and the increasing privatization of previously state and public functions.

In both Organization for Economic Cooperation and Development (OECD) countries and in developing countries, the traditional "social contract," so aptly described by an OECD publication as follows, is breaking down:

> Life is organised around an implicit "social contract" [*sic*]. Its two components, the gender contract and the employment contract, define the current division of family and labour market roles. Within the gender contract women assume the bulk of family care and domestic functions, while men are ascribed primary responsibility for the family's economic or financial well-being. The employment contract reinforces this division of labour by defining as its norm, the sole breadwinner in continuous full-time lifelong employment. (OECD 1994: 19)

As we begin the twenty-first century, women are increasingly entering the paid workforce while retaining their domestic and family care responsibilities. In OECD countries in 1997, women were about half of the active labor force (OECD 1999). Families with both parents working and single-parent families have increased dramatically, while two-parent families with one partner (usually the female) engaged in full-time child care and homemaking are much less common.

In response to the adjustments generated by globalization, women have entered both formal and informal paid labor markets in ever-increasing numbers in almost all countries. Flexible production and the global shift in capital and manufacturing have disrupted the "continuous life-long employment" aspect of the "social contract" for men and left many men in lower paying, less secure jobs with an increased likelihood of frequent job changes and long periods of unemployment. In developing countries such as Mexico, many have been drawn out of an agrarian subsistence economy into an urban context. Structural adjustment policies put in place to deal with the debt crisis in 1982 have disrupted further both the "gender contract" and the "employment contract" for men and women. In short, the world has undergone a "global shift" since 1971, a shift that has not only affected capital, production, labor, and the role of the state, but that has also changed gender relations in dramatic and significant ways. Whereas the reigning gender ideology of the pre-1971 period was one of man as provider and protector and woman as mother, wife, caregiver, and often provider as well, the new gender ideology as promoted by the United Nations is one that seeks to recognize all human beings as authentic without determining reproductive, gendered, ethnic, national, or racial attributes. Within this gender regime model, all equally have basic human rights.

IDENTITY AND RECOGNITION IN THE TRANSFORMATION OF GENDER REGIMES

Until recently globalization accounts did not consider the ways in which gender is integrated into the process. Gender categories not only define the identity of individual actors in various societies, but they also are present in the recognition or lack of recognition granted to individuals or categories of people by collectivities such as families, religious organizations, corporate organizations, nongovernmental organizations, cities, and states. In a society where all of the above collectivities ascribe more or less to the same "social contract" as defined by the OCED statement above, where they all "recognize" men and women as particular kinds of role players in the production and reproduction process, the identity of most individuals in that society is very likely to conform to a stable "gender order." Connell defines "gender regime" as "the state of play in gender relations in a given institution" (1987: 120). In other words, the actual practices that occur in a given institution can differentiate patterns of gendered division of labor and subsequent patterns of gendered domination and subordination. Connell argues that gender relations characterize all kinds of institutions. Every institution (here he includes formal organizations like schools, but also other more diffuse institutions like markets, or the state, or even streetcorner peer group life) engages in practices that construct various kinds of femininity and masculinity. In thinking about Mexico and the United States, relevant institutions would include the family, religious institutions, schools, land owning institutions, such as the Mexican *ejidos* (an agricultural community that is also a unit of production). Other relevant institutions encompass corporations, political parties, nongovernmental organizations, including international organizations, and local, state, and national governments. Because all of these institutions are interrelated in a society, changes in the gender relations or gender regime in one set of institutions can affect the gender relations or gender regimes in other sets of institutions.

The relationship between the personal identity held by members of various institutions in a society and the recognition that those institutions confer on their members may be a stable relationship or it may be a dialectic one. Individuals may struggle to change their own identities, but to be successful, the new identity must be recognized by someone. In the case of gender relations, to have a lasting impact, a new identity on the part of women needs to be recognized and acknowledged by others linked together in an institution. The process can work in the opposite way as well. An established institution can give recognition to a new kind of gender relationship and suggest a new identity for its members, an identity that many if not most of the members may not initially hold themselves. If the individual is experiencing some contradictions in her gender identity, she may resolve that contradiction by adopting the new gender identity. A change in gender regimes within an institution may come from within the institution or it may come from outside influences either on the formal procedures and stated beliefs of the institution or on the identities and life struggles of members of that institution.

Gender orders can be ideal norms posited by a variety of entities: religions, secular leaders, politicians, an international institution, or other civic leaders. Legal gender relations codes can be posited by states (or their delegates in instances where religious institutions are authorized to establish civil and family codes), the United Nations, and courts at all levels of government, including world courts. These codes can also be unrealized norms, standards to be sought, but only partially implemented in a geopolitical area.

A thesis of this chapter is that changes in gender regimes in the United States and Mexico are occurring because of a complex interplay among economic and social forces that generate contradictions in the lives of groups of women. These contradictions can lie dormant without the powerful insertion of alternative options for gender relations being made visible and feasible, or they can erupt into political resistance, political consciousness, or political activity to change gender relations in one or more institutions. A brief review of the literature reveals three general processes by which women who were politically inactive and without explicit political consciousness have become politically active in ways that tend to lead to gender regime change. One of these is when outside forces threaten the family and women's ability to perform their family and reproductive responsibilities. In these circumstances, some women will violate the traditional gender rule against political activism to defend and perform their traditional gender roles, that of being mothers who care for families and put food on the table. An example would be the eighteenth-century European women who engaged in bread riots to protest the high price of wheat and grain (Bouton 1993; Thompson 1971). The activism of mothers of "disappeared" people in repressive states is another example of women being driven to political action because of a disruption in their own ability to carry out traditional gender roles involved in the family. Las Madres de Plaza de Mayo who arose under the military dictatorship in Argentina in the 1970s is an example. Such activism also occurred in Mexico with the founding in 1974 of the Comité Nacional Independiente Pro-defensa de Presos, Perseguidos, Detenidos-Desparecidos y Exiliados Políticos (Committee in Defense of Political Prisoners, Exiles, and Disappeared People) by a mother whose medical-student son "disappeared." This organization, begun by a mother trying to protect her child, evolved into a presidential campaign in 1982 with the mother, Doña Rosario Ibarra de Piedra, running as the first woman candidate for president in Mexico (Carrillo 1990).

Another variation on this theme comes with the kind of disruption that comes with the withdrawal of state support for social services and welfare that previously had been in place. Women see these forms of support as essential to the survival of themselves and their children and are willing to break traditional family gender regime rules that demand quiescence and obedience to fight as mothers defending the family. The structural adjustment policies imposed on developing countries as a condition for loans from the International Monetary Fund (IMF) and the international financial community have stimulated a number of women throughout the world to become politically active in ways they would never have been before. For example, throughout the 1970s, Mexico's urban poor struggled to obtain land, housing, and public services. In 1979, regional popular organizations from thirteen states met in Monterey to form Coordinadora Nacional de Movimiento Urbano Popular (National Council of the Urban Popular Movement [CONAMUP]). Most of the participants in this coalition were women, although they were not the leaders. The women were placed up front when the group confronted police in their efforts to avoid land evictions and in their pleas to officials for roads, running water, and sanitation (Stephen 1992: 83).

By 1983, the women in CONAMUP had formed a Women's Regional Council to obtain services such as health centers, running water, schools, titles to land for housing, cooking gas, school lunches, cooperatives, and other economic amenities that help women perform their household duties (Stephen 1992: 84). Gender regime change is not *necessarily* an outcome of this kind of political activity, however. This type of activity often does little to alter the gendered division of labor and often means that women are working a triple shift. They are responsible for family maintenance, for making ends meet in the informal or formal economy, and in addition they work as political activists. The projects on which they work tend to reinforce the gendered division of labor in the traditional community (Stephen 1992: 90). Nonetheless, these disruptions can also start the process of gender regime change.

A second kind of contradiction that might lead to political activism and gender regime change is the change in the political consciousness of women as they first enter the waged labor force. Globalization has been feminizing the labor force all over the world. Whether this leads to gender regime change is the subject of considerable debate and research. Some argue that young women entering the assembly line workforce are empowered in their families and liberated somewhat by their earnings, which allow them to buy a few consumer goods and break away from family control (Chowdury 1997). Tiano (1991), in a study of *maquila* and domestic workers in Mexicali, found that two-thirds of the domestic and electronics workers and over half of the garment workers said that they would keep working even if they did not need the money. This finding suggests that the work is not totally disagreeable. Pena (1991, 1995) documented the shop floor resistance of female *maquiladora* workers to show that these workers do engage in forms of resistance. A study comparing the gender role identification of electronics and garment *maquiladora* factories found that the older, less "desirable" garment workers who had already participated in a strike action were more likely to have more egalitarian views of gender relations than a group of younger, unmarried, more highly educated women from an electronics factory (Young 1991). Safa (1995: 182), in comparing women workers in Puerto Rico, the Dominican Republic, and Cuba, notes that paid employment empowers women only under certain circumstances depending on state policy, the control that women have over resources, and the nature of the household economy. She argues that becoming a critical contributor to the household economy or being a married woman who participates substantially in the waged labor force are conditions that are most likely to promote a woman's empowerment. Single women, or those whose earnings are a substitute for male earnings, are less likely to become empowered because they must assume responsibility for family survival and are usually overburdened. Critical to women's empowerment is control of key economic resources such as wages, income, and property (Benería and Roldán 1987; Blumberg 1991; Safa 1995; 175). Young married women who, along with their husbands, work in the waged labor force and share in household budget decisions are the most empowered. Higher educational levels, for both men and women, lower fertility, legal unions, and state support for women's equality also contribute positively to women's empowerment. Safa also argues that state policies (minimum wage, currency devaluation, union support, occupational segregation), regardless of women's participation in the labor force, are critical determinants. She concludes that in Latin America and the Caribbean men are recognized and see themselves primarily as workers with family responsibilities, while women identify and are recognized as wives and mothers with economic responsibilities (Safa 1995: 182–185).

Other studies show that often young women working in factories are carefully kept under the control of male plant managers and supervisors at work, are forced to work long hours for wages that are below the subsistence level, are sexually harassed at work, and in other ways are demeaned and marginalized, making political resistance almost impossible. For women in these circumstances the workplace is but an extension of the patriarchal authority that these women experience in the home (Haj 1992; Salaff 1986).

While the act of joining the paid labor force does not automatically create a new consciousness or a new gender regime for women workers, often it can create what Erik Olin Wright calls the "permeability" of gender and class boundaries. Wright explores the interrelationship between gender regimes and class regimes in various institutions (Wright 1997).

> In some class structures, friendships, marriages, churches and sports clubs are largely homogeneous with respect to class. In such cases, class boundaries can be thought of as highly impermeable. In other class structures, these social processes frequently bring together people in different class locations. When this happens, class boundaries become relatively permeable. (Wright 1997: 149)

He finds that class does not strongly influence the sex distribution of housework even in the advanced countries of Sweden and the United States (Wright 1997: 304). In other words, gender regimes are remarkably similar in upper and lower classes. Class boundaries do not necessarily challenge gender regimes, although men do much more of the housework in all classes in Sweden than they do in the United States (Wright 1997: 289). However, in comparing the United States, Sweden, and Japan in the workplace, Wright finds three other factors that do challenge class and gender regimes. He identifies these as property, expertise, and authority, or "three exploitation mechanisms in the class structure" (Wright 1997: 158).

Property involves ownership of capital. Authority involves being in a managerial or supervisory position, and expertise involves having expert knowledge or expertise in the workplace (Wright 1997: 158). When the boundaries of any of these three factors crosscut class or gender regimes, they can penetrate gender or class boundaries to create potential sites of contestation and change. For example, the denial of gendered property or property rights, or the recognition of more egalitarian gendered property rights, can create a contestation site. Expertise can also contest gender regime boundaries. As women obtain more access to higher education and technical training, this expertise level may change gender regimes in the workplace. More egalitarian gender regimes in the workplace in turn might have an impact on gender regimes in the family. In a study of women in the electronics industry in Guadalajara, Mexico, Luisa Gabayet (1993) found that in most cases, male workers were more highly skilled, better paid, and had more job stability than women workers. However, when women are able to obtain training and jobs that demand that training, women are often able to command higher salaries than the males in their households. She cites the example of Wang.

> The production processes carried out at Wang require more training than those in other electronic factories. The women hired there have had several years of work experience in other electronic plants and have received a longer training period at Wang. This implies that management is interested in keeping its trained labor force, and translates into better salaries and fringe benefits. It is important to add that the women working at Wang were the only women in all the sample who received higher salaries than the men in their households. All the other women in the sample, even if their education level was higher than that of their brothers or husbands, earned less than the men. (Gabayet 1993: 14)

Although this example does not prove that gender regimes have changed in the households or families of these women, it does suggest that the homogeneity of the gender regimes in various institutions in the society, in this case family and workplace, have been reduced. The gender regime boundaries have become more permeable.

Finally, authority boundaries can affect gender regimes. For Wright, authority is personal managerial authority in the workplace. Wright notes that in the United

States, workplace managerial authority gaps between the sexes were smaller than they were in Sweden and minuscule compared to those in Japan (Wright 1997: 359–360). In other words, workplace gender regimes in the United States are more egalitarian with regard to managerial/supervisory positions than are workplace gender regimes in Sweden, Norway, or Japan. Managerial authority boundaries are more permeable in the United States for women than they are elsewhere.

Wright's concept of "permeability" of gender regimes in a society and his exploration of how property, expertise, and authority can create the conditions for this permeability in the workplace highlight some of the ways that contradictions are created for women. He does not document the action these women might take or the consciousness that they might develop because of these changes, but he does show that different countries have different levels of permeability for gender relations and suggests that permeable conditions will make gender regime change more probable.

In the United States, women have been stimulated to political action and gender regime change by some of the same factors mentioned above. While the early intellectual leaders of the women's movement in the United States, Elizabeth Cady Stanton and Susan B. Anthony, were motivated by an ideology of equality for women, many of the leaders of the suffrage movement, including leaders of the Women's Christian Temperance Union, the National Consumer's League, and the Women's Trade Union League, supported giving the vote to women to enable them to be able to better fulfill their gender roles as wives and mothers (McGlen and O'Connor 1995: 7).

War as well as economic changes, including globalization, have also stimulated gender order change in the United States. During World War II, women went to work in the defense industry and dramatically changed gender relations in the workplace. Globalization in the 1970s has reduced high-paying assembly line jobs, thereby undermining the "family wage." Women have gone to work to add to the family income because the nation's growing service economy needed their skills.

Another extremely important factor generating gender regime change in the United States during the women's movement in the 1800s and in the 1960s and 1970s was the liberal political ideology of the U.S. Constitution and the Bill of Rights, both based on abstract notions of universal individualism. The extension of citizen's rights to African Americans and to women was a logical solution to a glaring contradiction between the ideals of the nation and reality. The women's movement and supportive political leaders were able to use the freedom of association and speech within the civil society to challenge the old gender order established in the national legal code, the Constitution, the Bill of Rights, and federal statutes regulating gender relations and practices.

Although it took close to two centuries, the substance of the ideal gender order was successfully contested; and by the 1970s the legal gender order against which particular gender regimes, relations, and practices were to be judged within the

United States was changed by the federal government, first by the executive, then the legislative, and then the judicial branches. The new de jure, more egalitarian gender order then became the criterion by which de facto relations and practices were to be judged. This ideological component of consciousness raising and political recognition is not indigenously available in many countries that do not have a liberal tradition or democratic laws and institutions. However, it is available internationally through the International Human Rights Movement and can be a significant factor in gender regime change.

This discussion leads to the third way in which gender regimes can be altered— through the politics of international recognition. If different institutions in a society have different gender regimes, then we would expect that contestation over gender relations might be high as opposed to a society where all institutions have homogeneous gender regimes. Identifying with or being recognized by another state or institution with a different gender regime can generate a site of contestation and gender regime change. The forces of globalization can generate a diversity of gender regimes in a society's institutions by engaging in a kind of recognition politics. The United Nations strategy, with its World Congresses on Women and its twelve-point Platform for Action, is an example of attempting to develop an international standard, a new international gender regime that can be an alternative to existing traditional gender regimes. This standard can then be used to permeate more traditional gender regime boundaries in particular institutions. The Convention to Eliminate Discrimination Against Women (CEDAW) is an example. Illustrative of this on a more personal level is the story of the young woman from a highland village in Thailand who, upon returning from Beijing after the Fourth United Nations Congress on Women in 1995, went to one of the village elders and, fortified by her newly acquired status of international traveler, informed the elder that it was not internationally acceptable for him to beat his wife and that he should stop.

The methodology undergirding the International Human Rights Movement is based on trying to make international human rights law more responsive to women in three ways: by working from women at the grassroots up through the state to the creation of international human rights law, and by attempting to go from international law down to see "how the state can implement women's rights and how it [the state] can be held accountable as an actor both internationally and nationally" (Knop 1993: 75). The third method involves rethinking the most fundamental concepts of international law and sovereignty. Or as Kathleen Jones puts it: "We can replace the voice of the sovereign master not with babble but with efforts to recognize and admit responsibility for patterns of relationships that sovereign boundaries aim to negate" (quoted in Knop 1993: 76).

Finding and organizing around the contradictions that arise when gender regime boundaries are challenged by economic or political disruptions, by gendered property changes, managerial authority changes, or expertise changes represents the "up from the grassroots" method. Radihiki Coomaraswamy argues for this approach because she believes "that the future of human rights in South Asia does not lie with international treaties and states but with movements in civil society. She attributes social change to the coming together of the state and civil society as mobilization and awareness, while the role of the state is articulation and implementation" (quoted in Knop 1993: 75). Using this approach, women "can strive to develop international civil society which is going to be a very heterogeneous combination of NGOs [nongovernment organizations], independent experts and informal groups" (Knop 1993: 75).

The second approach of going from international law down involves getting equal representation of gender-conscious women on all international bodies. It also involves using international organizations such as the United Nations and the International Labor Organization (ILO), and agreements such as CEDAW and NAFTA, to negotiate with nation-states and even with individual transnational corporations for the recognition and enforcement of women's human rights. In discussing what it means to use a human rights methodology, Diane Orentlicher argues that it means "promoting change by reporting facts." To hold governments accountable "requires NGOs to: (a) carefully document alleged abuses; (b) clearly demonstrate state accountability for those abuses under international law; and (c) develop a mechanism for effectively exposing documented abuse nationally and internationally" (quoted in Thomas 1993: 83). To work, women need to get the facts, build consensus internationally and locally, and create mechanisms to expose the abuse and bring international, national, and local pressure to bear (Thomas 1993: 86).

In summarizing some of the ways that women move from being powerless and politically inactive to becoming more politically aware and politically active we have identified three different situations. One is when women act to conserve the traditional gender regime of the family and the household when it is being challenged by economic or political forces. A variation on this occurs when in responding to disruptions in their reproductive and nurturing capabilities women also advocate a new gender regime. This may become more likely as globalization of information makes alternative models more readily available. A second kind of politics occurs when gender regimes become more permeable, when different institutions that interact with one another have different gender regimes. Here the focus is on the workplace as well as on the interaction between the workplace and the family and other institutions. The feminization of the labor force can create at least some gender regime permeability, a situation where activists can become important in raising consciousness and thereby moving gender relations from a patriarchal to a more egalitarian gender order. The third situation does not involve women's identity reformation as much as it involves a politics of gender regime contestation and recognition, often backed by sanctions, among states, courts, local governments, and transnational corporations. Here again is political space for activists to develop sites of contestation that can affect a politics of recognition in institutions that regulate these sites.

STRATEGIC SITES OF CONTESTATION

The various processes by which gender regimes change are likely to unfold in particular circumstances where globalization gives rise to sites of contestation. Saskia Sassen has spoken about the importance of identifying strategic sites where such current processes of globalization can be studied (Sassen 1996: 14). She sees the "nexus between subsistence economies and capitalist enterprise" as one such site in situations involving export agriculture. A second site is "the nexus between the dismantling of an established 'labor aristocracy' in developed countries with shadow effects on an increasing sector of developed economies and the formation of an off-shore proletariat." A third strategic site is represented by global cities as they become "strategic sites for the valorization of leading components of capital and for the coordination of global economic processes" (Sassen 1996: 14). Global cities are also places where large numbers of women and immigrants invisibly service the decision-making centers of the global economy. The fourth strategic site identified by Sassen concerns issues of sovereignty and international law generated largely by immigrants who the U.S. courts have come to consider as individuals under a Human Rights Code rather than as citizens. She suggests that the transformation of sovereignty under the impact of globalization has opened political space for "women (and other hitherto largely invisible actors) to become visible participants in international relations and subjects of international law" (Sassen 1996: 15).

What do these four sites have in common? The first two are sites of major economic disruption, disruption of routinized economic processes, and accepted patterns of gender relations. The latter two have a different base. Sassen argues for the importance of global cities as strategic sites because of the close proximity and interdependence of the powerful and the powerless, which raises awareness of class and power differentials. This seems to be a quite different reason from the previous two. The final strategic site is also quite different. Here she shows us how the Human Rights Code, one that presumably recognizes all human beings as having authenticity, regardless of race, sex, ethnicity, or nationality, is being accepted in U.S. courts of law for individuals, not just for citizens. What all four of Sassen's strategic sites have in common is that they are sources of blatant contradictions brought on by globalization. What is not clear is whether the contradiction exists in the minds of those involved in the disruption or whether it exists only in the minds of analysts or jurists. What we would like to suggest is that in each of these strategic sites there is a possible dialectic occurring between identity and recognition and it is this dialectic that is the locus of gender regime changes. While those in the Marxist tradition tend to look for change in the process by which the consciousness or identity or standpoint of workers or women is changed, what those in a Hegelian tradition would also note is that for change to occur, the new identity of the workers (or the women) must be recognized and that that is as critical a political project as is the politics of consciousness raising or identity formation.

GENDER REGIME CONTESTATION IN FOUR
STRATEGIC SITES INFLUENCED BY NAFTA

The first part of this chapter has established a conceptual framework for analyzing globalization and gender regime change. The second half will apply this framework to analyze four strategic sites of gendered contestation associated with NAFTA. This is not meant to be a comprehensive survey of such sites in Mexico or the United States, nor is it meant to illustrate all of the gendered responses or consequences of the globalization forces that NAFTA represents. Each situation is one in which Mexican women, or in some cases American and other women, have been stimulated to become politically active in response to conditions or events that can be broadly attributed to the globalization processes that NAFTA represents. In each instance, the forces of globalization have increased the diversity (and in some cases, the proximity) of gender regimes within and among the institutions involved in the strategic site or, as in the case of Chiapas, disrupted the existing traditional gender regimes. The four examples seek to show changes in gender regimes by pointing to changes in the identity of individual women and in the recognition by institutions of new gender regimes. They also show how both national and international elements of civil society play a large role in the contestation of gender regimes as represented by NAFTA. Two of the strategic sites involve contestation over property. This applies to the case of Chiapas and the Zapatistas and to the case of the *colonia* of Maclovo Roja. The case of sexual harassment in the EMOSA (Exportadora de Mano de Obra, S.A.) *maquiladora* illustrates the contestation of different gender regimes as institutionalized in Mexican law as opposed to U.S. law. It also illustrates the role of NGOs in bringing this contestation into different decision-making arenas such as U.S. and Mexican courts, U.S. labor unions, and transnational corporations. The case of pregnancy testing and the Human Rights Watch action is another example of political and legal contestation between the different legal gender regimes of the United States and Mexico, one that is currently testing the labor side agreement mechanisms of NAFTA. Again the role of the Human Rights Watch as an NGO plays a critical role.

THE CHIAPAS SITUATION

Chiapas is a state in the south of Mexico on the border of Mexico and Guatemala. It is a strategic site for studying globalization because it represents a confrontation between subsistence agriculture and the forces of globalization in the form of the region's potential for capitalist development and the structural adjustment policies imposed on Mexico in 1982 by the IMF. These policies called for privatization, an increase in exports and cutbacks in government welfare, and other support programs. They clashed dramatically with Mexico's postrevolutionary vision, which had in the past been dedicated to a government-directed import substitution policy of development that emphasized communal landholdings in a semi-subsistence rural economy along with a corporatist structure of negotiations and compromises between the ruling party, the Institutional Revolutionary Party (PRI), and other organizations such as the Confederation of Mexican Workers (CTM), the National Confederation of Campesinos (CNC), and the National Confederation of Popular Organizations (CNOP). To lessen the pain of the structural adjustment policies, the PRI used its network of government spending relationships to ensure that the leaders of indigenous villages, urban workers, business interests, and professionals continued to deliver the vote to the PRI at election time. The neoliberal structural adjustment policies decreased services to women, children, and the elderly, imposed wage and price freezes, allowed privatization of the collectively held *ejido* lands, encouraged the cultivation of cash crops in fruit and coffee with governmental assistance, and then withdrew these forms of aid. Instead of heeding the cries of distress from small plot farmers, indigenous peoples, and agricultural laborers, the government promoted large-scale capitalist developments in agriculture, cattle, oil, hydroelectric power, and lumber in Chiapas, all of which encroached upon the traditional land claims of the people.

To deal with the dislocation that neoliberal reforms inevitably produce, President Salinas created a National Solidarity Program (PRONASOL) in 1990, which has used government funds to buy off opposition and strengthen support (Nash and Kovic 1997: 170–173). The problem with the program is that it has not reached or been effective in the jungle areas of Chiapas. Because of the natural resources of Chiapas in lumber, hydroelectric power, cattle, and minerals, the government has been particularly active in displacing small farmers in the region.

On New Year's Day, 1994, the day that NAFTA went into effect, the Zapatistas, along with over eight hundred indigenous men and women, staged a carefully timed revolt by forcibly entering and taking the municipal headquarters of San Cristóbal de Las Casas, Ocosingo, Las Margaritas, and Altamirano to protest the NAFTA agreement and its exclusion of the interest of small plot farmers and other indigenous people. They were responding to the fact that between 1982 and 1992, the government had condoned the expulsion of over twenty thousand Indians from their villages, often by local political bases loyal to the PRI (Nash and Kovic 1997: 180–181).

Resistance in Chiapas, 1982 to 1994

The first meeting of what was to become the Zapatista Front of National Liberation (EZLN) or the Zapatistas' army was in November 1983 (Bellinghousen 1996: 8). Their plan was to build a grassroots army with a broad community base. Cecelia Rodriguez, spokesperson for the Zapatistas in the United States, explained the grievances of the group in a 1997 telephone interview.

The well-known stance of Mexico is that it has accepted its Indian people. As evidence of this face they will show you, for example, the portrayals of Indian symbols and Indian culture in tourist guides. But the reality is that Indian Peoples are accepted only as museum pieces. In fact, their most basic needs—which is land and the ability to hold it in the traditional way—has never been addressed. So the struggle taking place today is not about owning a piece of property. It is about a relationship to a way of life. The issue of land comes up because NAFTA and the intrusion of the global economic pattern of development, or neoliberalism, is systemically destroying their relationship to the land. Therefore, basic to the Zapatista demands is the resolution of land issues. But the movement is also about other critical issues—health, housing, education, the right to self-government, the right to elect their own officials and not those selected by established political parties. These demands, I think, are a very radical departure from the normal political life of Mexico. (Rodriguez 1997: 7)

In 1992, the privatization policies of the federal government took a particularly aggressive turn with the reform of the Agrarian Reform Law. This reform allowed collectively held *ejido* lands to be sold. The new law had a particularly disastrous effect on many farmers in Chiapas who had been encouraged to grow cash crops such as coffee and fruit with some assistance from the government in marketing and credit. In 1992, this government aid ended, leaving many farmers in debt and consequently forced to sell their land (Nash and Kovic 1997: 180–181). In other cases, local political bosses expelled peasants from their villages. Most of those expelled were women, as the raids were justified as efforts to eliminate Protestants (most of whom are women) (Nash and Kovic 1997: 180). To expel people for religious reasons is illegal in Mexico. Ironically, women have traditionally not had access to *ejido* land under Mexican law except through male relatives (husbands or sons), yet it is they more than others who were expelled. This kind of action on the part of the authorities, be they local bosses, or the federal government, has changed the consciousness and identity of many local women. Women have taken a central role in the Zapatista movement. Nash and Kovic (1997) report that 30 percent of the Zapatista army are women who have renounced childbearing to take part in the armed conflict. The Zapatista platform, "Commitments for Peace," includes several planks that concern helping women in their role as mothers: demands for gynecological and obstetric care, child care centers, and public funds to feed children. Other demands focus on economic issues such as education, projects to improve farming, baking, and craft making, as well as better transportation systems for bringing products to markets (Nash and Kovic 1997: 182). While the Zapatista platform clearly makes demands for land, it does not ask for equal rights for women to the land.

In 1992, the Zapatistas renewed their women's equality campaign. According to an account by Subcomandante Marcos, the major spokesman for the Zapatistas in Mexico, Susanna, a Tzotzil woman, had the job of making the rounds of dozens of communities, speaking with groups of women to pull their ideas together into the "Women's Law" proposal (Marcos 1994). Cecelia Rodriguez notes that in 1992 there were "hundreds of community assemblies and a great deal of political education that women Zapatista leaders like Comandante Ramona and Comandante Ana Maria conducted in the communities" (Rodriguez 1997: 9). The result was a document entitled "Revolutionary Laws of Women," which put forth the following ten points:

> Women, regardless of their race, creed, color or political affiliation, have the right to participate in the revolutionary struggle in a way determined by their desire and capacity.
>
> Women have the right to work and receive a just salary.
>
> Women have the right to decide the number of children they will have and care for.
>
> Women have the right to participate in the affairs of the community and hold positions of authority if they are freely and democratically elected.
>
> Women and their children have the right to primary attention in matters of health and nutrition.
>
> Women have the right to education.
>
> Women have the right to choose their partners and are not to be forced into marriage.
>
> Women shall not be beaten or physically mistreated by their family members or by strangers. Rape and attempted rape will be severely punished.
>
> Women will be able to occupy positions of leadership in the organization and hold military ranks in the revolutionary armed forces.
>
> Women will have all the rights and obligations elaborated in the Revolutionary Laws and Regulations. (*Dark Night Field Notes* 1997: 10)

These Women's Laws were passed by the Clandestine Revolutionary Indigenous Committee (CCRI) in March 1993 and came to be known as the Revolutionary Laws and also as the "first uprising" of the EZLN (Marcos 1994).

After over a decade of organizing, planning, and resistance, which was met by an increasing level of violent repression, the Zapatistas staged an uprising on New Year's Day, 1994, the day that the North American Free Trade Agreement was to go into effect. Women were among the leaders of this revolt. The government, in response, engaged in what the Zapatistas call "low intensity warfare," which consists of cutting off water supplies to villages and refugee camps; filling the roads and cities with military trucks, soldiers, and equipment; hassling and sometimes killing villagers on the way to their fields; raping village women and bringing prostitutes into the area. The Zapatista movement countered by seeking and securing international attention and support. By 1996, the National Commission for Democracy in Mexico (NCDM) had been established in El Paso, Texas, and was publishing a monthly newspaper in English and Spanish titled *Libertad*. The NCDM also established a National Women's Committee, headquartered in the Chicano Studies Department at Pima Community College in Tucson, Arizona, "to support the resistance of women against the devastation of neoliberal restructuring, especially in Mexico and the US by combating the low-intensity warfare being directed at women in Chiapas" (NCDM, March 1996: 5). Another kind of international outreach involved hosting a conference called the Encuentro, which brought hundreds of people from forty-four countries (mostly Europe and the Americas with a smattering of countries from Asia, Africa, and the Middle East). France sent a big delegation of hundreds of people, while other countries had only one or two representatives. From July 27 to August 3, 1996, these international visitors were taken on an arduous journey to five different indigenous communities in the mountains of Chiapas where they discussed what could be done to combat neoliberalism by building a "global network of communication between struggles . . . a network of autonomous struggles reaching up from below to exchange experiences and solidarity" (Flood 1997: 33). A "Giving Voice to Silence" campaign began in the United States with El Comité Emiliano Zapata, California (Oakland, Berkeley, Bay Area) in September 1996, and Cecelia Rodriguez undertook a speaking tour of college campuses in the United States (NCDM, March/April 1998). Student groups from campuses from Chicano studies programs along the border have been going on trips to Chiapas as international observers. The Mexican government responded by deporting Spanish, Canadian, United States, Belgian, and German observers in the region and by harassing and deporting other sympathetic observers (mostly students) from the United States (NCDM, May 1998: 2; Preston 1998: A6).

When asked about the role of women in the Zapatista movement, Cecelia Rodriguez responded by saying:

> The patriarchal culture brought by the Spanish is still present and powerful in Mexico. It hasn't been transformed as it has perhaps in other parts of the world. So, for Indian women to take up arms as Zapatistas is a profound event. It all began pretty much as a recognition of their role and the quality of their lives. For example, at a very young age (the age of fourteen), you have to abide by an arranged marriage. You don't have a choice in how many children you have, and by the age of 35 your life is pretty much finished. . . . It was these terrible living conditions that prompted the women to decide to change it and to decide to change it in this way. They are now commanders and soldiers, and within the army itself they have established a different set of norms. For example, men and women have to do chores equally. Men cook, just the way women cook. Men take care of children. Women give orders just like men give orders, and they do the tasks that men do. (Rodriguez 1997: 9)

Comandante Ramona, an artisan, a central leader of the Zapatista movement, and a member of the CCRI explains the reasons for the change in her own words.

> We, for sure, were already dead. We didn't matter at all, I left my community to look for work because of the same need: I didn't have a way to live. When I got to a new place, I began to learn that women's conditions aren't the same in the rural areas. There I began to understand and develop an awareness of the differences: I began to learn about the organization and that women need to organize too.

The women have come to understand that their participation was important in order to change this bad situation; that's why they, although not all of them, are participating in the armed struggle. . . . We are hungry: our nutritional base is tortillas and salt. We cook beans when we have them, but we hardly ever have milk or meat. We lack many services that other Mexicans have. I want all women to wake up and plant in their hearts the need to organize because with our arms folded we cannot build the free and just Mexico that we all want . . . in the jungle the girls are malnourished, and when they are girls, they are already mothers. The majority die in childbirth, leaving many children orphaned. We do not have food or schools; we do not know Spanish. Everything drags down our happiness and health. (NCMD, March/April 1998: 5)

Identity and Recognition in Chiapas

What has happened in the Chiapas conflict is a change in gender regimes, at least in the institution of the EZLN. Over a third of the EZLN soldiers are females who have agreed not to have children while they are in the army (Nash and Kovic 1997: 182). Women are apparently accepted as generals and military leaders. The fact that the indigenous communities in Chiapas have always made their decisions by gathering all families in a village to make decisions and choose leaders may make the gender regime change in the EZLN an easier transition than it would otherwise be. The assumption of equal participation for all is not an alien concept. Another important contributing factor to gender regime change in Chiapas is the presence of international groups throughout the region for some period of time. In 1985, over 365 international organizations had offices in San Cristóbal de las Casas (telephone interview with Dr. Laura Gonzales, University of Guanajuato, May 10, 1998).

THE UNITED STATES–MEXICO BORDER

Perhaps nowhere in the world are the contradictions and disparities generated by globalization more apparent than along the U.S.-Mexican border. The large differences and close proximity between Mexico, an indebted developing nation, and the United States, the dominant developed economy in the world, make the interactions and changes in this region particularly interesting. While the border *maquiladora* industries predate the 1994 North American Free Trade Agreement, they were the precursors of conditions and situations that NAFTA has magnified and expanded as Mexico has moved to a more industrialized and export-oriented economy.

As with other cases of industrialization coming to primarily agricultural countries, the sexual division of labor has been a key component in the *maquiladora* story. Initially, the *maquilas* were primarily Fordist assembly plants employing mostly women. The *maquilas* were established in 1965 as a part of the Border Industrialization Program. The idea was to allow transnational corporations to divide the production process into multiple stages and to locate the most labor intensive of these processes on the Mexican side of the border while eliminating the tariffs, duties, and other regulations that might pose barriers to free trade and investment between the two countries. Planning, research and development, product design, skilled labor processes, capital-intensive production techniques, and even sometimes final assembly (for tax purposes) all would occur in the United States, while labor-intensive stages of production would be simplified and deskilled for minimally skilled low-wage workers on the Mexican side of the border. Originally, *maquila* plants were limited to the border region and were perceived as a regional development program. In 1972, *maquilas* were allowed in the interior, except in highly industrialized areas (Kopinak 1996: 10).

Most *maquila* industries were in the garment and electronic industries and employed young women aged 16 to 24 in highly routinized, unskilled, assembly line work. In these early years, women constituted approximately 85 percent of the *maquila* workforce (Fernández-Kelly 1983: 209). By 1975, this figure had dropped to 78 percent and by 1988 only 64 percent of *maquila* workers were women. Part of this decline is due to the growth of other *maquila* industries such as furniture making and transportation, which traditionally employ men. In response to Mexico's desperate economic situation of 1982, President de la Madrid in 1983 made the *maquila* industries a centerpiece for his program of export development and foreign investment by making administrative changes that encouraged and facilitated both domestic and foreign companies to operate *maquilas*. Government incentives were particularly aimed at the automobile and computer industries, industries that used the latest high-tech and robotized methods of production, and that tended to hire males. Overall, women's employment in the *maquilas* increased from around 42,000 to 172,000 between 1975 and 1988 while the rate of increase in men's employment increased at twice that rate going from around 13,000 to 96,000 in that same time period (Sklair 1989: 167; Tiano 1994: 25; Kopinak 1996: 12). Even in the electronics and garment industries, the percentage of women workers declined between 1980 and 1987. Women in the electronics industry declined from 80 to 72 percent, in the electrical machinery industry from 85 to 74 percent, and in the garment and textile industries from 84 to 79 percent (Tiano 1994: 24). In spite of this trend, the majority of workers in the *maquila* industries continue to be women, and the garment, textile, and electronic industries continue to constitute the majority of the *maquila* industry. The NAFTA agreement of 1994 among the United States, Mexico, and Canada has expanded the program even further. By 1996, approximately one-third of the formal labor force in Mexico was employed in the *maquiladoras*, up from about 5 percent in 1982 (Federal Reserve Bank 1996). While situations vary at different places on the border, many of the workers drawn into the border *maquila* factories come from other parts of Mexico. They bring with them the expectations and gender relations of peasant agricultural families or the urban poor.

Working conditions for the women and men in the *maquiladora* industries are uneven. Some *maquila* industries pay more than the minimum wage and more than a worker could earn in alternate employment. Many if not most *maquila* industries, however, pay very low wages, do not meet health and safety standards, do not provide safe working conditions, and often violate the human rights of their employees in terms of sexual harassment, pregnancy testing, and union busting activities. Many engage in toxic waste dumping in places inhabited by people. In Tijuana in 1998, the average wage was U.S.$3.60 a day. Living expenses in Tijuana remained quite high. They were 80 percent of those in San Diego, just across the border, and gasoline was 90 percent higher than it was in San Diego (interview with Mary Tong of the Coalition for Justice in the Maquiladoras, April 15, 1998, Northridge, California). Along the Texas border, the average wage in the *maquila* industry was up to about U.S.$4.00 a day take-home pay or from U.S.$20 to U.S.$26 a week for a forty-five- to forty-eight hour-week (telephone interview with Sister Susan Mika of Coalition for Justice in the Maquiladoras, May 11, 1998).

Another important aspect of the border *maquiladoras* is the living conditions in which the workers live when they are not inside the factories. Most live in squatter's communities, which along the border are typically called *colonias*. composed of old wooden pallets, scrap metal, shipping cardboard, and adobe. Often these are located in rather undesirable places like dry river beds that flood seasonally or windy desert areas. Many do not have electricity or sanitation facilities and are dependent on water being brought by truck. In Tijuana, laborers get to work on buses that the factories send around to pick up workers. According to Mexican law, squatters can lay claim to unused land after living on it for five years, and in ten years can own the land. This has become a source of conflict as the *maquila* industry has grown and more land is needed for industrial parks.

COALITION FOR JUSTICE IN THE *MAQUILADORAS*

In this border environment, a major source of political activity and political organizing has come from an international coalition of NGOs called the Coalition for Justice in the Maquiladoras (CJM). The CJM was founded in June 1989 after Sister Susan Mika put together a meeting of religious, labor, environmental, and women's groups in Matamoros, Mexico. The group included the Benedictine Sisters and the Sisters of Mercy, the American Friends Service Committee Border Program, the National Toxics Campaign, the American Federation of Labor-Congress of Industrial Organizations (AFL-CIO), the Despacho Obero of Juarez, and the Interfaith Center on Corporate Responsibility. The mission statement for the organization states: "We are a transnational coalition of religious, environmental, labor, Latino and women's organizations that seek to pressure U.S. transnational corporations to adopt socially responsible practices within the maquiladora industry, to ensure a safe environment along the U.S.-Mexico border, safe work conditions inside the maquila plants and a fair standard of living for the industry's workers" (CJM 1996). Originally, the CJM included groups that were primarily U.S.-based. This has changed dramatically as the coalition has grown. The executive board in 1998 was 50 percent Mexican.

Partially as a result of coalition activities, three different workers' centers have been established along the border. One of the oldest is the Support Committee for the Maquiladoras founded to work in the Tijuana–San Diego area in January 1993 by Mary Tong. Others include the Worker's Center in Cuidad Juarez (CETLAC) founded by three unions, the United Electrical Workers, the Teamsters Union and the Mexican union, Authentic Labor Front (FAT). A third workers' center was founded in 1997 in Nuevo Laredo by grassroots organizers. Organizers from these workers' centers along with organizers from other grassroots organizations such as the Pastoral Juvenil Obrera, the American Friends Service–sponsored Border Committee of Women Workers (or the Comité Fronterizo de Obreras [CFO]) collaborate with the CJM on the most difficult organizing work. Many of these organizers are former women *maquila* workers called *promotoras,* who move around daily to different *colonias* to recruit *maquila* workers to come to "orientation meetings." *Promotoras* first try to spend enough time with new re-cruits to gain their trust and convince them that they have something to gain by coming to a group meeting to learn about Mexican labor law and also about the International Labor Organization treaties that Mexico has signed. Ideally these meetings include workers from the same factory who can be encouraged to share stories. The *promotoras* attempt to learn from the workers what is going on in various factories, what the working conditions are like, and what strategies might be feasible. They often have to be very careful in this work because the bosses of the *colonias* may be in league with the *maquiladora* owners and be willing to re-port any suspicious activity in the *colonias* to the *maquiladora* owners (telephone interview with Sister Susan Mika, May 11, 1998). This kind of activity forms the basis for some of the coalition's actions. Some develop out of requests for sup-port from *maquiladora* workers themselves, complaints about health or safety sit-uations, or events such as severed limb accidents, or deaths from toxic waste dumps. In the ten years since the coalition has been in existence, it has waged over thirty campaigns over issues of environmental contamination, health and safety issues, wages and benefits, and community infrastructure.

SEXUAL HARASSMENT AT EMOSA MAQUILADORA IN TIJUANA

A sexual harassment offense occurred in Tijuana at a company picnic given by Exportadora de Mano de Obra, S.A. (EMOSA), a Tijuana satellite of U.S.-based American United Global, also known as National O-Ring located in Downey, California. The 150 women workers at EMOSA earned U.S.$5 to $7 a day in-specting O-rings made by National O-Ring and used in automobiles and other products. At the company picnic in September 1994, the CEO of National O-Ring, John Shahid, was in attendance. As in previous years, the company picnic included a bathing suit contest. Employees charged that during the bathing suit contest, Mr. Shahid videotaped the women in the contest, focusing on their crotches and bottoms. The women asked Shahid for the tape. He refused and later supplied a tape with the bathing suit contest omitted. The women filed a sexual harassment complaint with the Mexican Justice Department and the Mexican state labor board. When the authorities began to investigate, American United, the parent company for National O-Ring, suddenly closed the plant without paying any of the severance pay required by Mexican law. The women then filed a suit (*Aguirre vs. American United Global*, BC118159) in the Los Angeles Superior Court bringing sexual harassment charges under the U.S. law and a claim under the Mexican statute that fines companies for not providing severance pay. Because of the vagueness of the NAFTA labor agreement, which says that each of the three trading partners should enforce its own labor laws, where a case like this should be tried is hazy. Mexico really does not have any civil sexual harassment law, and criminal harassment carries a fine of around U.S.$80. The severance pay law, however, is a Mexican law. To resolve this impasse, the Tijuana/San Diego–based Support Committee for Maquiladora Workers, led by Mary Tong, called up the United Auto Workers who worked in plants that used the O-rings made by American United Global. The United Auto Workers had a clause in their contract with Ford, GM, and Chrysler that these companies would agree not to use any parts made under unfair labor practice conditions. The unions made this information known to the CEOs of the automobile companies. The result was that after eight months of legal action, demonstrations, and letter writing, American United Global agreed to pay 118 former workers at EMOSA a settlement package that met their expectations (CJM Newsletter 6 (1) Spring 1996: 11; interview with Mary Tong, April 15, 1998, Northridge, California; telephone interview with Maria Robinson of Support Committee for Maquiladora Workers, May 10, 1998).

The political conditions in Tijuana surrounding the *maquiladoras* make this action particularly significant. The state government of Baja is run by the National Action Party, a free-trade group that has its own official union, CROC (Revolutionary Conference of Workers and Peasants), and close ties with the Maquila Owners Association in Tijuana. *Maquilas* that attempt to raise wages are punished by this group as are workers who attempt to organize an independent union or who otherwise express resistance to management. In this climate, to observe women at EMOSA outraged enough to risk the blacklisting that they could certainly face because of their willingness to file a lawsuit is significant information about the kind of identity the women were willing to claim for themselves.

THE *COLONIAS*: THE CASE OF MACLOVIA ROJAS

Still another arena of female political activity on the border lies in the *colonias*. Just as the women in Chiapas become politically active when they are evicted from their villages, claims by others on *colonia* land can also create a space for political action for women. As illustrated above in the discussion of the organizing activities of the Coalition for Economic Justice and its affiliated Workers' Centers, the *colonias* are critical to the strategy of learning exactly what is going on in the *maquiladora* plants and attempting to organize workers to form a union or do something about the injustices. As described above, the Coalition for Justice in the Maquiladoras and its worker center satellites use the *colonias* as strategic places to organize. The organization can be directed at injustices in the *maquiladoras*, at attempts to unionize, or can concern *colonia* conditions. Although *maquiladora* owners' associations and various political bosses may attempt to control political activities including political speech in the *colonias*, the *colonias* can be an important political space for women. A *colonia* named Maclovio Rojas in Tijuana is a good example. There a woman named Hortensia Hernandez has become a major political activist along with two men in leading the fight to keep the *colonia* in the hands of the current settlers. The *colonia* includes about 1,300 families on a windswept desert area outside of Tijuana. These families have been living in the *colonia* since 1958 and under Mexican law are entitled to lay claim to the land after living on it for five years. After ten years, they become the owners of the land under current Mexican law. The *colonia* residents filed for title after eight years to the state of Baja California. The state has refused to recognize their claim. This has led to protests and marches. The three major leaders including Hortensia Hernandez have been arrested and jailed for periods of time. The *colonia* leaders as well as observers from the American Friends Service Committee and the Regional Border Workers Support Committee (CAFOR) believe that the government wants Maclovio Rojas's land because it is large and flat and quite suitable for sale to transnational corporations. They also argue that Maclovio Rojas is known to be predominantly of the opposition PRD (Partido de la Revolucion Democratica [Party of the Democratic Revolution]) party and not of the PAN (Partico de Acción Nacional [National Action Party]), which controls Baja, or the PRI, which controls most of Mexico (*Borderlines* 1996). For these reasons, Maclovio Rojas is being pressured as a *colonia*. The result is a strengthening of resistance and new opportunities for women's political activity as the women join together with men to defend and fight for their homes. The *colonias* are also extremely important as sites for union organizing.

HUMAN RIGHTS WATCH AND THE CASE OF PREGNANCY TESTING

Still another area of political awareness that is being generated in women along the border comes from the issue of pregnancy testing. Under Mexican law, an employed woman can receive six weeks of maternity leave with full pay both before and after birth (making a total of twelve weeks). The coverage is provided by social insurance (United Nations 1995: 138). To avoid paying these benefits, companies do all they can to keep from hiring pregnant women. This includes requiring women workers to provide a urine test as a condition of employment. Some companies will hire workers only on a temporary twenty-eight-day basis to coincide with the woman's menstrual cycle. If the woman becomes pregnant, she is not rehired. Other companies require women to show their bloody sanitary pads once a month to prove that they are not pregnant. The Mexican law does not specifically prohibit pregnancy testing; however, the Mexican constitution prohibits job discrimination according to sex. Other International Labour Organization (ILO) and United Nations agreements, to which Mexico is a signatory, proclaim a commitment not to discriminate in job hiring on the basis of sex. This political space is one that is being exploited by Human Rights Watch, the National Association of Democratic Lawyers in Mexico, and the International Labour Rights Fund, who have completed a study documenting the abuse based on interviews with fifty women in forty different factories along the border in 1995 and 1996 (Eggerton 1997). Human Rights Watch is pursuing the human rights methodology described above with this case. The study has documented the instances of pregnancy testing by transnational corporations all along the border in considerable detail. Using the study, Human Rights Watch filed a complaint against Mexico in the National Administrative Office (NAO) of the United States Department of Labor charging that Mexico had failed to establish mechanisms to provide recourse to workers who experience this violation of the NAFTA agreement. The NAO held hearings in November 1997 in McAllen, Texas, and brought female workers from Mexico to testify. In March 1998, the NAO found that pregnancy testing was definitely occurring but also determined that it was unclear what the law was concerning this matter in Mexico. The next level of adjudication according to the NAFTA labor agreement is "ministerial consultation," whereby officials of the U.S. Department of Labor meet with their counterparts in Mexico. One of the problems with this is that no definition exists of what constitutes "consultation." The Mexicans claim that pregnancy testing does not violate Mexican law. U.S. women are protected from pregnancy testing by the Pregnancy Discrimination Act of 1978 and also by the individual's constitutional right to privacy, a right that is not granted by Mexico to Mexican citizens. At the moment, the case is stalled at this "ministerial consultation" level. The third level of adjudication involves a "committee of experts" to convene and issue a report.

While pursuing the issue at the intergovernmental level, the Human Rights Watch has also taken its report to major U.S. transnational corporations that operate *maquiladora* factories on the border. General Motors and ITT Industries both have voluntarily agreed to discontinue the practice of pregnancy testing; however, others have not (telephone interview with La Shawn Jefferson of Human Rights Watch, May 20, 1998).

CONCLUSION

Forces of globalization that create new institutions (such as *maquiladora* factories and the *colonias*) or that alter gender relations in other institutions to create a diversity of gender regimes in the institutions in a society create the possibility for change in the gender order of the entire society. Usually this does not occur automatically, but rather depends on activists and organizers to generate identity change. The *promotoras* and the leaders of organizations such as the Coalition for Justice in the Maquiladoras are crucial to the creation of these political spaces. Changes in gender relations in the workplace regarding property, expertise, and the occupation of authoritative positions by women help create gender regime permeability and new political spaces for women. Globalization also contributes to creating political spaces for women by opening legal and political contestation between powerful institutions with regard to differences in their respective gender regimes. Disputes over pregnancy testing or sexual harassment juxtapose the different legal gender regimes of Mexico and the United States, of transnational organizations, and of local governments with that of the international human rights gender regime. They put gender on the agenda in places where such contestation has never before occurred, and present the opportunity for asserting the authenticity of that international standard.

10

Democratization and Gender Politics in South Korea

Bang-Soon L. Yoon

INTRODUCTION

Rapid industrialization and democratization in the Republic of Korea (hereafter referred to as South Korea) has transformed its society significantly, opening new political spheres for women in civil society. However, due to South Korea's peculiar socioeconomic and political context, women's political space has been largely confined to the extra-political arena. There are poor linkage mechanisms between women's elective, grassroots movements and the formal political arena. There is an urgent need for analysis of the reasons for the absence of such mechanisms.

Beginning in the early 1960s, South Korea embarked on a three-pronged industrialization strategy characterized by export-led industrialization, a developmental state model of economic planning, and the *chaebol* (family-owned large conglomerate) -centered industrial structure. In the following three decades, South Korea's industrialization proceeded within the framework of a growth-first and distribution-later formula. Economic growth and national security were identified by the Park Chung Hee regime (1961–79) as the two fundamental policy goals of the nation. These two policy goals were symbiotic: economic growth is a necessary condition for protection of the South from the hard-line communist North's military aggression; while national security also serves as a necessary condition for smooth economic growth. The North/South tensions persist even though the Cold War has ostensibly ended. These policy postures inevitably restricted many democratic elements in civil society, especially in the form of restrictions on interest-group activism, civil liberties, and civil rights.

South Korea's hypergrowth model of industrialization, often achieving double-digit annual growth rates (average annual GNP growth rate in each decade in the 1970s, 1980s were 8.6 percent and 8 percent respectively, and 8.1 percent in 1995) (NSO 1999: 238), has further consolidated men's power in society's rigid gender hierarchy, which is based on Confucian values. Rapid industrialization nonetheless transformed women's role in the economy and education dramatically and provided new potential for women's political participation. In the economic arena, women's labor force participation has expanded remarkably, growing from 36 percent of all women in 1960 to 49 percent in 1996. The educational sector also demonstrated a phenomenal growth of women's educational levels that rose from an average 4.7 years in 1970 to 9.3 years in 1995 (KWDI 1997: 77).

South Korea's economic growth was based on export-led industrialization deeply networked into the globalizing world economy.[1] At the beginning of South Korea's industrialization in the 1960s and 1970s, women's employment was clustered into the low-wage manufacturing sector for export. Feminization of labor in export industries was a primary characteristic, and women workers were publicly recognized as the "industrial backbone" or "industrial soldiers" of South Korea's "economic miracle." In the 1970s various types of work-related human rights violations sparked women's labor union activism. Women-centered labor activists engaged in peaceful, radical, and militant tactics, and college students also joined with blue-collar, working-class women in their labor union activism. Significantly, women's labor activism has opened a new "strategic site" for women outside the private sphere (Sassen 1996; Bayes and Kelly 1998). Furthermore, women's labor activism and human rights movements further evolved into a critically important force in the acceleration of the massive scale movement for democracy of the late 1980s.

The years 1987–92 marked a monumental transition point for South Korean democracy when pressures from civil society forced the governing elites to redefine the society-government relationship. A highly centralized bureaucratic-authoritarian system, within which South Korea's hypergrowth economy had been pursued, was forced to open its boundaries to demands for participation. Consequently, a direct election system for president was reinstated and civil rights and civil liberties were expanded, which facilitated interest group activities. South Korea's transition to democracy has been held up as a proven example of Huntington's "Third Wave" democracy movement (Huntington 1991).

Social scientists in past years have begun to chart this "democratization" process (Choi, Sang-Yong 1997; Hahm and Rhyu 1999). Such efforts have assumed gender neutrality in theory and methods. As such they have failed to recognize the inputs women have brought to South Korea's democratization, as well as the impact the transition to democracy has had on women's participation in the public sphere. For example, women have been active in the labor movement but not in formal politics. Research to date also has not sufficiently examined the gender distribution or redistribution of social rewards, resources, power, sanctions, and responsibilities. Furthermore, mainstream social science has so far focused its analyses on macro-level, formal institutions of government and linkage politics; therefore, women's participation at the grassroots level in nonelective roles through which women mobilize for social change has been excluded. The relationship between women's economic and political participation has also failed to receive a primary research focus in South Korea's democratization studies.

Women's political participation, when measured by representation in the formal institutions of government, is extremely poor, largely unaffected by the highly acclaimed transition to democracy. Women's power in political institutions is by and large dependent on male patrons in power elite circles such as in government and parties. Outside the formal political institutions, however, women's political participation (i.e., labor activism in the 1970s) has been strong, even before the highly visible democratization movements of the late 1980s. During the transition to democracy, women's "street politics" were crucial (Yoon, Jung-Sook 1997). Women's nongovernment organization (NGO) political activism continues to expand both in organizational structure, social issue-raising, as well as in decision-making processes with positive results, even leading to policy changes. Women in South Korea have also shown increased levels of political consciousness concerning gender inequality as well as social injustice, demanding appropriate reforms.

Four questions are raised as to why this consciousness has not yet translated into formal political power. First, how has the transition to democracy affected women's political marginalization in representative politics? Second, how has South Korea's industrialization provided women with "strategic sites" for political opportunities, and what are the mechanisms mobilized by women? Third, how do women's civil organizations perform, and how effective are they in policy-making? And finally, how has women's political activism in South Korea been influenced by international feminism? This chapter examines these issues from institutional, legal, and political cultural perspectives.

South Korea's democratization did not occur in a vacuum. South Korea's outward-oriented and rapid industrialization has set the parameters of its polity; consequently, the gendered nature of democratization in South Korea has been contextualized by the globalization of the economy. Most significantly, globalization has dictated a rapid pace for political change. This has allowed the androcentric power structure to remain largely intact. South Korea's unique geopolitical situation as a divided nation has supported a militarism that has had ramifications for women. Confucianism, which determines social hierarchy based on class, gender, seniority, and officialdom, still dictates a male-oriented political culture in South Korea, albeit with a moderating gloss.

WOMEN IN THE MARGINS

The first constitution, adopted in 1948, allowed universal suffrage, guaranteed equality before the law, and created no formal legal barriers restricting women's political participation as voters and as elected officials. However, women's political space in formal government institutions has been extremely limited in every category, and their presence has been no more than token or symbolic in nature. In the executive branch of government, a little over a dozen women have served at the ministerial level since 1948, each with a brief tenure in office. Under a strong and paternalistic presidential system (applying both to authoritarian military regimes and civilian regimes including the current Kim Dae-Jung government), women political appointees were very vulnerable to political climate changes.[2]

Women's participation rate in the national level bureaucracy in 1996 was 13 percent. Of these, 98 percent were civil servants at lower ranks (below the fifth grade) without significant decision-making power. Local government bureaucracy shows a similar pattern of women's employment. In government committees, only 8.5 percent of committee members were women (in 1996), and they were clustered into committees on women's affairs and health and social welfare (KWDI 1997: 305–307). The judiciary has been the least accessible area for women. Until 1978, only 8 women passed the government-administered bar examination. Although the mid-1990s marked a rapid growth rate (thirty-one women passed the exam in 1994), underrepresentation of women was characteristic: between 1985–95, 3.9 percent (rose to 5.2 percent in 1995) of judges and 0.53 percent (rose to 1 percent in 1995) of prosecutors were women (Ministry of Political Affairs II 1995: 206–207).

Women's representation, measured by numbers of women in the National Assembly (NA), as shown in table 10.1, is very low, especially in an international context. Among the forty-three countries surveyed by Nelson and Chowdhury (1994: 774–775), South Korea ranked thirty-eighth. Women's poor representation is particularly ironic, given the slight majority of female voters over male (of the total of 31,488,294 eligible voters, women accounted for 50.8 percent or 15,998,015 persons in 1996). In contrast to the United States, however, only a narrow gender gap existed in voting turnout rate (in 1996, voter turnout rates were 65.3 percent for male and 62 percent for female) (Kim, Won-hong 1997: 8). Between the first NA (1948) and the fifteenth (which ends in 2000), as shown in table 10.1, women on average have represented 2.2 percent of the NA seats. Despite the monumental democratization movement of the late 1980s, women's representation in the NA since 1988 is a meager 2.6 percent of total seats, thus marking no real difference or improvement from the predemocratization era.

Political roles played by women NA members in South Korea further indicate their marginal contribution to women's political life at the societal level. Their legislative history shows that they were either uninterested or indifferent to women's issues, such as labor or family law reforms. Some were coopted by authoritarian governments with negative effects on women's interests or demands. Their roles were no more than tokenistic window-dressing. Women cabinet members have exhibited a similar pattern of behavior (Sohn 1994).

Table 10.1   Women in National Assembles in South Korea (1948–2000)

Nat'l. Assm.	Term	# of Women Representatives	Total # of Representatives	% of Women Representatives
1	1948.05–1950.05	1	200	0.5
2	1950.05–1954.05	2	210	1.0
3	1954.05–1958.05	1	203	0.5
4	1958.05–1960.07	3	233	1.3
5	1960.07–1961.05	1	233	0.4
6	1963.12–1967.06	2	175	1.1
7	1967.06–1971.06	3	175	1.7
8	1971.07–1972.10	5	204	2.5
9	1973.03–1979.03	12	219	5.5
10	1973.03–1980.10	8	231	3.5
11	1981.04–1985.04	9	276	3.3
12	1985.04–1988.05	8	276	2.9
13	1988.05–1992.05	6	299	2.0
14	1992.05–1996.05	7	299	2.7
15	1996.05–2000.05	9	299	3.0
	Total	**78**	**3,532**	**2.2**

Source: Lee, Bum-Joon & Associates, ed., *Politics and Women in the 21st Century* (Seoul: Nanam, 1998, p. 74).

An examination of South Korea's power structure and recruitment process reveals the structural barriers that women candidates face. For example, among the total 78 NA women members (thirteen women served two terms or more) between 1948 and 1996, only nineteen (24 percent) were elected directly by district constituencies whereas the remaining 59 (76 percent) were indirectly elected through the nonelected, party-nominated "national constituency" seats system.[3] The original idea of the national constituency system was first introduced by Park, Chung Hee in 1973 in the name of Yujong Hoi, which became an important tool to centralize presidential power, thus moving South Korea toward hard-line authoritarianism. Under martial law, the Yushin (Revitalization) Constitution was promulgated in 1972, allowing Park an unlimited tenure in power as president, enabling him to exercise emergency power at will as well as permitting him to appoint one-third of the NA members for Yujong Hoi seats. In addition, the president would be elected indirectly by an electoral college largely made up of hand-picked, pro-government individuals. The Yushin system was a huge setback for democratic ideals, which stunted the power and authority of the legislative and judiciary branches of government and the free competitive party systems as well. Manifestly, the Yujong Hoi was developed and evolved into the national constituency system to give proportional representation to society's diverse constituencies, such as business, media, arts, educational entities, and *yoseong kye* (the women's community). Latently, however, it was a cooptation tool used by government ruling parties to gain support for the authoritarian government's political agendas, which were often highly controversial, unpopular, or strongly opposed by the public. Noteworthy is that during the ninth session (1973–79), the first session after the introduction of the Yujong Hoi NA seats, the number of women NA members more than doubled (table 10.1), reaching a record high number of twelve, of whom ten were handpicked by the ruling party. During the hard-line authoritarian rule of Park, Chung Hee and later Chun, Doo-Whan (1980–88), women's representation rate in the NA was consistently higher than at other times, ranging from 2.9 percent to 5.5 percent. In the name of representing *yoseong kye,* a few elite women were selected by the ruling parties to serve in the national constituency seats. Most were not career politicians, nor had they political backgrounds such as prior experience in government offices or in political parties. Popular nominees were women college professors with Ph.D.s, or leaders of conservative women's organizations, which were often regarded in the public eye as pro-government organizations. Among the fifty-four women national constituency seat members of the NA, 39 percent were former college professors, whereas career politicians were extremely few in number (Chang and Kim 1995: 161–183).[4]

Political parties in South Korea have been correctly characterized as personalist, boss-centered, (nearly all are males), and androcentric and they have very weak mass membership bases. This applies to both government and opposition parties. Although women's party membership has increased remarkably over time—in the ruling parties, women's party membership rose from about 20 percent in the 1960s to 40 percent in the 1980s, and to 56 percent in 1995—women have no real power in party decision-making. In the ruling party, women in the mid-1990s accounted for between 4.4 percent (two women among forty-five high-ranking party officials) and10 percent (one woman among ten senior party advisors) of key decision-making posts (Ministry of Political Affairs II 1995: 201). Few women have been lucky enough to be selected to serve in the party's leadership roles, but their value is largely symbolic and with short tenure, especially when other important qualifications such as political fund-raising are lacking.[5]

Women party leaders in fact were often excluded by the male culture so dominant in South Korea's party politics. For example, many important party decisions would be made in evening meetings held at Kisaeng House,[6] male-oriented restaurants, or drinking places, which systematically excluded women. Informal rules are very powerful in Confucian political culture, and people are supposed to behave according to their social standing. Women party members must intuitively judge the situation and read male colleagues' attitudes to decide whether to be included, and this decision is very important for women's political survival.[7]

Furthermore, NA's national constituency seats for women were regarded as *Il-whoi yong* (one-time use only) by power holders and would be "disposed of" after one term—disposed of like Kleenex as some locals say. Incumbency in South Korea's legislative politics has not played a significant role, reflecting political instability. Between 1948 and 1996, the total NA membership distribution was 59.7

percent of first-term members; 22.4 percent of two-term members; and the rest were three- or more term members. Even when such a weak incumbency system is recognized, women NA members' legislative life expectancy has been shorter than males on average due to their dependency on patronage politics. Of those fifty-four women NA members from the national constituency category, about 20 percent served more than two terms (KWDI 1995: 170–184). Literally none of the women national constituency member of the NA continued their careers in district electoral politics. Barriers (e.g., party endorsement, fund-raising, voter hostility) are still too high for women candidates to challenge in the districts.

The military juntas of Park and Chun possessed weak political legitimacy due to their irregular seizure of power by military coup (1961 and 1980 respectively). To cope with their political legitimacy problems, they assumed hard-line authoritarian rule, adopted a highly paternalistic patronage system as a managerial tool, and focused on rapid economic growth as well as defense as primary policy goals. Park orchestrated the military's rise to the center of the power elite. South Korea under Park was characterized as a bureaucratic-authoritarian political system wherein political power was centered around the president. However, a centralized and powerful presidency emerged from what Fernando H. Cardoso (1979) calls a "pact of domination," a hierarchically structured symbiotic alliance among different subgroups in the elite circle (e.g., the military and the technocrats). Technocrats (e.g., scientists and economists), as junior partners of the military power elite, were rewarded under Park's patronage for their functional merits and political legitimization (Yoon, Bang-Soon L. 1992b: 4–26). Technocratic power was not only an outcome of Park's power but also an important element in the maintenance of Park's power, which suffered from a weak political legitimacy, for technocrats, as Lee, Hahn-Been (1968) calls "task elites," were essential to accomplish the developing state's economic goals upon which Park's own political legitimacy (the military coup) rested (Yoon, Bang-Soon L. 1992a). In building the bureaucratic-authoritarian "pact of domination," patronage was widely used to reward task elites and other selective groups in society (e.g., *chaebols*). Recruitment of a large number of intellectuals (e.g., college professors) to work for the public research and development system or government was another example.

Patronage is an important part of South Korea's political culture that has deeply permeated both the public and private sectors, government institutions, as well as political parties, and both men and women have been subject to it. However, the patterns of patronage show a gender difference. For males, their functional merit attracted the patron's attention as "task elites," whereas for women, sexuality per se appears as a crucial factor rather than their expertise. A few elite women were recruited as NA members (in the national constituency seat category) or party leaders essentially for their symbolic value, irrespective of their functional merits. For example, although women college professors have been sought-after targets of political recruitment, their "Kleenex tissue paper" role clearly indicates their value is no more than tokenistic. Informal rules are also forceful in patronage politics, as one feminist activist put it: "For women to be recruited by male patrons in the government or political party, they should somehow appeal to that male patron—either due to their physical beauty or other character such as being smart—without losing femininity, and so on. Anyhow, you should be liked by the male patron to be selected. Money is another important criterion."[8]

Despite the fact that male "task elites" were institutionally recognized by power elites as junior partners, women elites under the patronage politics system lack such recognition. Their identity is blurred, and they do not have their own power bases for further career development in politics. In sum, while patronage has played a crucial role in the inclusion of women in the formal political sphere, few elite women have been selectively admitted to government and political party organizations on their own initiation. Almost all have been beneficiaries of gendered patronage politics. Therefore, their space within formal institutions has been very vulnerable. When gaps arise between the government's agenda and women's agenda, these token women often sided with the government transmitting government values to the society rather than the reverse. This gendered structure facilitated very few opportunities to promote women's interests and to expand women's political space at the societal level.

Since the late 1980s, however, women NA members have played more positive roles in transmitting a women's agenda into decision-making as is exhibited by passage of some important laws concerning women. This issue will be discussed later. Furthermore, since the early 1990s, there has been an increasing awareness among women voters regarding women's political participation in government institutions, and the political community (e.g., politicians, political parties) seems to be more responsive to women's interests. As a product of the democratization movement, there have been many reforms in the electoral system. Direct election for president was reinstituted, and the autonomy of local government was restored in 1991. In the recent local elections, the number of women running for local government council has increased although their success rate is still low (in 1995, women elected officials at city- and province-level government legislature was only 5.7 percent) (KWDI 1997: 305).

INDUSTRIALIZATION AND THE LABOR MOVEMENT: OPENING STRATEGIC SITES FOR WOMEN'S POLITICAL PARTICIPATION

Globalization of the world economy influenced women to become politically active both in and outside of formal political institutions. Particularly, women's political activism in nonsystemic spheres vastly expanded, challenging traditional gender orders and altering gender relations or what Connell (1987) calls the "gender regime." Of particular interest is the way women, who would otherwise be silent or inactive in politics, have become politically active. Literature lists three situations that served as instruments for women to become politically active, thus leading to gender regime change (Bayes and Kelly 1998; see also chapter 9, this text): when motherhood (e.g., family and reproductive responsibilities of women as nurturers or protectors of family members' welfare) has been challenged due to outside forces; when women's labor force participation raises the political consciousness of women as seen, for example, in the labor movement; and when gender orders of a given society are challenged by international standards. This latter type of gender regime change is "through a politics of international recognition," as exemplified by various codes as well as resolutions of the various UN conferences on women. Analyses of South Korean women's political activism outside of formal institutions confirm the above theses. Such analyses also suggest we look closely at the dynamic nature of women's entrance into public space, their struggle as well as the limits of such political activism to function as a conversion machine to gain formal political power.

The global economy has had a tremendous impact on women's work and on women's political activism in South Korea. The initial surge of women's employment took place in the 1960s when the government aggressively launched industrialization plans, and henceforth there has been positive linear progress in women's employment. The labor force participation rate of women of fifteen years old and above steadily increased so that nearly 50 percent of women now work outside the home. Women's employment in the 1960s and 1970s was primarily in the low-wage, low-skill-based export manufacturing sector, and unmarried young women were a major labor force. In 1960, of the total female labor force, only 6.3 percent of women worked in the manufacturing sector, but in just the two decades of Park's export regime, the number swelled to about 22 percent (the male versus female ratio rose from 73:27 in 1960 to 64:36 in 1980). Within the manufacturing sector, women's work was highly concentrated in low-wage and labor-intensive processing or assembly industries for exports such as textiles, clothing, leather processing, and fabricated metals. As of the 1980s, 71 percent of women in the manufacturing sector were employed in such industries (Kim, Soo-Kon, 1984, 19–21). Such feminization of export industries was the direct result of South Korea's export-led industrialization strategies, and young, unmarried female workers with low education levels were aggressively drawn into the labor market in order to take competitive advantages in the international division of labor. Female workers were particularly preferred for their willingness to work for lower wages (Cho, Seehwa 1993, 96–97). Female workers in fact worked longer hours for less than half of males' wages (42 percent in 1975, 44 percent in 1982). Since the late 1970s labor shortages in export industries have opened up employment opportunities for married women in the manufacturing sector. Over time, South Korea's tertiary sector industry also expanded remarkably, absorbing large numbers of women workers.

The "feminization of clerical work" phenomenon visibly emerged in South Korea in the 1970s, and women's inflow into the service industries became a major feature of women's work outside the home. In 1996, 57 percent of the total number of clerks, service workers, and shop/market sales workers were women, and of the total women employed, temporary work and part-time work accounted for 53 percent and 78 percent respectively (KWDI 1997; Yoon, Woo-Hyun 1998). The clerical women's labor movement of the 1970s and 1980s, focusing on sex discrimination, was an important element of the women's labor movement in South Korea, which positively resulted in many legal reforms in women's favor.[9] The impact of globalization of the South Korean economy on women workers once again captured social attention in the past few years when South Korea experienced an economic crisis followed by the International Monetary Fund's (IMF) bailout in the late 1997. Massive scale economic restructuring took place in order to meet the IMF's guidelines, resulting in a harsh blow to women's employment, particularly for married women workers. Newly emerged was the IMF *Chonyo* (IMF Maidens), referring to those married women workers who disguised their marital status or to those unmarried single women workers who postponed their planned marriage to avoid layoffs. The IMF Maidens situation nonetheless energized women's NGOs to focus on women's labor issues, demanding legal and policy reforms for gender equity in employment (Korean Working Women's Network 1997, 1998; *Hankuk Yeosong Minwoo Hoi* 1998).

The early stage of South Korea's industrialization was based on a developmental state model wherein government played centralized, interventionist, and directive roles (Yoon, Bang-Soon L. 1992a, 1992b). It was the bureaucratic-authoritarian government under several military regimes that empowered the *chaebols*, a unique product of the South Korean model of political economy,[10] whereas workers were put under repressive labor controls through various policy measures (Launius 1984, 1991; Lee, Young-Hwe 1989). Government had a tight grip on controlling organized labor as well as other organized interest-group activities (e.g., student demonstrations) by using both ideological and physical tools: anti-communism as an ideological device (Lee, Hyo-Jae, 1989, 1996) and highly brutal police forces as a physical tool. A special law was passed in 1971 that prohibited organized labor unionization and banned any labor activities in foreign-invested firms. This occurred around the same time that the government promulgated foreign capital investment laws and that export-processing zones were created to lure transnational corporations. Inasmuch as the women workers constituted a majority of the workforce in foreign investment factories, women workers were hardest hit. In the Masan Export Processing Zone, largely based on small-scale Japanese capital, 60 percent of the laborers were women (Lee, Hyo-Jae 1989, 265). Government labor policies placed further restrictions using national security as an excuse (anti-communism) to limit workers' rights to negotiation and collective bargaining, and labor-management disputes were to be resolved by government-led reconciliation methods, which in effect provided preferential treatment to big business such as the *chaebol*. Big business further manipulated labor management using sex differences in wages, promotion, job classification, retirement age, and so forth.

Gender implications of the statist model and the *chaebol*-controlled economy are significant. Women's employment opportunities and the pattern of women's employment were directly affected by government's export-led policies and structural changes in industrial sectors, which ironically provided the basis for the women's labor movement. Cho Soon-Kyoung (1994, 284) notes:

> Since the 1970s, the continuous growth in the employment of women has been the material base for the development of the women's labor movement. Their specific problems as women workers (equal pay for equal work, protection of motherhood, the right to labor, equal advancement between sexes) can occur only under the condition of employment. If women are blocked from participating in wage labor, these issues can barely be raised. This indicates that hereafter the development of the women's movement in Korea depends on the maintenance and growth of women's employment.

Unlike the popular image of Asian women, whose femininity, motherhood, sexuality, passivity, docility, and hard-working nature at the workplace may capture the observer's immediate attention, female factory workers were at the forefront of industrial labor activism in South Korea. Particularly in the mid-1970s until the democratization movement in the mid-1980s, the industrial labor movement was sustained by female factory workers who stood against exploitative working conditions (e.g., poor wages, hazardous work environments, and violation of human rights), repressive labor policies, and abusive government agencies such as the police (Lee, Hyo-Jae 1996, 263–267). Despite their roles as *Sanop* or *Suchul Jonsa* (industrial or export soldiers) euphemistically praised by the export regime and corporate leaders, young women factory workers' wages barely allowed a subsistence living (Cumings 1997: 370). Their struggles were threefold—against repressive government, against management, and against male labor union leaders who, often coopted by government, suppressed women workers' demands (Launius 1991). Young women factory workers in the export industries were a true vanguard of industrial labor activism, and they contributed to the eventual collapse of the military-authoritarian regime of Park, Chung Hee and to the massive democratization movement in the 1980s. The Y. H. Trading Company's (manufacturing wigs and garments) women workers' labor activism in the late 1970s is a good case in point. When the company planned to close due to mismanagement, women workers seized the leading opposition political party's building (lead by Kim, Young-Sam Park). A women worker's death caused by excessive use of physical force by police ignited larger anti-government social unrest (labor and student demonstrations), particularly in Seoul, Masan, and in Pusan, where the opposition leader Kim's political home is based. Disputes among President Park's entourage over how to handle such social unrest led to Park's assassination by his own intelligence director in 1979, which ended Park, Chung-Hee's eighteen-year tenure in power and terminated the anti-democratic Yushin system. Young women's struggle for factory workers' rights was more powerful in overthrowing the Yushin regime than any other social groups or NA members.

Women-centered labor activism in the 1970s stemmed from many factors. First there was the feminization of the export industry. For an export-regime, sensitive to the changing nature of international labor markets, a feminized labor force in the export sector was functionally necessary to maintain South Korea's comparative advantage via wage control or limit on labor unionization. This situation made women workers "semi-proletarianized," and they became ever more vulnerable to structural changes of the world economy and positioned in unstable employment status on the margins of society (Chang, Kyung-Sup 1995). Labor control in the export industries or other strategic industries, such as steel, oil refinery, machinery, shipbuilding, and so forth, was crucially important for the sake of a stable supply of workers, and at the deeper level, for maintaining regime stability for these power elites (e.g., Park, Chung Hee and Chun, Doo-Whan) who suffered from lack of political legitimacy. Second, although women workers lacked other resources of power with no support from outside their social class (e.g., middle class, women's organizations), collective bargaining was a viable tool to fight for their rights and improve their working conditions.

Significantly, women industrial workers brought new agenda items such as rights and equality issues that had been lacking in South Korea's traditional women's movement. They also introduced new tactics in the women's protest movement and further opened new political space for negotiation with the government and male power holders (business owners) for reforms with positive results in many cases. Due to government's tight control on labor, throughout the 1960s and 1970s, labor protests occurred infrequently (about one hundred cases each year), but they were militant once they occurred. Women's labor activism occurred within this context and it has several characteristics. First, South Korea's labor movement in the 1970s was characterized by production line factory women, especially in labor-intensive, feminized export factories. The death of a male worker, Chun, Tae-Il, who self-immolated in protest of abusive labor practices by his company, in the Chunggye garment industry energized the female garment industry workers' labor union movement. Chun's mother, Lee, So-Sun, a housewife, emerged as the leader in organizing labor activism in the garment industry. Her leadership role in labor and human rights continues to the present in collaboration with other mothers whose sons and daughters became political activists for social reforms. As some other highly visible cases indicate, women-clustered export industries were the main arena for women's labor movement: Haetae Cookie Company (1972), Dong-il Textile (1972–78), Taekwang Industry (a sweater factory, 1973–74), Bando Trading (garments, 1974–81), Y. H. Trading Company (1975–79), Namyoung Nylon (1977), Chonggye Union (garments, 1980–85), Wonpoong Union (worsted and woolens, 1980–92), and Motorola (a U.S. firm, 1987–88).

Second, in terms of protest strategy, women's labor activism often became very militant, adding new tactics to women's conventional protest movements (e.g., peaceful marches, signature-gathering, letter-writing, and public hearings). In some cases (the Y. H. Trading Company and Dong-il Textile), women laborers even took off all their clothing to block the riot police forces and corrupt male labor union leaders.

Third, women's labor protests took place in isolated, sporadic incidences involving a relatively small number of workers organized locally at the individual factory level. Due to legal barriers, coalition building with other social groups, or industry-based, larger-scale strikes were virtually impossible. And yet, women workers were determined, exhibited solidarity as workers, and were class-conscious. Company-run dormitories were important "strategic sites" for labor meetings without interferences from the management, and for building class-consciousness.

Fourth, the women factory workers' labor struggle is significant in that it raised such issues as rights and equality. While lacking a feminist consciousness, they clearly demanded worker's rights and nondiscriminatory equality at work (e.g., against sex discrimination in wages, promotion, job classifications). Some of their claims were met positively. In the Haetae Cookie Company, women workers' demand to reduce working hours to eight hours a day was accepted by the management (Lee, Hyo-Jae 1996: 269). Women laborers' agenda for rights and equality are, as a matter of fact, new to the women's movement in South Korea. Throughout its long women's movement history, focal issues were nonwomen-specific, larger social issues such as nationalism, anti-colonialism, national independence (during the first half of the twentieth century), liberation and anti-communism (particularly during the post-war era), and democratization and national unification (in recent decades). Women's campaign for their own rights and equality did not emerge until the early 1970s when industrialization became a new social agenda and there were larger numbers of women wage-earners. Women's work experience outside the home increased women's workloads as workers and mothers, for a supportive system for motherhood (e.g., child care or elderly care centers) did not exist. Women's struggle against urban poverty (e.g., slum area housewives' anti-redevelopment demolition struggle), together with the farm women's movement (e.g., to protect their cattle or crop prices from imported items), has also contributed to adding new agendas to the women's movement (Lee, Hyo-Jae 1996).

Fifth, women's global factory work places clearly became part of a new political space. Most factory workers were migrants from poverty-stricken rural areas whose political interests found no place in South Korea's formal political institutions, nor would these interests be articulated via social organizations (e.g., women's organizations). Many work-related improvements, while far from ideal, were obtained through their own struggle, at their own initiation, and with little support from outside their work system. Women's organizations prior to the 1980s were conservative and elite- and middle-class-centered, with little support given to the women workers' labor movement. There was no evidence of political women working to improve workers' rights. They lacked a feminist consciousness. Furthermore, as elite women with a different class standing, they sided with government rather than with workers. Workers had nothing with which to bargain, for the majority of women obtained NA seats through patronage politics, not by direct election by voters. So far, not a single woman in the NA had blue-collar, urban poverty, or farming backgrounds (for male NA members, it is also very rare). Fellow male union members insisted on a male-dominant gender hierarchy in the labor union activism. The women's labor movement, however, was assisted by outsiders who educated them to develop a class consciousness for the labor struggle. Those actively involved were activist religious groups with international connections such as the Urban Industrial Mission (UIM), a Protestant group deeply involved in the Chonggye Garment Workers Union protests, and the Catholic Jeunes Ouvriers Chretiens (JOC), also known as the Young Christian Workers. In addition, college students' night school was heavily involved in raising worker consciousness. UIM and JOC, in addition to their pastoral activities, provided education on labor laws, labor-management relations, and labor leadership for union activism. Thanks to UIM's education, women's labor organization membership grew visibly from 24.4 percent in 1970 to 36.7 percent in 1989, and the number of women assuming labor leadership roles also increased (Lee, Hyo-Jae 1996: 268). The JOC, a Maryknoll church-related activist organization, also provided women workers with leadership training, particularly through the *Tusa* (fighter) system, focused on union activism. The Night School system is a "counter-hegemonic workers" educational program that emerged in South Korea that was run by church groups, college student activists, and labor unions to develop working-class consciousness, culture, and an identity to serve the labor movement (Cho, Seewha 1993, 2–3).[11] Usually located in church buildings (thus safe from government intervention), the Night School originally began to educate youth working in factories. Gradually the Night School became radicalized by student teachers from the colleges interested in social reform and functioned as a stepping stone in the late 1980s and early 1990s for college student activists to join the labor force *incognito*. Nonetheless, the Night School functioned as a liaison between the workers and intellectuals, and that coalition-building was an important element of South Korea's democratization movement. Although both male and female college students taught at the Night Schools, there were more male teachers than female. Overall, the major constituencies of these labor education programs were young female workers (Cho, Seewha 1993). Inasmuch as religious organizations were involved, women workers felt safe and were able to develop a class consciousness free from government surveillance. Even the Korean Central Intelligence Agency could not figure out whether it was religion or communism that influenced women workers to be labor activists (Ogle 1990).

Since the 1980s South Korea's labor activism has shown a new pattern. Male workers in the heavy and chemical industries emerged as central figures, and a "masculine" character surfaced in terms of scale, militancy, organizational development, and leadership. Parallel to male-led labor activism was the alliance of intellectuals and workers in a joint labor movement. Within this framework, college- students, both male and female, would take a leave of absence from school to work as factory workers. Their goal was to raise working-class consciousness and help organize labor union activism. The government's dealings with college-student labor activism have been gender-specific by using sexual violence against women (e.g., rape, fondling, stripping of clothes, and other types of sexual assault), whereas male students would be conscripted for compulsory military service with short notice (all males above eighteen are subject to this and serve for over two years). Physical torture is a commonly used method in police interrogation, but sexual violence was used only against females as a state device to control women labor activists as well as women student activists. This issue will be discussed further shortly.

WOMEN'S MOVEMENT AND DEMOCRATIZATION

The women's movement in South Korea has evolved because of Korea's particular history of colonization, division of the nation into North and South at the end of the war, modernization, and democratization. Its ideological orientation, issues, organizational structures, and strategies, as well as membership, are reflective of these peculiar and political contexts over time. Of particular interest is the kind of issues raised and why, and how they are linked to institutional politics. A brief review of the women's movement since the post-war era is in order.

Unlike Western democracies, Korea lacked the experience of an evolution of a democratic civic society that focused on values such as individualism, equality, and political and economic rights. Due to colonization (1919–45) and partition (1945), national independence, liberation, as well as patriotism occupied the center stage of women's movement during the first half of the twentieth century. In the post-war era, when nation-building as well as law and order became fundamental policy goals, women's activism focused on narrow issues (e.g., anti-communist education) within a strong anti-communist ideological framework. Women's organizations also became the object of political mobilization (e.g., to join with various social reconstruction projects after the Korean War, to create a women's unit in the army and police, to participate in the government-sponsored anti-communist rallies, and so forth). Government outlawed the Chosun Women Alliance, the main women's organization since the colonial era, as left-wing women took control of the organization and membership grew to 800,000 in 150 branch offices. The Korean Women's Organization was created by the government and was filled with right-wing women (Chung, Hyun-Back 1997: 23). Such government intervention only allowed anti-communist positions, thus limiting women's issues. Social reform–oriented issues such as justice, rights, equality, or class were hard to raise within this political context. Women's suffrage in South Korea was given as a gift by outsiders (under MacArthur's military government after the end of World War II, the first constitution was drafted) in contrast to the United States, where women had aggressively fought for it for over half a century. Women's organizations in South Korea grew out of this unique context of pro-government and anti-communism, receiving financial aid from the government. From the outset of women's activism, the government used women's organizations as a tool for political mobilization. The tradition of objectifying women and mobilizing them for the government's purpose carried into later years with significant implications for gender politics in South Korea. Women became the major subjects of political mobilization in the New Community (*Saemaul*) Movement in the 1970s and 1980s, in government-organized anti-communism rallies, and in election campaigns by political parties (many of the women mobilized were paid per diem). The government-sponsored the New Community Movement, started by President Park, initially aimed at rural modernization, spread all over the nation covering a wide range of social life, such as education, business, politics, and culture, became the first major tool to mobilize a massive number of women into the political process. Residents in every district would have *Dong* (lower administrative unit of government) -based *Saemaul* meetings, and women were the major participants.[12] These meetings were crucially important for the government in mass mobilization to deliver the government agenda as well as promote ruling-party political candidates during election campaigns.

The women's movement in the 1960s was by and large led by few leaders without mass membership. Its weak organizational structure and funding allowed some leaders to "privatize" the organization (i.e., by becoming a major funding source, leaders used the organization for their personal interests rather than promoting organizational interests), or to be coopted by government. As a matter of fact, female political appointees in the cabinet, government committees, and NA members in the national constituency seats have been selected from this pool of women by power elites in the government and political parties. Such an organizational situation not only created disunity between the leadership and the rank-and-file members, but also made it difficult to raise such issues as women's political rights, human rights, gender equality, and workers' rights as supreme agenda items, particularly given South Korea's authoritarian political system. The women's movement in the 1960s was "conservative" with issues limited to certain areas (e.g., consumer protection, self-help, and friendship), and often women's activities were government "guided" (e.g., sponsored). Women's organizations did almost nothing to raise social consciousness or political awareness regarding women's status or women's rights (Lee, Hyo-Jae 1996).

The first major breakthrough in South Korea's women's movement took place in the 1970s and was caused by four factors that are internal and external in nature. Internally, first of all, was the women workers' labor struggle (as noted earlier). Second, the repressive political system of the Yushin era was challenged by the student protest movement that demanded democratization and the guarantee of individuals' basic rights. Thus, "radical" elements were added to traditional and conservative women's groups activism. Third, in academia, women studies courses were offered allowing young intellectuals to be aware of gender inequality and feminist-consciousness. And externally, the UN Women's Conference (1975 in Mexico), and the UN declaration of the Decade for Women allowed women in South Korea an international perspective via, for example, comparative data gathering. Women college students began to join with the broader democratization movements in the 1970s and began to work with women industrial workers in the labor union activism. Women student activists also helped industrial workers to raise their social consciousness and to reexamine their human rights situations. Some of them further joined with other established women's organizations such as the Korean Church Women United and challenged the government's sex tourism policies (Yoon, Bang-Soon L. 2000).

The political situation in the early 1980s under another military junta of Chun, Doo Whan, however, did not allow mass-based social activism and it adversely affected the women's movement. In the late 1980s a new regime headed by Roh, Tae Woo began to allow some increased freedom of speech and association. The wave of people power was too strong for political rulers to suppress the public demand for democratization. The latter part of the 1980s was characterized by a massive "democratization" movement in South Korea. Student workers, intellectuals, and middle-class citizens participated in this reform movement, often in violent protests. Male and female students, in particular, exerted significant power.

Democratization as a political process involves two distinctively different components: transition to democracy and consolidation of democracy (Huntington 1991). South Korea in the late 1980s marked a great transition, moving from bureaucratic-authoritarian to democratic rule. The initial transition to democracy in South Korea no doubt expanded more people's input in the formal political realm. The consolidation of democracy, which involves internalization, practice, implementation of rules and institutions, and even the establishment of democratic political culture, however, is far from complete, particularly from a gender equality point of view. Nonetheless, women's involvement in South Korea's democratization movement was significant in the successful transition to democracy, and it opened a new era for the women's movement by adding new dimensions to its agenda, strategies, organizational structures, and developing collaborative working relationships with government institutions.

Women's activism was most significant in the following areas. First, new "progressive" issues were raised, focusing on human rights such as anti-torture against social activists or political dissidents, anti–sex torture against female activists during police interrogation, and freedom of speech. Second, women's "street" politics strategy propelled the anti-government, democracy movement with wider mass support from the society. Two incidents contributed to the successful transition to democracy in South Korea: Kwon In-Sook's sex-torture (1986) and the death of Park Chong-Chul (1987). In both cases, women's organizations played crucial roles. In the former case, Kwon, a female college student activist who disguised herself as a worker to enter the factory in support of the labor movement, was sexually assaulted by police during investigation of her "anti-government" activism. With the support of women's organizations and 166 human rights lawyers (the largest defense team ever formed in South Korea's judicial history), Kwon was released from jail while the police officer was imprisoned. This case was monumental in challenging state power, which used sexual assault or "sex-torture" as a control tool only against females during police investigations, reportedly since the late 1970s. Such gender-specific control mechanisms that surfaced in Kwon's case angered the public and raised public awareness about the relationship among state, sex, and gender. Women's activism in sexuality issues as well as growing public awareness has helped to reveal the infamous imperial Japanese wartime sexual slavery case with some positive results (Yoon, Bang-Soon, L., 2000).

The Park, Chong-Chul case, involving the death of a male college student from water torture by police, and its cover-up also exposed the government's abusive power. When Park's death was not reported in the local media, which was under government control, some women activists leaked the news to the public by demonstrating in front of the National Security Planning Board, thus energizing a full-scale, mass-based anti-government protest movement for democracy. Together with another monumental demonstration case organized by women activists such as "the Day for Banishment of Tear Gas" (June 18, 1987), women's activism on human rights issues propelled South Korea's democratization movement (Yoon, Jung-Sook 1997). Third, small-scale, single-issue-based women's organizations were mushrooming during in the early part of the 1980s, such as "Another Culture," "*Pyongwoo Whoi*," "Countermeasures Committee for Women Worker's Right to Live," "the Countermeasures Committee against Sexual Torture," and "Women's Coalition Boycotts against Payment of Viewers' Fee to the Korean Broadcasting System," against government control of media (Yoon, Jung-Sook 1997). Moreover, they created an umbrella organization for coalition. Made up of twenty-four small-scale, single-issue "progressive" or "radical" women's organizations, the Korean National Council of Women (KNCW) was created in 1987 and played a crucial role at many different stages of South Korea's democratization movement (e.g., Kwon's sex-torture, Park's water-torture case, and the anti–tear gas campaign) with clear agenda items. KNCW's activism focused on human rights as the central issue and demanded the reinstitution of the direct election for the presidency (Yoon, Jung-Sook 1997).

Fourth, women's organizations worked closely with international women's organizations and built coalitions with the outside world (e.g., UN networks, Christian church women's organizations, and international seminars such as Women and Tourism organized by the Korean Church Women United in 1988). These entities effectively worked to bring some women's issues onto the policy agenda later (e.g., Korean's government's welfare program for the survivors of the Japanese wartime sexual slavery and other women-friendly legislation).

Despite the fact that women's activism outside formal political institutions has been crucial during the transition to democracy, no visible progress is noticeable as yet in women's representation in the government, political parties, or in economic decision-making. Women's NA membership in the immediate postdemocratization period clearly shows no improvement at all (table 10.1). The failure of women's grassroots activism to be linked with representation politics may be explained by two reasons. First, as noted above, one of the salient features of the South Korean model of democratic transition is what Huntington refers to as a "transplacement model" (Huntington 1991). Within the framework of the predemocratization era power structure, government, and elites, virtually all males survived the democratic social transition and maintained the status quo. Furthermore these power elites also maintained the peculiar form of androcentric political culture throughout the process of democratic reform. More civilians have been added to formal politics; some former anti-government political opponents entered into government institutions; two longtime major political opponents, Kim, Young-Sam (1992–98), and Kim, Dae-Jung (1998–current), even became presidents. As yet, such change is within the existing male power structure, with little redistributional effect for males and females. As a matter of fact, key political leaders who control government and political parties are the same male figures who have been in power since the 1960s (Kim, Jong-Phil, a military officer who joined Park, Chung Hee in the 1961 military coup, later serving as prime minister and in other important posts, is the current prime minister under Kim, Dae-Jung), or 1970s (former president Kim, Young-Sam and the current Kim, Dae-Jung). It is as if the U.S. politics of the 1990s were still under the leadership of Lyndon Johnson, George McGovern, or Richard Nixon. Transition to democracy weakened military power to a degree, but under the current unstable party system, civilian politicians, both ruling and opposition parties, still need the support from the old-time military elites (due to regional politics). At the most, while the transition to democracy has consolidated men's power with some changes, it has little impact on the redistribution of power between men and women in political space, for women have never been real members of the power elite club in South Korea.

Second, the women's movement per se is also responsible for the failure to convert women's grassroot power into formal political power. Women's activism has since the 1970s focused on democratization and rights issues, such as workers' and human rights, but their agenda was broad-based, not specifically focused on women's situation as women. The lack of feminist consciousness was a characteristic of the women's movement in the 1970s and 1980s regardless of whether a person was involved with traditional "conservative" organizations or "progressive, radical" organizations. When democratization was a larger social issue, women's activism was more influential. Yet, when it came to women-centered issues, few gains were obtained. This issue is particularly significant given South Korea's "transplacement" model of democratization, and man-centered political system as well as patriarchal political culture. Women's organizations pursued a nonpolitical involvement and a separatist strategy. KWAU, for example, had regulations to restrict its members from joining political parties (Yoon, Jung-Sook 1997: 15). Furthermore, there were other restrictions that have discouraged members from pursuing interests in formal politics:

> In the 1987 presidential election, some leaders of KWAU who were involved in the "critical support" campaign for an opposition party [UDP] were strongly criticized by most of the member organizations in its general assembly in 1988. A chairperson of one member organization, who individually supported the People's Party [the radical party] without open discussion with its members, was forced to resign by members of the organization. After these dissents, even though leaders and staff members have personally supported different political parties, the issue of the engagement with political parties has been restrained. (Yoon, Jung-Sook 1997: 15)

It was not until the early 1990s, that women's organizations aggressively began to seek women's representation in formal politics, as local governments were allowed to elect city council members and local legislators directly. Beginning in the mid-1990s, KWAU departed from its earlier nonpolitical, separatist position by supporting its leaders for political candidacy. Among the three NA members from the KWAU leadership since 1987, for example, two left for the NA without formal approval from the KWAU, but in 1996, former KWAU president Lee, Mi-Kyung was officially approved by KWAU to become an NA member. In policy-making processes, women's organizations, both "conservative" and "radical," often worked together for legal reforms or institutional changes related to women's issues. Coalition building based on feminist consciousness has become effective with many legal reforms. Most significant women-friendly legal reforms have been promulgated within the past ten years: the revised Family Law (1989), the Equal Employment Act (1989 and 1995), the Basic Law on Women's Development (1995, 1996), the Mother-Child Welfare Act (1989), the Childcare Act (1990), the Special Act on Sexual Violence (1993, 1997), the Nationality Law (1997), the Special Law on Punishment of Family Violence Crimes and the Law on Prevention of Family Violence and Protection of Victims (1997). The Basic Law on Women's Development, in particular, recognizes the importance of NGOs' role in achieving gender equality. Based on this law a Women's Development Fund was created, as well as the First Basic Plan for Women's Policy (1998–2002). But the law failed to integrate fully diverse voices of women's organizations as well as lacked an implementation mechanism (Choi, Young-Hee: 1998). In the case of the Equal Employment Act, it was abruptly passed by the NA in order for the ruling party to win in the presidential election (Cho, Sungsook 1988: 3). Nonetheless, these legal changes provide the context from which further legal reforms or policy changes may take place in the future.

CONCLUSION

In South Korea, women have been poorly represented in formal political institutions, whereas women's activism outside the formal political space has been strong. Women's extremely marginal representation is associated with the peculiar power structure of South Korea, which has systematically excluded women in terms of formal representation. The bureaucratic-authoritarian, patriarchal nature of the political system and the developmental state model have joined to keep women powerless in the formal political sphere. Furthermore, personality-centered politics, the patronage political system, and an androcentric male culture were additional factors keeping women politically incapacitated.

Nonetheless, in the extra-systemic area, women's political participation has been significant in South Korea. The main impetus was the globalizing South Korean economy as well as its developmental state. The growth of women's employment became the basis of women's labor struggle. Women's labor activism has clearly opened a new political space for women, primarily in raising issues. Actual policymaking, however, began much later, beginning in the late 1980s when larger numbers of women joined in the democratization movement and raised women-specific social issues. The young women's factory industrial labor movement was crucial in opening new political spaces for women. Given the continuous growth of women's employment outside the home, labor-related issues will continue to capture women's attention in the near future.

As an export-dependent nation, global economic changes have been critical in determining gender relations in the workplace, leading to large political implications. The emergence of the so-called IMF Maiden clearly shows how women's work has altered as the global economic regime intervened and restructured local industry. The South Korean case reveals the connection between the global economy and women's power. The IMF Maiden phenomenon energized more women's groups to become engaged in public debates related to gender equity in employment issues, pressuring the government for policy reforms. Some policy changes have been made recently in favor of women, although they are far from complete. Such recent policy changes, however, became available through the organized efforts of women's groups and women politicians who became more gender-conscious and under the so-called women-friendly policies of President Kim, Dae-Jung. If the women-friendly theses are accurate, it may again confirm the patronage nature of the South Korean political system. With an absence of the president's interest, such policy changes may not be possible.

Lastly, this chapter discussed the issue of why women's contributions to the transition to democracy had virtually no impact on women's representation in electoral politics. In terms of power structure, South Korea's transition to democracy was based on a transfer of power among the already established male power elites; it did not open doors to include women. The nonpolitical, separatist strategy pursued by women's organizations has resulted in some influence for women.

Further research is needed on this process. In the past few elections, women's organizations have aggressively been involved in demanding the creation of a quota system, fair elections, and enlarged electoral districts with multiple-member districts and limited campaign spending. As yet, their impact on women's political representation remains limited. Nonetheless, the growth of organized women's groups at the NGO level, as well as government's positive responsiveness in South Korea (e.g., new women-friendly laws), suggests that both nonelectoral politics as well as electoral politics need to be included in social science research.

NOTES

1. The term "globalization" of economy is broadly defined inclusive of international economy, for it evolved over a period time into the global economic system, and its coexistence can be detectable.

2. In spring 1999, for example, Ms. Sohn, Sook, a leading actor, who was appointed as the Minister of Environment by President Kim, Dae-Jung, was forced to resign within less than two months in office. Sohn, as an outspoken supporter of Kim, was selected and yet her theatrical roles while in office sparked a controversy that no longer guaranteed Kim's patronage.

3. Under this system each party before the election makes a rank-ordered list of candidates, and the national constituency seats will be proportionally assigned to a party in correspondence with the percentage of seats that each political party wins in a direct election in districts. If a party wins 60 percent of the seats in its districts, then it wins 60 percent of the national constituency seats.

4. When a party is interested in recruiting women leaders, the recruitment pool is from the outside and the recruitment from the rank-and-file-members are extremely rare. Although about twenty-six women NA members in national constituency seats indicated their party posts on their resumes, only limited numbers have actual political experience either as party members or in government institutions.

5. Interview with Ms. Park, Young-Sook, Seoul, Korea, September 5, 1998. Park was a deputy chair of the leading opposition party led by Kim, Dae-Jung.

6. The *Kisaeng* House, similar to Japan's Geisha House, was a popular place for high-level decision making among politicians and corporate leaders, particularly in the 1970s. The visibility of Kisaeng House has diminished over a period of time as other forms of restaurants targeting male clientele emerged.

7. Former deputy chair of Kim, Dae-Jung's party said during an interview that in the beginning of her party leadership, she just accepted dinner meeting invitations. Later, she could figure out by looking at the name of the restaurant whether the place was for men or for both genders and, if the place was known for men's parties, she would excuse herself. On one occasion, during an NA official visit to Japan, a male party leader asked her not to join them for the dinner. Interview with Ms. Park, Young-Sook, Seoul, Korea, September 5, 1998.

8. Interview data in Seoul, August 1999.

9. Female workers, as commonly practiced in banks, were to sign a mandatory employment contract with a promise to quit their jobs upon marriage. A court decision in the

mid-1980s involving a female insurance company employee defined women's retirement age at twenty-five because women in South Korea customarily marry at age twenty-six. Gender-specific discriminatory retirement age requirements were commonly practiced in the 1980s in "women's jobs" across social sectors: twenty-eight-year retirement age for typists, telephone operators, assistant nurses; twenty years for elevator operators; twenty-five years for administrative assistants (Lee, Kwang-Taik 1989: 20).

10. The emergence of a corporate state, the *chaebol*, and South Korea's "miracle economy" are parallel. Government patronage politics allowed for the *chaebol*'s hyper growth, which in turn provided large sums of a slush fund for politicians. Two former presidents, Chun, Doo-Whan and Roh, Tae-Woo, were jailed for collecting astronomical slush funds, or in local terms "political governance money." Political corruption has been a serious problem for decades and it corresponds with the emergence of the corporate state in the 1960s.

11. As the "management-side counterpart" of the Night School, factory schools were created at industrial sites with a clear target of young factory production workers in labor-intensive export sector industries. Created in 1976, the factory schools were located within the walls of factories, attended by only factory workers, and would offer middle and high school curricula. The latent function is to isolate young female workers from militant labor activism by using education as a device. The factory school system was a tool of cooptation, although the educational benefits per se should not be discredited (Cho, Seewha 1993).

12. Multiple reasons explain why women became the major participants in these meetings. Such meetings required passive participation (listening to what government says), which is considered more suitable to women. Timing of such meetings were either in the daytime or in the early evening when a majority of males were working, and they were residence-based. Whatever is concerned with house or family is supposed to be women's affairs, not men's.

11

Transforming Governance Agendas: Insights from Grassroots Women's Initiatives in Local Governance in Two Districts of India

Suranjana Gupta

A CONSTITUTIONAL MANDATE FOR ENGENDERING GOVERNANCE

The constitution of India, adopted in 1950, directed all state governments to organize local governments and give them the powers necessary to govern effectively (Jain 1996). However, the decentralization and devolution envisaged in the constitution did not take place. The local self-governing institutions remained ineffective for a number of reasons. Elections to local self-governments (LSGs) were not conducted regularly, LSGs were dominated by privileged sections of the population, and neither finances nor decision-making powers had been adequately devolved to LSGs. In 1993 the 73rd amendment provided a mandate to strengthen the local governing institutions at all three levels of the district, the block, and the village.

Some significant features of the amended act as it now stands are as follows:

- The act states that elections should be held every five years to constitute the local governing bodies. In case of dissolution, elections will have to be held within six months.
- At all three levels seats will be filled by direct elections.
- At each of the three levels, a minimum of one-third of the seats will be reserved for women. One-third of the offices of chairpersons of the *panchayat* (the Hindi word for the local governing body at the village level) will be reserved for women. At all three levels, seats will be reserved for scheduled castes and scheduled tribes in proportion to their population in the state. In addition, the offices of chairperson of the *panchayat* would be reserved for scheduled castes and scheduled tribes in proportion to their population.
- The local governing body at the village level, the *panchayat* will be accountable to the village assembly, or *Gram Sabha*, which is comprised of all registered voters. The village assembly must be called at least four times a year.

- The act provides for a specially constituted Finance Commission in each state to devolve finances to local self-government institutions.
- The national and state governments have to provide adequate finances to allow LSGs to function properly. In addition, LSGs may also raise their own funds.
- LSGs are empowered to prepare plans for basic services and economic development, which they will also be responsible for implementing.

WOMEN, DEVELOPMENT, AND GOVERNANCE

Elections to LSGs brought 3.4 million men and women across India into local governing institutions (Government of India 1998). More than one million of these members are women, most of whom have entered the public arena for the first time. While women's presence in local government is necessarily the first step toward participation in governance, it can hardly be considered sufficient. As members of local governing bodies, elected women are expected to be involved in microlevel planning of health services, primary education, water, basic services, and infrastructure as well as poverty alleviation programs. This means building women's capacities to articulate their interests and to intervene in planning processes. Society ascribes a different set of roles to men and women, which in turn determine the different ways in which they contribute to and benefit from their living environment (Beall 1996). These differences frequently go unacknowledged within a "gender-neutral" planning process. Therefore, to impact the way in which resources are allocated, women must not only articulate their interests within the planning processes but they must also transform the planning process itself to make it more responsive to gender issues, while incorporating the values of democratic participation.

Putting Women's Concerns on the Agenda

In Latur and Osmanabad districts of India, a nongovernmental organization called Swayam Shikshan Prayog (SSP) is working with women to build women's capacities to participate meaningfully in governance. Already an alliance of organized women's groups and elected women have made some headway in changing the face of local governance.

Women's collectives have been responsible for accessing information on development programs from administrative offices and disseminating this information. They have assisted communities and individuals in accessing state resources earmarked for development. They are monitoring the functioning of primary health centers and primary schools. In recognition of the women's abilities to monitor and supervise the functioning of development programs, the district administration has ensured that women are part of the village-level vigilance committees monitoring fair-price shops that sell subsidized food, grain, and fuel. Women's collectives are also ensuring that the village assembly, a forum for civic engagement, is attended by large numbers of women. While women's presence in large numbers at these meetings is in itself a sign of women's empowerment, women have gone a step further by putting on record their demands for resources and services.

In short the women's collectives along with the elected members are ensuring that women's development needs are put on the agenda of governance. Support from communities is evident in their willingness to contribute their own resources for local development facilities, be they in the form of land, labor, money, or materials. In addition tax collections have increased significantly.

The perspective that informs the initiatives discussed here begin with the understanding that for women in poor communities, gender interests are inextricably linked to the allocation of resources. These concerns are only acknowledged and addressed when women articulate their priorities within institutional spaces and go on to negotiate greater access and control over resource distribution and use. Thus, efforts to include the poor, women in particular, in local governance necessarily involves addressing their access and control over resources and services. By addressing practical development issues of the community, many of which are traditionally male dominated, women's collectives are in fact addressing strategic gender concerns by entering new spaces, demonstrating their competencies to manage resources, thus renegotiating their roles within communities vis-à-vis the state.

Three elements are then at the heart of engendering governance:

1. Opening up spaces for women's participation, particularly in the context of local planning.
2. Building women's capacities to address local development agendas by articulating their concerns, interacting with other actors, building alliances among women's collectives, and managing local resources.
3. Creating new institutional arrangements that respond to the needs of poor women through partnerships with mainstream institutions. Arguably the most significant relationships in this case are the community-state partnerships.

Alliances Between Women in Formal and Informal Political Spaces

While the discussion on political participation appears to emphasize the presence (or absence) of women in formal political structures, there is growing evidence that elected women need the support of women's collectives if they are to voice women's concerns in planning.

In Latur and Osmanabad it is the alliance between women's collectives *outside* formal political institutions and women *within* local governing bodies that are emerging as the nucleus of leadership at the village level. It is this leadership that is spearheading the transformation of local governance. Without the support of women's collectives outside formal political spaces, elected women are often an isolated minority whose participation in decision-making remains tokenistic.

SAVINGS AND CREDIT GROUPS

The support for elected women comes from organized savings and credit groups. In India, savings and credit groups (SCGs) that have mushroomed all over the country have been instrumental in building women's capacities to intervene in local village-development issues. The SCG is a village-based association of individuals, usually women, who meet regularly to create a pool of savings from which members may borrow at terms mutually agreed upon. The SCG sets in motion two kinds of learning processes. The first has to do with collectively managing resources. Women learn how to handle a fund that is collectively owned. Loans have to be prioritized, funds must be accounted for, and interest rates must be decided upon.

The second learning process has to do with the mobilizing and organizing aspect of the SCG. The SCG has the ability to bring people together on a regular basis (since savings have to be collected regularly) and provides a space for women to share day-to-day problems. While men have many opportunities to interact at the village level, few such spaces exist for women. The women's SCG becomes a valued part of their lives not only because it provides access to credit but also because it represents a space that is owned by women alone.

The collective decision-making with regard to savings and lending activities enables women to learn about collective mobilization and management of resources and people, thus laying the foundations for the group to intervene in local development processes.

As women's groups mature they swiftly make the transition from addressing household concerns through credit to participation in the public sphere, where they address community issues such as water, sanitation, healthcare, poverty alleviation programs, and the public distribution system. The financial activities of these collectives provide women with both the confidence and the resource base to intervene in local development processes. For instance women have taken bridge loans from the SCGs for the construction of toilets as part of a government-funded sanitation program.

The capacity-building aspect of SCGs is critical here because very often dominant groups use the inexperience of marginalized groups to restrict their entry into planning and decision-making.

COMMUNITY-STATE PARTNERSHIPS: INSTITUTIONALIZING CHANGE

The involvement of large numbers of people along with building alliances with the state are at the core of strategies that seek to institutionalize women's partic-

Figure 11.1

Institutionalization

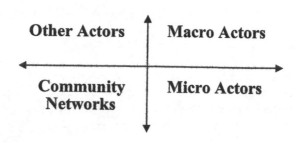

ipation in governance. Institutionalization is seen as the process by which routinized ways of functioning are created (Gurumurthy 1998) based on shared perceptions and practices that are independent of actors (UNDP 1997a). This definition translates into two areas for action: the first is creating a widespread network of community actors through horizontal learning processes. The other is eliciting support for women's initiatives from other actors in order to legitimize women's participation. At the micro end of this spectrum of "other actors" are village, block, and district officials; while at the macro end, arguably the most significant actor is the state (see Figure 11.1).

Partnership Between the State and Women's Groups in the Post-Earthquake Rehabilitation Process

In September 1993, the two districts of Latur and Osmanabad were devastated by an earthquake. The state-led rehabilitation program that followed focused on strengthening houses through participation of local communities. This became the starting point for a large-scale transition from rehabilitation to development. From the state government's standpoint the challenge was to promote community participation and to increase the stake of homeowners, women's groups, and communities in the rehabilitation program. It was apparent that there was an urgent need to get the government to create a more flexible approach that could accommodate the needs of communities. It was therefore essential to invest in creating mechanisms to facilitate information flow to and from community groups. Four hundred sixty-nine active women's collectives worked in partnership with the government, acting as mediators between communities and state officials to address housing needs of communities. As a result, communities took ownership of the rehabilitation program.

In the course of the rehabilitation process, women's groups undertook several tasks.

Information dissemination on earthquake safe construction techniques.

- Motivating households to participate in the program.
- Problem solving and grievance redressal for those who were unable to access the government funds or materials for the reconstruction process.
- Demonstrating collective construction and collective purchase of construction materials.
- Monitoring and supervising construction activities.
- Providing feedback to officials the district administration has endorsed, after having demonstrated their capacities to manage and supervise projects.
- Having demonstrated their competence in the activities mentioned above, state officials became supportive of the women's groups to run several other village-level development projects.

REORIENTING STATE OFFICIALS

The incentives built into bureaucracies demand that officials be primarily concerned with managing macropolicies (Zazueta 1995) and directives from "above." While there may be demands from below, there are rarely any incentives to respond to these. Even where macropolicies have created a favorable environment for grassroots participation in planning, frequently these policies are not reflected in operational mechanisms that enable information flow and dialogue between planners and local communities. Addressing this problem is one of the central challenges for those working toward more decentralized, democratic gender-sensitive governance.

From the outset it was evident that it would not be enough to simply train newly elected members—men and women—on fulfilling their responsibilities as local government officials. If they were going to function effectively they would require considerable support from other actors. Decentralized governance and all that it entails is as unfamiliar to district planners as to communities and newly elected members of local governing bodies.

THE TRAINING PROCESS

Capacity-building strategies designed to promote decentralized governance have therefore focused on bringing information to elected members as well as district officials. The training processes have sought to identify the new roles and new powers granted to local governments and their elected members and officials. This capacity-building also entails understanding what support the administration can provide at the various levels. The clarification of roles has led to the exploration of community-state partnerships in terms of what skills and resources each partner can bring to such collaborative relationships. Most importantly the training process sought to make visible gender concerns in local planning.

The SSP team, together with the district officials, designed a two-tiered program to train and orient elected members of 1,400 village-level governing bodies in two districts. In the first level of training a local resource pool of trainers was created by local officials comprised of technical personnel, women functionaries, and experienced women leaders. This resource team in turn trained elected members. The result was a local resource team in every village. Having interacted with officials in learning forums elected members became more confident of approaching them in the future. Field visits were also undertaken in order to showcase initiatives of women-headed LSGs and outcomes of women's participation in local governance.

ENGAGING WITH THE STATE

One of the greatest constraints to participatory planning is that there are no established systems and mechanisms for the state to engage with communities. This is all the more pronounced in the case of women. A block level (administrative units that make up a district with each block consisting of approximately one hundred villages) forum has therefore been designed to create opportunities for women's groups and elected women to interface with officials. The forum was used to provide feedback to officials, communicate problems, and put forward demands of the communities. For officials these forums represent an opportunity to widen their information base for planning since it draws people from so many villages. Such accurate information on user groups would otherwise be delayed and distorted when routed through "the proper channels." Such dialogue forums also play a significant role in consensus building on future programs and policies.

Interacting with officials in their territory is unquestionably intimidating for poor women because these spaces are usually male-dominated environments that are hostile to anyone who is an "outsider" to the system. For many rural women whose mobility is traditionally restricted, visits to administrative offices represent an empowering experience in terms of increased control over their mobility (Gurumurthy 1998). But for a few women these visits become the first step toward the "demystification" of the state. In a sense, they provide an elementary-level understanding of how state resources are administered, thus laying the groundwork for future advocacy efforts of women's collectives.

In the discourse on globalization it has been clearly recognized that groups adversely affected by recent global trends and those representing their interests often do not understand the new alignments and forces at work and therefore are unable to adequately address the problems emerging from these macrotrends. Less attention is paid to the fact that similar attempts to understand existing alignments and forming new ones have to be made at the microlevel if grassroots democracies are to function effectively.

A CRITICAL MASS OF ACTORS

Creating a widespread network or a critical mass of actors is an intrinsic part of reconfiguring institutional arrangements. Women derive tremendous strength from interacting with large numbers of women who are involved in addressing similar issues. The feeling of solidarity through regular interaction among women's collectives energizes them and enriches the learning process in that it expands the pool of experiences from which to learn. From an advocacy perspective, widespread participation is necessary to demonstrate the viability of community-based solutions to the state and to leverage resources and support mechanisms from the state to accommodate the needs of communities. While the state will often disregard the demands of a few, it can rarely afford not to engage with—or not to respond to—demands of larger numbers. State support is won not by coercion, but by the demonstration of large numbers of women's groups' abilities to scale up operations by mobilizing community support and managing local development projects.

HORIZONTAL PEER LEARNING

The most effective way for women to learn is through a process of collective analysis of their own experiences and those of their peers. When ideas and experiences are passed on through a community-led learning process, rather than a top-down nongovernment organization (NGO) led training process, each community tends to assimilate innovations and transfer learning in a unique manner, refining them to suit local environments. Most importantly, communities are prepared to take ownership of these new arrangements that they have been responsible for designing.

In practice, the commitment to horizontal learning and widespread networks of community actors translates into the creation of a variety of collective learning forums such as exposure visits, study tours, and information fairs. These learning forums have been effectively used for mobilizing women's collectives and increasing access to information and experiences, all leading to experimentation and innovations by women's collectives. For instance, most of the SCGs in Latur and Osmanabad districts have not been organized by an NGO-led training process but by a spontaneous learning process in which new groups have been mobilized and guided by the older, more experienced groups.

COMMUNITIES AS GATE-KEEPERS OF KNOWLEDGE

Involving women's collectives in development planning relies on the ability of women to build an information base that is owned by women. Where women are transforming development processes and setting precedents in good governance, these innovations must be disseminated through various means. Horizontal learning strategies where women learn from their peers are an attempt to retain community actors as gatekeepers of knowledge. Databases created by grassroots women's groups through supervision and monitoring of local services and participatory planning exercises can become powerful tools for negotiations with the state. Most importantly the knowledge base created by communities create a good base for planning.

VILLAGE ASSEMBLY: FORUM FOR CIVIC ENGAGEMENT

Organized women's groups have also been responsible for bringing large numbers of women to participate in village assemblies in large numbers. The village assembly is supposed to be held at least four times a year. In many villages where the local governing bodies had not called village assemblies, elected women and women's groups set a precedent by taking the initiative to calling the village assembly meetings to gain community support for various development programs they were initiating. By ensuring that the local governing body members attended participate, these meetings attained official village assembly status.

The village assembly has been effectively used by women's collectives to voice their concerns by raising questions and demands related to fund allocations, basic needs, and infrastructural facilities for communities. This forum is being used to ensure that elected members take action on resolutions passed at previous village assembly meetings and to disseminate information with a view to consensus building on development plans. In effect, the presence of women's groups in the village assembly represents civic engagement with local governments, through which communities are demanding greater accountability and transparency in governance.

EXPANDING PARTICIPATION

In the context of the state, participation continues to be a somewhat nebulous term, open to reinterpretation by different state agencies. But underutilized budgets, unmet targets in development programs, and pressures from donor agencies to fulfill "participation" requirements compel the state to involve women's groups in development programs. However, their involvement is generally in the form of implementers who will ensure efficient service delivery, rather than as potential planners and decision-makers who will redesign development programs and then run them. Many women's collectives, however, have accepted these terms of engagement. They have used their participation in government programs as an opportunity to build their capacities by learning about the program and understanding the administrative hierarchy that manages it. Once familiar with the officials and the program, women have provided constructive feedback on how programs can be modified to benefit them. In doing so women's collectives have expanded their own spaces for participation. This in turn will provide new learning opportunities and feed into the creation of new terms of engaging with the state and more meaningful participation in governance. Each learning loop strengthens women's abilities to negotiate the planning process and to claim a space for women in the domain of governance, demonstrating that they can indeed be worthy allies, rather than just beneficiaries in development planning.

Women's initiatives in addressing practical gender concerns facilitated by SSP point to the fact that women's participation in governance is gradually moving from mere presence in public spaces to a consolidation of their position as legitimate actors in planning and decision-making processes. That this is being recognized by the state administration is evident in that a more demand-oriented approach to development planning is emerging. It is a process that is placing information, resources, and choices in the hands of women's groups. These women's collectives are being perceived as leaders who represent community interests. In short the women's initiatives in local development have created a dynamic process of negotiation through which grassroots women's collectives are building a new consensus in which women are being seen, not as passive beneficiaries, but as active partners in local governance.

12

Engendering the Japanese "Double Standard" Patriarchal Democracy: The Case of the "Comfort Women" and Military Sexual Slavery

Kinhide Mushakoji

DEMOCRACY AND DEMOCRATIZATION

Hidden clandestine sectors within "democratic societies" where undemocratic practices remain dominant set the limits to the process of democratization. In this chapter, using the sex sector of the global economy and the double standards of discourse that legitimizes it as my focal point, I argue that these limits to democratization can be removed only by engendering this process. This discourse, maintained by patriarchal power, tolerates in the sexual-slavery sector extramarital sexual activities of the masculine citizens, while stigmatizing the women exploited in this sector, thus enabling it to avoid recognizing that this sector affects the sanctity of the patriarchal family institution and the human rights of women. In these hidden sectors, the critique of the undemocratic nature of masculine institutions is diverted from them to women in the sex sector. These women become personalized targets who receive unjustified stigmatization in place of the institutions victimizing them. I will clarify the epistemological structure of the double standards discourse supporting this hidden sector of gender-based enslavement and discrimination through an analysis of the discursive space of the "Comfort Women" debate that took place in Japan in the 1990s. This debate was a rare occasion when sexual slavery was brought into the arena of public debate. This debate consisted of three opposing positions, each of which proposed different solutions informed by different discourses. This example reveals the importance of deconstructing the double standards discourse. I complete this deconstruction by combining the universal formal discourse drawn from the Enlightenment that is exogenous to the non-Western world with the personalized and engendered version of the endogenous discourse of "caring." This chapter is written with the basic conviction that all hidden sectors where gender and racial discriminations are practiced by the "democratic" state and civil society should be divulged and deconstructed.

The ethical standards of democracy remain embedded in the implementation of universal values and due processes that have provided legitimacy to modern nation-state democracies. Modern states, such as *Rechtsstaaten*, welfare states, and national-security states, have helped promote human rights, human development, and human security. Nonetheless, one must recognize that none of these states has fully implemented the democratic ideal. In fact, a close look at all "democratic" states reveals hidden sectors that are so well integrated into these "democratic" societies that anti-human-rights and anti-democratic behaviors are tolerated. In most cases, these hidden sectors are not the creation of bad people. Rather, they are cultural patterns built into the sociopolitical system that enable even the most "advanced democracies" not only to tolerate their existence, but also to coexist and draw profits from them. The process of democratization has gradually divulged these hidden sectors, eliminating some of them and internalizing others. The colonial empires, such as those of the United Kingdom and France, were democratic in basic electoral terms within their own territorial borders, but contained numerous undemocratic, colonial societies, especially in Africa, Asia, and Latin America. Decolonization eliminated colonialism but perpetuated neocolonial relations. Traditional forms of slavery, such as that of nineteenth-century United States, have been abolished; but other contemporary forms of slavery, such as bonded slavery accompanying trafficking in women and children, still exists.

Within those societies that have otherwise reached a stage of democracy that observes universal principles of human rights, rule of law, and governmental accountability to its citizens, democratization can be understood as a process of exposing, deconstructing, and eliminating the remaining, hidden undemocratic sectors. The contradiction between the ideal and these sectors is why the study of these hidden sectors provides a good entry point in understanding the process of democratization itself. The mechanisms that permit the occlusion of these hidden sectors establish double standards that enable proclaiming universal democratic values of freedom and equality while legitimizing the existence of the occluded sectors and the creation of exceptionally discriminated social categories (Mushakoji 1997).

Democratization is not only a process of establishing electoral and representative systems of governance, it is first and foremost a process of human liberation. Carole Pateman (1996: 5–12) has noted that to assume that democratization ends when a formal institution takes a democratic appearance is incorrect. In her presidential address at the 26th World Congress of the International Political Science Association, she specifically discussed the questions of "Democratization and Democracy" and how the exclusion of women as political actors was occluded by the mores of the time. She also noted how particular political methods related to "democracy" depend on citizens having basic elements of personal security. She insisted on the following two points: (1) "The argument that democratization, rights and citizenship required radical changes in the relationship between men and women within marriage and within other institutions, began in earnest long before, in the 1790s. . . . Yet even today, all too few students are taught this tradition of political argument" (pp. 7–8). And, she also stated that (2) "Much of the controversy about the character and meaning of democratization centers on social equality, but even the minimal conception of democracy as a political method agrees that security of the person is fundamental to the operation of the political method. Whether the method operates successfully in this respect is an issue that requires more attention than it receives from political scientists" (p. 9).

Pateman's analysis highlights the importance of paying more attention to an expansion of our understanding of democratization as an integral part of democracy if we wish to promote gender equality. The feminists in the twentieth and even in the eighteenth centuries raised the issue of gender equality and equity, not only in elections but also in marriage and other "private" institutions. For them, democracy had no meaning unless the democratic methods and institutions were able to guarantee the security of women. At the turn of the twenty-first century, a majority of political theorists understand that marriage remains one of the most visible institutions still needing to undergo a process of democratization. But, the sexual slavery institutionalized in the prostitution sector is barely recognized as a problem requiring special attention in the process of the democratization of societies. It remains the most hidden institution where the security of women is not guaranteed and where the state and civil society persist in occluding the reality of their insecurity. Sexual slavery is one of the most undemocratic hidden institutions built into contemporary democracies still requiring "democratization."

The debate in Japan of the 1990s about state compensation to the "Comfort Women," the victims of military sexual slavery instituted by the state of Japan during World War II, provides an opportunity to examine the hidden clandestine nature of this institution and its foundation on a particular epistemological occultation. This contemporary public debate in Japan provides us with clues about the epistemological structure of this socially constructed system of occlusion. This blatant violation of women's rights has been brought to public attention and has raised the question of whether the state should assume its responsibility and make compensation to the victims, or whether it should be volunteers among the Japanese people who would contribute "atonement money" to them. The debate provides a good occasion to study the different interpretations of the discourses about military sexual slavery, and more generally about sexual slavery in general. It helps us find how this hidden clandestine sector of society practicing sexual slavery can continue to exist in societies asserting basic universal democratic values. In the exceptionally serious case of the "Comfort Women," the contradiction between the prostitution sector and democratic values becomes clear, while in "normal" situations it remains unseen and unnoticed.

This type of public debate did not occur in Europe during or since the Enlightenment during that continent's process of democratization even though formal universal values of human rights were proclaimed. The different agencies that worked for democratization in this period converged in demanding the creation of a legal state that would be in the service of the citizens and the civil society composed by them. The law was the chief tool in the hands of the people, and through them in the hands of the state, to enable democratization. According to the French Constitutionalists, the state was supposed to build *règles de droit* (rules of law) grounded in the *idées de droit* (ideas of the law) and thereby establish the necessary means to enforce the rules using the power of the state, the only modern institution with the legitimate monopoly of coercive force. Through such application of the *idées de droit*, the state was supposed to eradicate the undemocratic patriarchal discourse present in the traditional societies and contribute to the elaboration of *gesellschaft*-like human relations and social institutions (e.g., human rights and free market economy) (Burdeau 1949).

This process of democratization has spread all over the world as this message was transmitted as part of the colonial message of the Western powers. The democracy movement has built a powerful coalition of different "modernizing" social strata that have led the process of decolonization and of democratization. The struggle between the democratizing forces and the reactionary supporters of the traditional discourses continues. The process of democratization, however, is now taking different forms, and the state and civil society in different non-Western countries are the loci of different processes of hybridization combining the *gesellschaft*-based modern discourses with *gemeinschaft*-like traditional discourses. The "Comfort Women" debate reflects this hybrid situation existing in many non-Western societies where the traditional moral discourse of charity, sympathy, and caring coexist informally alongside the formal ethical/legal discourse about individual universal rights (Bowden 1997). This ethics of "caring" has served the purpose of opposing despotic rule through the creation of more humane caring relationships within communities. This *gemeinschaft* set of ethics became the target of systematic attack by the forces of Enlightenment and democratization, because it uses a patriarchal discourse and avoids questioning the absolute power of traditional rulers.

The most common formula undergirding democratization in twentieth-century democratic societies combines formal public institutions based on a democratic universal discourse with private informal institutions supported by traditional discourse. This combination together enables societal members, especially men and women, to behave toward each other according to an ethical double standard. As already noted, the discourse undergirding this double standard is informally based on traditional discourses about good *gemeinschaft*-like human interactions of charity, sympathy, and caring. Such double standards create democratic states with a set of universal norms and a set of due process rules that coexist with a society composed of members with moral sentiments addressing specific situations where not only are some undemocratic actions tolerated but also sometimes even recommended privately in spite of the public legal constraints. These constraints imposed by the modernizing state typically follow the tradition of the premodern patriarchal state and are often perceived in non-Western societies as only coercive. The modernizing bureaucracy, on its side, applies law, or the *règles de droit*, because it is what the modern state is expected to do to be recognized as "civilized." This application of the *règles de droit* is therefore done with no reference to the *idées de droit* that have been developed in the West and still lack effective support in the non-Western society.

The *règles de droit*, even understood as a legal embodiment of corresponding *idées de droit*, as has been the case in the North Atlantic democratic states, have gradually lost their utopian function of leading democratization processes and have turned into constitutional norms supporting the status quo of the existing democratic state. This trend has gradually turned the concept of the "rule of law" from an ideology of "democratization" into a concept that is used by the Western industrial democracies to legitimize their hegemonic pressure on the nondemocratic states of the non-Western regions. Inside the "democratic" societies of the North, feminists and spokespersons for other socially oppressed groups have been developing a critique of this formal democracy. In the eyes of these "outsiders," discrimination is maintained in the private and informal sectors of the formally democratic society. Public life is controlled by the universal, formal *règles de droit*. Once a liberating force, these rules of law are increasingly powerless to transform the discrimination in these sectors and to advance the dignity, rights, and identity of the oppressed living within them. A strong need remains for developing a different process of democratization even in the more advanced, industrial democracies. Particularly with regard to women, the formal democratic institutions of the public sector exist, but anti-democratic tendencies still remain strong.

As already stated, two ethical standards, one formally democratic and the other pragmatically undemocratic, currently characterize the contemporary form of democracy. For democratization to occur, first we must develop a social and political process to promote the universal *idées de droit* that will activate the *gesellschaft*-like formal sector of the civil society. This development will reestablish the universal *idées de droit* as the foundation for the currently petrified *règles de droit*. Second, for this democratization to proceed we must develop a democratic discourse that directly opposes the undemocratic discourses of the informal *gemeinschaft*-like institutions. Only by means of this double-pronged approach will positive social movements be able to address the structural and ideological forces currently enabling victimization and oppression within society's occluded sectors.

The "prostitution" sector of contemporary society represents not only a case of serious violation of the fundamental rights of the prostituted women and girls. More generally, this sector is an especially interesting case revealing the two ethical standards that lead to the lack of resistance of twentieth-century democratic societies to undemocratic tendencies. The coexistence of two ethical standards and discourses facilitates the justification of sex industries as a necessary evil in spite of the fact that they are institutions enslaving their victims in opposition to the fundamental values that have led, in other sectors, to a fairly successful process of democratization (Truong 1990).

In the name of such fundamental values, state compensation to the victims of state-run military sexual slavery would be self-evident. Even if sex industries were tolerated as a necessary evil, a state-run public brothel, an institution enslaving women from colonies and militarily occupied territories would be an unacceptable violation of individual women's rights requiring state compensation. Consequently, if such values actually prevailed, any debate about such enslavement would focus on whether the reported violations had taken place and on the legal aspects of compensation. The debate would not focus on whether such compensation should involve the state or the people of the responsible country. In Japan, however, a traditional discourse does exist and it has led to a different approach to the "Comfort Women" issue, a discourse that ignores this modern discourse attempting to apply the universal logic of human rights. The traditional discourse does not insist on universal human rights and state compensation toward those whose rights have been violated by it. This traditional discourse has existed in Japan since the feudal age when some enlightened people wanted to "humanize" the patriarchal social order through a religious/moral insistence on charity, sympathy, and caring toward the needy members of the community with no reference to their intrinsic rights and entitlements (Hanochi 1997, 1998). The opposition of these two discourses, which is common to all the non-Western countries engaged in a process of modernization and Westernization, helps clarify the double-standard epistemology defining the prostitution sector as both a public institution and a hidden private sector.

The "Comfort Women" debate deals with a special wartime situation that does not necessarily implicate the private, prostitution sector. However, the continuity between the state-run "Comfort Women" military sexual slavery and the private commercial sexual slavery is an integral part of this debate, and therefore, it has created a discursive space where the "Comfort Women" case is embedded in the broader debate on the contemporary sex industry and prostitution sector in Japan where the exploitation of women from East and Southeast Asian countries continues even though it is now conducted by private interests and not by the state (Hanochi 1998).

The initial reason for denouncing the state of Japan for its institutionalization of the "Comfort Stations" was discrimination against women from the subjugated, less-developed countries dominated by the military supremacy of Japan, either as colonies or as occupied territories. The recent development of the Japanese globalized sex industry has provided a more current major focal point of deep concern among post-colonial and anti-discrimination opinion leaders, who find that the contemporary form of industrial sexual slavery is a sexist and racist exploitation of the women from Japan's economic sphere of influence, quite similar to the "Comfort Women" exploitation of women from Japan's militarily occupied territories.

THE CASE OF THE "COMFORT WOMEN":
SEXUAL SLAVERY BY THE JAPANESE MILITARY

The state-run military sexual slavery case known as the "Comfort Women" is a case where the state of Japan used its power as colonial ruler and/or as military occupier to institutionalize a military brothel system, "recruiting" by abduction, deceit, and other constraining means women and girls from its colonies and occupied territories to work in the military brothels established and run by and for the Imperial Armed Forces. In this case, the usually clandestine sector of sexual slavery became a state institution. This institution was based on a blatant violation of the fundamental rights and dignity of the victims. In this situation, the victims, declared by the Universal Declaration on Human Rights to be "born free and equal in dignity and rights," were discriminated against and exploited by the Japanese military personnel within state-run brothels called "Comfort Stations." That the state of Japan explicitly created and sponsored these brothels, modeled on the traditional public brothel system, makes the action especially unacceptable and illustrates in an extreme way the commodification of women by the Japanese state and society.

The Japanese society, more precisely its male members, have to face the fact that traditional, ethical double standards legitimizing the prostitution sector in general and the public brothel system in particular have helped justify this blatant abuse of women's rights. The Japanese state, according to the universal principles accepted by all modern democratic states, must be held responsible for this state-run military sexual slavery, that is, for the "Comfort Stations" and the "Comfort Women." The responsibility of the Japanese state and people has become the object of public debate after half a century. All these years, the existence of the "Comfort Women" was vaguely known but was occluded from public awareness. The victims were ashamed to disclose their past due to the stigma of prostitution. This is a direct consequence of one side of the double standard discourse that stresses the exclusive role of the patriarchal family institution as having a monopoly on legitimate sexual intercourse, thereby facilitating treating women in prostitution as "bad women." Only when the debate in the United Nations about women's rights and violence against women, especially during armed conflict, drew public attention did some of the victims get the courage to speak publicly. Members of various feminist movements also began to demand state compensation from the government of Japan for the victims. The case triggered a public debate in Japan that helped externalize the different value judgments about sexual slavery hidden in the minds of Japanese citizens.

The position of the Japanese government was that international law does not require the state of Japan to pay compensation to the "Comfort Women." The government tried to pacify the objections raised by the advocates of the "Comfort Station" victims in their own countries as well as in Japan by setting up an Asian Women's Fund. Through this fund, the Japanese government supported distributing to the victims atonement money collected from Japanese citizens, while simultaneously denying responsibility for compensating the victims. This support created a strong dissatisfaction among many citizens who had launched a movement to help the victims. The movement leaders decided to crush the fund. In their eyes the fund had been built to justify the government policy of avoiding state compensation and public recognition of state wrongdoing (Yoshiaki 1997: 38–45). This institutionalized violence against women by the state itself was not just a crime committed by it, but also involved the Japanese civil society, since the "Comfort Stations" were a variant of the public brothel system, the hidden sector of the Japanese society where the males in this highly patriarchal society still practice sexual slavery. Although the form of the brothels and their regulation by the state varied in different regimes and historical conditions, the essence of the system is longstanding. The case of the "Comfort Women" is not only an act of the state that requires compensation; it is also the consequence of an institutionalized practice of sexual slavery that continues to thrive in contemporary Japan. The practice of sexual slavery is daily becoming a more and more serious ethical and pragmatic issue as the sex industry becomes increasingly globalized and more widespread.

To define in a purely legalistic manner how the Japanese state and civil society must cope with the case of the "Comfort Women," with state-run military sexual slavery, is insufficient, for the case requires coming to terms with the private sense of discrimination and stigmatization of the victims of the sexual slavery caused by the patriarchal Japanese culture. Unless a new discourse of caring for these victims triggers a transformation of the attitude of the Japanese vis-à-vis the prostitution sector, state compensation will only strengthen the stigmatization of the women in prostitution. The compensation will be made because the "good women" of the colonies and occupied territories of Japan were forced to become "bad women," not because their human rights were violated.

In the case of "prostitution" the two ethical standards enable accepting the institution as a necessary evil and not unjust as such, while simultaneously stigmatizing the women in prostitution as "bad women." Under such ethics, occultation occurs. The wrong committed to the victims, "good women" turned by force into "bad women," should be redressed, but the institution, brothels called "Comfort Stations," were not considered bad in themselves, if they had "normal" "bad women" (i.e., women in prostitution) working there. The national sense of morality operating within the institutional framework of the existing state order is unable to recognize that its policy of creating the "Comfort Station" institution is questionable and unethical. Instead, the double standard promotes the view that the victims should be compensated, but the state should not be penalized. According to the above-mentioned traditional discourse on charity, sympathy, and caring, the stigmatized and brutalized women become the objects of sympathy and atonement, but this discourse denies any links with a universal discourse on rights and responsibilities. The opposition between the public legal position and a private sense of sympathy and caring constrained by conventional double standards about prostitution has led the debate into a complex exchange of statements based on different discourses reflecting particular interests and beliefs. This exchange, as well as the facts of the situation, creates an ideal case for analyzing the double standard regarding the hidden sector of prostitution and sex industries not only in feudal imperialist Japan but also in the "democratized" Japan of the post–World War II period.

Put in its historical context, the "Comfort Women" case involving state-run military sexual slavery can be described as follows. In the latter half of nineteenth century, modern Japan developed a new domestic order corresponding to the requirements of a modernizing capitalist state with a cohesive and expansionist orientation. The state-regulated brothel sector was a clandestine and yet important unit of this domestic order. Meiji Japan was built as a patriarchal, capitalist, state-controlled society unified by the emperor. This patriarch was the mediator and integrator of the familial/capitalist, developmentalist Japanese society; and the society was one that created a gender division of labor with a production sector dominated by its male population, a reproduction sector where women were forced to play the role of wives and mothers, and a third brothel sector where sex slaves were provided to the male population as a bonus and an encouragement to their productive activities.

The state of Japan throughout its modern history skillfully used the patriarchal male-centered double standard on trafficking and prostitution in order to strengthen its domestic and external power as a modern state. First, the domestic political economic structure of modernizing Japan in the latter half of the nineteenth century maximized its capacity to produce goods indispensable for its industrialization by developing a well-integrated and docile masculine labor force and a parallel traditional patriarchal family structure enabling it to reproduce this docile masculine labor force through equally docile wives/mothers.

This division of labor between factories and families was complemented by the public brothel system that served as a "safety valve" by permitting extramarital sexual satisfaction for its masculine labor force. When Japan began its external expansion through colonization and military aggressions, the same means was militarized in support of military "virility(!?)" and safety from venereal diseases as the Imperial Army invaded neighboring countries from the 1930s through the end of World War II in 1945.

The Japanese government created the "Comfort Stations" as a military brothel system. The victims of this prostitution system, the "Comfort Women," and the ethical issues involved were concealed from public attention after the defeat of Japan in 1945, while sexual slavery, which had turned into a growing commercialized sex industry, prospered. In the early 1970s Japanese women concerned about the growing sex tourism toward Korea were told by their Korean sisters that a military version of sexual slavery had existed in the form of military sexual slavery before 1945 (Matsui 1997: 53–58). Already in the 1970s, Japan was exploiting the women of East and Southeast Asia in countries it was dominating economically.

The Japanese people were involved in this institutionalized gender violence and continue to be involved in it. The Japanese people, accepted and reproduced throughout their history a male-dominant, patriarchal, ethical double standard discourse that stigmatized as "bad" the women prostitutes involved in commercial prostitution while considering the existence of brothels and the extramarital satisfaction of male sexual needs a necessary evil for maintaining male morale and the strength of the nation.

In the Edo period, the public brothel system was a place where the masculine members of the society, irrespective of their status and rank, developed an "egalitarian" brothel culture called the *kuruwa* culture. In the modernizing Japan of the Meiji era, the government, which had adopted Western laws and formal institutions, maintained the public brothel as an institution useful for supporting the modernization and industrialization of Japan. Before the World War II defeat, this exercise in violence against women victimized both Japanese women and women from the countries colonized by Japan. Now that the public brothel system has been abolished, commercial, global sex industries have replaced it, exploiting women from a variety of developing countries. In this historical context of colonialism and neocolonialism, the debate surrounding the "Comfort Women" and military sexual slavery unmasks an ethical double standard that promotes sexist and racist exploitation of women within Japan's sphere of influence.

The "Comfort Station" was a wartime, state-imposed version of the modern Japanese public brothel system, different only in its brutal military aspect and its sponsorship by the state itself. Women as a group were the most affected of the victims of militarist Japan, which committed many atrocities and other violations of the human rights of the peoples in the regions occupied or colonized by it. Yet, many observers of Japan, both in its military and economic expansionist phases, ignored the crucial importance of the different forms of violence against women, especially as it was conducted in the prostitution sector of military and commercial sexual slavery, until the "Comfort Women" issue drew international attention and triggered a debate polarizing the Japanese civil society in the 1990s.

THE DISCURSIVE SPACE OF THE DEBATE
ABOUT STATE COMPENSATION

The debate about state compensation to the victims of the Japanese state-run military sexual slavery called "Comfort Women" and about the role of the Asian Women's Fund involved different discourses about the legal responsibility of the state and the moral obligations of the society. The "Comfort Women" debate interests us particularly because the discursive space created by the different discourses used in this debate helps us divulge and determine the complex epistemological construct that defines the prostitution sector. Setting aside the debate about whether state-run military sexual slavery did or did not exist (a debate that resembles the one on the existence of the Holocaust and has no direct implication to our concern on sexual slavery itself), the most important divide in the debate was about the legal and moral responsibility of the state of Japan and of the Japanese people.

This point has been made in an unambiguous manner by the UN Special Rapporteur on Violence Against Women, Its Causes and Consequences, Ms. Radhika Coomaraswamy.

> The Special Rapporteur sees the Fund, as created, as an expression of the Japanese Government's moral concern for the fate of "comfort women." However, it is a clear statement denying any legal responsibility for the situation of these women and this is reflected in particular in the desire to raise funds from the private sector. Although the Special Rapporteur welcomes the initiative from [a] moral perspective, it must be understood that it does not vindicate the legal claims of the "comfort women" under public international law. (Report of the Special Rapporteur 1996: Para. 134)

This statement helps identify and classify the three different positions taken by the Japanese government and by different sectors of the Japanese civil society in the debate over state compensation and the Asian Women's Fund. These positions differ, as we said already, in terms of their interpretation of the legal and moral responsibility of the state of Japan and of its citizens.

The first position is officially proclaimed by the Foreign Ministry of Japan, which denies any legal ground for state compensation vis-à-vis the victims of the state sexual slavery. The Foreign Ministry argued that the state of Japan deals only with other states and cannot enter into legal rapport with victims without negotiating with the states with which Japan has already completed state-to-state compensation (with the exception of North Korea). The government additionally asserts that it can only be bound by international conventions and treaties signed prior to the sexual enslavement of the "Comfort Women." Those signed after the fact cannot be applied. Since no state commitments existed at the time of the "Comfort Stations," to claim compensation now represents a retroactive application of legal obligations. This argument does not negate the universality of human rights as legal norms. It simply does not recognize the universality of human rights qua *idées de droit*. Such recognition would make possible a retroactive application to itself of the idea of crimes against humanity, which would include crimes related to violence against women exercised by states during violent conflicts (Iwamatsu 1998: 93–140). The Japanese state position is a legalistic one that ignores the *idées de droit* underlying the concept of state compensation and instead insists on a narrow legalistic interpretation of the *règles de droit*. It is a typical legal approach of non-Western states that have introduced rules of law with no prior process of democratization having generated the new *idées* for the new *règles*. Such discourse represents the formal side of the double standard discourse on the prostitution sector. This discourse recognizes the legality of prostitution without establishing the rights of the women who are exploited in it. The denial of any responsibility to give compensation to the "Comfort Women" victims is logically correct so long as one adopts this discourse.

The second position was taken by movements and intellectuals critical of the government policy (including myself) who considered it essential to safeguard the universal application of human rights by having the state of Japan assume full responsibility for past violations of the fundamental rights of the "Comfort Station" victims (Nihon no Senso Sekinin Shiryo Centre 1999). Those upholding this position believed that state compensation to individual victims was not only a valid practice but also an act of rectification expected from any responsible party, whether a private person or a state. Not to recognize that states could deal directly with private persons, as was practiced in the European Human Rights Regime, was to deny that human rights norms could apply to states in any situation. From the perspective of the second position, military sexual slavery was a crime against humanity that could and should be applied retroactively. Furthermore, because Japan had ratified the 1923 Convention against trafficking, the Japanese state had already recognized prostitution and sexual slavery as illegal when the Imperial Army instituted the "Comfort Women" enslavement policy. This position, in spite of its call for compensation for blatant abuses of human rights, did not advocate that the state take moral measures of atonement to try to transform the Japanese patriarchal, ethical standard that still promotes sexual slavery (Sengo-Hosho Jitsugen Campaign 1996). The need for the Japanese state to give compensation to the victims of the military sexual slavery it institutionalized is legally self-evident, especially when one refers to the *idées de droit* on human rights, especially women's rights about violence against them. This discourse, however, leaves undefined the exploitative nature of the prostitution sector and the loss of dignity of the women exploited in it.

Within this second position compensation might have to be given to "good women" who were forcefully degraded to become "bad women" in prostitution. However, such compensation would be required by the state only because the state had used its power to coerce women into state institutionalized sexual slavery. The state would not be held responsible in those cases where states tolerate and only regulate such institutions. The second position does not force the issue of the state having to assume the responsibility of omission, that of not protecting women's rights as human rights. Such an omission appears less serious than the responsibility of commission of forced sexual slavery by the state of Japan. In my view, however, such an omission needs to become the concern of the international community. This is especially the case for military-base sexual slavery regulated by the base authorities.

The third position was held by those who supported the government's decision to establish the Asian Women's Fund, which would be paid for by private citizens and organizations but would allow the Japanese government to avoid making state compensation. The Ministry of Foreign Affairs under the instruction of the socialist Prime Minister Murayama invented this face-saving compromise to appease the politicians while keeping intact the position of the government bureaucracy. The Ministry of Foreign Affairs held that no legal grounds existed for state compensation, but that the government could establish a fund to receive donations from the Japanese people to express their desire to apologize to the victims. This formula was a skillful move to avoid assuming state responsibility. The fund payments were a clear replacement for state compensation and would foreclose any further objections to the Japanese government's decision to refuse giving compensation to the victims. Supporters of the second position, however, argued that this use of the fund implied that a state's legal obligations, based on universal rights, could be replaced by legally meaningless acts based on a moral concern. This replacement of a universal *idées de droit* by a personalized sense of "caring" was unacceptable for the second position.

The government, which never did revise its position, took a decision contradicting itself by establishing the Asian Women's Fund as a concession to the third position with the support of citizens who did not necessarily recognize the legality of the government's refusal to give compensation, but who wanted to express their sense of guilt and sympathy to the victims of the military sexual slavery. Many of them believed that since state compensation was unlikely, the minimum moral obligation of the Japanese people was to express their deep feeling by giving the victims atonement money. A sense of urgency to take some measures to support the victims whose age did not permit further delay supported this action. This was a natural conclusion to be drawn from their discourse emphasizing personal "caring" of each of the individual victims.

Practically all the supporters of the fund available for contact did not believe in the formal argument that state compensation is a necessary condition that should logically precede any moral measures. Many recognized the need of state compensation but placed greater importance on the need to develop a humane discourse expressing guilt and the will of the Japanese people to compensate the victims at least partially. In contrast to the holders of the second position, a few lawyers and law professors preferred the more humane "caring" approach of the Asian Women's Fund to the Western universalist legal argument demanding state compensation. Many of the supporters of the Asian Women's Fund preferred to define the case of the "Comfort Women" as an unfortunate case of gender violence caused by the combination of specific cultural and historical circumstances. Their discourse was, thus, basically a *gemeinschaft*-like private one, stressing charity, sympathy, and caring on the personal level.

We have already stressed the fact that this discourse is quite different from the formal, universal, *gesellschaft*-like discourse of those who demand state compensation. "Atonement" is a concept belonging to a *gemeinschaft*-like moral discourse, quite different from the concept of "compensation" based on an *idées de droit* of formal and universal rights calling for state responsibility. The distinction between a legal measure based on the concept of responsibility and a moral measure based on a vague sense of guilt combined with a sentiment of sympathy is not clearly perceived by most of the supporters of the fund (Sengo-Hosho Jitsugen Campaign 1996, note 6).

The advocates of the third position did not negate the universality of human rights norms, but tried to develop a personalized nonconfrontational moral discourse without either denying or confirming the validity of the *idées de droit* proclaimed by the holders of the second position. They neither rejected nor accepted these ideas as the basis of the *règles de droit* regarding state compensation as the holders of the first and second positions did. For the supporters of the fund, it was important, if not sufficient, to take an action of moral atonement, which was undoubtedly akin to the human rights discourse, to the extent that it emphasizes, as does the Universal Declaration of Human Rights, "the spirit of brotherhood" (and sisterhood?!) (Onuma, Shimomura, and Wada 1998). The position of the supporters of the Asian Women's Fund is in line with the universal *idées de droit* of human rights, but it does not support its formal universal application in the form of *règles de droit*. "Sisterhood" is in their case personal and informal and overlooks completely the legal responsibility of the state. This third position uses a discourse directly inherited from the premodern *gemeinschaft*-like ethics that attempts, as we saw before, a rectification of the despotic rule of imposed law, through a patriarchal benevolent ethics of "caring."

The supporters of the fund avoided contesting the legal arguments of the Japanese Ministry of Foreign Affairs that deny the need for any legal measures that would recognize the responsibility of the state of Japan. Unlike the confrontational proclamation of the legal responsibility by the holders of the second position, those who hold the third position take a noncritical attitude vis-à-vis the government. By avoiding a discussion of the issues of the legal responsibility of the state of Japan, their highly moral discourse resembles so many status-quo–oriented discourses that appeal to the conscience of the power holders rather than making universally valid demands in a confrontational way.

The exclusion of the imperative requirement of state compensation from the third-position discourse has a definitely negative effect on human rights promotion and democratization. It helps the government of Japan in its attempt to divert world public opinion from the question of state compensation to the "Comfort Station" victims. The state is, nevertheless, the target of verbal attacks by the Japanese right-wing movements who deny any responsibility, legal or moral, for the "Comfort Women." The right wing sees the attention given to the case as a ploy promoted by the left wing. The Foreign Ministry meanwhile continues to avoid being identified with this extremist position, thanks to its support for the Asian Women's Fund that it helped create as a means for satisfying the expressed wish of the socialist Prime Minister Murayama.

The sense of guilt and the sympathy toward the victims of one's own group could have existed in any society, premodern and nondemocratic, as part of the moral discourse of any religion that stresses kindness and compassion toward other human beings. The conflict between such moral discourse and a universal recognition of state responsibility in the modern *idées de droit* is the result of an opposition between a traditional discourse and a modern one. The conflict between the second and the third positions, thus, represented the two discourses that are normally compartmentalized in the public and the private life of the Japanese society (and of other non-Western societies), which democratizes in the public domain while maintaining its traditional discourse in private life. This debate, deeply rooted in the modernizing Japanese culture, attracted everybody's interest and diverted the attention of both social movements and of the public media from any confrontation between the first and the second positions. As a consequence, the Japanese government did not have to discuss the legality of its refusal to make compensation to the victims of its military sexual slavery.

The majority of the "Comfort Women" victims themselves, in spite of their material interest in accepting the "atonement" money, sided with the second position arguing that the Asian Women's Fund's atonement money was an attempt by the Japanese government to escape its responsibility. This caused a painful division among the victims in the Philippines.

In response to the criticism about replacing state compensation, the Asian Women's Fund developed an extremely meaningful new program called *Songen Jigyo*, or activities regarding the dignity of women. The program funded activities to fight against different forms of violence against women, including trafficking of women and children, and different efforts to transform the patriarchal culture in Japan and in other Asian societies. These activities are based on a recognition that social and cultural traditions accepting prostitution as an institution while stigmatizing the women in prostitution were at the root of the state-run military sexual slavery and continue to be a root cause of privatized commercial sexual slavery.

Recognition of the above contradiction leads to recognizing also that the Enlightenment discourse cannot simultaneously condemn the prostitution sector as an institution of sexual slavery and proclaim that the women in prostitution are exercising a legally acceptable activity. If the women in prostitution have to be destigmatized, then their work will need to be legally acceptable. This means that women in prostitution should be equally respectable as women in the family. Such recognition can only take place if the sex sector is defined as a normal industrial sector, not as a clandestine sector exploiting women as sex slaves.

The case of the "Comfort Women" military sexual slavery is a typical example of the patriarchal power that distorts gender relations by legitimizing the slavery institution and the masculine exploiter, while failing to accept the legitimacy of prostitution that would endanger the family (the key institution in any patriarchal society). This dilemma can be overcome only by a creative application of the discourse of caring, not in its patriarchal conformist version, but in its creative version proposed by some feminists. One can deconstruct any kind of stigma if one cares genuinely about an individual, since caring addresses the person herself, and the label of "sex slave" looses its derogative value in front of one's care about the victim as a person.

Only when some feminists raised their voice against the Japanese military sexual slavery did the victims get the courage to tell publicly that they had been "Comfort Women," a stigmatized status that could not have been announced publicly unless they were assured by the anti–"Comfort Women" movement that they were cared for and had nothing to fear from public opinion. Only when a significant portion of the public realized that the "Comfort Women" was an unacceptable institution of sexual slavery, and its victims were not to be stigmatized as "Comfort Women" but rather cared for and "atoned" as victims, were the "Comfort Women" able to come forward.

The double standard discourse justifying other kinds of sexual slavery, military or commercial, should be deconstructed in the same way, by an application of a universal *idées de droit* condemning the sexual slavery institution combined with a personalized caring approach to the women in prostitution, whose dignity should be cared for with no distinction between them and women in families.

Activities of the *Songen Jigyo* were based on the realization that the state-run military sexual slavery of the "Comfort Women" was but an extreme case of the sexual exploitative culture that still supports the operating, globalized sex industry of Japan. To eradicate this problem will require more than a onetime state payment to the victims of "Comfort Stations." Critics of the *Songen Jigyo* argued that it is a means of deflecting the criticism the Asian Women's Fund received for trying to give atonement to the "Comfort Women."

In spite of this shortcoming, the third position has an advantage over the second because it attempts to treat the victims of the military sexual slavery not as abstract human persons possessing universal rights but also as living and mortal individuals who should be cared for as individuals in their concrete environment, each with specific needs—material and moral. Most participants in debates over the hidden sex sector typically discuss it as an object of abstract discussions while ignoring individual women. The discourse adopted by the holders of this third position, however, efficiently put into question the very labeling of individual women as wives, mothers, or women in prostitution. In other words, this discourse can lead to questioning categories imposed by the patriarchal state and society in order to strengthen its power over the labeled women.

CONCLUSION

The above description of the three different positions in the "Comfort Women" debate reveals an important lacuna. The aforementioned statement by Ms. Coomaraswamy makes crystal clear the need for the state and the people of Japan to: (1) recognize the legal responsibility of the state of Japan toward the victims of its military sexual slavery, giving them due apologies and compensation; and (2) make efforts to transform the patriarchal brothel culture of Japan so that no kind of sexual slavery will be able to victimize women and girls, whether from within Japan or from the neighboring countries of Japan. The Japanese people must assume this important moral responsibility. This combination of legal and moral responsibilities is unfortunately not implemented, let alone proposed, by any of the agents involved in the "Comfort Women" debate. Neither the state nor the Asian Women's Fund nor the movements demanding state compensation propose an integral approach to the "Comfort Women" issue, coping with both the legal and moral aspects of the problem.

This is a fourth and most preferable position, one that adopts a discourse that can combine a legal and a moral approach to the "Comfort Women" question as well as cope with all forms of sexual slavery. The only way to deconstruct the double standard discourse is by establishing unambiguously the illegality of the sex sector on the one hand, and on the other hand proclaiming the responsibility of the society to accept the women in prostitution as equal in dignity with women in the family sector, eliminating all grounds for discrimination and stigmatization.

The difficulty in arriving at this position is partially created by the opposition that has developed during the debate between the holders of the second and the third positions. Yet, a more fundamental problem lies in the very nature of the two discourses and their relationship to the double standard discourse on the hidden clandestine sex sector.

The difficulty in joining the second and the third positions discussed above is due to the contradiction between their discourses. Their discursive orientations stress respectively, (1) the priority of universal human rights standards grounded in individual rights and dignity, and (2) the ethical position that "caring" for an individual victim's welfare is more precious than any legal regulations. As we saw already, one cannot take sides between these two positions if the hidden prostitution sector of the Japanese society is to be democratized. The double standard discourse that continues to justify the existence of this sector combines a public discourse and a private discourse that have to be corrected simultaneously. The application of universal human rights *idées de droit* and *règles de droit* is indispensable to deconstruct the institutional frameworks of the prostitution sector. A personalized caring of the exploited women is also indispensable if one wants to avoid justifying the sex industries while removing all stigma from the women in prostitution. Their rights and dignity do not emanate from the legality of the prostitution sector but from their personal dignity that cannot be violated even on the private, informal level. A measure that applies the *règles de droit* about state compensation toward its victims of human rights violation is a necessary condition for the rectification of this affront. An additional extralegal effort by the Japanese society transforming the masculine stigmatization of the "bad women" in the prostitution sector needs to be added, and the two together will constitute the sufficient conditions for overcoming the double standard discourse at the base of the sexual slavery, state-run or private, military or commercial institutions.

The case of the "Comfort Women" debate shows the difficulty of democratizing a situation where two opposite movements, one against the institution and the other caring for the victims, have to be developed simultaneously. The difficulty comes from the fact that the former needs to adopt the discourse of the Western Enlightenment tradition while the latter has to ignore it and develop an endogenous discourse, a democratized version of the traditional caring discourse. One movement needs to engage in the legal fighting for the institutionalization of formal democracy based on universal *idées de droit*. The other needs to stress the insufficiency of a formal introduction of exogenous values in the public life of the state and to insist on the necessity of developing a process of democratizing private community life based on a new endogenous social and cultural discourse.

The combination of the two discourses goes against the law of the excluded middle that helped to create all the modern dichotomies of public/private, universal/particular, legal/moral, and so forth. This dichotomy helped the double standards discourse that compartmentalize two logics: one about the institution, the other about the individual members. The new discourse should deconstruct these dichotomies and combine in an integral whole the legal application of a universal *idées de droit* to the hidden sector while simultaneously applying the moral approach of a particular and personalized, societal caring for its members.

We may conclude in more general terms that the patriarchal power continues to impose on democratizing societies a double standards discourse based on a formal acceptance of exogenous democratic *idées de droit* while ignoring their practical violation in particular concealed clandestine sectors of the society. In these hidden sectors, the critique of the undemocratic nature of specific institutions is diverted toward personal targets, mainly vulnerable and exploited women who receive unjustified stigmatization in place of the institution victimizing them. Engendering democracy, even in existing "democratic" countries, implies the elimination of the hidden sector of enslavement and discrimination, especially the sex industry sector that enslaves and commodifies women. It is important to take note of the fact that this effort requires a deconstruction of the public/private, modern/traditional, legal/extralegal dichotomies, even of the sexual slavery/right to prostitution opposition that originates from the double standards patriarchal discourse. All hidden sectors where gender and racial discriminations are practiced by the democratic state and civil society should be divulged and deconstructed. The dichotomous discourses that occlude the true structures of the patriarchal and neocolonial exploitation should also be transformed into a more just and more caring discourse.

13

Democratization: Reflections on Gendered Dislocations in the Public Sphere

Mary E. Hawkesworth

Democratization has been celebrated by politicians, political scientists, and political theorists as one of the most important achievements of the late twentieth century. In its most rudimentary form, democratization is defined as a transition from various types of authoritarian regime and command economies to liberal democracy and capitalism. In Africa, Asia, the Pacific, Eastern Europe, Latin America, and Russia democratization is characterized as a process of transition through which regimes that have been bureaucratic authoritarian, military dictatorships, and/or state socialist move toward an elective system of governance and a capitalist market (Saint Germain 1994).

To all who have been taught that democratic governance respects the dignity of human beings, affords rights and immunities to individuals, prevents abuse of power by government officials (or provides remedies for removal of abusive governments), fosters individual freedom, encourages collective action to achieve political benefits, provides opportunities for political innovation, and maintains mechanisms through which citizens can hold governments accountable, democratization does indeed seem an accomplishment worth celebrating. The establishment of fundamental freedoms for citizens through the constitutional protection of certain civil liberties (freedom of thought, speech, press, association, freedom from particular forms of governmental abuse, and freedom to participate in politics by voting and standing for election) and the provision of fundamental fairness through the rule of law and a range of entitlements to certain standards of living secured by the state certainly seem to be hallmarks of progress. When considered in the context of the claim advanced by some international relations scholars that in the twentieth century democratic governments have not made war against one another, the growth of democracies across the globe seems to hold the promise of a new era of peace in international affairs.

Given such optimistic expectations for democratization, the recent findings of feminist scholars come as something of a shock. Evidence drawn from women's lives around the globe suggests that democratization produces gendered redistributions of resources and responsibilities that make women worse off. "In Central and Eastern Europe, the level of women's participation in national legislatures fell precipitously when democratic elections were held, ranging from 20–30% in 1987 . . . to less than 10% in Poland, Czechoslovakia and Hungary in 1990" (Jaquette and Wolchik 1998: 10). In the 1995 elections, women constituted 10 percent of the legislators in the Czech Republic, 18 percent in Slovakia, 11 percent in Hungary, and 13 percent in Poland and Bulgaria (Jaquette and Wolchik 1998: 11). In Latin America, women are also markedly underrepresented in elective offices, holding only 5 percent of the seats in the legislative assembly in Brazil, 9 percent in Peru, and 14 percent in Argentina (Jaquette and Wolchik 1998: 11). Despite two hundred years of feminist political mobilization, women hold less than 12 percent of the formal political offices in nations across the globe. In more than one hundred countries women hold no elected offices in their national assemblies (Nelson and Chowdhury 1994).

The economic indicators of democratization are also troubling. The United Nations 1997 Human Development Report notes that the economies of more than one hundred nations were better off fifteen years prior to 1997 than they were in 1997. In Central and Eastern Europe women's unemployment has skyrocketed[1] as access to child care and reproductive freedom have been severely constricted (Bystydzienski 1992; Rai, Pilkington, and Phizacklea 1992). Some Eastern European women have resorted to prostitution as a means of survival as the global "traffic in women" surges despite the rampant dangers of AIDS. In Africa, Asia, and Latin America structural adjustment policies since the 1970s have imposed drastic cuts in social spending, contributing to the growing impoverishment of women and children. According to the United Nations Development Fund for Women (UNIFEM) women constitute nearly 70 percent of the world's 1.3 billion poor. The 564 million rural women living in poverty in 1990 represented a 47 percent increase above the number of poor women in 1970. Structural adjustment policies increase women's participation in waged labor at a time when global competition is driving wages down. Thus women find themselves working more hours in paid labor, playing crucial roles in the informal sector, and assuming increased responsibility for family subsistence. "These shifts in work patterns often have an impact on gender relations in the home not always to the benefit of women" (Craske 1998: 106).

In a period coincident with the increasing strength of feminism as a global movement, how can we make sense of democratization's gendered dislocations? If democracy is understood as a mode of governance that respects the dignity of human beings, affords rights and immunities to individuals, fosters individual freedom and development, and encourages collective action to achieve political benefits, then why are these gendered effects so palpable? And how can such blatant inequities continue to fall below the threshold of visibility and concern for mainstream social scientists, politicians, and the press?

The failure of social scientists to notice growing political and economic inequities may be related to an ideological immunity afforded by certain analytic concepts accredited within the social science disciplines. A gulf separates popular understandings of key political concepts such as democracy from social science definitions of these concepts. Since the eighteenth century, for example, liberal political theorists have routinely argued that pragmatic considerations such as population size, time constraints, limited citizen knowledge or interest, and the need for stability, necessitate that democracy be understood as a system of representative government. Within social science, the conception of democracy as "rule of the people, by the people, and for the people" has been supplanted by a conception of democratic elitism, rule by an elite chosen through popular participation in free and fair elections. Mainstream social scientists confidently assert that prime ministerial/parliamentary systems and presidential/republican systems converge on this point: meaningful democracy in the late twentieth century is synonymous with rule by a popularly elected elite. Thus as operational indicators of democratization, social scientists tend to focus upon the existence of "free and fair elections." But in focusing on "popular participation in elections," mainstream social scientists have been remarkably gender-blind. Examining the political behavior of men but advancing claims about citizens, women's participation as voters, candidates, or elected officials disappears. Assumptions about the normalcy of hierarchy and research methods insensitive to gender may explain why democratization's gendered dislocations fail to be noticed by mainstream scholars, or by the press and politicians who ground their analyses in scholarly accounts of political transformations. But how are we to make sense of the gendered dislocations themselves? Why is democratization making women worse off?

Feminist theory can help us understand some of the factors contributing to democratization's gendered dislocations. Feminist scholarship has demonstrated that claims concerning the "neutrality," "objectivity," and "inclusivity" of mainstream approaches in political theory and social science are deeply suspicious. A hallmark of feminist critique within the humanities, social sciences, and natural sciences has been the identification of androcentrism in theories, methodologies, and substantive research findings. The notion of androcentrism suggests that assumptions, concepts, beliefs, arguments, theories, methods, laws, policies, and institutions may all be "gendered." They may tacitly or explicitly privilege one gender at the expense of the other.[2] Social practices may be gendered in diverse ways. Exclusionary practices that bar women from participation lie at the most overt end of a gendered spectrum. But practices that are officially "gender-blind," "gender-neutral," or "equal opportunity" may also be gendered if they are rooted in experiences typically associated with men but not with women or if certain factors make it more difficult for women than for men to achieve the same outcome by following the same procedures.

Many of the processes associated with democratization are gendered. The model of liberal democracy that democratizing nations are urged to emulate is drawn from Euro-American experiences. The most advanced of the Western liberal democracies have very poor records in areas of gender equity. With the exception of the Scandinavian nations, which are perhaps better categorized as social democracies, women are drastically underrepresented in positions of power in liberal democratic nations, holding only 12–21 percent of the positions in the legislative bodies. In the most advanced capitalist economies (e.g., the Group of 7 nations—the United States, Canada, Great Britain, Germany, France, Italy, and Japan with Russia sitting as a nonvoting member), women are still confronting a glass ceiling that is remarkably low. Very few women are able to translate their education and professional experience into the positions in the highest ranks of the corporate sector. Less than 5 percent of the senior management positions in the corporate sector are held by women. At the opposite end of the economic spectrum within advanced capitalist nations, women are overrepresented among the poor. In the United States, for example, women and their children constitute 80 percent of the poor, a higher percentage than exists globally.

If democratizing nations are seeking to replicate the Euro-American model of male-dominant democratic elitism within a capitalist economy, then perhaps it should not be such a surprise that women are faring less well than men. Many of the tools that democratizing nations are being offered to guide their transitions have been criticized by feminist scholars for perpetuating gender inequities.

Consultants currently offering advice on democratic consolidation are drawing heavily on "modernization theory," which assumes that capitalism will itself produce liberal democracy, which in turn will elevate women's status. On this view, integrating women into the modern labor force is deemed the basis for their liberation. This assumption is predicated upon a belief that modern methods of production will generate modernist belief systems, including commitments to representative government. Specifically, the adoption of modern machine technologies is expected to promote norms of rationality, universalism, and egalitarianism, which in turn engender mobility and achievement. In principle, these rules of "modern" society negate ascription standards—including gender—as determinants of the individual's socioeconomic and political status. Thus opportunities for women are expected to expand as technological advancement makes production less a function of physical strength. Greater employment opportunities supposedly contribute to higher aspirations and expectations as women begin to recognize their own economic power. On this view, inclusion of women in the modern industrial economy contributes to a greater open-mindedness, resulting in the destruction of the patriarchal ideology that has justified women's exclusion from the "socially valued" productive sphere and from participation in the institutions of state.

The assumptions that inform modernization theory (i.e., the process is linear, cumulative, expansive, diffuse, and fundamentally occupied with the modern/traditional value dichotomy) inform democratization as well. According to this model, remedies for gender inequity in developing societies require only legal and institutional reforms. Observable differences between men and women in developing, or developed, societies is said to be merely a failure of the diffusive element of the model, not a problem in the process of democratization or the economic restructuring central to it.

Feminist scholars who have studied women in development have found that the assumptions of modernization theory have not been born out in development projects in the global South (or for that matter in the industrialized nations). Inclusion of women in industrial production can coexist with traditional belief systems and traditional patterns of women's subordination. Indeed, inclusion of women in industrial production need not supplant women's performance of traditional roles. Feminist political economists are in the process of documenting the simultaneous growth of the formal, informal, and subsistence economies. Many women in the global South and in former Soviet-bloc states are simultaneously involved in light industry jobs, provision of a range of services within the informal sector, and subsistence agriculture to produce the food to keep their families alive. Such a "triple shift" need not challenge established patterns of women's subservience. Feminist scholars have also demonstrated that "development" is far from linear and cumulative. A modicum of progress in one aspect of social transition can be off-set by setbacks in other areas of life. Consider, for example, the increase in domestic violence that can be coincident with a woman's increasing economic independence.[3] Or consider the astonishing transformation of some young male anti-apartheid activists in South Africa, who since 1995 have renamed themselves the South African Rapists Society and adopted sexual violence against women as the outlet for their "displaced political energy." Contrary to the assumptions of modernization theory, the impressive political empowerment of South African women under the African National Congress government and the dramatic increase in the number of women in the South African parliament since the creation of the new constitution coexists with a huge increase in violence against women. Indeed South Africa now has the highest percentage of violence against women in the world: 60 percent of intimate relationships involve violence.

Modernization theory also fails to acknowledge the extent to which Westerners implementing development projects in the global South have replicated Western patterns of male dominance in their choice of trainees and employees in both industrial and agricultural development projects. Indeed, Western development "experts'" assumptions that farming is men's work led to the displacement of women subsistence farmers and the spread of mass starvation and environmental crises as land farmed by women for subsistence crops was taken over for male-controlled production of export crops. In addition to structural adjustment policies developed in response to the international debt crisis that require countries to increase productivity and exports while decreasing government spending on social welfare, and colonial land policies that accorded men legal entitlement to land, misguided development policies have created food, fuel, and water crises in rural areas in the global South that have made women's lives vastly more difficult.

However erroneous the assumptions underlying modernization theory, feminist scholars point out that Western "experts" continue to recommend adoption of key tenets of modernization theory as part of the process of democratization. As a result, democratization is producing gendered patterns of skilling and deskilling, gendered differences in political rights and economic opportunities, gender-specific political visibility and invisibility, while subtly and unsubtly regendering the identities of citizens (Alvarez 1990; Funk and Mueller 1993; Jaquette 1989; Miller 1991; Nelson and Chowdhury 1994; Peterson and Runyon 1999; Radcliffe and Westwood 1993; Saint Germain 1994).

In recent work, a number of scholars have emphasized the importance of the development of "civil society" to ensure the success of democratization. Within the works of Western democratization experts, civil society is typically conceived in terms of a voluntary sector of organizations and interest groups that provide a means for organized citizen action. The cultivation of civil society is said to be beneficial because it encourages citizens to organize to promote their interests and fosters ties among like-minded people across divisions of race, class, ethnicity, and gender. Private interest organizations create alternative power centers outside the state, provide an opportunity for learning leadership and developing political skills, and can provide not only a means of political communication, but a mechanism for tracking government performance and holding governments accountable. Like the popular construction of democratization, such an account of civil society sounds uniformly beneficial.

Discussions of civil society have been proliferating over the past decade. Some commentators use the term broadly to encompass all civic, economic, religious, and voluntary institutions that fall outside agencies of government. Such an encompassing definition makes sense in describing the emergence of a host of institutions in the aftermath of the fall of authoritarian regimes. But the conception of civil society that dominates the discussions of American democratization experts has a narrower and more pluralist cast. Incorporating assumptions from theorists such as Hobbes, Locke, Hume, Madison, Hegel, and de Tocqueville, this narrower conception of civil society should give feminist scholars cause for concern. Feminist critiques of the conceptions of human nature informing classic liberal and republican conceptions of civil society suggest that some of the core concepts are gendered in subtle and not-so-subtle ways (Brown 1988; Di Stefano 1996; Hirschmann 1992; J. Scott 1996; Tronto 1993). The notion of the autonomous individual as a self-interested maximizer, who forms bonds with others to advance private interests, haunts these discourses. Construing the "self-made" individual as someone with no ties to family or community gives rise to a notion of association as purely instrumental. The individual joins only those groups that will advantage him or her and abandons any group that fails to accomplish that end. Positing the pursuit of private interest as the primary concern of the individual in civil society, politics itself is construed instrumentally as a limited public process of interest accommodation.

Feminist scholars have suggested that the radical individualism underlying the instrumental model of civil society and of politics is fundamentally at odds with women's experiences, the life cycle and needs of citizens, and the beliefs of women political activists about the appropriate reasons for participation in social groups (Hirschmann 1992; Flammang 1997; Jaquette and Wolchik 1998). The gendered dislocations associated with democratization provide good reason for interrogating the productive power and exclusionary effects of "scientific" discourses promoting radical individualism and instrumental politics. In an excellent study of women and democratization in Latin America, and Central and Eastern Europe, Jane Jaquette and Sharon Wolchik point out that women were actively involved in the initial and most dangerous stages of democratization: organizing against oppressive regimes, mobilizing as citizens, demanding the transformation of the political system, and standing publicly against authoritarian rule. In this critical stage of democratization, women understood their political roles very differently than as autonomous individuals. Like the Mothers of the Plaza de Mayo in Argentina, women came to the political arena as members of families, carrying obligations and aspirations that could not be subsumed under the rubric of self-interest. They understood their political project to be very different from private interest group activity, seeking not personal advantage but a much broader social goal of changing both the substance and style of political activity (Jaquette and Wolchik 1998: 13).

Rather than rejecting the self-understandings of these courageous women activists and subsuming their political engagement under the rubric of some form of "enlightened self-interest" to fit democratization experts' model of civil society, it is useful to consider the implications of their self-understandings in relation to their glaring absence from later stages of democratization. Jaquette and Wolchik document the displacement of women in Latin America and Central and Eastern Europe from political activity after the downfall of the old regime and during the period of "democratic consolidation." In tracing this displacement of women, Jaquette and Wolchik note that women's growing absence can be tied to the resurrection of traditional party apparatus and politician-client relations, which supplant the large-scale, participatory, citizen coalitions crucial to the overthrow of the old regimes. While political parties come in many different varieties, the kinds of parties being fostered by U.S. democratization experts are the "nonideological," undisciplined, "pragmatic" interest-accommodating parties characteristic of American political life.[4] Women and politics scholars have amassed a great deal of evidence that such political parties are more hostile to women's political participation than are average citizens. Thus the resurgence of interest-accommodationist party activity, mandated by democratization experts as essential to competitive elections, may help explain some of democratization's gendered dislocations, for it signifies an extinction of hopes. Women's hopes for a different kind of politics—more participatory, more oriented toward social justice and less dependent on self-interest and money—are eradicated with the institutionalization of an old (and traditionally hostile to women) political organization. As women's "interests" are aggregated by political parties, they are "tamed," stripped of any transformative content. Parties' efforts to aggregate interests, to devise platforms that can appeal to a wide range of voters, including conservative men and women, require the elimination of "nonconsensual issues," such as reproductive freedom and economic justice, from the partisan agenda (Valenzuela 1998). Indeed, the insistence of many autonomous women's movements that issues of justice must be addressed in politics has provided grounds for accommodationist political parties to resist the integration of women into politics, especially in key decision-making positions. Appealing to the need for "political realism" and the necessity of "compromise," male party elites can reject women candidates ostensibly for their lack of pragmatism. Praise for women's "superior ethical standards" can thus serve to marginalize women as traditional parties simultaneously insist that politics is not an arena for ethical purists. Under the banner of neoliberalism, seasoned party cadres can insist that the role of government is to foster "self-help strategies," not social justice (Craske 1998).

Democratic consolidation has also been characterized by a shift in the kinds of political engagements deemed to be effective, or even possible, for women. During the earliest stages of democratization, women mobilized across class and ethnic divisions in participatory movements that emphasized the importance of solidarity and skills-building for all participants. For participants in autonomous women's movements the creation of a "democratic space" in which women could learn and grow through participation in decision-making was crucial to the politicization of women, for it helped women cultivate the skills to transform their everyday lives and practices. Under democratic consolidation, nongovernmental organizations (NGOs), staffed by well-educated professionals and funded by international agencies, become the primary vehicle for women's interaction with governmental institutions. NGOs have been extremely important in keeping women's issues on the political agenda and in providing essential services for women in democratizing nations. Yet, the efficiency and professionalism required for NGOs' success exists in uneasy tension with the inclusive solidarity of participatory women's movements.

Teresa Caldeira (1998) has pointed out that the emergence of NGOs as the premier women's organizations under democratic consolidation raises important concerns. Because NGOs are dependent upon external funding, granting agencies have the power to set priorities for NGO activity. No matter how beneficial these priorities may be for women, priorities set by international agencies disempower local women who can no longer set their own agendas. Sabine Lang (1999) has noted that although feminist NGOs may have been created out of participatory social movements, several factors mitigate their ability to maintain social movements. At the most minimal level, because NGOs are dependent upon soft money, they must develop the fixed organizational structures, professional staff, and fiscal accountability necessary to be entrusted with major grants by funding agencies. They cannot afford the fluidity of a mass-based voluntary movement. Their agendas must be narrowly focused and presented in terms of realizable goals and objectives in order to demonstrate their efficacy. The energy required for the grant writing essential to organizational survival leaves little time for mass mobilization. In some circumstances, the competition among NGOs for funds could hinder strategic coalition building, placing NGOs in the uncomfortable position of being financially dependent upon institutions and organizations that pure political principle would lead them to confront (e.g., tobacco money, Nestle, Delcon shield). In addition, the professionalization of NGO staff necessary to attain the respectability required not only to receive funds from international agencies, but also to establish a reputation as an authoritative voice on women's needs and interests replicates inequalities and privileges among women rather than eroding them.

Although cautioning against any "blanket assessments of feminist NGOs as handmaidens of neo-liberal planetary patriarchy," Sonia Alvarez has noted several recent developments that threaten NGOs ability to "advance a progressive policy agenda while simultaneously articulating vital linkages among larger women's movement and civil society constituencies" (1999: 181). Under democratic consolidation as the political rewards and material resources to support consciousness-raising and women's political empowerment dry up, feminist NGOs are increasingly pressed into the role of "gender experts." As global pressures are brought to bear upon governments to develop "gender sensitive policies," feminist NGOs who possess policy-specialized staff, previous experiences with UN programs, and a record of international funding are recruited by governments to provide technical advisory services. In keeping with neoliberal privatization efforts, NGOs are hired as consultants for gender policy assessment, project execution, and social services delivery, especially in the area of poverty alleviation policies. But this changed relationship to the state also changes NGOs' relationship with autonomous women's organizations. "Consulted as experts who can evaluate gender policies and programs rather than as movement organizations that might facilitate citizen input and participation in the formation and design of such policies, feminist NGOs' technical involvement in policy assessment . . . does not necessarily translate into effectual gender policy or women's rights advocacy" (Alvarez 1999: 192). Indeed, increasing dependence upon government grants for their very livelihood may undermine the ability of feminist NGOs to criticize government policy and "to pursue more process-oriented forms of feminist cultural-political intervention—such as consciousness-raising, popular education or other strategies aimed at transforming those gender power relations manifest in the realms of public discourse, culture, and daily life—forms of gendered injustice that defy gender-planning quick fixes" (Alvarez 1999: 198).[5]

Reviewing twenty-five years of transnational women's activism, Amrita Basu (1995, 1999) has suggested that women's NGOs have been particularly effective when a national government's repression or indifference constrains local feminist activism and when an international appeal involving civil and political rights to provide a remedy can be made. Operating in the post–Cold War era, NGO's likelihood of success increases when their goals can be formulated in the language of liberal human rights. Noting that the hegemonic rhetoric of human rights is fast becoming the discursive limit of permissible social change, Basu points out that women's NGOs have been much less effective in addressing economic justice issues—the issues of water, firewood, land, and employment—that have been the focal point of so much local feminist activism. To note that transnational feminist activists, however dedicated, have not succeeded in overthrowing global capitalism or the devastating structural adjustment policies imposed by the International Monetary Fund and the World Bank hardly seems a scathing indictment. For what fair-minded person could expect feminist NGOs to accomplish in a decade what socialist revolutionaries have failed to do over the past 150 years?

But if our goal is to understand democratization's dislocation of women, then perhaps there is more to be said about the circumscribed sphere of feminist NGO's success. Again, the insights of Teresa Caldeira (1998) are particularly helpful. Caldeira has suggested that operating within the boundaries of "public/private" set by neoliberal conceptions of civil society, NGOs provide services that the state is unwilling or unable to provide. Once accepted within the purview of NGO activity, what might once have been considered a matter of public policy is subtly redefined as a project of a private organization. Thus the context of women's struggles subtly changes. What was once understood as a political struggle of citizens about the boundaries of justice can now be construed as a dispute over private resources. In changing the framing assumptions from a discourse of citizenship and justice to a discourse of competition for scarce resources or material provision to meet private need, women's goals are resignified as "private." In working with NGOs on projects vital to their physical safety and economic survival, women in democratizing nations are reprivatized. Although hailed as the hallmark of women's incorporation into the new civil society, NGOs simultaneously manifest the tendencies toward privatization and growing inequalities characteristic of neoliberal political systems. NGOs must be understood, then, as both crucial vehicles for the advancement of certain women's interests under resurgent capitalism and as an effect of the dismantling of welfare state structures, and as such complicit in the delegitimation of social rights and the privatization of women. In their mode of operation and in the unintended consequences of their action, NGOs affirm entrepreneurial individualism as a privileged mode of political agency and displace participatory politics.

The institutionalization of a particular liberal conception of civil society, the incorporation of women into civil society through NGOs, and the promotion of accommodationist political parties as the central elements of democratization are routinely depicted as progressive developments, but this may be another instance where structures that count as progressive for men have markedly different consequences for women. Indeed, it might be helpful to understand the resurrection of civil society and the accreditation of accommodationist parties as active processes of gendering public space. By valorizing institutions at odds with women's hopes for participatory politics and long associated with the exclusion of women as the key components of democratization, public space is symbolically reclaimed as male space.

To illuminate the process of gendering public space, it might be useful to consider two contemporary examples at great remove from democratization—the Serbian incursion in Bosnia and the regime of the Taliban in Afghanistan. The genocidal war in Bosnia was gendered. As women's rights activists have documented, rape was used as a strategic weapon in that war. The Serbian army made a strategic decision to rape Muslim women as a means of demoralizing the Bosnian men. The citizenship of women (Serb or Bosnian) was not at issue; women were viewed as mere means to achieve psychological and military objectives. Such an intentional dehumanization constitutes political space as male space. Indeed the sphere of political contestation is actively created as a threat to women, as a space in which to dehumanize and violate women. In Afghanistan, the Taliban have issued edicts prohibiting women from showing themselves in public unless fully veiled and accompanied by a man. They have also prohibited girls and women from attending schools and practicing professions. The forced enclosure of women is implemented by publicly administering heinous punishments, including death, to any who refuse to comply. The Taliban have invented a version of Islam at great remove from the foundational texts of their religion and the lived religious practices in their nation. On the basis of this invention, they are attempting to forge gendered political identities by enacting them with brutal force. Through this process they are producing political space as exclusively male. As long as defiance means likely death, the Taliban will succeed in their eradication of women from the public world.

A process so blatantly enacted by the Serbs and the Taliban can also have far more subtle manifestations. I suggest that the incorporation of certain gendered concepts within the neoliberal definition of democratization and the entrenchment of gendered institutions as the defining characteristics of democratization contribute to a very subtle structuring of public space as male terrain. The construction of women committed to participatory politics and economic justice as too idealistic or too unrealistic for political life marginalizes women just as successfully as did the Victorian pedestal. Working in two directions at once, it supports men's claims that idealistic women are inappropriate political actors, while simultaneously convincing women that the tawdriness of interest group politics is not worth their time and effort. The perpetration of violence against women by some men provides justification for other men to assume the familiar mantle of women's protector, while leaving women wondering how politics can help them when violence ensnares them in their most intimate relationships.

The gendered dislocations accompanying democratization are indisputable. Does it make sense to interpret them in terms of a subtle restructuring of political space as male terrain? I believe that there are two compelling reasons to do so. The first reason draws upon recent work by feminist historians that suggests that this has happened before. In the eighteenth and nineteenth centuries, a universalist rhetoric of democracy afforded a mechanism for men to claim exclusive political rights and entrench those claims in a wave of constitution-making. In the case of the American Revolution, the French Revolution, and again in the United States in the period of Reconstruction, some men accorded themselves exclusive constitutional privileges and immunities against the vocal opposition of women who had participated intensively in the overthrow of the old regimes. In establishing male gender as a constitutional criterion for full citizenship, some women who had rights of participation, including voting privileges, lost those rights (McDonagh 1999; Case 1999; Barkley Brown 1997). Such powerful historical precedents caution against dismissing democratization's displacement of women as inconsequential.

The second reason to take this interpretive frame seriously looks to the future rather than the past. If those in the global community committed to the full realization of women's citizenship understand democratization as a process of reclaiming public space as male, then it might be possible to identify national and international strategies more supportive of women's political inclusion.

Some of the tactics adopted by contemporary women's rights advocates can be read as efforts to thwart the reconstitution of political space as male space. Rather than relinquish political parties and elective offices to men, feminists in a num- ber of nations have pressed for the creation of policies to break male control of party apparatus and elective offices. In response to this pressure, some seventy-five political parties in more than thirty nations have established quotas to ensure that women are recruited as party candidates at least in proportion to their membership in the party (Leijenaar 1998). Some nations have established constitutional provisions mandating equitable representation of women. India, for example, requires that women hold one-third of local elective offices. (Similar legislation at the federal level was defeated, in part, because lower-caste parties feared that the legislation would privilege higher-caste women.) France has just passed a constitutional amendment guaranteeing women equal access to governing offices and now moves into the enormously complex stage of statutory implementation.

The Platform for Action based on the Fourth World Conference in Beijing called upon governments "to commit themselves to establish the goal of gender balance in governmental bodies and committees, as well as in public administrative entities, and in the judiciary, including inter alia setting specific targets and implementing measures to substantially increase the number of women with a view to achieving equal representation of women and men" (paragraph 190a).

Feminists in autonomous women's movements and in some NGOs have attempted to contest prevailing assumptions concerning civil society. Rather than accept norms of self-interested actors, they have struggled to reclaim civil society as a space for women's empowerment and collective action. Feminist activists have pressed governments and international agencies to complete "gender impact analyses" prior to the adoption and implementation of policies. Monique Leijenaar (1998) has suggested that those in a position to democratize states and international consultants working with them should conduct gender impact analyses of all aspects of democratization in order to identify "best practices" to foster women's political participation. Feminist activists have also used litigation in international tribunals in an effort to hold their governments accountable for violations of women's rights recognized in international treaties, such as the Universal Declaration of Human Rights, and the Convention on the Elimination of All Forms of Discrimination Against Women.

Widespread awareness that democratization currently institutionalizes practices that are hostile to women, hamper or preclude women's inclusion, and regulate women's access to decision-making could bring new life to these feminist efforts. Contesting the reconstitution of political space as male space can illuminate the gulf between democratization and democracy in ways that may help women in "mature" liberal democracies learn from the experiences of women in democratizing nations. Governments cannot continue to claim to be democratic if they allow half their populations to be grossly underrepresented. Emerging liberal democracies, like their mature counterparts, have embraced a rhetoric of equal opportunity only to mask systemic inequality. By construing women's absence as a deprivation of public roles, women's rights advocates have a powerful means to challenge the legitimacy of any democratic consolidation that privileges men. Contesting gender power in liberal democratic institutions may help feminists repoliticize their emancipatory struggles. Holding political parties and elected officials accountable to inclusive norms of democracy may be one way to reopen the very old question of whose lives are to count politically and whose interests are to be served through democratic decision-making. Perhaps it might also reopen the question of what kind of democracy is possible in the twenty-first century, thereby resurrecting the emancipatory impulse of feminist social movements.

NOTES

1. In certain parts of the former Soviet bloc, women's unemployment reached 80 percent in the aftermath of democratization. A decade later the majority of women remain out of paid work in Russia. (See Jaquette and Wolchik 1998; Sperling 1998.)

2. In principle, a gendered practice could privilege men or women. But the history of male dominance has resulted in systematic male power advantages across diverse social domains. Feminist usage of the adjective "gendered" reflects this male power advantage. Hence a gendered practice is synonymous with androcentic practice in common feminist terminology. This equation also draws upon linguistic terms that characterize the male as unmarked/universal and the female as marked/other. Within this framework, the allegedly neutral and inclusive term, gender, reflects the universal/male norm.

3. A good deal more research is needed to make sense of such increasing violence against women. Since the issue of domestic violence was politicized only in the 1970s, it is difficult to know to what extent the rate of violence has increased and to what extent increased rates of reporting and changed police practices account for an apparent increase. In some nations undergoing democratization, local feminist activists have argued that increasing male frustration related to economic strains are producing an increase in domestic violence; others have linked the increase in domestic violence to a form of "backlash" against increasing independence of women.

4. These stand in marked contrast to the programmatic and disciplined parties characteristic of many European social democratic states.

5. Alvarez notes that depending on the size and mission of the institution, as well as its technical profile, state funds account for 10–25 percent of feminist NGOs operating budgets in Chile and 40–50 percent of feminist NGOs budgets in Colombia (1999: 196).

References

Adams, Patricia, and Lawrence Solomon. *In The Name of Progress: The Underside of Foreign Aid.* London: Earthscan Publications Ltd., 1991.

Agarwal, Bina. *A Field of One's Own, Gender and Land Rights in South Asia.* Cambridge: Cambridge University Press, 1994.

Aglietta, M. *A Theory of Capitalist Regulation.* London: NLB, 1979.

Allan, L. Review of Mulgan's "Maori, Pakeha and Democracy." In *Australian Journal of Political Science* 25, no. 2 (1990): 372.

Altvater, E. "Markt und Demokratie in Zeiten von Globalisierung und ökologischer Krise." In *Vernetzt und verstrickt,* edited by E. Altvater, A. Brunnengräber, M. Haake, and H. Walk, 241–256. Münster: Westfälisches Dampfboot, 1997.

Altvater, E., and B. Mahnkopf. *Grenzen der Globalisierung.* Münster: Westfälisches Dampfboot, 1996.

Alvarez, Sonia. *Engendering Democracy in Brazil: Women's Movements in Transition Politics.* Princeton, N.J.: Princeton University Press, 1990.

———. "Advocating Feminism: The Latin American Feminist NGO 'Boom.'" *International Feminist Journal of Politics* 1, no. 2 (1999): 181–209.

Amin, Samir. *Les Défis de la Mondialisation.* Paris: L'Harmattan, 1996.

Anderson, F. "Women in Australia." In *Australia: Economic and Political Studies,* edited by M. Atkinson, 259–270. Melbourne: Macmillan, 1920.

Anwar, M. *The Myth of Return.* London: Heinemann, 1979.

Arizpe, Lourdes, and Carlota Botay. "Mexican Agricultural Development Policy and Its Impact on Rural Women." In *Rural Women and State Policy, Feminist Perspectives on Latin American Agricultural Development,* edited by Carmen D. Deere and Magdalena Leon, 67–83. Boulder, Colo.: Westview Press, 1987.

Australian Geographic Society. *The Australian Encyclopedia.* Sydney: Australian Geographic Society, 1988: 2142.

Bakker, I. *The Strategic Silence: Gender and Economic Policy.* London: Zed Books, 1994.

Banks, O. *Faces of Feminism: A Study of Feminism as a Social Movement.* Oxford Martin Robertson Press, 1981.

Barkley Brown, Elsa. "Negotiating and Transforming the Public Sphere: African American Political Life in the Transition from Slavery to Freedom." In *Women Transforming*

Politics, edited by Cathy Cohen, Kathleen Jones, and Joan Tronto, 343–376. New York: New York University Press, 1997.

Basu, Amrita. *The Challenge of Local Feminisms: Women's Movements in Global Perspective*. Boulder, Colo.: Westview Press, 1995.

———. "Mapping Transnational Women's Activism: Globalizing the Local, Localizing the Global." Paper presented at the Institute for Research on Women, Rutgers University, October 11, 1999.

Bauman, Z. "Glokalisierung oder: Was für die einen Globalisierung, ist für die anderen Lokalisierung." *Das Argument* (1996): 653–664.

Bayes, Jane H., and Rita Mae Kelly. "Political Spaces, Gender, and NAFTA." A paper presented at the Out of the Margin/IAFFE Conference. Amsterdam, the Netherlands, June 2–5, 1998.

Beall, Jo. *Urban Governance: Why Gender Matters*. Gender in Development Monograph Series. New York: UNDP, 1996.

Becker, Gary S. *A Treatise on the Family*. Cambridge, Mass.: Harvard University Press, 1981.

Becker-Schmidt, R. "Geschlechterdifferenz—Geschlechterverhältnis: soziale Dimensionen des Begriffs 'Geschlecht.'" *Zeitschrift für Frauenforschung*, no. 1–2 (1993): 37–46.

Bell, S., and B. Head. *State and Economy in Australia*. Melbourne: Oxford University Press, 1993.

Bellinghousen, Hermann. "EZLN's 13 Years Celebrated in La Realidad." *Libertad* 8 (Nov.–Dec.). El Paso, Texas, National Commission for Democracy in Mexico: 1996.

Benería, Lourdes, and Martha Roldán. *The Crossroads of Class and Gender: Industrial Homework, Subcontracting, and Household Dynamics in Mexico City*. Chicago: University of Chicago Press, 1987.

Berger, P. L., B. Berger, and H. Kellner. *The Homeless Mind: Modernization and Consciousness*. New York: Vintage, 1973.

Bloom, F. T. "Struggling and Surviving: The Life Style of European Immigrant Breadwinning Mothers in American Industrial Cities, 1900–1930." *Women's Studies International Forum* 8, no. 6 (1985): 609–620.

Blumberg, Rae Lesser. "A General Theory of Gender Stratification." In *Sociological Theory*, edited by R. Collins. San Francisco, Calif.: Jossey-Bass, 1984.

———, ed. *Gender Family and Economy: The Triple Overlap*. Newbury Park, Calif.: Sage Publications, 1991.

Bonacich, E. "A Theory of Middlemen Minorities." *American Sociological Review* 38 (1973): 583–594.

Borderlines. "Tijuana Colonia Protests Government-Led Eviction Attempt." vol. 4, no. 9 (October 1996): 10. Silver City, N.M.: Interhemispheric Resource Center.

Bourdieu, P. "Die Sachzwänge des Neoliberalismus." *Le Monde diplomatique* (March 1998): 3.

Bouton, Cynthia A. *The Flour War: Gender, Class, and Community in Late Ancien Regime French Society*. University Park: Pennsylvania State University Press, 1993.

Bowden, Peta. *Caring: Gender-Sensitive Ethics*. New York: Routledge, 1997.

Brodie, J. "Shifting the Boundaries: Gender and the Politics of Restructuring." In *The Strategic Silence*, edited by I. Bakker, 46–60. London: Zed Books, 1994.

Brown, Wendy. *Manhood and Politics*. Totowa, N.J.: Rowman & Littlefield, 1988.

Bryce, J. *Modern Democracies*, vol. 3. New York: Praeger, 1921.

Buijs, G., ed. *Migrant Women: Crossing Boundaries and Changing Identities*. Oxford, UK: Berg Publishers, 1993.

Burdeau, Georges. *Traite de Science Politique*. Paris: Librarie generale de droit et de jurisprudence, 1949.

Bystydzienski, Jill, ed. *Women Transforming Politics: Worldwide Strategies*. Bloomington: Indiana University Press, 1992.

Caldeira, Teresa. "Justice and Individual Rights: Challenges for Women's Movements and Democratization in Brazil." In *Women and Democracy: Latin America and Central and Eastern Europe*, edited by Jane Jaquette and Sharon Wolchik, 75–103. Baltimore: Johns Hopkins University Press, 1998.

Cardoso, Fernando H. "On the Characterization of Authoritarian Regimes in Latin America." In *The New Authoritarianism in Latin America*, edited by David Collier, 33–57. Princeton, N.J.: Princeton University Press, 1979.

Carrillo, Teresa. "The Women's Movement and the Left in Mexico: The Presidential Candidacy of Dofla Rosarlo Ibarra." In *Chicana Voices: Intersections of Class, Race and Gender*, edited by National Association for Chicano Studies editorial committee, Teresa Cardova, chair, 96–113. Albuquerque: University of New Mexico Press, 1990.

Case, Mary Anne. "Assessing the Categories: Should Political Representation Be Organized by Race, Gender, or Sexuality." International Conference on Politics, Rights, and Representation. University of Chicago, October 14, 1999.

Castells, M. *The Rise of the Network Society: The Information Age: Economy, Society and Culture*, vol. 1. Oxford: Blackwell Publishers, Ltd., 1996.

Castles, S. *Immigration and Australia: Myths and Reality*. Sydney, Australia: Allen and Unwin, 1998.

Chafetz, J. S. *Gender Equity, An Integrated Theory of Stability and Change*. Newbury Park, Calif.: Sage, 1990,

Chakrabarty, D. "Postcoloniality and the artifice of history: Who speaks for Indian pasts?" *Representations* 37 (Winter 1992): 1–26.

Chandler, A. *The Visible Hand: The Managerial Revolution in American Business*. Cambridge: Harvard University Press, 1977.

Chang, Kyung-Sup. "Gender and Abortive Capitalist Social Transformation: Semi-Proletarianization of South Korean Women." *International Journal of Comparative Sociology* 36, no. 1–2 (June 1996):61–81.

Chang, Sung-ja, and Kim, Won-hong. *The Supportive Measures of the Political Parties for Increasing Women's Participation in Politics*. Seoul: Korean Women's Development Institute, 1995.

Chatterjee, P. "Colonialism, Nationalism and Colonized Women: The Contest in India." *American Ethnologist* 16, no. 4 (November 1989): 622–633.

Cheng, L., and L. Evans. "Transnational Migration and the Formation of an International Professional-Managerial Class." Paper presented at the annual meeting of the American Sociological Association, Cincinnati, August 1991.

Cho, Seewha. "Gender, Labor and Schooling: Factory Schools at Textile Mills in South Korea." Ph.D. diss. University of Wisconsin–Madison, 1993.

Cho, Soon-kyoung. "The Limits and Possibilities of the Women's Movement in Korea." In *Gender Division of Labor in Korea*, edited by Hyoung Cho and Pil-wha Chang, 275–291. Seoul: Korean Woman's University Press, 1994.

Cho, Sungsook. "Toward a Grass-roots Women's Movement in Korea through Class Consciousness." Presented at NWSA 1988, Minneapolis, Minnesota, June 22–26, 1988.

Chodorow, N. *The Reproduction of Mothering: Psychoanalysis and the Sociology of Gender*. Berkeley: University of California Press, 1978.

Choi, Sang-Yong. *Democracy in Korea: Its Ideals and Realities*. Seoul: Korean Political Science Association, 1997.

Choi, Young-Hee (Korean National Council of Women). "Women in Korea: Achievements and Challenges." Presented at the Third East Asian Forum, country paper, 1998.

Chowdury, D. P. "Child Labour in Asia." Lecture given at Indian International Centre, Delhi, India, January 10, 1997.

Chung, Hyun-Back. "Together and Separately: 'The New Women's Movement' after the 1980's in South Korea." *Asia Women* 5 (Fall 1997): 19–38.

CJM (Coalition for Justice in the Maquiladoras). *Annual Report 1996*. Newsletter 6, no. 1 (Spring 1996).

Commonwealth of Australia. *Bringing Them Home: National Inquiry into the Separation of Aboriginal and Torres Strait Islander Children from their Families*. Canberra: Australian Government Publisher, 1997.

Connell, R. W. *Gender and Power. Society, the Person and Sexual Politics*. Stanford, Calif.: Stanford University Press, 1987.

Craske, Nikki. "Remasculinisation and the Neoliberal State in Latin America." In *Gender, Politics, and the State*, edited by Vicky Randall and Georgian Waylen, 100–120. London: Routledge, 1998.

Crompton, Rosemary. *Class and Stratification: An Introduction to Current Debates*. Cambridge, Mass.: Polity Press, 1993.

Cumings, Bruce. *Korea's Place in the Sun*. New York: W. W. Norton and Co., 1997.

Dark Night Field Notes. "Revolutionary Laws of Women." Chicago, Ill.: Dark Night Press, 1997.

Dasgupta, S. D. "Marching to a Different Drummer? Sex Roles of Asian Indian Women in the United States." *Women and Therapy* 5 (1986): 297–311.

Dasgupta, S. S. *On the Trail of an Uncertain Dream: Indian Immigrant Experience in America*. New York: AMS Press, Inc., 1989.

De Tocqueville, A. *Democracy in America*. New York: Harper and Row, 1988.

Deere, Carmen D., and Magdalena León. "Introduction." In *Rural Women and State Policy, Feminist Perspectives on Latin American Agricultural Development*, edited by Carmen D. Deere and Magdalena León, 1–7. Boulder, Colo.: Westview Press, 1987.

Dembele, Demba Moussa. African External Debt, Structural Adjustment and Development. Unpublished manuscript, Washington, D.C.: African Policy Forum, 1996.

———. "Pladoyer pour les femmes Ouest Africaines dans la Convention de Lome. In *Africa: Gender, Globalization and Resistance*, edited by Yassine Fall, 123–158. Dakar, Senegal: AAWORD. Imprimerie St. Paul, 1999.

Demirovic, A., and K. Pühl. "Identitätspolitik und die Transformation von Staatlichkeit: Geschlechterverhältnisse und Staat als komplexe materielle Relation." Edited by E. Kreisky and B. Sauer. *Politische Vierteljahresschrift* 28 (1997, Special Issue): 220–240.

Denoon, D. *Settler Capitalism: The Dynamics of Dependent Development in the Southern Hemisphere*. Oxford: Oxford University Press, 1983.

Devi, Indira M. *Women, Education, Employment and Family Living: A Study of Emerging Hindu Wives in Urban India.* Delhi: Gian Publishing House, 1987.

Di Stefano, Christine. "Autonomy in the Light of Difference." In *Revisioning the Political*, edited by Nancy Hirschmann and Christine Di Stefano, 95–116. Boulder, Colo.: Westview Press, 1996.

Die Gruppe von Lissabon. *Grenzen des Wettbewerbs.* Munich: Luchterhand, 1997.

Dinnerstein, M. *Women Between Two Worlds: Midlife Reflections on Work and Family.* Philadelphia, Pa.: Temple University Press, 1992.

Domrese, R. J. "The Migration of Talent from India." In *The International Migration of High-level Manpower: Its Impact on the Development Process, Committee on the International Migration of Talent.* New York: Praeger, 1970.

Economist, The. "Africa for the Africans: A Survey of the Sub-Saharan Africa." September 7, 1996 (10-page survey between pp. 52–53).

Eggerton, Laura. "Abuse Part of Job at Mexican Firms." *The Globe and Mail.* Mexico City, Mexico, October 14, 1997.

Eisenstein, Hester. "Femocrats, Official Feminism and the Uses of Power." In *Playing the State. Australian Feminist Intervention*, edited by Sophie Watson, 87–103. London: Verso, 1990.

Elson, Diane. "Micro, Meso, Macro: Gender and Economic Analysis in the Context of Policy Reform." In *Strategic Silence. Gender and Economic Policy*, edited by I. Bakker, 33–45. London: Zed Books, 1994.

———. *Male Bias in the Development Process.* Manchester: Manchester University Press, 1995.

Fall, Yassine. "Macroeconomic Reforms in Sub-Saharan Africa: What Position from the Women's Movement in Policy Advocacy?" *Democraties Africaines*, no. 6 (April–June 1996): 68–74.

Faludi, S. *Backlash.* New York: Crown Publishers, 1991

Faver, C. A. *Women in Transition: Career, Family and Life Satisfaction in Three Cohorts.* New York: Praeger, 1984.

Federal Reserve Bank, Dallas/El Paso Branch. *Business Frontier* 3 (1996).

———. "Mexican Border Industrialization, Female Labor Force Participation, and Migration." In *Women, Men, and the International Division of Labor*, edited by June Nash and Maria Patricia Fernandez-Kelly, 205–223. Albany, N.Y.: SUNY Press, 1983.

———. "Broadening the Scope: Gender and International Economic Development." *Sociological Forum* 4 (1989): 11–35.

Fernández-Kelly, M. P., and S. Sassen. "Recasting Women in the Global Economy: Internationalization and Changing Definitions of Gender." In *Women in the Latin American Development Process*, edited by C. E. Bose and E. Acosta-Belén, 99–124. Philadelphia: Temple University Press, 1995.

Flammang, Janet. *Women's Political Voice: How Women Are Transforming the Practice and Study of Politics.* Philadelphia, Pa.: Temple University Press, 1997.

Fletcher, C. *Aboriginal Self Determination in Australia.* Canberra: Australian Institute of Aboriginal and Torres Strait Islander Studies, 1994.

Flood, Andrew. "Notes from the Field: The Encuentro in La Realidad, Mexico July 17, 1996–August 3, 1996." *Dark Night Field Notes* (Winter/Spring 1997): 31–33.

Franzway, S. *Staking a Claim: Feminism, Bureaucracy and the State.* Sydney, Australia: Allen and Unwin, 1989.

Fraser, N. *Unruly Practices: Power, Discourse and Gender in Contemporary Social Theory*. Minneapolis: University of Minnesota Press, 1989.

——. "Struggle Over Needs: Outline of a Socialist-Feminist Critical Theory of Late-Capitalist Political Culture." In *Women, the State, and Welfare*, edited by L. Gordon, 199–225. Madison Wi.: University of Wisconsin Press, 1990.

Friedman-Kasaba, K. *Memories of Migration: Gender, Ethnicity, and Work in the Lives of Jewish and Italian Women in New York, 1870–1924*. Albany, N.Y.: SUNY Press, 1996.

Friese, M. "Modernisierungsfallen im historischen Prozeß. Zur Entwicklung der Frauenarbeit im gewandelten Europa." *Berliner Journal für Soziologie* 2 (1995): 149–162.

Fujime, Yuki. "Sei no Rekisi gaku" (The History of Sex). In *Gender non Nihon-Shi* (The History of Gender in Japan), vol. 1, 87–110, 315–330. Tokyo: Fuji Shuppan, 1998.

Funk, Nanette, and Magda Mueller. *Gender Politics and Post-Communism*. New York: Routledge, 1993.

Gabayet, Luisa. "Women in Transnational Industry: The Case of the Electronics Industry in Guadalajara, Mexico." Texas Papers on Mexico: Institute of Latin American Studies, University of Texas at Austin. Paper no. 90-04, 1993.

Garcia, V., and L. Gonzalez. "Finding and Enumerating Migrants in Mexican Enclaves of the US Northeast: The Case of Southern Chester County, Pennsylvania". Center for Survey Methods Research, United States Bureau of the Census, Suitland, Maryland, 1995.

——. "Guanajuatense and Other Mexican Immigrants in the United States: New Communities in Non-Metropolitan and Agricultural Regions." Working paper, Julian Samora Research Institute, Michigan State University, 1999a.

——. "Mexican Enclaves in the US Northeast: Subsistence Agriculture in Guanajuato, Mexico, and Migration to Southern Chester County, Pennsylvania." Working paper, Julian Samora Research Institute, Michigan State University, 1999b.

——. "Problem Drinking and Transnational Mexican Farmworkers: Preliminary Findings on Predisposing Factors in their Homeland." Paper presented at the 98th Annual Meeting of American Anthropological Association, Chicago, Ill., 1999c.

Garcia, Victor. "Surviving Farmwork: Economic Strategies of Chicano/Mexican Households in a Rural California Community." Ph.D. diss., University of California, Santa Barbara, 1992.

——. *Results from an Alternative Enumeration in a Mexican and Mexican American Farm Worker Community in California. Ethnographic Evaluation of the Behavioral Causes of Undercount*. Report #12. Washington, D.C.: Center for Survey Methods Research, Bureau of the Census, Department of Commerce, 1995.

Gardner, Brian. *The East India Company: A History*. New York: Dorsett Press, 1971.

Garfinkel, H. *Studies in Ethnomethodology*. Englewood Cliffs, N.J.: Prentice-Hall, 1967.

Gaye, Daffe, and Mamadou Dansokho. "Mondialisation et Globalisation: Les nouveaux habits de l'imperialisme." *Democraties Africaines* (1997): 39–43.

Geertz, C. *The Interpretation of Culture*. New York: Basic Books, 1973.

Giddens, A. *The Constitution of Society*. Cambridge, Mass.: Polity Press, 1984.

——. *Konsequenzen der Moderne*. Frankfurt am Main: Suhrkamp, 1995.

——. *The Third Way: The Renewal of Social Democracy*. Cambridge, Mass.: Polity Press, 1998.

Gonzalez, Laura. *Respuesta Campesina a la Revolución Verde en el Bajío*. México: D. F. Universidad Iberoamericana, 1992.

———. "Proyecto Redes de Migrantes Guanajuatenses." *Pa'l Norte,* Boletín de la Dirección de Atención a Comunidades Guanajuatenses en el Extranjero, no. 4 (1995): 14–16.

———. "Political Brokers, Ejidos, and State Resources in Guanajuato, Mexico." Ph.D. diss., University of California, Santa Barbara, 1996a.

———. "CALI-GUA, la Red de Migrantes que Unen a California con Guanajuato." *Pa'l Norte,* no. 11 (1996b): 14–16.

———. University of Guanajuato. Phone interview with Jane Bayes, May 10, 1998.

Gonzalez, L., and J. Hernandez. "Migrantes, Quiénes Son y Cuántos Son." *Alternativas* 2, no. 4. Revista de la Procuraduría de los Derechos Humanos de Guanajuato (1998): 7–10.

Gordon, L. "Gender, State and Society: A Debate with Theda Skocpol." *Contention* 2, no. 3 (Spring 1993): 139–155.

Government of India, *Annual Report 1997–98.* Ministry of Rural Areas and Employment. 1998.

Griffin, K. *Green Revolution: An Economic Analysis.* Geneva: UN Research Institute for Social Development, 1972.

———. *Political Economy of Agrarian Change, An Essay on the Green Revolution.* Cambridge: Harvard University Press, 1974.

Grimshaw, P. *Women's Suffrage in New Zealand.* Auckland, New Zealand: Auckland University Press, 1972.

———. *Paths of Duty.* Honolulu: University of Hawaii Press, 1983.

Grimshaw, P., and A. May. "Inducements to the Strong to be Cruel to the Weak: Authoritative White Colonial Male Voices and the Construction of Gender in Koori Society." In *Australian Women: Contemporary Feminist Thought,* edited by N. Grieve and A. Burns, 92–106. Melbourne, Australia: Oxford University Press, 1994.

Groneman, C. "Working-Class Immigrant Women in Mid-Nineteenth-Century New York: The Irish Woman's Experience." *Journal of Urban History* 4, no. 3 (1978). 39–51.

Gurumurthy, Anita. *Women's Rights and Status: Questions of Analysis and Measurement.* New York: UNDP Gender in Development Monograph Series, 1998.

Hagen, E., and J. Jenson. "Paradoxes and Promises. Work and Politics in the Postwar Years." In *Feminization of the Labor Force,* edited by J. Jenson, E. Hagen, and C. Reddy, 3–16. New York: Oxford University Press, 1988.

Hahm, Chaibong, and Sang-young Rhyu. "Democratic Reform and Consolidation in South Korea: The Promise of Democracy." In *Democratization and Globalization in Korea,* edited by Chung-in Moon and Jongryn Mo. Seoul: Yonsei University Press, 1999.

Haj, Samira. "Palestinian Women and Patriarchal Relations." *Signs* 17, no. 4 (1992): 761–778.

Hamilton, R. *The Liberation of Women.* London: Macmillan, 1978.

"Hankuk Yeosong Minwoo Hoi." *Pyongdung* 12 (July/Aug. 1998).

Hanochi, Seiko. "Mou-Hitotsu no 'Anzen Houshou' no Kakuritsu ni mukete: josei NGO 20 Nen no Power (Towards an Alternative Security: The Power of 20 Years' Struggle by Women's NGOs)." *Gunshuku Mondai Shiryou* 196 (1997): 330–333.

———. "The State of the Fight Against Patriarchy in the Prostitution/Trafficking Sector in Japan." In *Resurgent Patriarchy: Feminist Constructions and Movement in Asia,* edited by Urvashi Butalia, 203–221. Hong Kong: ARENA Press, 1998.

Haraway, D. *Modest Witness: Second Millennium. Femaleman Meets Oncomouse.* New York: Routledge, 1996.

Hartmann, Heidi I. "The Family as the Locus of Gender, Class and Political Struggle: The Example of Housework." In *Theorizing Feminism: Parallel Trends in the Humanities and Social Sciences*, edited by C. Herrmann and Abigail J. Stewart, 171–197. Boulder, Colo.: Westview Press, 1994.

Hartz, L. *The Founding of New Societies*. New York: Harcourt Brace, 1964.

Harvey, D. *The Condition of Post-Modernity*. Oxford: Blackwell, 1989.

Held, D. "Democracy, The Nation State and the Global System." *Economy and Society* 20, no. 2 (1991): 138–172.

HELP, ed. *Asia no Josei ni yotte Nihon no Mondai ga Mietekita: Josei no Ie HELP 10 Nen no Ayumi* (The Problems of Japan Become Visible Thanks to Asian Women: 10 Years of the House of Women). Tokyo: HELP, 1996.

Hewitt de Alcantara, C. *Modernizing Mexican Agriculture: Socioeconomic Implications of Technological Change 1940–1970*. Geneva: UN Research Institute for Economic Development, 1976.

Hirsch, J. *Der nationale Wettbewerbsstaat*. Berlin-Amsterdam: Edition ID-Archiv, 1995.

Hirschmann, Nancy. *Rethinking Obligation*. Ithaca, N.Y.: Cornell University Press, 1992.

Hirst, Paul, and Grahame Thompson. *Globalization in Question*. Cambridge, Mass.: Polity Press, 1996.

Hood, Jane. *Becoming a Two-Job Family*. New York: Praeger, 1983.

Horta, K. "Chad, Cameroon 'Oil Pipeline Project.'" *Africa Agenda,* no. 11 (June 1997a): 30–32.

Hossfeld, K. "Their Logic against Them: Contradictions in Sex, Race, and Class in Silicon Valley." In *Women Workers and Global Restructuring*, edited by K. Ward, 149–178. Ithaca, N.Y.: Cornell University Press, 1990.

Hughes, R. *The Fatal Shore: A History of the Transportation of Convicts to Australia, 1787–1868*. New York: Pan Books, 1988.

Huntington, Samuel P. *The Third Wave*. Norman: University of Oklahoma Press, 1991.

Iwamatsu, Shigetoshi. "The Dual Structure of Aggression of the Japanese Ruling Elite." In *Sensou Sekinin to Kaku Haizetsu* (War-time Responsibility and the Abolition of the Nuclear Bomb, 93–140). Tokyo: Sanichi Shobo, 1998.

Jain, Devaki. *Panchayati Raj: Women Changing Governance*. Gender in Development Monograph Series. New York: UNDP, 1996.

———, ed. *The Women's Movement in Latin America: Feminism and the Transition to Democracy*. Boston: Unwin Hyman, 1989.

Jaquette, Jane, and Sharon Wolchik. *Women and Democracy: Latin America and Central and Eastern Europe*. Baltimore: Johns Hopkins University Press, 1998.

Jefferson, La Shawn. Human Rights Watch. Phone interview with Jane Bayes, May 20, 1998.

Jennett, C. "Aboriginal Affairs Policy." In *Hawke and Australian Public Policy*, edited by C. Jennett and R. Stewart, 245–283. Melbourne: Macmillan, 1990.

Jensen, J. M. *Passage From India: Asian Indian Immigrants in North America*. New Haven, Conn.: Yale University Press, 1998.

Jenson, J., E. Hagen, and C. Reddy. *Feminization of the Labor Force. Paradoxes and Promises*. New York: Oxford University Press, 1988.

Jessop, B. "Regulation Theories in Retrospect and Prospect." Paper presented at the International Conference on Regulation, Barcelona, June 16–18, 1988.

———. "Veränderte Staatlichkeit." In *Staatsaufgaben*, edited by D. Grimm, 43–73. Baden-Baden: Nomos, 1994.

Kabiria, Nazli. "Culture, Social Class, and Income Control in the Lives of Women Garment Workers in Bangladesh." *Gender and Society* 9, no. 3 (1995): 289–309.

Kamerman, S. B., and A. Kahn. *Childcare, Family Benefits, and Working Parents: A Study in Comparative Policy.* New York: Columbia University Press, 1981.

Kelly, Rita Mae. *The Gendered Economy.* Newberry Park, Calif.: Sage, 1991

Kelly, Rita Mae, and M. Boutilier. *The Making of Political Women.* New York: Nelson-Hall, 1978.

Kelly, Rita Mae, with Phoebe Stambaugh. "Sex-role Spillover: Personal, Familial, and Organizational Roles." In *Workplace/Women's Place: An Anthology*, edited by D. Dunn, 19–31. Los Angeles: Roxbury, 1997.

Kerber, Linda. *Women of the Republic: Intellect and Ideology in Revolutionary America.* Chapel Hill: University of North Carolina Press, 1980.

Kerchner, B., and G. Wilde, eds. *Staat und Privatheit.* Opladen: Leske and Budrich, 1996.

Kim, Soo-Kon. *Analysis of Korean Women's Labor Force Participation Factors* (Korean). Seoul: Korea Development Institute, 1984.

———. *A Study of the Fifteenth General Election and the Women Candidates.* Seoul: Korean Women's Development Institute, Women's Studies Forum, 1997.

Kirkby, D. "The Politics of Paradox: Paid Work and the Liberation of Women, 1970–1990." In *Studies in Gender: Essays in Honour of Norma Grieve*, edited by P. Grimshaw, R. Fincher, and M. Campbell, 235–245. Melbourne: University of Melbourne, 1992.

Knop, Karen. "Beyond Borders: Women's Rights and the Issue of Sovereignty." In *Ours By Right: Women's Rights as Human Rights*, edited by Joanna Kerr, 75–77. London: Zed Books, 1993.

Kopinak, Kathryn. *Desert Capitalism: Maquiladoras in North America's Western Industrial Corridor.* Tucson: University of Arizona Press, 1996.

Korea League of Women Voters. *Survey into the Actual Conditions of Female Workers in Korea: Centering Around the Kuro and Kumi Industrial Complexes.* Seoul, ROK, 1980.

Korean Overseas Information Service. *Korea's Reform and Globalization: President Kim Young Sam Prepares the Nation for the Challenges of the 21st Century.* Seoul: KOIS, 1993.

Kramer, S., and J. Masur, eds. *Jewish Grandmothers.* Boston: Beacon, 1976.

Kreisky, E., and B. Sauer, eds. *Feministische Standpunkte in der Politikwissenschaft.* Frankfurt am Main: Campus, 1995.

———, eds. *Das geheime Glossar der Politikwissenschaft.* Frankfurt am Main: Campus, 1997.

Kulawik, T. "Autonomous Mothers? West German Feminism Reconsidered." *German Politics and Society*, no. 24–25 (1991–92): 67–86.

Kulawik, T., and B. Sauer. *Der halbierte Staat.* Frankfurt: Campus, 1996.

Kurz-Scherf, I. "Krise der Arbeit—Krise der Gewerkschaften." *Weibblick*, no. 25 (1996): 20–29.

KWDI. Annual Report. *Programs to Assist Political Parties in Women's Political Participation.* Seoul: KWDI, 1995.

———. *Annual Statistics on Women 1997.* Seoul: KWDI, 1997.

Landes, Joan. *Women and the Public Sphere in the Age of the French Revolution.* Ithaca, N.Y.: Cornell University Press, 1988.

Lang, S. "The NGOization of Feminism." In *Transitions, Environments, Translation*, edited by J. W. Scott, C. Kaplan, and D. Keates, 101–120. New York: Routledge, 1997.

Lang, Sabine. "The NGOization of Social Movements." Paper presented at the International Conference on Politics, Rights, and Representation, University of Chicago, October 17, 1999.

Larner, W. "The 'New Boys': Restructuring in New Zealand, 1984–94." *Social Politics* 3, no. 1 (1996): 32–56.

Launius, Michael. "The State and Industrial Labor in South Korea." *Bulletin of Concerned Asian Scholars* 16, no. 4 (1984): 2–10.

——. "State-Labor Relations in Democratizing South Korea." *Pacific Focus* 6 (Spring 1991): 39–58.

Lee, Hahn-Been. *Korea: Time, Change, and Administration*. Honolulu: East-West Center Press, University of Hawaii, 1968.

Lee, Hyo-Jae. *Women's Labor Movement in Korea*. Seoul: Jung Woo Sa, 1989 (revised and expanded edition 1996).

Lee, Kwang-Taik "The Status of Employment Discrimination in Labor Field and Directions for Improvement." In *Debates on the Implementation of Male-Female Equal Employment Labor,* 15–27. Seoul: KWDI (in Korean), 1989.

Lee, Young-Hwe. *Labor Relations and Labor Movement in Korea*. Seoul: Younghak Publishing Company (in Korean), 1989.

Leijenaar, Monique. "Gender and Good Governance." Paper presented at the Annual Meeting of the American Political Science Association. Boston, September 3–6, 1998.

Lemoine, M. "Die Arbeiter Zentralamerikas als Geiseln der 'maquilas.'" *Le Monde diplomatique*, die Tageszeitung, March 1998, pp. 14–15.

Leonard, K. I. *Making Ethnic Choices: California's Punjabi Mexican Americans*. Philadelphia: Temple University Press, 1992.

Liddle, Joanna, and Rama Joshi. *Daughters of Independence, Gender, Caste and Class in India*. London: Zed Books, 1986.

Lindsey, L. *Sex Roles: A Sociological Perspective*. Englewood Cliffs, N.J.: Prentice-Hall, 1994.

Mackinnon, C. "Feminism, Marxism, Method and the State." *Signs* 7, no. 3 (1983): 515–544.

Mahnkopf, B. "Die 'Feminisierung der Beschäftigung' — in Europa und Anderwo." *Weibblick* 718 (1997): 22–31.

Mann, P. S. *Micro-Politics: Agency in a Postfeminist Era*. Minneapolis: University of Minnesota Press, 1994.

Marcos. "The First Zapatista Uprising" Letter to *La Journada*, Mexico City, 26 January 1994. Published in *La Journada* (January 31, 1994). Translated by Johathan Fox, *Celebrating the Struggles of Women*. El Paso, Tex.: Comision Nacional por la Democracia en Mexico, 1994.

Margolis, Jane. "El Papel de la Mujer en la Agricultura del Bajío." Master's thesis, Department of Anthropology, Universidad Metropolitana Iztapalapa, 1982.

Martin, P. "Liberale Marktwirtschaft als höchstes Stadium der Menschheit." *Le Monde diplomatique* (June 1997): 14.

Matsui, Yayori. *Asia tono Rentai* (Solidarity with Asia). Ajia Josei: Shiryo Center (Asian Women's Documentation Center), 1997: 53–58.

Mazumdar, S. "Race and Racism: South Asians in the United States." Pp. 25–38 in *Frontiers of Asian American Studies,* edited by G. Nomura, R. Endo, S. H. Sumida, and R. C. Long. Pullman, Wash.: Washington University Press, 1989.

McDonagh, Eileen. "Democratization and Gender in American Political Development: Woman Suffrage and the Contradiction Model." Paper presented at the Conference on Framing Equality: Inclusion, Exclusion and American Political Institutions. Eagleton Institute of Politics, Rutgers University, March 25–26, 1999.

McDowell, L. *Capital Culture: Gender at Work in the City.* Oxford: Blackwell, 1997.

McGlen, Nancy E., and Karen O'Connor. *Women, Politics, and American Society.* Englewood Cliffs, N.J.: Prentice-Hall, 1995.

Messner, D. "Netzwerktheorien: Die Suche nach Ursachen und Auswegen aus der Krise Staatlicher Steuerungsunfähigkeit." In *Vernetzt und verstrickt,* edited by E. Altvater, A. Brunnengräber, M. Haake, and H. Walk, 27–64. Münster: Westfälisches Dampfboot, 1997.

Mika, Sister Susas. Coalition for Justice in the Maquiladoras. Phone interview with Jane Bayes, May 11, 1998.

Mill, John Stuart. *Selections,* edited by Stefan Collini. Cambridge, UK: Cambridge University Press, 1989.

Miller, Francesca. *Latin American Women and the Search for Social Justice.* Hanover, N.H.: University Press of New England, 1991.

Ministry of Political Affairs II. *Republic of Korea. The 50 Years Korean Women's Development.* Seoul: Ministry of Political Affairs II, 1995.

Mogelonsky, M. "Asian Indian Americans." *American Demographics* (August 1995): 32–39.

Mulgan, R. *Maori. Pakeha and Democracy.* Auckland, New Zealand: Oxford University Press, 1989.

Mushakoji, Kinhide. "Multilateralism in a Multicultural World: Notes for a Theory of Occultation." In *The New Realism: Perspectives on Multilateralism and World Order,* edited by Robert W. Cox, 83–108. New York: Macmillan, 1997.

Nash, John F. "The Bargaining Problem." *Econometrica* 18 (1950): 155–162.

———. "Two Person Cooperative Games." *Econometrica* 21, no. 1 (1953): 128–140.

Nash, June, and Christine Kovic. "The Reconstitution of Hegemony: The Free Trade Act and the Transformation of Rural Mexico." In *Globalization: Critical Reflections,* edited by James H. Mittelman, 165–185. Boulder, Colo.: Lynne Rienner, 1997.

NCDM (National Commission for Democracy in Mexico)–1996; Nov./Dec. 1996; March/April, 1998; May 1998. *Libertad.* El Paso, Tex.: National Commission for Democracy in Mexico, USA March.

Nelson, B. "The Origins of the Two-Channel Welfare State: Workmen's Compensation and Mothers' Aid." In *Women, the State, and Welfare,* edited by L. Gordon, 123–151. Madison: University of Wisconsin Press, 1990.

Nelson, Barbara J., and Najma Chowdhury, eds. *Women and Politics Worldwide.* New Haven, Conn.: Yale University Press, 1994.

New South Wales. Issues Paper: *Aboriginal Representation in Parliament.* Sydney, Australia: New South Wales Government Printer, 1998.

Nielsen, J. M. *Sex and Gender in Society, Perspectives on Stratification.* Prospect Heights, N.J.: Waveland, 1990.

Nihon no Senso Sekinin Shiryo Centre, ed. "Symposium: Nationalism to ianfu 'mondai.' " (Nationalism and the "Comfort Women" Problem). In *Yujo* (Traditional Women in the Prostitution of Traditional Japan), edited by Aoki Shoten and Nishiyama, Matsunosuke. Tokyo: Fuji Shuppan, 1999.

Nishiyama, Matsunosuke, ed. *Yujo* (Traditional Women in the Prostitution of Traditional Japan). Tokyo: Fuji Shuppan, 1979.

NSO (National Statistical Office). *Major Statistics of Korean Economy*. Seoul: NSO, 1997, 1999.

OECD (Organization for Economic Cooperation and Development). *Women and Structural Change: New Perspectives*. Paris: OECD, 1994.

———. *Labour Force Statistics 1977–1997*. Paris: OECD, 1999.

Ogle, G. E. *South Korea: Dissent within the Economic Miracle*. New York: Zed Books, 1990.

Ong, P., E. Bonacich, and L. Cheng. *The New Asian Immigration in Los Angeles and Global Restructuring*. Philadelphia: Temple University Press, 1994.

Onuma, Yasuaki, Michiko Shimomura, and Haruki Wada, eds. *Ianfu Mondai to Asia Josei Kikin* (*"Comfort Women" and the Asian Fund*). Tokyo: Tcshindo, 1998.

Ostner, I. "Arm ohne Ehemann? Sozialpolitische Regulierung von Lebenschancen für Frauen Im internationalen Vergleich." *Politik und Zeitgeschichte* (Sept. 1, 1995): B36–37/95.

Palerm, J. V. "A Binational System of Agricultural Production: The Case of the Mexican Bajío and California." In *Mexico and the United States Neighbors in Crisis*, edited by D. G. Aldrich and L. Meyer, 311–367. Riverside: University of California (UC: Mexus) and Borgo Press, 1992.

———. *Los Nuevos Campesinos*. Mexico City: Universidad Iberoamericana, 1998.

———. "Las Nuevas Comunidades Mexicanas en los Espacios Rurales de los Estados Unidos: a Propósito de una Reflexión acerca del Quehacer Antropológico." *Areas, Revista de Ciencias Sociales*. Murcia, Espana: Universidad de Murcia, 1999, pp. 153–179.

Parekh, B. "Review of P. James's *Nation Formation: Toward a Theory of Abstract Community*." *Nations and Nationalism* 4, no. 2 (1998): 273–274.

Pateman, Carole. *The Sexual Contract*. Stanford, Calif.: Stanford University Press, 1988.

———. "Democracy and Democratization: 1991 Presidential Address, 16th World Congress, IPSA." *International Political Science Review* 17, no. 1 (1996): 5–12.

Pena, Devon. "Tortuosidad: Shop Floor Struggles of Female Maquiladora Workers." In *Women on the U.S.-Mexico Border: Responses to Change*, edited by Vicki L. Ruiz and Susan Tiano, 129–154. Boulder, Colo.: Westview Press, 1991.

———. *Terror of the Machine: Technology, Work, Gender, and Ecology*. Austin: University of Texas Press, 1995.

Peterson, V. Spike, and Anne Sisson Runyon. *Global Gender Issues*. 2nd ed. Boulder, Colo.: Westview Press, 1999.

Pimentel Rodríguez, M. G. "Diagnóstico de Salud, Comunidad La Ordeña, Moroleón, Gto." Informe del Servicio Social realizado de febrero de 1994 a febrero de 1995 y entregado a la UNAM y a la Secretaria de Salud del Estado de Guanajuato, 1995.

Pleck, E. "The Old World, New Rights, and the Limited Rebellion: Challenges to Traditional Authority in Immigrant Families." *Research in the Interweave of Social Roles: Jobs and Families* 3 (1983): 91–112.

Pozzetta, G. E., ed. *Ethnicity and Gender*. Hamden, Conn.: Garland Publishing, 1992.

Preston, Julia. "Both Carrot and Stick Fail in Chiapas." *New York Times*, May 17, 1998: A6.

Pyke, Karen D. "Women's Employment as a Gift or Burden? Marital Power Across Marriage Divorce and Remarriage." *Gender and Society* 8, no. 1 (1994): 73–91.

Radcliffe, Sara, and Sallie Westwood, eds. *Viva: Woman and Popular Protest in Latin America*. New York: Routledge, 1993.

Rai, Shirin, Hilary Pilkington, and Annie Phizacklea, eds. *Women in the Face of Change: The Soviet Union, Eastern Europe and China*. London: Routledge, 1992

Ralston, H. *Lived Experiences of South Asian Immigrant Women in Atlantic Canada: The Interconnection of Race, Class and Gender*. Lewiston, N.Y.: Mellen Press, 1996.

Ramu, G. N. *Women, Work and Marriage in Urban India, A Study of Dual and Single-earner Couples*. New Delhi, India: Sage, 1989.

Reeves, W. P. *State Experiments in Australia and New Zealand*. London: Grant, 1902.

"Report of the Special Rapporteur on violence against women, its causes and consequences." Ms. Radhika Coomaraswamy, in accordance with Commission of Human Rights resolution 1994–45. Report on the mission to the Democratic People's Republic of Korea, the Republic of Korea and Japan on the issue of military sexual slavery in wartime. United Nations, Economic and Social Council, E/CN.4/1996/Add.1, 4 January 1996. Para. 134.

Rodriguez, Cecelia. "Conversations with Cecelia Rodriquez," telephone interview with Cecelia Rodriguez by Ryan Werner of KOPN (NPR) Radio in Columbia, Missouri, Chicago: *Dark Nights Field Notes* (Winter/Spring 1997): 6–9.

Roediger, D. R. *Towards the Abolition of Whiteness*. New York: Verso, 1994.

Ross, A. *The Hindu Family in Its Urban Setting*. Toronto: University of Toronto Press, 1960.

Safa, Helen I. *The Myth of the Male Breadwinner: Women and Industrialization in the Caribbean*. Boulder, Colo.: Westview Press, 1995.

Safilios-Rothschild, Constantina. "Socio-Economic Determinants of the Outcomes of Women's Income Generation in Developing Countries." In *Women, Employment and the Family in the International Division of Labour*, edited by Sharon Stichter and Jane L. Parpart, 221–228. London: Macmillan Press Ltd., 1990.

Saint Germain, Michelle. "Women, Democratization, and Public Policy." *Policy Sciences* 27 (1994): 269–276.

Salaff, Janet W. "Women, the Family, and the State: Hong Kong, Taiwan, Singapore—Newly Industrialized Countries in Asia." In *Women in the World 1975–1985*, 2nd ed., edited by Lynne B. Iglitzin and Ruth Ross. Santa Barbara, Calif.: ABC-CLIO, 1986.

Sanday, P. *Female Power and Male Dominance*. Cambridge, UK: Cambridge University Press, 1981.

Sassen, S. "Toward a Feminist Analytics of the Global Economy." *Indiana Journal of Global Legal Studies* 4, no. 1 (Fall 1996): 7–41.

Sawer, M. *Sisters in Suits*. Sydney: Allen and Unwin, 1990.

Sawer, M., and M. Simms. *A Woman's Place: Women and Politics in Australia*. Sydney: Allen and Unwin, 1984, 1993.

Schmitter, P. C. "Still the Century of Corporatism?" *Review of Politics* 36, no. 1 (1974): 85–131.

Scott, Catherine. *Gender and Development: Rethinking Modernization and Dependency Theory*. Boulder, Colo.: Lynne Rienner, 1996.

Scott, Joan Wallach. *Only Paradoxes to Offer: French Feminists and the Rights of Man*. Cambridge: Harvard University Press, 1996.

Sen, Amartya. "Economics and the Family." *Asian Development Review* 1, no. 2 (1983): 14–21.

——. "Gender and Cooperative Conflicts." In *Persistent Inequalities*, edited by Irene Tinker, 123–149. New York: Oxford University Press, 1990.

———. *Development as Freedom*. New York: Alfred A. Knopf, 1999.

Sengo-Hosho-Hoan Jitsugen. *Kojin Hosho no Jitsugen ni Mukete Jitsugen* (A Conceptualization of War-Time Compensation Act: Towards the Realization of Individual Compensation). Tokyo: Toshin-do, 1996.

Sethi, R. C. "Smells Like Racism." In *Race, Class, and Gender in the United States: An Integrated Study*, edited by P. S. Rothenberg, 154–164. New York: St. Martin's Press, 1998.

Sharma, Ursula. *Women's Work, Class, and the Urban Household: A Study of Shimla, North India*. London: Tavistock Publications, 1986.

———. *Women, Work and Property in North-West India*. London: Tavistock Publications, 1990.

Siddiqi, M. U., and E. Y. Reeves. "A Comparative Study of Mate Selection Criteria among Indians in India and the United States." *International Journal of Comparative Sociology* 27, nos. 3–4 (1986): 226–233.

Simms, M. "The Australian Feminist Experience." In *Australian Women: Feminist Perspectives*, edited by N. Grieve and P. Grimshaw, 227–239. Melbourne, Australia: Oxford University Press, 1981.

———. "Democracy Freedom and the Women's Movement in the Philippines." In *Politics of the Future: The Role of Social Movements*, edited by C. Jennett and R. Stewart, 340–354. Melbourne, Australia: Macmillan, 1989.

Sklair, Leslie. *Assembling for Development: The Maquila Industry in Mexico and the United States*. Boston: Unwin Hyman, 1989.

Slaughter, M., and P. Swagel. *Does Globalization Lower Wages and Export Jobs?* Washington, D.C.: International Monetary Fund, 1997.

Smith, J., and I. Wallerstein. *Creating and Transforming Households. The Constraints of the World-Economy*. Cambridge: Cambridge University Press, 1992.

Smock, A. "Conclusion: Determinants of Women's Roles and Status." In *Women: Roles and Status in Eight Countries*, edited by A. Smock and J. Zollinger. New York: John Wiley, 1977.

Sohn, Bong-Scuk. "Women's Political Engagement and Participation in the Republic of Korea." In *Women and Politics Worldwide*, edited by Barbara J. Nelson and Najma Chowdhury, 437–447. New Haven, Conn.: Yale University Press, 1994.

Sperling, Valerie. "Gender Politics and the State during Russia's Transition Period." In *Gender, Politics, and the State*, edited by Vicky Randall and Georgian Waylen, 143–165. London: Routledge, 1998.

Standing, Hilary. "Resources, Wages and Power: The Impact of Women's Employment in Urban Bengali Household." In *Women, Work, and Ideology in the Third World*, edited by Haleh Afshar, 232–257. London: Tavistock Publications, 1985.

Steinberg, S. *The Ethnic Myth*. New York: Antheneum, 1981.

Stephen, Lynn. "Women in Mexico's Popular Movements: Survival Strategies Against Ecological and Economic Improverishment." *Latin American Perspectives* 19, no. 1 (Winter 1992): 73–96.

Stetson, D. M., and A. Mazur, eds. *Comparative State Feminism*. Thousand Oaks, Calif.: Sage, 1995.

Strange, Susan. *The Retreat of the State: The Diffusion of Power in the World Economy*. Cambridge: Cambridge University Press, 1996.

Supapung, Nayana: "Thai-Japanese NGOs' Cooperation to Assist Thai Female Migrants: Progress and Problems in Terms of Networking and Human Rights." In

International Female Migration and Japan: Networking, Settlement and Human Rights, edited by Meiji Gakuin, 131–138. Tokyo: PRIME (International Peace Research Institute), 1996.

Suret-Canale, J. *Afrique Noire Occidentale et Centrale: l'Ere Coloniale (1890 a 1945)*. Paris: Editions Sociales, 1964.

Sy, J. Habib. *Telecommunications Dependency: The African Saga (1850–1980)*. Nairobi, Kenya: Regal Press Kenya Limited, 1996.

Sydney Morning Herald. January 5 and May 1, 1999.

Thomas, Dorothy Q. "Holding Governments Accountable by Public Pressure." In *Ours By Right: Women's Rights as Human Rights*, edited by Joanna Kerr, 82–88. London: Zed Books, 1993.

Thompson, E. P. "The Moral Economy of the English Crowd in the Eighteenth Century." *Past and Present* (February 1971): 76–136.

Thurow, L. S. *The Future of Capitalism*. New York: Penguin Books, 1997.

Tiano, Susan. "*Maquiladoras* in Mexicalli: Integration on Exploitation?" In *Women on the US Mexico Border: Responses to Change*, edited by Vicki L. Ruiz and Susan Tiano, 77–104. Boulder, Colo.: Westview Press, 1991.

———. *Patriarchy On the Line: Labor, Gender, and Ideology in the Mexican Maquila Industry*. Philadelphia: Temple University Press, 1994.

Tomioka, Emiko, and Mutsuko Yoshioka. *Nihon no Joseito Jinken* (Women and Human Rights in Japan). Tokyo: Fuji Shuppan, 1995.

Tong, Mary. Coalition for Justice in the Maquiladoras. Personal interview with Jane Bayes, April 15, 1998 at California State University, Northridge.

Tong, Mary and Robinson, Maria. Support Committee for Maquiladora Workers. Phone interview with Jane Bayes, May 10, 1998.

Triandis, H. C. "The Self and Social Behavior in Differing Cultural Contexts." *Pychological Review* 96, no. 3 (1989): 506–520.

Tronto, Joan. *Moral Boundaries*. New York: Routledge, 1993.

Truong, Thanh-Dam. *Sex, Money, and Morality: Prostitution and Tourism in Southeast Asia*. London: Zed Books, 1990.

UNDP. *Human Development Report*. New York: Oxford University Press, 1995.

———. (United Nations Development Program). *Reconceptualising Governance*. New York: UNDP, 1997a.

———. *Human Development Report*. New York: Oxford University Press, 1997b.

———. *Human Development Report*. New York: Oxford University Press, 1998.

UNESCO. *Report on the State of Education in Africa: Education Strategies for the 1990s: Orientation and Achievements*. Dakar, Senegal: Breda, 1995.

United Nations. *Women in a Changing Global Economy: 1994 World Survey on the Role of Women in Development*. New York: United Nations, 1995.

U.S. Bureau of the Census. *Statistical Yearbook*. Washington D.C.: Government Printing Office, 1970.

———. *Statistical Abstracts*. Washington, D.C.: Government Printing Office, 1995.

———. *Statistical Abstracts*, nos. 11 and 13. Washington, D.C.: Government Printing Office, 1997.

Valencia, Reynaldo. "*Persistencia y Expansion de sistemas Agricolas Tradicionales: el Caso del Huamil en el Bajío.*" Master's thesis in Social Anthropology. UAM-Iztapalapa, Mexico, D.F., 1981.

Valenzuela, Maria Elena. "Women and the Democratization Process in Chile." In *Women and Democracy: Latin America and Central and Eastern Europe*, edited by Jane Jaquette and Sharon Wolchik, 47–74. Baltimore: Johns Hopkins University Press, 1998.

Ward, K., and J. L. Pyle. "Gender, Industrialization, Transnational Corporations, and Development: An Overview of Trends and Patterns." In *Women in the Latin American Development Process*, edited by C. E. Bose and E. Acosta-Belen, 37–64. Philadelphia: Temple University Press, 1995.

Warning, Marilyn. *Counting for Nothing: What Women Value and What Women Are Worth.* Toronto: University of Toronto Press, 1999.

Wichterich, C. *Die globalisierte Frau: Berichte aus der Zukunft der Ungleichheit.* Hamburg: Rowohlt, 1998.

WILPF (Women's International League for Peace and Freedom). *Justice Denied! Human Rights and the International Financial Institutions.* Geneva: WILPF, 1994.

World Bank. *Sub-Saharan Africa: From Crisis to Sustainable Growth: A Long-Term Perspective Study.* Herndon, Va.: World Bank, 1989.

Wright, Erik Olin. *Class Counts: Comparative Studies in Class Analysis.* Cambridge, UK: Cambridge University Press, 1997.

Yamawaki, Keizo. "An Overview of the Influx of Foreign Workers to Japan." In *International Female Migration and Japan: Networking, Settlements, and Human Rights*, edited by Meiji Gakin, 9–28. Tokyo: PRIME (International Peace Research Institute), 1996.

Yans-McLaughlin, V. "A Flexible Tradition: South Italian Immigrants Confront a New York Experience." *Journal of Social History* 7, no. 4 (Summer 1974): 429–445.

Yasuaki Onuma, Michiko Shimomura, and Haruki Wada, eds. *Ianfu Mondai to Asia Josei Kikin* ("Comfort Women" and Asian Women Fund). Tokyo: Toshindo, 1998.

Yoon, Bang-Soon L. *State Power and Public R&D in Korea: A Case Study of the Korea Institute of Science and Technology*, Ph.D. diss., University of Hawaii at Manoa, 1992a.

———. "Reverse Brain Drain in South Korea: State-led Model." *Studies in Comparative International Development* 27, no. 1 (Spring 1992b): 4–26.

———. "Politics of Agenda-Building: Imperial Japan's Military Sexual Slavery Case." In *Handbook of Global Social Studies*, edited by Stuart Nagel and Amy Robb, 163–181. New York: Marcel Dekker, 2000.

Yoon, Jung-Sook, "Reconsidering Autonomy in the Women's Movement: A Strategy of Korean Women's Associations United." Unpublished M.A. thesis, University of Sussex, 1997.

Yoon, Woo-Hyun. "Employment Issues: Status and Tasks." Seoul, Korea: Federation of Korean Women's Organizations (Hankuk Yoyun), 1998.

Yoshiaki, Yoshimi. "'Jugun-Ianfu' Mondai towa." (What Is the "Comfort Women" Problem) Asia Forum ed. Moto "Ianfu" no Shogen: 50 Nen no Chinmoku wo Yabutte (Testimony of the Former "Comfort Women": Breaking 50 Years of Silence) *Koseisha*, 1997: 38–45.

Young, B. "Politik und Ökonomie im Kontext von Globalisierung." In *Politische Vierteljahresschrift*, edited by E. Kreisky and B. Sauer, 137–151. Sonderheft: Geschlechterverhältnisse im Kontext politischer Transformation 28, 1997.

———. *Triumph of the Fatherland: German Unification and the Marginalization of Women.* Ann Arbor: University of Michigan Press, 1999.

Young, Gay. "Gender Identification and Working Class Solidarity among Maquila Workers in Cuidad Juarez: Stereotypes and Realities." In *Women on the U.S.-Mexico Border:*

Responses to Change, edited by Vicki L. Ruiz and Susan Tiano, 105–128. Boulder, Colo.: Westview Press, 1991.

Yung, J. *Chinese Women of America*. Seattle: University of Washington Press, 1986.

Zazueta, A. *Policy Hits the Ground*. Washington, D.C.: World Resources Institute, 1995.

Zeleza, Tiyambe. *A Modern Economic History of Africa: The Nineteenth Century*. Vol. 1. Dakar, Senegal: Codesria, 1993.

INTERNET SOURCES

Ethyl Corporation vs. Government of Canada: <http://www.nassist.com/mai/ethylx.html>

Korean Working Women's Network (in Korean), 1997: <http://www.kwwnet.org>

Korean Working Women's Network (in Korean), 1998. "IMF's New Liberalism: Attack and Employment Issues." 1998: 1–43: <http://www.kwwnet.org/English/index.html>

MAI & Human Rights: <http://www.citizen.org/pctrade/MAI/What%20is/mailhuman3.htm>

OECD website: <http://www.oecd.org>

Index

Aboriginal Representation in Parliament, 18

Aborigines, 17, 19, 23–24

acculturation, 109–10

Adams, Patricia, 54

Afghanistan, Taliban in, 233

AFL-CIO, 165

Africa: Bretton Woods institutions in, 57–59, 61–62, 69; Chad oil project, 10, 62, 67–68; under colonialism, 9, 51–52, 68; debt cycle in, 53–55; and debt management, 9–10, 55, 58, 62, 63–66, 71–72; Exxon/Shell/ELF oil consortium in, 67, 70–71; human underdevelopment in, 52–53, *65*; and investment/trade deregulation, 59–62; literacy rate in, 52, 53, *65*; Lomé Convention, 10, 50, 56–57; neoliberal policy agenda for, 55–56; privatization policy in, 68–70; regional integration in, 72–74;

Africa Growth and Opportunity Act (AGOA), 60–62

African National Congress, 227

Aglietta, M.A., 27

agrarian capitalism, 29

Agrarian Reform Law (Mexico), 160

Agriculture: in Africa, 52, 56–57; in Mexico, 10, 11, 77, 82–83, 160; and modernization theory, 227–28

Aguirre vs. American United Global, 167

AIDS, in Africa, 49, 53

Allan, Lyall, 18

Altvater, E., 28–29, 44

Alvarez, Sonia, 228, 231

American Friends Service Committee, 165, 168

American United Global, 166–67

Amin, Samir, 50

Anderson, F., 22

androcentrism, 225

"Angel of the House", 18

Anthony, Susan B., 154

Anwar, M., 110

Argentina, 16, 143, 224

Arizpe, Lourdes, 77

Asians in U.S.: and immigration law, 97–98. *See also* Indian (Asian) women in U.S.

Asian Women's Fund, 140, 214, 216–17, 218, 219, 220

Association of African Women for Research and Development (AA-Word), 67

Association of Democratic Lawyers in Mexico, 169

Australia. *See* Oceania settler societies

Bajío region, Mexico, 78, 82–88

Bakker, I., 37

Bando Trading, 183

Banks, O., 21

255

Barkley Brown, Elsa, 234
"Barred Zone" Immigration Act, 97
Basu, Amrita, 231–32
Baumann, Z., 28
Bayes, Jane H., 1–14, 11–12, 147–70, 172, 179
Beall, Jo, 196
Becker, Gary S., 122, 123–24
Becker-Schmidt, Regina, 39
Bell, S., 21
Bellinghousen, Hermann, 159
Benedictine Sisters, 165
Benería, Lourdes, 152
Benetton, 33
Berger, B., 109
Berger, P.L., 109, 116
Bill of Rights, 154
Blumberg, Rae Lesser, 103, 152
Bonacich, E., 98, 103, 110
Border Committee of Women Workers, 166
Border Industrialization Program, 163
border industries. *See maquiladora* industries
Border Workers Support Committee (CAFOR), 168
Bosnian War, 233
Botay, Carlota, 77
Bourdieu, P., 43
Bouton, Cynthia A., 150
Bowden, Peta, 208
Brazil, 224
breadwinner gender regime, 9, 10, 35, 36, 38, 106
Bretton Woods institutions: in Africa, 57–59, 61–62, 69, 73. *See also specific names*
British East India Company, 2
Brodie, Janine, 42
Brown, Wendy, 228
Bryce, J., 16, 22
budgetary policy, neoliberal, 55
Buijs, G., 100
Burdeau, Georges, 208
Burma, sex trafficking in, 143, 145
Burton, Clare, 23
Bystydzienski, Jill, 224

Caldeira, Teresa, 230, 232
Cambodia, 32, 143, 145
Canada, 9, 16, 21
Capitalism: agrarian, 29; industrial, 29, 30, 35–37; informational, 29–30
Cardosa, Fernando H., 177
Carrillo, Teresa, 150
Case, Mary Anne, 234
Castells, M., 28, 29, 30, 31
Castles, S., 16
Catholic Jeunes Ouvriers Chretiens (JOC), 184–85
Chad oil project, 10, 62, 67–68
Chafet, J.S., 113
Chakrabarty, D., 115
Chandler, Alfred, 30–31, 35
Chang, Kyung–Sup, 182
Chang, Sung–ja, 176
Charter 77, 46
Chartists, 17
Chatterjee, P., 115
cheap-labor countries, 32–33
Cheng, L., 98, 99, 103, 110
Chiapas conflict, 158–63
child care, 40, 148
child labor, 11
child-rearing, 40, *104*, 107–8, 124
Chile, 16
China: comfort women in, 140; global factories in, 32; sex trafficking in, 143
Chinese Exclusion Act of 1907, 97
Chinese immigrants, 97, 115
Cho, Seewha, 180, 185
Cho, Soon-Kyoung, 181
Chodorow, N., 114
Choi, Sang-Yong, 172
Choi, Young-Hee, 191
Chonggye Garment Workers Union, 184
Chonggye Union, 183
Cho, Sungsook, 191
Chosun Women Alliance, 186
Chowdhury, Najma, 224, 228
Chowdury, D.P., 151
Christian Women's Union for Public Morality, 139
Chun, Doo-Whan, 176, 177, 182, 187
Chun, Tae-Ti, 183

Chung, Hyun-Back, 186
civil society, 228, 234–35
class: and gender regimes, 152–53; and
   income control, 122–23, 126; and labor
   force participation of women, 18,
   40–41; and political participation of
   women, 23
Coalition for Justice in the Maquiladoras
   (CJM), 165–66, 168
Cobbett, Richard, 17
Colombia, sex trafficking in, 143
Colonialism: in Africa, 9, 51–52, 68; and
   democratization, 206;
   economic/political components of, 2–3;
   in Oceania, 16
colonias: labor organizing in, 166;
   Maclovia Rojas resistance, 167–68
comfort women, 138, 139–40, 210;
   compensation of, 207, 211–12, 214–19;
   disclosure of, 211, 213, 220; public
   debate over, 205, 211, 212–13; state
   sponsorship of, 211, 212
Comite Pro-Defensa de Presos, Exiliados
   y Desaparecidos Politicos, 150
communications technology, and
   informational capitalism, 29–30
Confederation of Mexican Workers
   (CTM), 159
Connell, R.W., 1, 8, 34, 121, 147, 149,
   179
consumption, mass, 27
Convention Against Trafficking and the
   Exploitation of Prostitution of Others,
   141
Convention to Eliminate Discrimination
   Against Women (CEDAW), 13, 155,
   156
Coomaraswamy, Radhika, 140, 155–56, 215
cooperative conflicts, household, 122, 124
Coordinadora Nacional de Movimiento
   Urbano Popular (CONAMUP), 151
Craske, Nikki, 224, 230
"creative schizophrenia" theory, 109, 116
Crompton, Rosemary, 126

Dasgupta, S.D., 9, 97, 109, 115
debt cycle, 53–55

debt management, 9–10, 55, 58, 148;
   HIPC Initiative, 10, 62, 63–66, 71–72.
   See also structural adjustment policy
Declaration of Independence, 5
Deere, Carmen D., 77
Dembele, Demba Moussa, 57
Demirovic, A., 44
Democratization: and civil society
   concept, 228, 234–35; defined, 223;
   expansion, 5–6, 154; under federalism,
   9, 20–21; and indigenous peoples, 16,
   17–18, 23–24; of marriage, 207; of
   nonstate institutions, 6; in South Korea,
   172–73, 179, 182, 185–91; and U.S.
   policy, 8
democratization/gender regimes, 5, 6, 8,
   11– 13; and ethical standards, 12–13,
   206–9; and hidden undemocratic
   sectors, 205–6, 207; and human rights
   agenda, 7, 8, 11–13; negative impact
   on women, 5, 6, 13, 223–35; and
   personal security rights, 206–7; in
   private institutions, 207; in process *vs*
   consolidation phases, 12; and
   prostitution, 207–10; and quota system,
   7, 8, 12, 195, 234;
Denoon, D., 16, 21
Despacho Obero of Juarez, 165
Devi, Indira M., 123
Die Gruppe von Lissabon, 33
Dinnerstein, M., 111
Di Stefano, Christine, 228
Domrese, R.J., 99
Dong-il Textile, 183

Eastern Europe: Bosnian War, 233; labor
   force participation of women, 227;
   political participation of women, 224,
   229; sex trafficking in, 143, 224
economy: Keynesian welfare state, 27, 36,
   41–43; local, 4; market-oriented, 43;
   service, 23, 29. *See also* globalization
Education: in Africa, 53, 65; and gender
   regime change, 152, 153; in India,
   98–99, 111, 112–13; workers', 185,
   193–94n11
Eggerton, Laura, 169

Eisenstein, Hester, 44
El Comité Emiliano Zapata, 162
ELF-ERAP, 67
ELF/Exxon/Shell oil consortium, in
    Africa, 67, 70–71
elitism, democratic, 225, 226
Elizabeth I, Queen of England, 2
Elson, Diane, 40, 121
employment of workers. *See* labor force
    participation of women
Encuentro, 162
Enhanced Structural Adjustment Facility
    Program (ESAF), 63, 64, 66, 71–72
environment, 4, 8; and Chad oil project,
    67–68; and fishing agreements, 57; and
    maquiladora border industries, 165
equal employment opportunity (EEO)
    programs, 23
*Ethyl Corporation vs. Government of
    Canada*, 59, 61
Europe: -Africa trade, 51–52, 56–57;
    democratization in, 207–8;
    denationalization in, 27; and gender
    equity, 226; globalization impact on, 9;
    legalized prostitution in, 143–44;
    political participation of women, 150,
    224; women's movement in, 23. *See
    also* Eastern Europe
European Economic Community, in Lomé
    Convention, 56–57
Evans, L., 99
exchange rate policy, neoliberal, 55
Exportadora de Mano de Obra (EMOSA),
    166–67
export industry, 11
export zones, 32, 45
Exxon/Shell/ELF oil consortium, in
    Africa, 67, 70–71

Fall, Yassine, 9–10, 49–74, 56, 72
Faludi, Susan, 43
family wage, 3, 19, 23, 154
Faver, C.A., 109, 111, 117, 118
federalism, 9, 20–21
feminism: democratization critique of,
    225–29; and equality in private
    institutions, 207; immigrants' negative

view of, 115; on nation-state, 43–44;
    on prostitution, 139, 144. *See also*
    women's movement
Fernández-Kelly, M.P., 33, 38, 164
fisheries, and Lomé Convention, 57
Flammang, Janet, 229
Fletcher, C., 24
Flood, Andrew, 162
food supply, 4, 8, 10, 57
Fordist industrialization, 9, 27, 29, 35–37
foreign investment, 3, 8, 10; Multilateral
    Agreement on Investment (MAI),
    59–60
Franzway, S., 22, 23
Fraser, N., 42, 44
French Regulation School, 9, 29, 35
French Revolution, 5
Friedman-Kasaba, K., 99, 100, 114, 117,
    118, 119
Friese, M., 37, 41
Fujime, Yuki, 138
Funk, Nanette, 228

Gabayet, Luisa, 153
Garcia, A.M., 33
Gardner, Brian, 2
Garfinkel, H., 115
garment industry, 33, 87–88, 89, 164, 183
GATT (General Agreement on Tariffs and
    Trade), 58
Geertz, C., 119
gender, defined, 34
Gender Empowerment Index (GEM), 67
gender orders: defined, 34; of Fordist era,
    36, 37; norms and standards, 150;
    reconfiguration of, 37–40, 45
gender regimes: breadwinner model, 9, 10,
    35, 36, 38. 106; and class, 152–53;
    Connell's concept of, 1, 147, 149, 179;
    defined, 34, 149; in double
    wage-earner family, 38, 113; forces for
    change in, 150–56; and housework
    sharing, 123–36; and income control,
    122–36, 152; in India, 121–36; in
    Indian (Asian) immigrant family,
    103–17; and individualization, 38;
    institutionalized, 2, 4–5, 7; and

international standards, 155, 156, 179; in Mexican immigrant family, 10–11, 90–91, 92; in Mexico, 10, 11, 75, 77, 83, 86–87, 88–89, 91–92, 151–52; in Oceania, 18–20, 21–23; partnership, 9, 19, 129–30; patriarchal, 4, 7, 8, 127; political participation impact on, 150–51; and property, 18–19; separate spheres of activity, 18, 19, 25, *104*, 106; as social contract, 148, 149; in societal institutions, 149–50; and spousal power hierarchy, 103, 106, 113, 116; and spousal role reversal, *105*, 106, 107; in workplace, 152, 153–54. *See also* democratization/gender regimes; globalization/gender regimes

Gender-related Development Index (GDI), 67

General Agreement on Tariffs and Trade (GATT), 58

Gentlemen's Agreement of 1907, 97

Germany: democratization expansion in, 6; legalized prostitution in, 143; women's movement in, 44

Giddens, Anthony, 20, 28, 34

global cities, 31, 157

global factories, 32, 33, 45, 46, 87

globalization: components of, 2–3, 50; counter-tendencies to, 28–29; historical, 49; and immigration, 4, 8, 10, 77, 95, 97, 119–20; informal economy of, 32–33; intellectual origins of, 6–7; *vs* internationalization, 28; neoliberalist agenda in, 3–4, 23; network structures for, 30–33; rise of informational capitalism, 29–30; of sex trafficking, 138, 141, 142–43, 144–45; as "timeless time", 28; and U.S. policy, 8. *See also* Africa; Mexico

globalization/gender regimes, 3, 4, 6, 7, 8–13, 148–49; in Africa, 10, 50, 52, 57, 67–68, 70, 73–74; and international standards, 155, 179; and labor market, 27–47, 154; in Mexico, 10, 11, 75–76; positive aspects of, 45–46; sites of

contestation, 4, 6, 7, 8, 153, 157–69; in South Korea, 179–85

Gonzalez, Laura, 10, 75–94, 78, 163

Gordon, L., 34, 44

Green Revolution, 77, 78, 93–94

Grimshaw, Patricia, 19, 20, 21

Groneman, C., 114

Guanajuatenses in U.S., 89–91, 92

Guanajuato, regions of, 77–78

Gupta, Suranjana, 12, 195–204

Gurumurthy, Anita, 199, 201

Haetae Cookie Company, 183

Hagen, E., 36, 42

Hahm, Chaibong, 172

Haj, Samira, 152

Hamilton, R., 18

Hanochi, Seiko, 11, 137–46, 210

Haraway, D., 30

Hartmann, Heidi I., 124

Hartz, L., 16, 17

Harvey, D., 31, 33

Hawkesworth, Mary E., 1–14, 13, 223–36

Head, B., 21

Held, D., 44

Helsinki Declaration, 46

Hernandez, Hortensia, 168

highly indebted poor countries (HIPC), 52; debt relief initiative, 10, 62, 63–66

Hirsch, J., 28

Hirschmann, Nancy, 228, 229

Hirst, Paul, 28

HIV/AIDS, in Africa, 49, 53

Hood, Jane, 122

Horta, Korina, 67

Hossfeld, K., 39

household production, 18, 32–33, 38–39, 87

households, 39, 121–22

househusband concept, 106, 107

housework: and class, 153; devaluation of, 36; in immigrant families, 91, 116; and income control, 123–36; paid domestic help, 124, 125; and spousal role reversal, *105*, 106, 107; and triple shift, 39

Hughes, R., 17

human development index (HDI), 52
Human Rights Watch, 158, 169
human rights of women, 3, 7, 11–13;
  gesellschaft vs gemeinschaft views of,
  208, 217; *idées de droit vs règles de
  droit*, 208–9, 215; international
  recognition of, 11–12, 46, 155–56;
  international tribunals on, 235; and
  state accountability, 140, 156, 212–22.
  See also violence against women
Hume, David, 7
Huntington, Samuel P., 172, 173, 188, 189
Hydraulique Quebec, 69

Ibarra de Piedra, Rosaro, 150
idées de droit, 208, 209, 215–22
IMF. *See* International Monetary Fund
immigration: and acculturation, 109–10;
  associational, 100; Chinese
  immigrants, 97, 115; and
  empowerment of women, 117–19;
  globalization tied to, 3, 4, 8, 10, 77, 95,
  97, 119–20; and labor force
  participation, 89–90, 100, *104–5*, 113,
  114, 116; liberalization of Asian
  immigration, 97–98; restriction of
  Asian immigration, 97. *See also* Indian
  (Asian) women in U.S.; Mexicans in
  U.S.
Immigration Act of 1965, 97, 98
Immigration Reform and Control Act of
  1986 (IRCA), 94n6
India, 6, 11, 12; education in, 98–99, 111,
  112–13; income control/housework-
  sharing in, 122–36; local government
  in, 195–96; political participation of
  women, 195, 196–204, 234; savings
  and credit groups (SCGs) in, 198;
  traditional culture in, 112
Indian (Asian) women in U.S., 95–97;
  acculturation of, 109–10; antifeminist
  attitudes of, 115; behavioral duality of,
  109, 116–17; demographic
  characteristics of, 100–103;
  educational background of, 111,
  112–13; empowerment and selfhood
  of, 117–19; gender regimes of, 10–11,

103–17; generational differences
  among, 111–12; labor force
  commitment of, 117, 118; labor force
  participation of, 100, *104–5*, 107, 113,
  114, 116; lack of political awareness,
  114–15; migration patterns of, 97–100;
  and prejudice, 113–14; transnational
  identity of, 119
indigenous peoples, Oceania: gender
  relations of, 19; government models of,
  23–24; political rights of, 16, 17–18;
  and white women's activism, 21
individualism, 154
industrial capitalism, 29, 30, 35–37
Industrial Revolution, 49
inequality, in segmented labor market, 37,
  40–41
informal sector, 32–33, 47n2
informational capitalism, 29–30
Institutional Revolutionary Party (PRI), 159
Interfaith Center on Corporate
  Responsibility, 164
International Finance Corporation (IFC),
  67
internationalization, 28
International Labor Organization (ILO),
  156, 169
International Labour Rights Fund, 169
international law, 155–56, 157, 211
International Monetary Fund (IMF), 3–4,
  9, 45, 50, 151; HIPC debt relief
  initiative of, 63–66, 71–72; in Mexico,
  151, 153; political power of, 58; in
  South Korea, 180, 192
international organizations: in Africa,
  57–59, 61–62, 69; and gender regime
  standards, 155, 156, 179; and human
  rights, 46, 155, 156; neoliberalist
  agenda of, 3–4; as site of contestation,
  7, 157; and state, 45; women's, 22, 46.
  See also specific names

Jain, Devaki, 195
Japan, 12–13; modernizers *vs*
  traditionalists in, 139; patriarchal social
  order of, 137, 138, 139–40, 210, 213;
  phases of modernization, 138;

workplace gender regimes in, 154. *See also* comfort women; prostitution in Japan
Jaquette, Jane, 224, 228, 229
Jennett, C., 24
Jensen, J.M., 97
Jenson, J., 36, 42
Jessop, B., 27
Jones, Kathleen, 155
Joshi, Rama, 112, 124

Kabiria, Nazli, 123, 126
Kahn, A., 117
Kamerman, S.B., 117
Keita, Modibo, 66
Kellner, H., 109
Kelly, Rita Mae, 1–14, 10–11, 95–120, 113, 114, 147–70, 172, 179
Kerber, Linda, 5
Kerchner, B., 44
Keynesian welfare state, 27, 36, 41–43
Kim, Dae-Jung, 189, 190, 192
Kim, Jong-Phil, 190
Kim, Soo-Kon, 180
Kim, Won-Hong, 174, 176
Kim, Young Sam, 181, 189, 190
Kirkby, D., 23
Knop, Karen, 155, 156
Kopinak, Kathryn, 164
Korea: comfort women in, 140. *See also* South Korea
Korean Church Women United, 187, 189
Korean National Council of Women (KNCW), 189
Korean Women's Organization, 186
Kovic, Christine, 159, 160, 163
Kramer, S., 118
Kreisky, E., 34, 44
Kulawik, T., 44
kuruwa tradition of prostitution, 138, 214
Kurz-Scherf, I., 36
Kwon, In-Sook, 188

labor activism of women: in Mexico, 163–69; in South Korea, 181–85
labor force participation of women: Asian Indian immigrants, 100, *104–5*, 113,
114, 116; and empowerment, 117–19, 151–52; and family roles, 39–40, 42, *105*, 106–8, 148; in feminized labor market, 3, 6, 8, 10–11, 45, 151, 163–64, 180, 182; in Fordist era, 27–28, 29, 31, 35–37; gender regimes in workplace, 152, 153–54; in global factories, 32, 33, 45, 46; home-based work, 32–33, 87; and housework-sharing, 91, 116, 123–36; and income control, 122–36, 152; Mexicans in U.S., 38, 89–90; in Mexico, 32, 87–88, 153 (*See also* maquiladora industries); and modernization, 13, 226–28; and pregnancy testing, 12, 168–69; in segmented market, 18, 31–32, 40–41; in settler societies, 19, 23; in South Korea, 179–81, 192
labor migration, Mexico/U.S., 10, 77, 78, 81–82, 87
labor unions, 45–46, 166, 183, 184–85
Landes, Joan, 5
Lang, Sabine, 44, 230
Laos, 32, 143
Larner, Wendy, 40
Launius, Michael, 181, 182
Lee, Hyo-Jae, 181, 182, 183, 187
Lee, Mi-Kyung, 191
Lee, So-Sun, 183
Lee, Young-Hwe, 181
Leijenaar, Monique, 234
Lemoine, M., 32, 40, 45
Leonard, K.I., 97
León, Magdalena, 77
Liddle, Joanna, 112, 124
life expectancy, in Africa, 53, *65*
Lindsey, L., 114
literacy rate, in Africa, 52, 53, *65*
Locke, John, 7
Lomé Convention, 10, 50, 56–57
Los Madres de Plaza de Mayo, 150

McDonagh, Eileen, 5, 234
McDowell, Linda, 40
McGlen, Nancy E., 154
Mackinnon, Catherine, 22

Mahnkopf, B., 28–29, 33, 41
Mann, P.S., 40
Maori, 16, 18, 23–24
maquiladora industries, 11, 87–88,
    163–64; Coalition for Justice, 165–66;
    pregnancy testing by, 168–69; sexual
    harassment complaint in, 166–67;
    working conditions in, 164–65
Marcos, 160, 161
Margolis, Jane, 85
Martin, P., 43
Masur, J., 118
Matsui, Yayori, 213
May, A., 19, 21
Mazur, A., 44
Medellin drug cartel, 143
Messner, D., 30
Mexicans in U.S., 10; gender regimes of,
    90–91, 92; labor force participation of,
    38, 89–90; migration patterns of, 10,
    77, 78, 81–82, 87, 92, 94n6
Mexico: Agrarian Reform Law, 160;
    agricultural systems in, 10, 11, 77, 78,
    82–87; Asian Indians in, 97; Chiapas
    conflict in, 158–63; debt management
    in, 148; gender regimes in, 10, 11, 12,
    75, 77, 83, 86–87, 88–89, 91–92, 162;
    Green Revolution in, 77, 78, 93–94;
    Guanajuato areas of, 77–88; labor
    activism of women, 163–69;
labor force participation of women, 32,
    87–88, 153; Maclovia Rojas resistance
    in, 167–68; political participation of
    women, 150, 151, 159–63, 165–69;
    pregnancy testing issue in, 168–69; sex
    trafficking in, 143; sexual harassment
    complaint in, 166–67; structural
    adjustment policies in, 151, 158–59
migration. *See* immigration; Indian
    women in U.S.; Mexicans in U.S.
Mika, Susan, 165, 166
Mill, John Stuart, 1
Miller, Francesca, 228
modernization theory, 13, 226–28
Mogelonsky, M., 98
monetary policy, neoliberal, 55
mortality rate, in Africa, 53

motherhood/domesticity, 40, *104*, 106
Motorola, 183
Mueller, Magda, 228
Mulgan, R., 16, 24
Multilateral Agreement on Investment
    (MAI), 59–60, 61–62
multinational corporations. *See*
    transnational corporations
Murayama, Prime Minister, 217
Mushakoji, Kinhide, 12–13, 205–22, 206

NAFTA (North American Free Trade
    Agreement), 59
Namyoung Nylon, 183
Naples Club, 63, 64
Nash, John F., 122
Nash, June, 159, 160, 163
National Action Party, 167
National Commission for Democracy in
    Mexico (NCDM), 161–62
National Confederation of Campesinos
    (CNC), 159
National Confederation of Popular
    Organizations (CNOP), 159
National O-Ring, 166–67
National Solidarity Program
    (PRONASOL), 159
National Toxics Campaign, 165
nation-states: and denationalization, 27;
    and feminist agenda, 43–45; human
    rights accountability of, 140, 156,
    212–22; and internationalization, 28;
    and nonstate organizations, 45;
    Philadelphian *vs* Westphalian form of,
    20–21, 24–25; solidarity, 41. *See also*
    democratization
Natonal Consumer's League, 154
Nelson, B., 44
Nelson, Barbara J., 224, 228 African
    policy agenda of, 55–56; philosophical
    base of globalization, 3–4, 58
network society, 30–33
New Community Movement, 186
New Zealand. *See* Oceania settler societies
Nielsen, J.M., 113
Night School system, 185
Nishiyama, Matsunosuke, 138

Nkrumah, Kwame, 66
nongovernmental organizations (NGOs),
  women's, 230–32
North American Free Trade Agreement
  (NAFTA), 59, 147, 156; and Chiapas
  conflict, 158–63; labor agreement, 167,
  169; and Mexico-U.S. border
  industries, 163–65
Nyerere, Julius, 66

Oceania settler societies, 15–25; defined,
  15; democratization expansion in, 5,
  17–18; and federal system, 9, 20–21,
  24–25; gender relations in, 18–20;
  international migration to, 16–17;
  vacant possession in, 16; women's
  movement in, 21–23. *See also*
  indigenous peoples, Oceania
O'Connor, Karen, 154
Ogle, G.E., 185
Ong, P., 98, 103, 110
Onuma, Yasuaki, 249
Orentlicher, Diane, 156
Organization for Economic Cooperation
  and Development (OECD), 45, 57–58;
  membership and functions of, 59;
  Multilateral Agreement on Investment
  (MAI), 59–60; social contract of, 148,
  149
Ostner, I., 36

Pacific Islands, 15
Papua New Guinea, 15, 17
Para-statal, 47n4
Parekh, Bhiku, 20
Paris Club, 63, 64
Park, Chong-Chul, 188–89
Park, Chung Hee, 171, 176, 177–78, 180,
  182, 186
Partido de Acción Nacional (PAN), 168
Partido de la Revolucion Democratica
  (PRD), 168
Partido Revolucionario Institucional
  (PRI), 78
partnership gender regime, 9, 19
Pastoral Juvenil Obrera, 166
Pateman, Carole, 41, 44, 206–7

patriarchal gender regimes, 4, 7, 8, 127
patriarchal societies: double standard in,
  213, 222; Japan, 137, 138, 210, 213;
  Mexico, 162
peer learning, 202
Pena, Devon, 151
Peru, 224
Peterson, V. Spike, 228
Philadelphian system, 21, 24–25
Philippines, 15, 20; comfort women, 140;
  global factories in, 32, 45; sex
  trafficking in, 141, 144–45
Phizacklea, Annie, 224
Pilkington, Hilary, 224
Pleck, E., 114
political participation of women, 5, 7, 8,
  13; and Asian Indian immigrants,
  114–15; in India, 195, 196–204; in
  Mexico, 150, 151, 159–63, 165–69;
  motivating factors in, 150–51, 154,
  156; negative impact of
  democratization, 224, 226, 229–30,
  233–34; in nongovernmental
  organizations (NGOs), 230–32; in
  Oceania settler societies, 21–23; and
  quota system, 12, 195, 234; at sites of
  contestation, 157–69; in South Korea,
  173–79, 185–91. *See also* women's
  movement
poverty, 4, 8, 224, 226
Pozzetta, G.E., 110, 119
pregnancy testing, 12, 168–69
Preston, Julia, 162
privatization: in Senegal, 68–70; social
  service, 41, 151
production, Fordist model of, 27
property, 5, 18–19, 153
prostitution, 4; and democratic values,
  206, 207–10; and ethical double
  standard, 208–9, 211, 212–13, 220;
  globalization of sex trafficking, 138,
  141, 142–43, 224; legalized, 143–44;
  military sex industry, 141; in
  patriarchal capitalist societies, 137,
  139–40, 210, 213; sex tourism, 139,
  142, 143, 213. *See also* comfort
  women

prostitution in Japan, 11, 210;
  commercial brothel system, 141–42,
  213, 214; military sex industry, 141,
  213; in premodern (Edo) period,
  137–38, 214; state-regulated, 139,
  140, 141, 213; trafficking network in,
  142–43, 144–45, 214. *See also*
  comfort women
Pühl, K., 44
Pyke, Karen D., 122, 126, 130, 133
Pyle, J.L., 33, 39, 45, 46

quota system, 7, 8, 12, 195, 234

Rai, Shirin, 224
Ralston, H., 110, 119
Ramu, G.N., 112, 124
Reagan, Ronald, 43
Reddy, C., 42
Reeves, E.Y., 109
Reeves, W.P., 16, 17, 21
regional cooperation, in Africa, 72, 74
règles de droit, 208, 209, 215, 218, 221
Renaissance, 5
"Republican Motherhood", ideology of, 5
Revolutionary Conference of Workers and
  Peasants (CROC), 167
Revolutionary War, 5
Rhyu, Sang-Yong, 172
Robinson, Maria, 167
Robinson, Randal, 61
Rodriguez, Cecelia, 160–61
Roediger, D.R., 113
Roldán, Martha, 152
Ross, A., 111
Rousseau, Jean Jacques, 7
Runyon, Anne Sisson, 228

Safa, Helen I., 152
Safilios-Rothschild, Constantina, 122, 126,
  130
Saint Germain, Michelle, 223, 228
Salaff, Janet W., 152
Sanday, P., 103, 108
Sassen, Saskia, 27, 31–32, 33, 38, 40, 43,
  45, 46, 147, 157, 172
Sauer, B., 34, 44

savings and credit groups (SCGs), in
  India, 198
Sawer, M., 20, 22, 23
Schmitter, P.C., 35
Scott, Joan Wallach, 5, 228
Seattle protest, 7
Sen, Amartya, 121, 122, 124
Seneca Falls Declaration of the Rights of
  Women, 5
Senegal, privatization in, 68–70
SENELEC, 69
separate spheres of activity, 18, 19 *104*,
  106
service sector, 23, 29
settler societies: *vs* conquered states, 16.
  See also Oceania settler societies
sexism, 114
sex tourism, 139, 142, 143, 187, 213
sex trafficking. *See* prostitution
sexual double standard, 19, 208–9, 211,
  212–13, 220
sexual harassment, 12, 158, 166–67
sexual slavery, military. *See* comfort
  women
sexual torture, 188
Shahid, John, 166–67
Sharma, Ursula, 123, 124
Shell/Exxon/ELF oil consortium, in
  Africa, 67, 70–71
Shimomura, Michiko, 218
Sidiqi, M.U., 109
Simms, Marian, 8–9, 15–25, 20, 22
single parents, 38, 148
Sircar, Arpana, 10–11, 95–120
Sisters of Mercy, 165
Sklair, Leslie, 164
Slaughter, M., 16
slavery, 4, 5; sexual (*See* comfort women)
slave trade, 9, 50, 51, 68
Smith, Adam, 7
Smith, Joan, 39
Smock, A., 111
social class. *See* class
socialization, 114
social service jobs, 36
social service privatization, 4, 42, 151
Sohn, Bong-Scuk, 174

Sohn, Sook, 192–93n2
Solomon, Lawrence, 54
SONATEL, 69
Songen Jigyo program, 219, 220
Soni-Sinha, Urvashi, 11, 121–36
South Africa, 16, 45, 227
South Korea, 12; democratization in,
172–73, 179, 182, 185–91; global
factories in, 32, 45–46; industrialization
of, 171–72, 180–81; labor activism of
women, 181–85; labor force
participation of women, 179–81, 192;
military sex industry in, 141; political
participation of women, 173–79,
185–91; sex tourism in, 142, 143, 187,
213; sexual torture case in, 188
Standing, Hilary, 123
Stanton, Elizabeth Cady, 5, 7, 154
state feminism, 44
States. *See* democratizaiton; nation-states
Steinberg, S., 110
Stephen, Lynn, 151
Stetson, D.M., 44
Strange, Susan, 28, 43, 45
structural adjustment policy: in Africa,
63–66, 69–70, 71; in Mexico, 151,
158–59; and neoliberal agenda, 55;
poverty related to, 224
subcontractors, 32, 33
suffrage, 5, 17, 173, 186
suffrage movements, 5, 18, 22, 154
Supapung, Nayana, 145
Support Committee for the Maquiladoras,
166, 167
Suret-Canale, J., 51, 68
Swagel, P., 16
Swayam Shikshan Prayog (SSP), 196
sweatshops, 32, 33
Sweden, gender regimes in, 153, 154
Sy, J. Habib, 52

Taekwang Industry, 183
Taiwan, 32, 143
Taliban, 233
technology, information, 29–30
temperance movement, in settler societies,
19–20

Terra Nullius doctrine, 16, 24
textile industry, 33, 87–88, 89, 164, 183
Thailand, sex trafficking in, 141, 143, 145
Thatcher, Margaret, 43
Thomas, Dorothy Q., 156
Thompson, E.P., 150
Thompson, Grahame, 28
Thurow, L.S., 29
Tiano, Susan, 151, 164
Tocqueville, Alexis de, 18–19
Tolpuddle Martyrs, 17
Tomioka, Emiko, 139
Tong, Mary, 165, 166, 167
transnational corporations, 3, 8;
accountability of, 61; in export zones,
32, 45; in Fordist era, 30; global
factories of, 32, 33, 45, 46; and
household economy, 32–33; and
privatization policy, 69. *See also*
maquiladora industries
Treaty of Waitangi, 16
Triandis, H.C., 119
triple-shift, 39
Tronto, Joan, 228
Truong, Thanh-Dam, 210

United Auto Workers, 167

United Nations: and comfort women issue,
215; and gender regime standards, 155;
and sex discrimination, 169
United Nations Development Fund for
Women (UNIFEM), 224
United Nations Human Development
Report, 224
United Nations Human Rights Congress, 7
United Nations Women's Conference, 155,
187
United States: Africa Growth and
Opportunity Act (AGOA), 60–62;
democratization expansion in, 5;
democratization/globalization policy
of, 8; federalist system in, 21; gender
regime change in, 9, 155–56; and
Green Revolution, 93n3; informal
economy in, 33; and Multilateral
Agreement on Investment (MAI), 60;

as new settler society, 16; temperance
    movement in, 19–20; women's
    movement in, 5, 154; workplace
    gender regimes in, 153–54; Zapatista
    outreach in, 161–62. *See also* Indian
    (Asian) women in U.S.; Mexicans in
    U.S.
Urban Industrial Mission (UIM), 184
Uruguay, 16
Uruguay Round, 58

Valencia, Reynaldo, 78
Valenzuela, Maria Elena, 230
Vietnam, 32, 143, 145
violence against women: in Bosnian War,
    233; rate of, 236n3; in South Africa,
    227. *See also* comfort women;
    prostitution

Wada, Haruki, 218
wages: control of income, 122–26, 152;
    double wage-earner family, 38, 113;
    family, 3, 19, 23, 154; subsistence,
    32–33, 182
Wallerstein, Immanuel, 39
Ward, K., 33, 39, 45, 46
welfare state, 27, 36, 41–43
Westphalian model, 21, 24–25
Wichterich, C., 30, 32, 33
Wilde, G., 44
Wolchik, Sharon, 224, 229
Women's Christian Temperance Union,
    20, 154
women's movement: in Australia/New
    Zealand, 20, 21–23; in Germany, 44;
    and nation-state, 43–45; in South
    Korea, 185–91; suffrage, 5, 18, 22,
    154; in United States, 5, 154. *See also*
    feminism

women's organization, nongovernmental
    (NGOs), 230–32
Women's Rights Convention, Seneca
    Falls, 5
Women's Trade Union League, 154
Wonpoong Union, 183
Worker's Center in Cuidad Juarez
    (CETLAC), 166
working women. *See* labor force
    participation of women
World Bank, 3–4, 9, 45, 50, 58; Chad oil
    project, 67–68; HIPC debt relief
    initiative, 63–66, 71–72
World Conference on Women, Beijing, 46,
    234
World Trade Organization (WTO), 4, 7,
    45, 50, 58, 59, 61–62
Wright, Erik Olin, 152–54
WTO. *See* World Trade Organization

Yans-McLaughlin, V., 103, 106
Yaoundé Convention, 56
Y.H. Trading Company, 182, 183
Yoon, Bang Soon L., 12, 171–94, 178,
    180, 187, 188
Yoon, Jung-Sook, 173, 189, 190
Yoon, Woo-Hyun, 180
Yoshiaki, Yoshimi, 212
Yoshioka, Mutsuko, 139
Young, Brigitte, 9, 27–47, 44
Young Christian Workers (JOC), 184–85
Young, Gay, 152
Yung, J., 115

Zapatista Front of National Liberation
    (EZLN), 159–63
Zazueta, A., 200
Zeleza, Tiyambe, 51

List of Contributors

Jane Bayes, Ph.D., Professor of Political Science, California State University, Northridge, received her Ph.D. at the University of California at Los Angeles. She is the author of *Ideologies and Interest-Group Politics: The United States in a Global Economy and Minority Politics and Ideologies in the United States.* Her research interests are political economy, women and politics and public policy. She is the recipient of the SWAPA Award of the American Society for Public Administration for outstanding research on women. She served on the Board of Directors for the American Political Science Association from 1998–2000.

Yassine Fall, M.S. in Economics, Ph.D. candidate at The University of Texas at Dallas, is also the Executive Secretary of the African Association of Women for Research and Development (AAWORD) and an economist from Senegal. She graduated in economics from Howard University, Washington, D.C. and has conducted theoretical research as well as field research on gender and development issues in several countries throughout Africa. Her areas of expertise include macroeconomic policy, environmental management, emergency relief operations, child labor, argo-forestry and food security analysis.

Laura Gonzalez, Ph.D., Research Scientist, The University of Texas at Dallas, studied anthropology at the Iberoamericana University in Mexico City. She got her Master's and Ph.D. degrees in Anthropology at the University of California, Santa Barbara. Between April 1994 and September 1999, she worked at the Social Sciences Research Center at the University of Guanajuato. Laura is the Director of the Network of Guanajuato Migrants Project, Coordinator of the Permanent Research Seminar, and responsible for the research line on International Migration and US-Mexican Relations. The Iberoamericana University published her book *Respuesta Campesina a la Revolución Verde en el Bajío [Peasant*

Response to the Green Revolution in the Bajío Region]. Her doctoral dissertation: "Political Brokers, Ejidos, and State Resources in Guanajuato" is published as 85 Cuadernos del CICSUG, Number 3. She has been a member of the Mexico National Research System since 1996.

Suranjana Gupta, M.S. in Social Work, is a Research Associate with the Swayam Shikshan Prayog Project in India. Ms. Gupta has been working with this project in India for several years. She has been monitoring the progress being made in India to implement the constitutional mandate to have thirty percent of elected local government positions be held by women.

Seiko Hanochi, Ph.D. candidate in Political Science at York University, is also Secretary-General of the Japan Accountability Caucus following-up on the Fourth UN Conference on Women. She is currently conducting a research project on sexual trafficking of girls and women in Southeast Asia with special attention being paid to Japan.

Mary E. Hawkesworth, Ph.D., a Professor of Political Science and Director of the Center for the American Women and Politics (CAWP) at Rutgers-the State University of New Jersey. Dr. Hawkesworth is a major contributor to the fields of political theory, feminist theory, public policy, and women and politics. Previously she served as acting director of the University of Louisville's Women's Studies Program. Her books include *Beyond Oppression: Feminist Theory and Political Strategy* (Continuum, 1990), *Theoretical Issues in Policy Analyses* (SUNY, 1988), and *The Encyclopedia of Government and Politics* (Routledge, 1992). Her exploration of how to make our democracy worthy of feminist support has been widely read and has impacted women's groups and strategic thinking about public policy. The edited special issue on *Feminism and Public Policy in Policy Sciences* (1994) continues her work in this area, as does her article "Confounding Gender," in *Signs,* vol.22, no.3: 649–685. She is the 1997 recipient of the University of Louisville's Award for Outstanding Research.

Rita Mae Kelly, Ph.D. in Political Science, Indiana University, Dean of Social Sciences, the University of Texas, Dallas, also holds an Honorary Doctorate in Political Science from the University of Umea in Sweden for her "pioneering contributions to the field of women & politics [. . . and her . . .] ability to combine theory and empirical work [serving] as an inspiration for the researchers seeking to establish gender as an important analytic category within the discipline of Political Science." Kelly's recent books include *Gender Power, Leadership, and Governance* (University of Michigan Press, 1995, 2nd printing, 1997); *Advances in Policy Studies Since 1950* (Transaction Press, 1992, winner of the 1993 Policy Studies Organization's [PSO's] Aaron Wildavsky Best Book Award); *The Gendered Economy* (Sage, 1991, 4th reprinting); *Gender, Bureaucracy, and*

Democracy (Greenwood Press, 1989); *Women and the Arizona Political Process* (University Press of America, 1988); *Comparable Worth, Pay Equity, and Public Policy* (Greenwood Press, 1988); and *Promoting Productivity in the Public Sector* (MacMillan/St. Martin's Press, 1988). Other awards include the PSO's (1995) Merriam Mills Award; the SWAPA Distinguished Research Award (American Society for Public Administration, 1991); a Fulbright Fellowship, (Brazil, 1991); and the Women's Caucus of Political Science Outstanding Mentor in the Discipline Award (1991 and 1996). She is also former President of the Western Political Science Association, the Policy Studies Association, and has been or is a member of the boards of numerous other professional associations and academic journals. She was editor of *Women & Politics: A Journal of Research and Policy Studies* from 1985–1990.

Kinhide Mushakoji, Ph.D., is professor of International and Global Studies at Ferris Women's University, Japan. Dr. Mushakoji is a former president of the International Political Science Association and a founder and leader of the United Nations University. He has numerous publications on issues of human rights, international relations, and Japanese role in global politics.

Marian Simms, Ph.D., Professor of Political Science, Australian National University Canberra, Australia, is an international scholar known for her work on women and politics and the study of Australian politics and the Oceania region. She currently heads the Australian National Election Survey Project and is completing a comparative study of political parties in Oceania.

Arpana Sircar, Ph.D., is originally from Calcutta, India. Dr. Sircar received her B.A. in History with honors from Calcutta University, and her M.A. in History from Jadavpur University. In 1971, she came to the U.S. to continue her graduate studies, earning a second Master's degree in History from Northeastern University in Boston, and a Ph.D. in Humanities from the University of Texas, Arlington. She is currently teaching at Texas Weslayan University in Fort Worth, Texas. Dr. Sircar is the author of *Work Roles, Gender Roles, and Asian Indian Immigrant Women in the United States*.

Urvashi Soni-Sinha, Ph.D. candidate. M.S. in Economics, Warwick University, England, is originally from India, and is currently completing her degree in Women's Studies and Economics. Her dissertation focuses on export processing zones and their implications for gender relations and social change.

Bang-Soon L. Yoon, Ph.D., is an Associate Professor of Political Science and Women's Studies at Central Washington University. Dr. Yoon received her Ph.D. at the University of Hawaii, Manoa under a fellowship from the East-West Center, Honolulu, Hawaii. Her areas of specialty are state power, militarism, and sexual violence. Her recent research concerns the so-called "Comfort Women" taken as sex slaves by the Japanese military and the Japanese military's treatment and attitudes towards women during World War II.

Brigitte Young, Ph.D., is a Professor of Political Economy, at the University of Muenster in Germany. Dr. Young teaches courses on Feminist Theories and the State; Gender, Power, and the Economy; and several international issues of gender. She is the author of *Triumph of the Fatherland: German Unification and the Marginalization of Women* (1999), and *Prospects for Soviet Grain Production*. She was nominated by the German Parliament to sit on the highly prestigious Expert Commission (Enquete-Kommission) on "Globalization of the World Economy: Challenges and Answers" from 2000 until 2002. She is founder and co-director of a non-profit organization, the Center of Globalization and Media, at the University of Muenster (in cooperation with Prof. Dr. Ingrid Volkmer, Augsburg University). She also founded the Center on Globalization, European Integration, and Gender and in 1999 coordinated an international conference on "Feminist Perspectives on the Paradoxes of Globalization."